Restart

Sport After the Covid-19 Time Out

Edited by
Jörg Krieger, April Henning, Lindsay Parks Pieper

Restart

Sport After the Covid-19 Time Out

Edited by
Jörg Krieger, April Henning, Lindsay Parks Pieper

First published in 2022
as part of the *Sport and Society* Book Imprint
doi: 10.18848/978-1-957792-14-9/CGP (Full Book)

Common Ground Research Networks
University of Illinois Research Park
60 Hazelwood Drive
Champaign, IL 61820 USA

Copyright © Jörg Krieger, April Henning, Lindsay Parks Pieper, 2022

All rights reserved. Apart from fair dealing for the purposes of study, research, criticism or review as permitted under the applicable copyright legislation, no part of this book may be reproduced by any process without written permission from the publisher.

Library of Congress Cataloging-in-Publication Data

Names: Krieger, Jörg, editor. | Henning, April, editor. | Pieper, Lindsay
   Parks, editor.
Title: Restart: sport after the Covid-19 time out / edited by Jörg
   Krieger, April Henning, Lindsay Parks Pieper.
Description: Champaign, IL: Common Ground, 2022. | Includes
   bibliographical references and index. | Summary: "In the edited
   collection Restart. Sport After the Covid-19 Time Out, practitioners and
   international scholars explore the "restart" of sport and fitness
   following the initial period of lockdowns during spring 2020. The
   chapters provide insight and analysis into the sport and fitness
   landscape following the initial wave of the pandemic. Challenges for
   sport providers, consequences for sporting participants, and chances for
   new ways of practicing sports are the focus of the book. It therewith
   contributes to the contemporaneous data, analyses, and insights into the
   global sport landscape that has been impacted by the Covid-19 pandemic.
   The book presents a variety of interdisciplinary perspectives in a total
   of nineteen individual chapters, organized around five main themes:
   sporting events, the Olympic Movement, national perspectives, youth and
   fitness sport, and the role of the media"-- Provided by publisher.
Identifiers: LCCN 2022013886 (print) | LCCN 2022013887 (ebook) | ISBN
   9781957792125 (hardback) | ISBN 9781957792132 (paperback) | ISBN
   9781957792149 (pdf)
Subjects: LCSH: Sports--Social aspects. | Sports administration. | Sports
   and state. | Sports--Safety measures. | COVID-19 (Disease)--Social
   aspects. | Epidemics--Social aspects.
Classification: LCC GV706.5 .R465 2022 (print) | LCC GV706.5 (ebook) |
   DDC 796.06/9--dc23/eng/20220503
LC record available at https://lccn.loc.gov/2022013886
LC ebook record available at https://lccn.loc.gov/2022013887

Table of Contents

Introduction 1
Jörg Krieger, April Henning, and Lindsay Parks Pieper

List of Contributors 5

Part One
Sport Events and Leagues

Chapter 1 15
Strategic Covid-19 Safety-Protocol: Preparing to Restart the International 60+ Masters Small-Sided Football World Cup in Denmark 2021
    Scott D. Robertson; Harry T. Hubball, Lars Corlin-Christensen, Risto Kauppinen, George Fox, and Jorge Díaz-Cidoncha García

Chapter 2 33
"Celebrate this Victory in a Sensible Manner": Irish Media and the Restart of Gaelic Games in Ireland
    Seán Crosson and Marcus Free

Chapter 3 51
A League of their Own: Male Privileges in Australian Rugby League During Covid-19
    Jim McKay and Karen Brooks

Chapter 4 69
One Big Family: Return to Play by MLS Referees Driven by Friendship and the Love for the Game
    Yuya Kiuchi, Bill Dittmar, Scott Matteson

Part Two
The Olympic Movement

Chapter 5 83
Restart, Ready or Not? The Tokyo 2020 Olympic Games
  Helen Jefferson Lenskyj

Chapter 6 97
Lessons from Covid-19: The Organized Sport and its Responses to Climate Change
  Tim Sperber

Chapter 7 119
The Modern Olympic Games in a Post-Pandemic World
  Jeffrey O. Segrave

Chapter 8 135
Is the Olympic Values Education Programme (OVEP) Relevant in a Post-Covid-19 World?
  Hilla Davidov

Part Three
National Perspectives

Chapter 9 159
The Philippines: Restarting Sports in "Bubbles"
  Severino R. Sarmenta Jr.

Chapter 10 171
Fighting a Pandemic by Recommendations and Trust Sports in Sweden during Covid-19
  Johan R. Norberg, Karin Andersson, and Susanna Hedenborg

Chapter 11 187
Bring Back Our Sport: Power Play at the Resumption of Sport Activities in the Gambia
    Pascal Mamudou Camara

Chapter 12 201
What the Danish Covid-19 Lockdown and Re-Opening Can Teach us About Sports Participation and How It Can Be Promoted
    Jens Høyer-Kruse and Bjarne Ibsen

Part Four
Youth and Fitness Sport

Chapter 13 219
Covid-19 and The Shifting Role of Parent as Youth Sport Spectator
    Jerry F. Reynolds and Matt Moore

Chapter 14 235
Antigonish Multisport and the Maritime Bubble: A Commentary on the Possibilities of Youth Sport Programming in Post-Pandemic Rural Canadian Society
    Tom Fabian

Chapter 15 251
Change and Challenge: A Case Study of Distance and Touch in a Fitness Club After Lockdown
    Dominika Czarnecka

Chapter 16 263
Global Perspectives on Group Fitness Post Lockdown: Reflections of Les Mills' Trainers
    Karin Andersson, Jesper Andreasson, and Ulrike Vogl

Part Five
Media and Technology

Chapter 17 277
"A Hellish Version of Snakes and Ladders": Print Media Reporting on the Impact of Covid-19 on Professional Sport in England
   Kay Biscomb and Kath Leflay

Chapter 18 289
Ghost Games and Artificial Soundscapes: Sports Media and Fan Reactions to the Return of European Soccer Matches in Empty Stadia
   Jeffrey W. Kassing, Mary Helen Clark, Carrie Kaput, Trinity Winton, Keara Katayama, Suzanne Day, Isaiah Utley, and Aleah N. Fisher

Chapter 19 309
Esports, Repositioning and Enhancing Profitability Post Covid-19 Sports Lockdown: An Australian Case
   Michelle O'Shea, Sarah Duffy, and Daniel Roman

Introduction

Jörg Krieger, April Henning, and Lindsay Parks Pieper

Since the start of 2020, the Covid-19 global health pandemic has maintained a tight grip on all aspects of public life. The pandemic brought initially sport and physical activities to a halt during the near global lockdown in spring 2020. Mega-sport events, including the 2020 Olympic Games, and national sport leagues were canceled or postponed, while individuals who had regularly engaged in physical activity for leisure or health purposes found themselves unable to exercise–or at least as they normally would–due to governmental restrictions. Public gatherings were banned, public places and venues closed, and severe social distancing imposed. In most countries, such measures made it impossible for individuals to exercise in public indoor settings. Outdoor recreational activities were often also restricted to a reduced number of people exercising together. We covered the full extent of the challenges and consequences of the sport and activity "time out" due to the 2020 lockdown in our previous volumes *Time Out: National Perspectives on Sport and the Covid-19 Lockdown* and *Time Out: Global Perspectives on Sport and the Covid-19 Lockdown*.

Following the initial Covid-19 lockdown period, some areas began to reopen in autumn 2020. This restart included both elite and leisure sports. Previously postponed events commenced under new restrictions, while training and recreational activity facilities slowly reopened under new national or local regulations around physical distancing and hygiene. Approaches varied by sport, country, and even locality. Stakeholders within sport had to consider the spread of the virus, dangers of increased social interaction, governmental regulations, as well as financial implications. Resuming activities while avoiding becoming "spreader" events was the biggest challenge for sporting stakeholders when restarting competitions. In many countries, the challenges continue and several sports have restarted only to take subsequent time outs following new outbreaks of the virus.

Forced to adapt to pandemic restrictions, people adjusted their sport and physical activity practices when societies slowly reopened. The elite sport sector opened first in most countries, but often without spectators. Many professional leagues finished their lockdown-interrupted seasons or returned to play in empty stadiums, leading organizers to try different solutions to simulate live audiences. When Denmark became the second country in Europe to restart its football league (after Germany) at the end of May 2020, it made spectators in Aarhus visible to players on pitch-side screens (McVeigh 2020). Though the German Football League discouraged clubs from using artificial noise to replicate crowds, it eventually appeared in Bundesliga broadcasts to enhance the viewing experience (Lauletta 2020). Many leagues, including the U.S. National Football League (Jamieson 2021) and Australia's National Rugby League (Hytner 2020), used cardboard cutouts of fans to make stadiums appear at capacity when they resumed competitions. In Herning, the home city of Danish club FC Midtjylland, large screens were set up outside the stadium for spectators to watch the match from inside their cars (Wright 2020). Sport organizers found innovative and creative ways to adapt to pandemic restrictions that limited spectators, a crucial component of professional sport.

However, players, team officials, referees, media representatives, and other key personnel needed for the restart of elite sport also experienced, at times, extreme measures in order to participate. For many sports, bubbles were created that required all involved individuals to stay in a restricted area for days, weeks, and in some cases, months. This meant staying away from families, friends, and homes. Major League Soccer (MLS) in the United States was one of the first professional leagues to organize a bubble for its MLS Is Back Tournament in summer 2020. Teams traveled to Orlando, Florida, and remained on-site for the duration of the competition (Fusaro 2020). Many elite athletes also underwent quarantine restrictions to help stymie Covid-19 outbreaks. Upon arrival in the Women's National Basketball Association bubble, for example, all players underwent a mandatory four-day quarantine period (Maloney 2020). Even in competition, hygiene protocols had to be respected and most organizers required facemasks and social distancing, as well as time between events for cleaning. For example, the German football league required players to socially distance when celebrating goals (West 2020); the Jamaican Ministry of Sport outlined and necessitated sanitization protocols for the resumption of sport in the country (Ministry of Culture, Gender, Entertainment, and Sport 2021).

Covid-19 restrictions also applied to leisure sport participants. Even when leaders lifted some lockdown restrictions, most commercial fitness studios remained closed. Fitness and leisure sport participants had to reconsider their normal routines and come up with alternative ways to exercise. Substitute fitness equipment, such as big water bottles, heavy pieces of wood, or outdoor fitness facilities–and the ubiquitous online fitness class–became immensely popular as they allowed participants to do high-intensity workouts at home or in outdoor settings (Kaur et al. 2021).

Yet, when eventually permitted to engage in physical activities in indoor facilities, individuals still had to adhere to several sets of rules. These often included temperature checks, mask wearing, social distancing measures, and sanitization requirements. For example, several YMCAs required gym goers to wear face masks at all times, including when working out, for several months (Krize 2020). In team sports, training was only allowed in small groups and no full team training was possible. Direct contact, an essential feature in many competitions, remained prohibited. The pandemic is ongoing and sport and leisure event and facility availability remains precarious.

Despite these efforts, national authorities permitted the restart of sport in many areas, only to ban them again when infection rates started to rise. Thus in many ways, the "restart" of sport has been less of a smooth resumption of activities and more of a start and stop ordeal. This volume therefore focuses on the "restart" of sport and fitness following the initial period of lockdowns during spring 2020. We intend for the current volume to pick up from where the *Time Out* volumes left off and provide insight and analysis into the sport and fitness landscape following the initial wave of the pandemic. As such, it is also important to note that at the time of writing this introduction, national situations vary significantly. Whereas in some countries, such as Denmark, all restrictions have been dropped, citizens in most other parts of the world continue to face significant constraints. This has clear implications on fitness and leisure sport activities, and such varying circumstances have an impact on elite sport, too. In elite football, for example, clubs have refused to allow international players to represent their home countries, as they were required to isolate for two weeks upon their return. This led to a major stand-off between countries and clubs. Tensions and contexts such as these are the focus of *Restart*.

This volume is organized around five main themes. The first four chapters deal with the restart of sporting events in four countries: Denmark, Ireland, Australia, and the United States. These case studies offer insights into how sport leaders navigated different national Covid-19 protocols. This section is followed by an assessment of the Olympic Movement's challenges after its postponement of the 2020 Summer Olympic Games to 2021. These chapters also offer thoughts on the future of the Olympic Movement as it addresses the environmental, international, political, and educational issues highlighted by the pandemic. The third theme of the book is national perspectives on the restart. In four chapters, authors provide analysis of how national governments in very different geographical locations–two from Scandinavia and two from the Global South–handled sport during the re-starting phase. Youth sport and fitness are closely linked to governmental approaches and comprise the next theme of the collection. Both sectors depended heavily on health and safety regulations and the authors collectively demonstrate how participants, parents, commercial enterprises, and youth sport organizations were affected by such measures. Finally, the last three chapters look at the role of the media during the restart phase, both in reporting about sport and with regards to innovations and the implementation of new technology in staging and broadcasting elite sport.

Of course, as the pandemic is still ongoing, we do not anticipate this volume to be a final analysis of the restart period. It is inevitable that new analyses and information will emerge, and that much of what we think we know now will be reinterpreted in the next several years or even decades to come. What this volume does, however, is contribute contemporaneous data, analyses, and insights into the global sport landscape. It is our hope and expectation that future scholars will build on the contributions in this volume to further and deepen our understanding of the impact of the pandemic on sport.

References

Fusaro, Stefano. 2020. "MLS is Back Tournament: What It's Really Been Like after One Month Inside the Bubble." *ESPN*, August 3, 2020. https://www.espn.com/soccer/major-league-soccer/story/4152148/mls-is-back-tournament-what-its-really-been-like-after-one-month-inside-the-bubble.

Hytner, Mike. 2020. "Fan in the Stand: NRL Fans Can Pay for Cardboard Cutouts of Their Faces to Be PUt on Stadium Seats." *Guardian*, May 29, 2020. https://www.theguardian.com/sport/2020/may/29/fan-in-the-stand-nrl-fans-can-pay-for-cardboard-cutouts-of-their-faces-to-be-put-on-stadium-seats.

Jamieson, Amber. 2021. "Here's the Deal with the Fans in the Stadium for the Super Bowl." *Buzzfeed*, February 7, 2021. https://www.buzzfeednews.com/article/amberjamieson/super-bowl-stadium-crowd-size.

Kaur, Harleen, Tushar Singh, Yogesh Kumar Arya, and Shalini Mittal. 2021. "Physical Fitness and Exercise During the COVID-19 Pandemic: A Qualitative Enquiry." *Frontiers in Psychology* 11: 590172. doi: 10.3389/fpsyg.2020.590172.

Krize, Nikki. 2020. "Masks Required While Working out at the YMCA." *WNEP*, November 18, 2020. https://www.wnep.com/article/news/local/union-county/lewisburg-ymca-miller-center-masks-coronavirus/523-b64a7a02-ff72-4abe-8194-6ec03121813a.

Lauletta, Tyler. 2020. "Germany's Top-Flight Soccer League was Broadcast in the US with Fake Crowd Nose, and It Sounded Surprisingly Normal." *Insider*, May 27, 2020. https://www.insider.com/video-bundesliga-fake-crowd-noise-no-fans-2020-5.

Maloney, Jack. 2020. "WNBA 2020 Season: What We Knew About the League's Plan for COVID-19 Testing and Prevention." *CBSSports*, June 26, 2020. https://www.cbssports.com/wnba/news/wnba-2020-season-what-we-know-about-the-leagues-plan-for-covid-19-testing-and-prevention/.

Ministry of Culture, Gender, Entertainment, and Sport. 2021. "Minister Grange Announces Arrangements for Resumption of Sports without Spectators." *Jamaica Information Service*, February 5, 2021. https://jis.gov.jm/minister-grange-announces-arrangements-for-resumption-of-sports-without-spectators/.

McVeigh, Niall. 2020. "Denmark Returns to Action with Fans Taking Their Usual Place Via Zoom." *The Guardian*, May 28, 2020. https://www.theguardian.com/football/2020/may/28/denmark-returns-fans-virtual-stand-zoom-agf-aarhus-randers.

West, Jenna. 2020. Bundesliga Players Show Off Social Distancing Goal Celebrations." *Sports Illustrated*, May 16, 2020. https://www.si.com/soccer/2020/05/16/bundesliga-social-distancing-goal-celebrations-dortmund-video.

Wright, Chris. 2020. "Drive-in Football! Fans Watch at Stadium from Comfort of Cars, Limos and Quad Bikes." *ESPN*, June 2, 2020. https://www.espn.com.sg/soccer/blog-the-toe-poke/story/4105206/drive-in-football!-fans-watch-at-stadium-from-comfort-of-carslimos-and-quad-bikes.

List of Contributors

Karin Andersson is a PhD student of linguistics at the University of Ghent, Belgium. She also holds a Master degree in both Humanitarian Action from Uppsala University, Sweden, and in English and American Studies from the University of Vienna, Austria. Her upcoming interdisciplinary dissertation is an ethnographic study that deals with professional identities of group fitness instructors.

Jesper Andreasson is a Professor of Sport Science at Linnaeus University, Sweden. He holds a PhD in Sociology and has published articles and books in the field of gender studies, sociology of sport, health, and gym and fitness culture.

Kay Biscomb started her career as a PE teacher in secondary education in Botswana and England. After undertaking her first masters degree, she started her PhD at University of Gloucestershire, United Kingdom, under Professor Celia Brackenridge. She joined the staff at the University of Wolverhampton, United Kingdom, in 1996 and since then has been Head of Department and Associate Dean. Her research interests are media representation, equality, and identity issues in sport.

Karen Brooks is an Honorary Senior Research Fellow at the Institute for Advanced Studies in the Humanities at The University of Queensland, Australia. An award-winning teacher, she's also published widely on popular culture, gender, sex, media, youth culture, and education. A columnist/social media commentator on popular culture, media and politics for over twenty years, she's also the author of numerous works of best-selling historical fiction.

Pascal Mamudou Camara is a PhD student at the Institute of Sport History, German Sport University Cologne, Germany. Born and brought up in The Gambia, he holds a BSc in Sport Management from the Universidad Deportiva del Sur, Venezuela, and a MA in International Sport Development and Politics from the German Sport University Cologne. He also worked as a journalist and as Program Officer at the National Sports Council of The Gambia.

Lars Corlin-Christensen has a MSc in Food Science & Nutrition and has spent his entire career in the international food, biotech, and health business, mainly within scientific marketing and R & D. He chaired the first Centre for Food Research at University of Copenhagen, Denmark, has been an official representative in the European Industrial Research Management Association, and has been part of expert groups in the EU. Lars is the Chair-elect for the 60+ International Super Masters 5-a-side/Futsal World Cup. As a player, he has been active in organized football for more than fifty years and taken a number of leadership roles, and he is a former Chairman of the Akademisk Boldklub Copenhagen, Denmark.

Mary Helen Clark is a student in the MA program in Communication Studies at Arizona State University in Phoenix, United States. Her research interests include gender, micro-aggressions, and feminist theory.

Seán Crosson is a Senior Lecturer in Film in the Huston School of Film & Digital Media, Leader of the Sport & Exercise Research Group, and Co-Director of the MA Sports Journalism and Communication Programme at University of Galway. His previous publications include the monographs *Gaelic Games on Film: From silent films to Hollywood hurling, horror and the emergence of Irish cinema* (Cork University Press, 2019) and *Sport and Film* (Routledge, 2013), and the collections *Sport, Film and National Culture* (Routledge, 2021) and (as co-editor) *Sport, Representation and Evolving Identities in Europe* (Peter Lang, 2010).

Dominika Czarnecka is an Assistant Professor at the Center for Ethnology and Contemporary Anthropology at the Institute of Archaeology and Ethnology of the Polish Academy of Sciences in Warsaw, Poland. Her research focuses on the anthropology of the body, emotions, and senses; anthropology of sport; visual anthropology; the mechanisms of conceptualizing otherness and difference; and the post-Cold War military heritage of Central and Eastern Europe. Her previous publications include *Monuments in Gratitude to the Red Army in Communist and Post-Communist Poland* (L'Harmattan 2021) and the edited collection (with Dagnosław Demski) *Staged Otherness: Ethnic Shows in Central and Eastern Europe 1850–1939* (CEU Press, 2021). Her current project is "Through body in motion. Anthropological study of embodied experiences and identity transition of female fitness culture participants."

Hilla Davidov was part of the Israeli Olympic delegations from 2004 to 2016 and was an active member of the Judo professional Olympic entourage helping support the national team in winning three Olympic medals. Davidov has a BEd in Physical Education, Master of Arts Olympic Studies and an MBA (Marketing). Currently, she is a PhD candidate in the Olympic Studies program at German Sport University Cologne. Davidov was a member of the Israel Advisory Committee for re-designing the National Curriculum in Physical Education and received the World Fair Play Award in 2016. Davidov is a board member of the International Pierre de Coubertin Committee and the international Catchball federation president.

Suzanne Day holds an MA degree in Communication Studies and a BA in Organizational Communication from Arizona State University in Phoenix, United States. Suzanne has worked in the field of transportation demand management since 1990. Her work focuses on bicycling as transportation, cyclists as a community, and making streets safer for all users.

Jorge Díaz-Cidoncha García has played and coached for diverse football teams in Spain, Australia, and Switzerland. He has a BA in Sport Sciences, two MA degrees in Sport Management/Sciences, and a PhD in Sport Sciences focused on small-sided games. He also holds a UEFA PRO coaching license and a Technical Director's license by the Spanish Football Association. He currently works as FIFA's Youth Football and Grassroots manager in Zurich, Switzerland.

Bill Dittmar is the co-founder of Executive Fusion, Inc with his wife Heidi since 1991. He lives in Newport News, Virginia, United States. He is also the Co-Owner of Synergy Global 4U which is a private Virtual Campus featuring leasable offices, training classrooms, conference halls and a full virtual Expo Center. He is a member of the faculty at "The Honor Foundation" which specializes in training transitioning Navy Seals and Special Forces Operators for civilian life. He was a Major League Soccer (MLS) Referee from 1996 to 2015 and is currently an MLS Referee Coach for the Professional Referees Organization (PRO).

Sarah Duffy, PhD, is a Lecturer at Western Sydney University, Australia. Her doctoral thesis studied the consequences of the commercialisation of a common pool resource (CPR) and the influence of power and politics on CPR management. She is interested in the consequences of marketing in terms of fairness, quality of life and environmental sustainability for the stakeholders involved. She is currently researching how the Australian energy industry is responding to climate change and issues of gender in the workplace.

Tom Fabian is a Postdoctoral Fellow in Sport Anthropology at the University of Ottawa, Canada. He applies both historical and anthropological methods to sport, physical culture, and body culture. His main research interests focus on traditional games, university sport, and community sport. Current projects include sport for reconciliation in Indigenous communities, the history of the Universiade, and the environmental benefits of participating in traditional games. The impetus for the study herein stems from the fact that he lives in the small Nova Scotian town of Antigonish with his partner, offspring, and canine.

Aleah N. Fisher is a student in the MA program in Communication Studies at Arizona State University in Phoenix, United States. Her research interests include rhetoric and race and identity.

George Fox has a BA Hons in History from the University of Bristol, United Kingdom, and currently works for a financial firm in London, United Kingdom, as an Assistant Fund Manager. At Bristol, he was both a player and committee member for the university side whilst also coaching men's and women's teams.

Through his involvement with the university sides, he was recruited as a Tournament Director for the *International Super Masters 5-a-side World Cup*, a role he has continued to perform ever since.

Marcus Free is a Lecturer in Media and Communication Studies at Mary Immaculate College, University of Limerick, Ireland. He has published widely in international journals and scholarly collections on the intersections of sport, gender, race and national identity in film, print and broadcast media. He is co-author of *The Uses of Sport: A Critical Study* (2005) and co-editor of *Sport, the Media and Ireland: Interdisciplinary Perspectives* (2020).

Susanna Hedenborg is Full Professor in Sport Sciences at Malmö University, Sweden, and President of the Swedish Research Council for Sport Science. She has a background in social and economic history and her sport research has focused on gender issues, children and youth sport, and equestrian sports. She is involved in a research program on sports, outdoors, and environmental challenges.

Jens Høyer-Kruse is an Assistant Professor at the Centre for Sports, Health and Civil Society of the Department of Sports Science and Clinical Biomechanics, University of Southern Denmark. His main research interests consist of sports facilities, sports policy, sports geography, active living and sports participation. His current research focuses on the movement habits of the Danish population and the use and non-use of their surrounding areas and sports facilities.

Harry T. Hubball is a Professor in the Faculty of Education at The University of British Columbia in Vancouver, Canada. His research interests include Masters Football Coaching and the Scholarship of Educational Leadership. He is the founding Chairperson of the *International Masters 5-a-side/Futsal World Cup and Symposium* (2006–2022); Director and Head Coach of the *Inter UBC Masters Soccer Academy Program*; and he is an avid player of 50–60+small-sided football. He has published over twenty-five articles and has been invited to give masters football coaching sessions and related research presentations in over twenty countries.

Bjarne Ibsen is a Professor at the Centre for Sports, Health and Civil Society of the Department of Sports Science and Clinical Biomechanics, University of Southern Denmark. His main fields of research are sociological analyses of civil society, associations, volunteering, interactions between the voluntary and public sector, sports and civil society politics and physical movement habits.

Carrie Kaput is a student in the MA program in Communication Studies at Arizona State University in Phoenix, United States. She also holds a BSc in Political Science and a B.A. in Social Justice and Human Rights with additional emphasis in Public Policy and Sustainability.

Jeffrey W. Kassing is a Professor of Communication Studies in the School of Social & Behavioral Sciences at Arizona State University in Phoenix, United States. His research interests include sport and identity, sports media, and soccer. He is the Co-Director of the Sport, Media, and Culture Research Group at Arizona State University.

Keara Katayama is a student in the MA program in Communication Studies at Arizona State University in Phoenix, United States. Her research interests include religious communication with a focus on organizational leadership structures and procedures, interpersonal conflict, and rejection messages.

Yuya Kiuchi lives in Lansing, Michigan, United States, and is the graduate director of the GPIDEA online graduate programs and assistant professor in the Department of Human Development and Family Studies at Michigan State University, United States.

Kath Leflay is based in Sutton Coldfield, United Kingdom. After finishing her BSc in Sport in Society at Sheffield Hallam University, she worked in roles in sport management and sport development. She completed her MA in Sport and Popular Culture at Sheffield Hallam, and worked part time in further education teaching on BTEC level 3 Sports Studies and Sports Science courses. She completed her PhD in 2015 and is currently Principal Lecturer for Recruitment at the University of Wolverhampton, United Kingdom. She teaches across a range of applied sport sociology and sport development modules and is a research active in both sport sociology and teaching and learning.

Helen Jefferson Lenskyj is a Professor Emerita at the University of Toronto, Canada, where she taught sociology. Her work as a researcher and activist on gender and sport issues began in the 1980s, and she has published eight books critiquing the Olympic industry, as well as five books on gender and sport. Her most recent publication is *The Olympic Games: A Critical Approach* (Emerald, 2020). She completed her PhD at the University of Toronto in 1983 and was a Professor from 1986 until retiring in 2007. Her website is www.helenlenskyj.ca.

Risto Kauppinen, MD PhD, is a magnetic resonance imaging scientist in Bristol, United Kingdom, with a long-standing track record developing imaging techniques for improved diagnosis and treatment monitoring of common neurological disorders, including stroke, dementia, and cancer. He has been a keen grassroots footballer since youth and has been instrumental in organizing international senior football tournaments held in several European countries.

Scott Matteson is an instructor in the Department of Human Development and Family Studies at Michigan State University, United States. He is currently pursuing a Doctorate in Education from the University of South Carolina in curriculum and instruction with a concentration in educational technology. His research focus includes how the implementation of technology into classrooms influences student engagement through motivation, choice, and voice. He lives in Haslett, Michigan, United States.

Jim McKay is a Professor and Honorary Senior Research Fellow in the Institute for Advanced Studies in the Humanities at The University of Queensland, Australia. He has published widely on topics such as gender, race, nationalism, globalization, and popular culture, and is a former editor of the International Review for the Sociology of Sport.

Matt Moore is an Associate Professor and Chair in the Department of Social Work at Ball State University, United States. He is a former NCAA tennis player and current college coach (Anderson University). His research focuses on the integration of social work in sports from a macro perspective. He wrote the first ever Social Work in Sports textbook, has several publications on Sport Social Work, presented at dozens of national and international conferences. He was the recipient of the 2017 Excellence in Teaching Award at Ball State. He earned his MSW and Ph.D. from Indiana University, United States.

Michelle O'Shea, PhD, is a Senior Lecturer at Western Sydney University, Australia. Her research interests are in the areas of sport, culture and society. More specifically her research involves the critical examination of professional and non-profit sport organization functioning, addressing issues relevant to gender and diversity, sport organization community and societal impacts, sport marketing and social media communications, and fandom. Prior to joining Western Sydney University, her professional expertise was in Sport Marketing and Business Development.

Johan R. Norberg is Full Professor in Sport Sciences at Malmö University, Sweden. He has a background in history and his research is focused on sport policy, governance, and sport history. He was Chief Secretary of the Swedish Sports Committee of Inquiry between 2007 and 2008, and since 2010 he has been assigned to The Swedish Research Council for Sport Sciences, monitoring government support to sport.

Jerry F. Reynolds II is an Assistant Professor of Social Work at Ball State University in Muncie, Indiana, United States. His research explores family dynamics in youth sports. A former college athlete, he serves as Vice President of the Alliance of Social Workers in Sports and has been a volunteer coach at the youth, middle, high school, and collegiate levels. He holds a BSW from The Catholic University of America in Washington, DC, an MSW from the University of Michigan, and a PhD from Louisiana State University. He is married to Jennifer and they have three sons, Jack, James, and Jerry III.

Scott D. Robertson is a Doctoral Candidate and Teacher Educator at The University of British Columbia in Vancouver, Canada. His research interests include teacher autonomy and the dynamics of curricular relationships as well as mentoring and teacher education. He is also a secondary school teacher and an avid amateur footballer. His career as an educator began in 1990, coaching youth football, and in 1997 he also became a coach educator. He has coached amateur players and teams across most age and skill levels.

Daniel Roman is a Masters graduate from Western Sydney University, Australia. Having completed a Masters of Business Administration degree, he has brought along his passion for sport and business into a research capacity. His research interests include issues around fandom, innovative sport engagement techniques, particularly around digital and interactive devices, and exploring how contemporary sport knowledge can be applied in different settings. He has also attained professional expertise in sport marketing and participation and retention practices by working at a number of Australian sport organizations, specifically through his involvement in a membership department at one of Australia's most prominent clubs.

Severino R. Sarmenta Jr. is a Lecturer at the Department of Communication, Ateneo de Manila, Quezon City, Philippines, where prior to his retirement in 2017, he was Assistant Professor and twice department chair. Aside from academic work, he is an active sports broadcaster and writer and has covered Philippine and international sports events like the Seoul and Sydney Olympics, as well as three Asian Games editions. Recently, he was at the 2020 Tokyo Olympics as international commentator for Dentsu Broadcasting as well as for Philippine broadcast networks Cignal TV, One Sports and TV5.

Jeffrey O. Segrave is Professor of Health and Human Physiological Sciences at Skidmore College, United States. In 2005, he was appointed the David H. Porter Endowed Chair. His main area of scholarly interest lies in the socio-cultural analysis of sport; hence, he embraces an interdisciplinary approach that seeks to study sport at the intersections of history, sociology, philosophy and literature. His primary scholarly focus is on the history of the Olympic Games. He has published three edited anthologies—including *Olympism* (1980) and *The Olympic Games in Transition* (1988)—and more than 20 book chapters and 60 articles on sport in a wide variety of journals.

Tim Sperber is a PhD student at the Olympic Studies Centre and Institute of Sport History of the German Sport University Cologne, Germany. He has a BA in Sport Management and communication and a MA in International Sport

Development and Politics from the German Sport University Cologne. His PhD project Climate change and the Olympic Movement contributes to the field of sport ecology from a global perspective. The research aims to illustrate climate action and climate adaptation within the organized sport in Brazil, Germany, New Zealand, and South Africa.

Isaiah Utley is a graduate of the MA program in Communication Studies at Arizona State University in Phoenix, United States. He currently serves as the Marketing and Communications Manager at the Ice Den in Scottsdale, Arizona. His research interests include sport, social media, sport fandom, and sport politics/activism.

Ulrike Vogl is an Associate Professor at the Department of Linguistics of Ghent University, Belgium. Her research focus is on historical sociolinguistics, pragmatics, language ideology, and critical discourse analysis. Since 2019, she has collaborated on an interdisciplinary research project on the changing professional identity of group fitness instructors.

Trinity Winton is a graduate of the MA program in Communication Studies at Arizona State University. Her research interests include intrapersonal communication and communication within the American prison system.

Part One

Sport Events and Leagues

Chapter 1

Strategic Covid-19 Safety-Protocol: Preparing to Restart the International 60+ Masters Small-Sided Football World Cup in Denmark 2021

Scott D. Robertson; Harry T. Hubball, Lars Corlin-Christensen, Risto Kauppinen, George Fox, and Jorge Díaz-Cidoncha García

Introduction

An ageing population on a global scale has resulted in the significant growth of amateur / grassroots football competition at senior age groups. At local, national, and international levels, more and more people aged 55–70+ are playing traditional football, walking football, and futsal in small-sided formats, e.g., 3v3 up to 6v6 (Baker, Fraser-Thomas, Dionigi, and Horton 2010; Hubball, Reddy, Sweeney, and Kauppinen 2018; Hubball and García 2020; Hubball and García in press). However, in the context of return-to-play safety-protocols in response to the Covid-19 pandemic, very few studies examine the key adaptations and preparations for sporting event restarts that meet the unique health and safety needs and circumstances of competitive senior athletes, e.g., aged 60+ (McCartney, Sullivan, and Heneghan 2020). Meeting the needs and circumstances of senior players in an international seniors' sporting context, and also the coaches, referees, volunteers, and spectators who attend the event, is complex, multifaceted, and paramount.

This chapter presents key stakeholder perspectives regarding modification and adaptation of play conditions and event preparations for the restart of the two-day 2021 *International 60+ Masters Small-sided Football World Cup* (2021 IMSWC) at the Akademisk Boldklub FC in Denmark. This event was postponed due to the pandemic lockdown in 2020 and its ensuing restrictions and has since been rescheduled to take place on August 14–15, 2021. Specifically, this chapter examines the strategic development of evidence-based practice and representation, and the resulting depth of understanding about Covid-19 return-to-play safety-protocols designed in the context of a seniors' international sport competition. Readers may want to reflect on the following questions as they consider the

Covid-19 return-to-play safety-protocol (RSP) within their own international seniors' sporting event contexts.

> 1. How are key stakeholders in your seniors' sporting event context best represented within the governance structure for Covid-19 RSPs?
>
> 2. How do key situational factors, e.g., geographic region, venue/club context, allocation of people and funding resources, shape the modification or adaptation of play conditions and event preparations as you restart the international seniors (55–70+) sporting event in your context?
>
> 3. How are Covid-19 RSPs understood, interpreted, organized, delivered, experienced, and/or institutionalized in your context?
>
> 4. What are the most common best practices and challenges for implementing Covid-19 RSPs in your context?
>
> 5. How are effective Covid-19 RSPs evaluated and best supported in your context?

Drawing on interdisciplinary research and case study methodology, multiple data sources such as documentation analysis, focus group interviews, and survey questionnaires inform the strategic development of evidence-based practice for Covid-19 RSPs in the context of a seniors' international sport competition.

Theoretical Underpinnings

Strategic international tournament development is key to enhancing Covid-19 RSPs in diverse seniors amateur / grassroots small-sided football settings. In addition to accounting for the host organization and its geographical setting, strategic international tournament development emphasizes a number of related factors. In addition to inclusive organizational leadership, other factors include how the tournament is effectively planned, delivered, evaluated, and improved and how tournament leaders, officials, guests, team members, and spectators are authentically supported and engaged. In this context, "delivery" or implementation centers on multicultural football perspectives and the facilitation of intercultural engagement and adaptation pertaining to Covid-19 RSPs for the restart of the rescheduled 2021 IMSWC in Denmark (Blatter and Dvorak 2014; Krustrup et al. 2018; Skoradal et al. 2018; Franks, Lilley, Hubball, and Franks 2019).

Given varying levels of support and often limited resources in seniors amateur / grassroots football contexts, strategic international tournament development that is focused on research-informed and evidence-based practice provides a critical foundation for both quality assurance and quality enhancement in this regard (Century and Cancella 2016). For example, interdisciplinary sport science research (Mueller and Albrecht 2016; FIFA 2015; Baker, Fraser-Thomas, Dionigi, and Horton 2010; Reid and Arcodia 2002) provides key insights into the unique health and safety needs and circumstances of senior amateur / grassroots teams and players, as these relate to Covid-19 RSPs for international small-sided football tournaments:

- biomedical, e.g., WHO and host nation health ministry testing and vaccination guidelines

- physiological, e.g., injury prevention, cardiovascular health and fitness, strength, and flexibility

- psychological, e.g., theories of mental health, motivation, skills acquisition/adaptation, and active health

- adherence

- sociocultural, e.g., social, cultural, economic, historical, and political factors

- educational leadership, e.g., strategic coach inquiry, research methodologies, communities of practice

- event management, program development, implementation and evaluation, organizational leadership

- team and player development, health and performance analysis

The *Fédération Internationale de Football Association* (FIFA), the world governing body for football, in partnership with the *World Health Organization* (WHO), developed a practical assessment tool aimed at helping teams, clubs, and member associations toward a safe return to football (FIFA 2020). There are four main guidelines:

- Measures to facilitate a return to participation

- Risk assessment of football events

- Player health, fitness, and injury considerations

- Amateur and grassroots football

During a global pandemic, however, any return must carefully and respectfully weigh the benefits enjoyed by multinational seniors small-sided football participants with the profound potential of risk to health and safety brought about by social gatherings:

> The resumption of footballing activities can contribute many health, economic, social, and cultural benefits to a society emerging from the COVID-19 environment; however, all decisions about such a resumption must be made with careful reference to local and national public health guidelines. The important guiding principle is that the resumption of footballing activities should not compromise the health of individuals or the community. Furthermore, the resumption of footballing activities should be based on objective health information to ensure that activities are conducted safely and do not risk increased [sic] local Covid-19 transmission rates (FIFA 2020, 13).

While the frameworks above provide broad-based assistance for international tournament leaders and football associations / clubs / organizations, a strategic RSP that can meet the needs of senior amateur / grassroots small-sided football teams and players in an international tournament setting requires more customized, evidence-based practice. In such a context, we argue that strategic international tournament development to enhance Covid-19 RSPs is inherently situated, socially mediated, and locally constructed within broader communities of practice. For example, a host football organization within a particular cultural context and political landscape will have inherently situated strategic priorities, access to available resources, and levels of support that typically frame the tournament experience. The tournament's development will also be mediated by key stakeholder support and by engagement with respective on-site multinational tournament leaders, officials, coaches, and players. Finally, any conceptions of "quality" and "effectiveness" that pertain to understanding and improving the tournament will be inextricably bound within its localized contextual setting. As a result, implementing strategic international tournament development to enhance Covid-19 RSPs can be challenging for tournament leaders and football associations / clubs / organizations anywhere around the world.

Conceptual Framework

Building on previous research in this field, the following flexible, iterative, and heuristic framework has been adapted and applied in diverse senior amateur / grassroots small-sided football coaching settings (Hubball and García 2020; Hubball and García 2021). Strategic coach inquiry is central to each specific component of this conceptual framework (see Figure 1).

Figure 1: Strategic International Tournament Development Framework to Enhance Covid-19 Return-to-play Safety-protocol in Amateur/grassroots 55–70+ Small-sided Football Contexts (Hubball and García 2020; Hubball and García 2021).

Context Strategies

Context strategies influence all components of the conceptual framework and center on two broad considerations. First, they consider inclusive organizational leadership, e.g., representation of highly committed (and frequently volunteer) multinational tournament committee members with relevant expertise; networking; communication; and strategic coach inquiry skills for key roles and responsibilities. Second, they consider the fostering of a community of practice to enhance Covid-19 RSPs in the context of the 2021 IMSWC. Grounded in evidence-based practice, context strategies focus on conducting a comprehensive needs assessment, key among these being relevant research literature (see WHO / FIFA / Football Association / government health ministry guidelines). They also include on-line meetings, on-site visits, and the development of a detailed event planning document with the host organization in order to align a strategic purpose, e.g., institutional aims, objectives, values, and political landscape, with available resources, e.g., specialized leadership expertise, facilities, and equipment available to both the international tournament organization and host organizational setting (Wenger-Trayner and Wenger-Trayner, 2015).

Planning Strategies

Planning strategies take into account all components of the conceptual framework and focus on an evidence-based approach to strategic international tournament goals. Long-term goals can include a shared vision for future international tournament locations, venues, and practices while intermediate goals can include inclusive organizational communications and a multinational team-recruitment strategy. Short-term goals can include non-conflicting tournament dates, indoor or outdoor seasonal consideration, single or multi-day competition format, and program itinerary. As well, "Plan B, C, and D" contingencies for various Covid-19 conditions can be set in accordance with the estimated number of attending international teams. During the planning phase, it is critical to engage key international stakeholder representatives, such as with technology-enabled social media and web-based communication tools (Chambers, Glasgow, and Stange 2013) in order to enhance Covid-19 RSPs in the context of the 2021 IMSWC.

Covid-19 Return-to-Play Safety-Protocol Strategies

RSP strategies take into account all components of the conceptual framework and focus on multicultural perspectives and the facilitation of intercultural engagement, such as connecting senior athletes and participants in meaningful ways throughout the duration of the 2021 IMSWC (FIFA 2020; WHO 2021).

Impact Assessment Strategies

Impact assessment strategies take into account all components of the conceptual framework and focus on an evidence-based approach to authentic assessment and evaluation, i.e., quality assurance and quality enhancement, of international tournament practices pertaining to Covid-19 RSPs. Essentially, this involves judging the degree to which the international tournament goals are attained as well as assessing the international tournament's quality, effectiveness, efficiency, and even longer-term contributions, all of which can inform future decisions regarding what is highly valued and/or made explicit for further development or improvement. This process begins by identifying context-specific outcome criteria specifically pertaining to Covid-19 RSPs that can indicate success in an international tournament context. Common issues might include a reduction in the number of participating teams and countries, the effectiveness and/or efficiency of the Covid-19 safety-protocols, the experience of participating multinational teams and players, including any potential international competition barriers, the economic consequences of Covid-19 contingencies, and the quality of organizational leadership. Context-specific outcome indicators for international tournament success must be aligned with relevant evidence of impact in order to monitor positive change and enhance Covid-19 RSPs in the context of the 2021 IMSWC (Hamilton and Feldman 2014; Yin 2017).

Strategic Coach Inquiry

Strategic coach inquiry informs all components of the conceptual framework in order to provide evidence-based practice to enhance Covid-19 RSP in the context of the 2021 IMSWC (Coe, Waring, Hedges, and Arthur 2017).

Strategic coach inquiry involves the following factors:

- identifying context-specific priority outcomes / criteria / indicators, i.e., research objectives / questions, for further development and/or improvement

- consulting relevant literature and on-line sources to ground and inform context-specific international tournament practices

- selecting an appropriate context-specific educational research methodology, e.g., action research

- appreciative inquiry, case study research, ethnographic inquiry, phenomenological inquiry, self-study research, based on the practice context and outcomes / criteria / indicators

- selecting appropriate context-specific data collection methods, e.g., qualitative, quantitative, or mixed, in order to triangulate and align research priorities with evidence-based practice in the international tournament context, e.g., qualitative methods include survey tools and focus group interviews with international team managers, international tournament committee planning and debrief meetings, video analysis, international team performance records, and media reports

- developing a unique research design in order to operationalize as well as recognize the limitations of strategic educational inquiry and evidence-based practice in the international tournament context

- assessing appropriate and relevant, e.g., professional and academic, venues to disseminate strategic coach inquiry in the international tournament context

Through strategic coach inquiry, Figure 1 can help international tournament leaders to engage key stakeholder representatives across iterative components and phases of implementation, whether face-to-face or by way of technology-enabled social media and web-based communication tools. Altogether, this framework has provided a useful strategic international tournament development framework in order to enhance Covid-19 RSPs in the context of the 2021 IMSWC.

Method

Drawing on case study methodology employed over a twelve-month period, the purpose of this practice-based inquiry was to develop a strategic Covid-19 safety-protocol for restarting the 2021 *International 60+ Masters 5-a-side Football World Cup Tournament* in Denmark. This two-day amateur/grassroots international seniors' small-sided football tournament and symposia (Hubball, Mitchell, and Reddy 2010; Hubball, Reddy, Sweeney, and Kauppinen 2018) is hosted annually at football clubs / institutions / universities and organizations throughout Europe and the UK as follows:

Table 1.1: Annual Hosts International Seniors' Small-sided Football Tournament and Symposia

Year	Venue	Age Category
2022	November TBC, Doha, Qatar	60+
2022	Zurich, FIFA, Home of Football, Switzerland	60+ & 65+
2021	Copenhagen, Denmark	60+ & 65+
2020	Copenhagen, Denmark *Covid-19 cancellation	58+ & 65+
2019	Paris, France	58+ & 65+
2018	Bristol, University of Bristol, England	55+ & 65+
2017	Swansea, Swansea University, Wales	55+ & 65+
2016	Algarve, Portugal	50+
2015	San Sebastián, Spain	50+
2014	Verona, Italy	50+
2013	Real Sociedad, Spain	50+
2011	Antalya, Turkey	50+
2010	Birmingham, Aston University, England	45+
2008	Flizbach, University of Zurich, Switzerland	45+
2006	Chelsea School, University of Brighton, England	40+

The invitational grassroots international masters tournament is limited to men's representative teams of age-specific players selected from any club, community, institutional group, or football association. Participating teams include representatives from Belgium, Canada, England, France, Spain (FC Barcelona), Germany (Werder Bremen), Greece, Hungary, Holland (former national players), Ireland, Kenya, Morocco, South Africa, Oman, Switzerland, Turkey, U.S.A., Wales, Scotland, Finland, Norway, and Denmark, as well as a multinational United Nations team comprising 60+ players from Sweden, France, Finland, Denmark, and Canada.

Case study research methodology provides a rich description of the context of international tournament implementation. It is highly generative in nature and particularly well-suited to developing a strategic Covid-19 safety-protocol for restarting the 2021 IMSWC in Denmark. In order to investigate this phenomenon within its real-life practice context (Dionigi 2006; Pearson, Albon, and Hubball 2015), data analyses pertaining to specific Covid-19 conditions and re-start procedures in Denmark were drawn from relevant documentation such as WHO, FIFA, and Danish Health Ministry Covid-19 safety guidelines, as well as from focus group interviews and survey questionnaires, to assess the Covid-19 conditions locally as well as the restart procedures in Denmark. For example, focus group interviews were held with key multidisciplinary and multinational tournament stakeholder representatives, such as medical doctors, tournament host leaders, and an organizational committee of volunteer coaches, researchers, officials, and players. The focus groups were held from January to August in several formats: monthly for two to two-and-a-half hours per meeting; weekly for ninety minutes during the final six weeks (including on-site visits and preparations), and daily for forty-five minutes during the final week prior to kick-off. A synthesis and summary of each meeting's minutes was forwarded to all committee members, with a request for appropriate edits where necessary. Specific prompts for this inquiry are listed below:

- How are key multinational stakeholder perspectives best represented within the governance structure for the Covid-19 RSP?

- How are key situational factors, e.g., geographic region, Danish government, host club context, shaping the restart of the 2021 IMSWC in Denmark?

- What are the most common best practices and challenges for implementing a strategic Covid-19 safety-protocol for restarting the 2021 IMSWC in Denmark?

Qualitative data sources were analyzed using the constant comparative method through categorization and finally to thematization (Coe, Waring, Hedges, and Arthur 2017). Next, member checking was utilized to establish major themes and data patterns, and to discern complex commonalities, contradictions, and interactions pertaining to the development of a strategic Covid-19 safety-protocol for restarting the 2021 IMSWC in Denmark. The use of iterative and multiple data sources established the trustworthiness of the research findings through triangulation.

Results

Strategic Covid-19 Return-to-Play Safety-Protocol

Based on advanced Danish Government Health Regulations and Guidance regarding Covid-19 safety, significant accommodation and scheduling flexibility afforded by the Danish club hosts (reflecting spring-to-summer seasonal differences), and survey responses about vaccinations and confidence to travel internationally from participating senior multinational team managers and match officials, revised viable tournament dates were changed from the month of May to August 14–15, 2021, and customized Covid-19 RSPs for the restart of the 2021 IMSWC were updated to remain consistent with the highest current standards.

Significant measures have been developed to address specific Covid-19 concerns for this senior amateur / grassroots small-sided international football tournament. The following strategies are in addition to standard risk-assessment safety-protocols that have been developed for the 2021 IMSWC, such as ensuring competent officials, organizational staff and playable pitch conditions, responsive procedures in case of player injury or fatigue, suitable protection and footwear requirements, and weather contingencies. The following non-exhaustive list of strategies was established to provide customized measures for minimizing risk during the months of tournament planning, during which time this chapter was written. Due to rapidly changing Covid-19 pandemic circumstances, these strategies have and may still require continual adjustment, according to the realities of the situation until (and likely throughout) the tournament event itself.

Pre-Tournament Travel Assessments

- Check WHO guidelines

- Check Danish and national government travel advisories and restrictions, e.g., pre-trip vaccinations and/or pre-during-post tournament Covid-19 testing requirements

- Check airline, travel agent, hotel, and insurance advisories and restrictions

- Check FIFA / DFA and host Club football advisories and restrictions

- Require all tournament attendees to consult their primary care providers / GPs about any personal health risks that need to be considered (Covid-19 related and non-Covid-19 related diseases)

On-Site Tournament Leadership

- The two-day international tournament will strictly adhere to Danish Government / FIFA / DFA / host Football Club Covid-19 related health and safety regulations and guidance to minimize risks of spreading common infectious diseases, such as the common cold, influenza, and the Covid-19 viruses.

- For tracing purposes, only teams, players, officials, and guests that have been registered with the international tournament committee prior to the event may attend the two-day tournament and masters football research symposium.

- Host club officials, including the designated Covid-19 health and safety officer, medical doctor(s) and volunteer staff, will provide regular public health reminders, rules, and communications throughout the event, such as whether players and match officials are required to wear face covers and maintain 1.5m physical distancing, e.g., three-touch only ball rule, during warm-ups and competitive games.

- The guest speaker at the two-day international symposium, which is held at the host club venue in conjunction with the tournament on August 14–15, 2021, will be the Head Doctor of Leicester City Football Club (LCFC), a professional club in England. As part of his presentation, the guest speaker will address key aspects of Covid-19 safety protocols at LCFC as well as those implemented during the pandemic-stricken 2020–2021 English Premier Football League season.

On-Site Tournament Health Assessments for Entering the Venue

- All registered participants must sign the waiver, recommended by Danish authorities, acknowledging that they have read and agreed to abide by the customized Covid-19 safety-protocols.

- If authorized by Danish authorities, tournament attendees will be required to demonstrate a negative Covid-19 test document within three days prior to entry.

- Tournament attendees must be free of any Covid-19 symptoms such as fever, chills, cough, shortness of breath, sore throat and painful swallowing, stuffy or runny nose, loss of sense of smell, headache, muscle aches, fatigue, and loss of appetite; as a responsible organization, the host Club will notify their Health & Safety Authorities if any participant or member(s) of their team is identified with Corona virus symptoms.

- All tournament attendees will receive health screening via questionnaire and touchless thermometer reading that must record below 37.7 o C (100.4 o F).

On-Site Tournament Facilities

- All tournament attendees, e.g., spectators, volunteers, club staff, players, officials, etc., must adhere to physical distancing guidelines and remain 1.5m apart as well as use hand-washing hygiene and wear face covers at the tournament venue where appropriate.

- Tournament spectators will be located in separate marked areas at the host venue allowing no contact with tournament participants.

- The two-day tournament will be played in a round-robin format in an "Age Group / Cohort" of twelve small-sided teams or less, to a maximum of one hundred players per cohort. After Day One, games and twenty-hour break, teams will stay with the same Cohort for the new small-sided game format on Day Two.

- Tournament teams will arrive at the host venue at specified time-slots and will stay in specified (marked) areas. Each team will move as a group from their designated area to a scheduled game and avoid any on-or-off-pitch physical contact with opponents and officials (including handshakes, etc.). Team benches will be placed on opposite sides of the pitch.

- In order to avoid exposed time to opponents or teammates during small-sided games, players will be required to execute sideline kicks within a two-second maximum and execute corner kicks within a five-second maximum. The "wall" for the sideline free kick or a direct free kick will be maintained by only

> one player at a distance of 3m. Goalkeepers must wear gloves and should sanitize these at half-time.

- Minor injuries will be self-treated where appropriate; otherwise, first-aid / trainer / medical personnel will be equipped (with appropriate protection) to provide assistance.

Thus, health and safety practices in this international 60+ masters football tournament are inherently situated within Danish health and safety regulatory practice context, and they are socially mediated through a responsive international 60+ masters football community, i.e., via a diverse intercultural exchange and negotiation of shared understandings for inclusive international tournament health and safety practices. Finally, implementation of customized international tournament health and safety practices is personally enacted, i.e., across the range of multinational 60+ teams, players, officials and spectators, each tournament participant bears their own responsibility to enact tournament health and safety practices.

Discussion

Without question, the rescheduling of the 2021 IMSWC in Denmark has resulted in significantly increased workloads and time commitments for volunteer organization committee members as they face complex, uncertain, and constantly changing pandemic circumstances. In order to adapt and problem-solve successful solutions for tournament implementation, despite significant pandemic challenges, the tournament organizational leadership team has drawn on context factors represented in the conceptual framework, such as the fortuitous circumstances in Denmark regarding the national management of the pandemic as well as the country's reputation for high standards.

Of critical importance has been the inclusive, collaborative, responsive nature of the leadership team itself, each member having a vested personal interest that the tournament proceed and thus being determined to continually overcome set-backs and adversity. Also important has been the leadership team having adequate 'political clout', including the capability for rapid communication and decision-making between participating team managers and tournament officials, access to relevant venue support and on-site club resources, and even enough sway to have the local Mayor officially open the event! The Covid-19 situation also had direct implications for ongoing forecasting of event viability and rescheduling. This has prompted additional event communications, including on-line executive team meetings, e-mail surveys and memos to registered team managers and match officials, and tournament website updates that highlight critical benchmark timelines, the strategic development of the Covid-19 RSPs, and related financial considerations.

For example, withdrawal of several multinational teams due to Covid-19 concerns five months prior to the tournament presented potentially significant financial implications for the remaining majority of teams and, consequently, for the viability of the tournament. Furthermore, within one month prior to tournament kick-off, the United Kingdom (non-EU) with the exception of Wales was placed by Danish authorities on a travel Red list, a restriction permitting entry to Denmark, regardless of vaccinations, only with an "essential travel" verification certificate and a two-week quarantine requirement. This Red list designation for players from England, Scotland, and Northern Ireland resulted in the last-minute withdrawal by multiple UK-based teams, players, and match officials. As a result of this dynamic situation, urgent and necessary team recruitment strategies were launched to replace withdrawn teams with appropriate age-specific wait-list multinational and local teams for the two-day event in August 2021. A team refund policy consistent with tournament website information established that, under these unprecedented circumstances, only partial team refunds would be provided following the tournament (September 2021), once full structural costs could be taken into account. Overseen by a volunteer multinational tournament executive committee, the not-for-profit annual budget model functions solely from minimal team registration fee revenues, covering basic costs for facility rentals, match officials, a guest sport science speaker, team trophies, and participation medals.

Further health-related costs have fallen to participating teams and players representing North America, Europe, Nordic countries, United Nations, and the U.K., incurred by the requirement that international teams returning within 72 hours to their home countries are to be tested in centers within the Copenhagen region. Such costs can also be augmented by additional staff volunteer contributions at the host venue, such as the recruitment of an emergency medical preparedness team comprising physicians and others with appropriate expertise from among the pool of multinational players and team officials.

Finally, in addition to strategic development, impact assessment will be integral to the implementation of the strategic Covid-19 RSPs during the two-day 2021 IMSWC in Denmark. For example, quality assurance and enhancement data, i.e., for use in subsequent 2021 and 2022 international tournaments, will be collected during the August 2021 tournament. Subsequently, a one-month post-tournament follow-up will focus on analyses of relevant key stakeholder perspectives, such as team managers, players, and Akademisk Boldklub FC officials, and tournament documentation records, e.g., team registrations, budget accounting, the tournament director's field notes, and even news reports, such as localized newspaper coverage ("Wales Walk It" 2021) and a national ITV news report broadcast in the UK (Wales Walking Football 2021). Looking ahead, largely based on successful implementation of Denmark 2021, the next 60+ World Cup tournament scheduled for 2022 in Zurich is already at full capacity with twenty registered international teams and a substantial waitlist.

Altogether, such perspectives pertain first to the effectiveness and efficiency of the 2021 IMSWC's strategic Covid-19 RSPs, including any potential for further improvements, and second to the impact of the strategic Covid-19 RSPs on the participation experiences of the event's multinational participants. Therefore, following the event, further research will examine the effectiveness of the customized strategies that result from their implementation.

Conclusion

In the context of the current global Covid-19 pandemic, coaches and international event leaders around the world are responsible for the added health and safety needs and circumstances of amateur/grassroots seniors' (55–70+) athletes. Evidence-based practice from this inquiry suggests that strategic Covid-19 return-to-play safety-protocols can take many forms and provide a critical foundation for quality assurance and enhancement. Specifically, data suggest that adapted safety-protocols for amateur/grassroots international 60+ seniors football events during the Covid-19 pandemic focus on responsive age-appropriate risk assessment practices as well as related concerns such as facilities, equipment, travel, team participation (withdrawal and replacement issues), financial considerations, and restricted-play adaptations / experiences for limited physical contact.

Furthermore, critical leadership contributions (inclusive of multinational stakeholder representatives, increased organizational workloads, and complex "Plan B+" contingencies), key organizational supports, and evidence-based practices are essential aspects of the science, politics, and art of implementation. Although the international case presented is still a work in progress, both theoretically and practically, significant developments and commitments to safety-protocols have been made in preparation for meeting the unique age-related health and safety needs and circumstances of competitive seniors' players in the two-day 2021 IMSWC.

REFERENCES

Ashley, Laura Day. 2017. "Planning Your Research." In *Research Methods and Methodologies in Education* (2nd ed.), edited by Robert Coe, Michael Waring, Larry V. Hedges, and James Arthur, 34–43. London: Sage.

Baker, Joseph, Jessica Fraser-Thomas, Rylee A. Dionigi, and Sean Horton. 2010. "Sport Participation and Positive Development in Older Persons." *European Review of Ageing and Physical Activity* 7: 3–12.

Blatter, Joseph, and Jiri Dvorak. 2014. "Football for Health—Science Proves that Playing Football on a Regular Basis Contributes to the Improvement of Public Health." *Scandinavian Journal of Medicine and Science in Sports* 24, no. S1: 2–3. https://doi.org/10.1111/sms.12270

Century, Jeanne, and Amy Cassata. 2016. "Implementation Research: Finding Common Ground on What, How, Why, Where, and Who." *Review of Research in Education* 40, no. 1: 169–215.

Chambers, David A., Russell E. Glasgow, and Kurt C. Stange. 2013. "The Dynamic Sustainability Framework: Addressing the Paradox of Sustainment Amid Ongoing Change." *Implementation Science* 8, no. 1. http://dx.doi.org/10.1186/1748-5908-8-117

Danish Health Authority. n.d. "Current Covid-19 Conditions in Denmark." Accessed May 21, 2021. https://www.sst.dk/en/English/Corona-eng.

Dionigi, Rylee A. 2006. "Competitive Sport and Aging: The Need for Qualitative Sociological Research." *Journal of Aging and Physical Activity* 14, no. 4: 365–79.

FIFA, Fédération Internationale de Football Association. 2020a. "COVID-19: Medical Considerations for a Return to Footballing Activity." Last modified May 29, 2020. https://digitalhub.fifa.com/m/1646d5fc62614ee7/original/cpng0f3y5pclmxn0prdb-pdf.pdf.

———. "Making Football Truly Global: The Vision 2020–2023." Last modified February 26, 2020. https://digitalhub.fifa.com/m/a08ad6a73aa4d41b/original/z25oyskjgrxrudiu7iym-pdf.pdf.

———. "Grassroots." Accessed May 21, 2021. https://cdn3.sportngin.com/attachments/document/8546-2348967/FIFA_grassroots_en.pdf.

Franks, Chris, Tom Lilley, Harry T. Hubball, and Ian Franks. 2019. "Injury Prevention and Performance Enhancement: Tournament Strategies for O55+ Masters Football Teams and Players." *International Science and Football Association Newsletter Magazine* 3: 24–31.

Gibbs, Graham R. 2017. "Using Software in Qualitative Data Analysis." In *Research Methods and Methodologies in Education* (2nd ed.), edited by Robert Coe, Michael Waring, Larry V. Hedges, and James Arthur, 243–251. London: Sage.

Hamilton, Jennifer, and Jill Feldman. 2014. "Planning a Program Evaluation: Matching Methodology to Program Status." In *Handbook of Research on Educational Communications and Technology*, edited by Michael J. Spector, M. David Merrill, Jan Elen, and M. J. Bishop, 249–256. New York: Springer.

Hubball, Harry T., and Jorge Díaz-Cidoncha García. 2021. "International Perspectives of Strategic Team and Player Development in Diverse Amateur/Grassroots 60+ Small-Sided Football Contexts." *Global Research in Higher Education* 4, no. 1: 48–63. https://doi.org/10.22158/grhe.v4n1p48.

Hubball, Harry T., and Jorge Díaz-Cidoncha García. 2020a. "Research-informed and Evidence-based Quality Assurance and Enhancement in Amateur/Grassroots Football: Strategic Educational Inquiry for Coach Leaders/Administrators." *Global Research in Higher Education* 3, no. 4: 42–57. https://doi.org/10.22158/grhe.v3n4p42.

———. 2020b. "Strategic Program Development Practices to Enhance Grassroots 55–65+ Small-sided Football in Diverse International Contexts: The Art, Science, and Politics of Implementation." *Global Research in Higher Education* 3, no. 2: 34–51. https://doi.org/10.22158/grhe.v3n2p34.

Hubball, Harry T., Peter A. Reddy, Mike Sweeney, and Risto Kauppinen. 2018a. "Development and Impact of the International Masters/Veterans 5-a-side World Cup Football Tournament (2006–2017): A Scholarly Approach." *The International Journal of Sport and Society* 9, no. 2: 1–17. https://doi.org/10.18848/2152-7857/CGP/v09i02/1-17.

———. "Effective 3-a-side Game Formats and Team Strategies for Advanced Level O55–O70+." *International Science and Football Association Newsletter Magazine* 2: 14–16.

Hubball, Harry T. and Peter A. Reddy. 2015. "Impact of Walking Football: Effective Team Strategies for High Performance Veteran Players." *Journal of Sports Pedagogy and Physical Education* 6, no. 1: 13–27. https://doi.org/10.18848/2381-7100/CGP/v06i01/54114.

Hubball, Harry T., Steve Mitchell, and Peter A. Reddy. 2010. "Universities' Masters World Cup Soccer: Integrated Sports Science Research and Implementation of an International Masters Soccer Community." *World Leisure Journal* 52, no. 1: 48–60. https://doi.org/10.1080/04419057.2010.9674622.

Krustrup, Peter, Craig A. Williams, Magni Mohr, Peter Riis Hansen, Eva Wulff Helge, Anne-Marie Elbe, Maysa de Sousa, Jiri Dvorak, Astrid Junge, Amri Hammami, Andreas Holtermann, Malte N. Larsen, Donald Kirkendall, Jakob F. Schmidt, Thomas R. Andersen, Pasqualina Buono, Mikael Rørth Daniel Parnell, Laila S. Ottesen, Søren Bennike, Jens J. Nielsen, Amy E. Mendham, Abdossaleh Zar, Jacob Uth, Therese Hornstrup, Klaus Brasso, Lars Nybo, Birgitte R. Krustrup, Tim Meyer, Per Aagaard, Jesper L. Andersen, Harry T. Hubball, Peter A. Reddy, Knud Ryom, Felipe Lobelo, Svein Barene, Jørn Wulff Helge, Ioannis G. Fatouros, George P. Nassis, Jincheng Xu, Svein Arne Pettersen, Jose A. Calbet, André F. Seabra, António N. Rebelo, Pedro Figueiredo, Susana Póvoas, Carlo Castagna, Zoran Milanović, Jens Bangsbo, Morten B. Randers, and João Brito. 2018. "The 'Football is Medicine' Platform—Scientific Evidence, Large-scale Implementation of Evidence-based Concepts and Future Perspectives." *Scandinavian Journal of Medicine and Science in Sports* 28, no. S1: 3–7.

McCartney, Margaret, Frank Sullivan, and Carl Heneghan. 2020. "Information and Rational Decision-Making: Explanations to Patients and Citizens about Personal Risk of Covid-19." *BMJ Evidence-Based Medicine*. Last modified October 19, 2020. https://doi:10.1136/bmjebm-2020-111541.

Molanorouzi, Keyvan, Selina Khoo, and Tony Morris. 2015. "Motives for Adult Participation in Physical Activity: Type of Activity, Age, and Gender." *BMC Public Health* 15, no. 66. https://doi.org/10.1186/s12889-015-1429-7.

Mueller, Christoph E., and Maria Albrecht. 2016. *"The Future of Impact Evaluation is Rigorous and Theory-driven."* In *The Future of Evaluation in Modern Societies. Global Trends, New Challenges, Shared Perspectives*, edited by Reinhard Stockmann and Wolfgang Meyer, 283–93. New York: Palgrave Macmillan.

Reid, Sacha, and Charles Arcodia. 2002. "Understanding the Role of the Stakeholder in Event Management." *Journal of Sport and Tourism* 7, no. 3: 20–22.

Skoradal, May-Britt, Pal Weihe, Poula Patursson, Jann Mortensen, Luke Connelly, Peter Krustrup, and Magni Mohr. 2018. "Football Training Improves Metabolic and Cardiovascular Health Status in 55-to-70-Year-Old Women and Men with Prediabetes." *Scandinavian Journal of Medicine and Science in Sports* 28, no. S1: 42–51.

Tischer, Ulrike, Ilse Hartmann-Tews, and Claudia Combrink. 2011. "Sport Participation of the Elderly—The Role of Gender, Age, and Social Class." *European Review of Aging and Physical Activity* 8, no. 2: 83–91.

Trauer, Birgit, Chris Ryan, and Tim Lockyer. 2003. "The South Pacific Masters' Games Competitor Involvement and Games Development: Implications for Management and Tourism." *Journal of Sport and Tourism* 8, no. 4: 240–59.

Wales Walking Football. 2021. "ITV News. Interviewing the over 65s walking football World Cup champions. Wales walking Football Federation." Retrieved from https://www.facebook.com/watch/?v=3020191431571368.

"Wales Walk It at World Cup!" Football: Coedpoeth Duo are Celebrating, *Wrexham Leader*, August 25, 2021.

Webster, Brian, John Gainey, Nigel Hill, Lars Corlin Christensen, and Harry T. Hubball. 2020. "Effective Officiating Practices for an International Masters 5-a-side World Cup Football Tournament." *International Science and Football Association Newsletter Magazine* 4: 5–7.

Wenger-Trayner, Etienne, and Beverly Wenger-Trayner. 2015. "Learning in a Landscape of Practice: A Framework." In *Learning in Landscapes of Practice: Boundaries, Identity, and Knowledgeability in*

Practice-based Learning, edited by Etienne Wenger-Trayner, Mark Fenton-O'Creevy, Steven Hutchinson, Chris Kubiak, and Beverly Wenger-Trayner, 13–29. London: Routledge.

WHO. 2021. "Coronavirus Disease (Covid-19) Pandemic." Accessed May 21, 2021. https://www.who.int/emergencies/diseases/novel-coronavirus-2019

Yin, Robert K. 2017. *Case Study Research and Applications: Design and Methods* (6th ed.). Thousand Oaks: Sage Publications.

Chapter 2

"Celebrate this Victory in a Sensible Manner": Irish Media and the Restart of Gaelic Games in Ireland

Seán Crosson and Marcus Free

Introduction

This chapter will examine the media discourses surrounding the Gaelic Athletic Association's (GAA) recommencement of intra-county club and inter-county Gaelic Games competitions in Ireland in 2020. The timeframe will cover the period from the end of May until the men's All-Ireland Gaelic football final on December 19. As we have previously stressed (Crosson and Free 2021),[1] although Gaelic games are amateur they are the largest participant and spectator sports in Ireland, with players and administrators interconnected with all spheres of Irish society. For this reason, the media discourses surrounding the restarting of competitions highlight how the combination of a pragmatic, measured approach to emerging from the pandemic nationally, and enduring anxieties regarding the risks involved, was acutely registered in the GAA's proceeding with both club and the elite level inter-county competitions.

The chapter is mainly structured around two focal points. The first is the media discourses concerning the restart of club competitions, particularly the experience in county Cavan, where increasing rates of Covid-19 infection were related in the media to celebrations surrounding club games. We concentrate on internally conflicting currents within the local newspaper, *The Anglo-Celt* (and its contrast with national media discourses), as exemplary of local resentment towards Covid-19 restrictions imposed by the Irish government. Our second focus is the restart of the elite level inter-county All-Ireland championships in October 2020. We concentrate here on the GAA's Bloody Sunday centenary

---

[1] This chapter should ideally be read in conjunction with our chapter on the Spring 2020 lockdown (Crosson and Free 2021) which contains a more detailed overview of the GAA's history and specificity as a sports organization. The current chapter is also focused exclusively on men's GAA in Ireland; equally significant has been the impact of the pandemic on Gaelic games featuring women, and the relevant media coverage. It is not possible to address this complex issue adequately within this chapter though it is also the subject of ongoing research by the authors.

commemorative event in Croke Park, Dublin, on November 21, and its role in providing rhetorical justification for the restart and continuation of inter-county competitions as national morale boosters, despite their coinciding with a second wave of increasing Covid-19 infections.

The research employed methods in qualitative critical discourse analysis (Fairclough 2010) in order to identify the constructive roles and tensions between various tropes and rhetorical structures in selections of print, broadcast, podcast, and social media texts during this timescale. Given the huge volume of material, it was decided to concentrate mainly on the period in which concern grew regarding local club celebrations, and in which competitions were prematurely ceased; and the holding of the elite inter-county championships, with the "Bloody Sunday" centenary as an evidently major topic of extended media discussion. Searches were conducted in the LexisNexis database using "GAA" in conjunction with various terms ("Covid-19," "club," "county," "Bloody Sunday," etc.) in order to generate a primary corpus of articles in Irish national and local print media. Where available, national radio and television broadcasts, podcasts, and Twitter interactions that either referenced, or were referenced in, these articles were included in the corpus.

The Return of the Intra-County Club Competitions

As previously noted (Crosson and Free 2021), a broader movement was evident during the Spring 2020 lockdown to prioritize the GAA local club games' return to play over the elite inter-county championship (inter-county teams are representative sides drawn from local clubs). This was apparent in the GAA "roadmap" (June 5), permitting first club competitions (from July 31), then inter-county competition (from October 17) (GAAa 2020). Although later updated (June 12 and 30) the return dates did not change. However, the nature of this return (including provision/non-provision for a limited number of spectators) evolved as the Irish government adjusted restrictions in response to increasing (or decreasing) numbers of Covid-19 infections. It was envisaged that inter-county teams could resume collective training on September 14, with club activity concluding by October 11 and inter-county competitions commencing on October 17.

The movement towards a "split season" model, clearly separating club and inter-county competitions, and the increased streaming of games and national coverage of club competitions was generally deemed a success in end of year media commentaries. The playing of intra-county competitions prior to inter-county competitions created a designated space and higher profile for the former, thus affirming the GAA's local rootedness despite the usually higher media profile of inter-county competitions. On November 28, the GAA announced a "split season" approach would be adopted for GAA games in 2021, albeit with the inter-county All-Ireland Championship preceding the intra-county competitions this time. Club Players Association chair Micheál Briody hailed it as a "brilliant result" (Lanigan 2020b, 72). Seán Moran (2020b, 19) in *The Irish Times* also welcomed this:

> great legacy of 2020 to the GAA. After decades of agonising the GAA finally hit on the solution to what the Club Players' Association had termed 'the fixtures crisis'. Pandemic and lockdown forced the change and in the summer of 2020 with the return to play taking place in club championships, [...] players, unencumbered by the demands of [inter-county] managers, were free to train and play with their clubs.

However, this end of year positivity was preceded by controversy in the Autumn over uncontrolled celebrations at club fixtures. On July 10, the GAA had announced that in line with changing Government Public Health advice, supporters could return to Gaelic games at a much-reduced capacity of 200 in the South (Republic of Ireland), with up to 400 allowed to attend matches in the North (Northern Ireland) if appropriate "perimeter fencing with viewing access on all four sides" was in place (GAAb 2020). The north-south difference highlights the GAA's challenge of managing an all-Ireland Association covering two jurisdictions, with differing views of appropriate safety measures. Our focal county, Cavan, is in the province of Ulster, but is south of the border with the six of the nine Ulster counties that are within Northern Ireland.

Concerns were expressed regarding the return to play, particularly for an amateur organization, including by GAA historian Paul Rouse in a Newstalk "Off the Ball" radio interview:

> [The GAA] has presented itself as a community-based organization. It does not run itself in the professional context like the major leagues of European sport and of American sport who create essential bubbles to protect sportspeople. This puts the GAA in a very vulnerable position because if the coronavirus gets into clubs, it will spread across the community (Bogue 2020a, 34).

The local clubs' enmeshment with every sphere of Irish society, so extensively lauded for facilitating voluntary and charitable activities in the Spring, was identified here as a threat. Players could not be sequestered, and supporters were circulating in their communities anyway. Yet these concerns were played down by the Cavan county board Secretary, Liam McCabe, in the *Irish Daily Mail* on July 14, extending the discourse of managed risk that emerged in the late Spring lockdown period (Crosson and Free 2021, 307):

> we have to get on with life. If you don't want to get it then all you can do is stay at home. I am not worried about a club in Cavan getting it because, touch wood, they have not got it. (Clifford 2020, 49)

The first weekend of return to play (July 18 and 19) was generally viewed as a success in the media, despite the obvious challenges (Moran 2020a, 23). However,

GAA President John Horan expressed concerns regarding post-match celebrations: "sport and partying are not going to work at the moment" (Moran 2020a, 23). Furthermore, a major concern, given the impact on income, was the "restriction on crowds." The 200-limit included "teams, officials and media" (Moran 2020a, 23). Due to continuing high levels of Covid-19 infection, the government continued with existing attendance restrictions.

Exemplifying local dissent concerning the imposition of restrictions, Cavan's county football team manager, Mickey Graham, was scathing regarding the attendance limit. In an *Irish Independent* July 22 article, he described the 200 cap as a "joke." Graham blamed house parties, particularly, for spreading the disease and stressed the financial challenges GAA clubs and county boards were facing. He also emphasised the importance of the additional support and hope Gaelic games provide, in a theme reiterated across the media:

> The people turning up at club games [...] are just grateful to get back out. And it just shows what sport does. It definitely gives that feelgood factor and, come the depths of winter, you'd be hoping that the inter-county game can keep people occupied and give them something to look forward to (Roche 2020, 48).

A further requirement of the new regulations was for ticket only games, thus expediting the introduction of digital ticketing for club team supporters. However, as reported in *The Anglo-Celt* (McCarney 2020a, 1), demand for tickets presented considerable challenges for clubs, particularly with non-ticket holders turning up.

The Anglo-Celt is the major local paper in county Cavan. It is widely read across the county and in neighboring counties, with considerable coverage given to sport; its coverage reveals how local media closely interconnect with the GAA, and how different discursive strands variously collided and intersected across local and national media coverage. These ranged from acceptance of the National Public Health Emergency Team (NPHET) health and safety concerns and warnings, to libertarian defense of individual rights (with an emphasis also on individual responsibility), to populist defense of local communities, in which the GAA is embedded, as collective "units" under threat from outside interference, to the argument (illustrated by Graham above) that controlled outdoor environments were safer than gatherings in uncontrolled exterior or interior spaces.

As club championships progressed, the threat of Covid-19 infections among players was a recurring challenge. On August 6, The *Anglo-Celt* revealed that two championship matches had to be rescheduled due to "Covid concerns" (McCarney 2020b, 4). The same page also revealed (in an article continued from page 1) that County Cavan had "the highest number of Covid infections per capita in Ireland and Cavan General Hospital is one of 11 acute medical facilities to have reported a recent rise in suspected cases" (Enright 2020a, 1, 4). On August 18, the Irish government completely banned spectators, only permitting sporting events and matches "behind closed doors" (Department of the Taoiseach 2020a). The subsequent *Anglo-Celt* front page (Image 1) featured a startling photograph of supporters watching a club encounter on a hill overlooking a football ground, above the headline "This is morally wrong," a quote from county chairperson Kieran Callaghan. Stressing the irony of the arrangement, Callaghan continued:

> This [is] actually creating so many other unsafe situations and I urge spectators not to put themselves or anyone else at risk. At the weekend, we had […] numerous incidents with people trying to see the games. […We] are driving people away from a safe environment and towards unsafe environments (Fitzpatrick 2020a, 1, 4).

Image 1: The Anglo-Celt, 27 August 2020. (Photo: Adrian Donohue. Copyright: The Anglo-Celt. Permission to reproduce kindly granted by the publisher).

Callaghan also suggested that streamed games could potentially contribute to more indoor socialising: "we have people congregating in public houses and hotels to watch them." He further noted the mental health impact the decision would have on players and supporters, and described the financial impact for Cavan GAA as "horrendous" (Fitzpatrick 2020a, 1, 4).

The Anglo-Celt's Sports Editor, Paul Fitzpatrick, was particularly critical. Cavan's border location was significant as limited numbers were still permitted just kilometres away. On September 17, claiming that "The Nanny state is in charge now!" he argued strongly for relaxed restrictions around attendance:

> Personal autonomy has been pushed to the margins. […] This ostracisation of those who dare to dissent is a hallmark, surely, of an oppressive society, not a liberal one. A groupthink has descended here; the national media, in the main, has shifted left and those in the centre, or on the conservative side, have been left stranded. Four legs good, two legs bad, as Orwell put it (Fitzpatrick 2020b, 21).

The political statement here can be contested. Irish media have hardly "shifted left" in a media landscape characterised by increasingly concentrated ownership (Doughty Street Chambers 2016); the current government also principally consists of the centre-right Fine Gael and Fianna Fáil parties, with the Greens as junior partners. It may be indicative of a growing ressentiment during the pandemic more recently manifested in anti-lockdown protests (Lally, McGreevy and Pope 2021). The combination of libertarianism and localist populism is telling. Rogers Brubaker (2020, 8) has identified a "paradox" between libertarian and populist perspectives internationally in anti-lockdown arguments in that populism is ordinarily associated with nationalist protectionism while libertarianism focuses on individual liberty and economic freedoms. Here there is a rhetoric whose logic needs teasing out. The GAA is presented as a locus of community and cultural integration, with internally protected outdoor safe spaces in which social distancing can be controlled, but in order for this to happen there must be freedom of movement within the county to those spaces. This ideal combination is contrasted with an overly protectionist state that has ironically and inadvertently generated irresponsible movement, by supporters, to the margins of games; or to interior, typically domestic spaces where social distancing cannot be controlled.

Whether *The Anglo-Celt* merely represented, or actively fuelled "dissent" is a moot point, but the exercise of "personal autonomy" certainly continued as restrictions were openly flouted by some supporters in the weeks that followed in the aftermath of county club finals. "Cavan Day" (September 26) was a virtual festival to celebrate the county, its culture and society. The celebration coincided with the senior county club championship football final between Crosserlough and Kingscourt, a drawn game screened live by national broadcaster RTÉ. Beside a celebratory *Anglo-Celt* editorial the following week (October 1) (Editorial 2020a, 22), a letter published in response to Paul Fitzpatrick's September 17 article extended his theme of centralized control of everyday life, questioning the reliability of the Covid-19 test and relating it to wider infringements of civil liberties: "I do not trust our government or our mainstream media to be truthful and I fear the virus will be used to bring in other long-term restrictions and take away our constitutional rights" (Martin 2020, 22).

The replay of the Cavan senior county club championship football final was held on October 3 and reports emerged in the weeks that followed of Covid-19 regulation breaches in celebrations that followed (McDonagh 2020, 3; Begley 2020, 5; O'Regan 2020, 6). The GAA Management Committee was quick to respond to reports of breaches in Cavan and in other counties, announcing on October 5 an immediate ban on all club activity (Campbell 2020, 40; Farrell 2020). Responding to rising infections, the Irish government also introduced more severe restrictions (level 4) for counties Cavan, Monaghan, and Donegal from October 15, leaving the rest of the Republic on level 3 (Department of the Taoiseach 2020b). High rates of infections in the North also led to tightened restrictions there (The Executive Office 2020). Taoiseach (Prime Minister) Micheál Martin described (on October 14) the rate in Cavan in particular as "very worrying" (571 cases per 100,000 (the highest in the Republic) compared to a national figure of 190.7) (Hughes 2020, 1). The *Irish Times* alleged that GAA club activity in Cavan was a major contributor. Rates were described by a Cavan-based pharmacist as "off the scale," with eighty cases a day equivalent to "1200 in Dublin" (McDonagh 2020, 3).

The Anglo-Celt registered conflicting responses in its editorial of October 8 entitled "We are in Last Chance Saloon." Arguing that the government "couldn't continue to turn a blind eye to sport fans celebrating successes on the pitch" it contradictorily asked, "how do you expect the people not to celebrate?" Revealingly, it posited that "There is much talk of 'units' in all of these guidelines –family units and work units and pods in schools etc. But people from rural Ireland understand your parish is a unit in itself. Everyone is family" (Editorial 2020b, 22). This rhetoric chimed with Cavan county board PRO Susan Brady's reported expression of "no regrets" over hosting events and her stress on the enormous contribution GAA members made in supporting vulnerable people in their community during the pandemic, with Cavan GAA additionally providing its Kingspan Breffni stadium "as a HSE drive-thru test centre completely free of charge" (Enright 2020b, 3). The logic here was that the GAA's overall contribution outweighed the negative impact of match-related behavior it could not directly control.

However, the national *Irish Independent* newspaper featured a different view:

> sports activities [are] breeding grounds for infection, combining boisterous spirits and alcohol. […] There is particular frustration in Cavan this week that groups getting together after GAA matches have been among people who tested positive. They would all have returned to homes around the county (O'Regan 2020, 6).

The *Irish Daily Mail* reported that Ballyjamesduff in Cavan had the highest rate in the country ("rocketing" to 651.1 per 100,000), directly connecting this with recent GAA activity and celebrations, but highlighting internal town divisions:

> Local councillor Trevor Smith said: 'I'm hearing a lot about the new cases stemming from the aftermath of two recent football finals. 'There's a lot of hysteria being created at the moment.' [...] One business owner, who did not wish to be named, told the Irish Daily Mail that members and supporters of the club should have known better. 'There were huge celebrations following that match so it's no surprise at all why we have so many cases.' (Begley 2020, 5)

The *Anglo-Celt* nevertheless continued its coverage of the defense of the local GAA. In an article concerning mental health during Covid-19, local Fine Gael (a government coalition party) senator Joe O'Reilly insisted it was "wrong to blame" the GAA for post-match "misbehavior" and stressed that the GAA is "not some abstract body" but "created out of the communities from all over the county" (Enright 2020c, 29). The editorial of the same edition (October 22) also defended the GAA, calling "finger pointing and blame game [...] in some ways, more dangerous than the virus itself. A stigma is now developing to the point where people are afraid to admit they have Coronavirus, they feel like lepers, or are even afraid to even go for a test." (Editorial 2020c, 26).

"Hope and History Rhyme": The Bloody Sunday Centenary Commemoration and the all-Ireland Inter-County Championships

It was against this backdrop of controversy and defensive hyperbole that the elite level inter-county All-Ireland championships commenced on October 17. There was some disquiet regarding the legitimacy of their delayed start-up. Could even the GAA's top level players be on a par with elite professional athletes who could be sequestered to a higher degree, given GAA athletes' amateur status? For example, commenting on the ten recently reported Covid-19 cases in Fermanagh's inter-county team, on October 15 Shane McGrath (2020) in the *Irish Daily Mail* declared that the GAA's once "honorable and ambitious plan" to stage the inter-county championship was now being "dispatched into a blizzard." Nonetheless, the championship proceeded, minus spectators, and was uninterrupted by the Government's imposition of the Level 5 lockdown on October 21.

When, on November 28, the *Irish Times*' Jennifer O'Connell questioned a "case for GAA exceptionalism" that "really hasn't been made," she scathingly quoted a statement by Chief Medical Officer of NPHET, Tony Holohan in October. Referring to the GAA, Holohan said that it was "important to try to preserve some of that kind of activity to give us all something to look forward to." She also quoted his later statement (November 23), following provincial final celebrations:

> I think we have tipped too much as a country into a sense of blame and trying to find the latest person who is in breach of a particular guideline and trying to find a lamppost to hang them from.

That the NPHET CMO should echo the language used in the above local examples suggests that the GAA inter-county championship was indeed being afforded truly "exceptional" status. Indeed, the government awarded the GAA €15m to pay for their staging, "separate to any other windfall the Association might get" (Keys 2020b). Commenting on this, while reporting some current and past players' misgivings, Colm Keys (2020b) in the *Irish Independent* noted that the Government evidently saw the championships as a morale boosting "form of entertainment for many." It would also be a spectator-free television spectacle that could keep viewers at home.

When eventually played on November 21 and 22 the four men's All-Ireland provincial Gaelic football championship finals, which produced the overall competition's semi-finalists, took place as statistics for new Covid-19 cases were in decline in late November. This likely helped to allay fears. However, the "Bloody Sunday" centenary commemoration in Croke Park on November 21 was possibly most central to marginalizing criticism. On this day in 1920, during the Irish War of Independence, British forces fired upon players and supporters at a Dublin-Tipperary challenge match, killing fourteen. The commemoration was flagged, since early 2020, in the calendar of events for the "decade of centenaries" of Ireland's revolutionary period.[2] That the match outcomes produced the same semi-finalists as 1920 was widely noted in Irish media as an extraordinary coincidence with almost magical significance, including a very unexpected victory for Cavan (the county's first since 1997) in the Ulster Championship. Munster victors, Tipperary, had not won their provincial championship since 1935, and did so wearing a replica of the jersey the 1920 team wore in the fateful Bloody Sunday match. This inspired numerous variations on a theme in media reports—"historic parallels" (Ryan 2020), "fairytale finish" (Bogue 2020b), "remarkable symmetry" (Keys 2020a)—with a sense of teleological national destiny:

> "The hand of history is moving the chess pieces of Championship 2020" (Anon. 2020)
>
> "Ghosts of heroes past inspire Tipp and Cavan successes" (Boyle 2020b)
>
> "History smiling on Tipperary" (Fogarty 2020)
>
> "History repeating itself is no rare GAA occurrence" (Moran 2020b)

"Hand of history" is a phrase used by Tony Blair ("the hand of history is upon our shoulder") shortly prior to the 1998 Belfast "Good Friday Agreement" that concluded the Northern Ireland "peace process" (de Breadun 2018). Also used in

---

[2] See https://www.decadeofcentenaries.com/

relation to Tipperary's "historic" exploits was Irish poet Seamus Heaney's line (1990, 77), "once in a lifetime […] justice can rise up, and hope and history rhyme":

"Tipperary make hope and history rhyme" (Fogarty 2020)

"Can hope and history rhyme for Tipperary football on emotional day?" (Keys 2020c)

The line was quoted by Joe Biden in his 2020 United States Presidential campaign video, harking towards a post-Trump era of reconciliation. Its use here signifies a happy ending to Tipperary's provincial campaign that perhaps resonated with this general sense of ending in Irish media following Trump's replacement by a self-identified "Irish-American" dedicated to protecting the principle of an invisible border in Ireland following the U.K.'s Brexit departure from the European Union (Lynch 2020). The coincidental semi-final outcomes fuelled anticipation that a season "like no other" (a phrase used repeatedly during 2020 e.g., Moran 2020d; Gallagher 2020) might produce a correspondingly bizarre championship outcome, with both Tipperary and Cavan as "fairytale" (Bogue 2020b) contenders. These outcomes chimed with the theme, in Irish media, of ending and release pre-Christmas that culminated in the lifting of Level 5 restrictions in December, allowing for what Taoiseach Micheál Martin (November 19) called a "meaningful Christmas" (RTÉ News 2020).

The Bloody Sunday commemorative event involved a wreath laying ceremony, with Irish President Michael D. Higgins, honoring those killed in 1920. It was accompanied by the burning of fourteen torches in an otherwise darkened stadium, a reading of the details of their shortened lives by actor Brendan Gleeson, and a concluding video depicting them as they prepared to attend the 1920 match. The ceremony followed the broadcast of an RTÉ television documentary, *Bloody Sunday* on November 15, in turn based on Michael Foley's *The Bloodied Field* (2020); Foley also wrote the Gleeson monologue.

Although Bloody Sunday was crucial to the association of the GAA with the War of Independence in the post-Independence Irish state it was actually more of a cultural nationalist rather than militant nationalist organization (Cronin 1999, 87-91). The 1920 match was targeted by so-called "Black and Tan" Auxiliaries assisting the Royal Irish Constabulary police force following the assassination of fourteen suspected British agents that morning. Following independence in 1922 the names of all but Michael Hogan, the Tipperary footballer shot dead that day, were largely forgotten. Foley's (2020) meticulous research sought to reconstruct their lives, and is part of a turn in Irish social history towards the documenting of those indirectly or incidentally involved in the conflict (for example, Duffy (2016); Ferriter and Riordan (2017)). Two of the Bloody Sunday victims were children. A third was shot and buried in her wedding dress.

In RTÉ's commemoration broadcast, Foley commented that:

tonight is about connectedness and the fact that there's so many people can't be here, the people who are on my mind are the families of the victims. [...] we've all had to make sacrifices this year, and [...] I just hope that they're watching at home and they can feel the emotion that we're feeling here and that they know that [...] the whole country's with them tonight.

Although referring to the relatives of the dead, his words, over the torch lit occasion, were reminiscent of the government sponsored "shine a light" evening on April 11 2020 in honor of those who had died of Covid-19. On December 20 there was a similar initiative, "shine your light." The "connectedness" here surely evoked the enduring theme of seeking sustained connection despite the pandemic-imposed separation.

The broadcast also telescoped history, connecting the theme of the legitimacy afforded to the games' staging, given the GAA's laudable community activities (Crosson and Free 2021), with its historical significance. Presenter Joanne Cantwell directly paralleled the scale of the current pandemic challenges and the impact of Bloody Sunday, "One hundred years on and an Association and a country facing monumental issues of a different kind to those that caused the abandonment of a football match." Cantwell continued, "this year, haven't we been once again reminded [of] the importance of the GAA within the community and I suppose what tonight does is it reminds us of the place that it played in history and Irish culture?"

This honouring of innocent victims also contributed to a current theme, in Irish society, of postcolonial maturation, an honest reckoning with the past exemplified by Michael D. Higgins' "Machnamh 100 [...] forum for reflection on the War of Independence, the Civil War and the Partition of Ireland," commencing on December 4, 2020.[3] The commemoration contrasted with the "robust fetishization of military elements" (Crosson 2020, 104) in the 2016 Croke Park pageant, "Laochra" (the Irish for "warriors") commemorating the 1916 Rising. More painfully, and contentiously, this reckoning has involved Commissions of Inquiry into Ireland's twentieth century history of mass incarceration and abuse in industrial schools and, more recently, "mother and baby homes" (O'Halloran 2021).

The commemoration also had a quasi-religious format and tone. Sport's ritualistic structure, formal ceremonies, honoring of its celebrities as deified figures and direct invocation of Christian belief have been widely noted (e.g., Birrell 1981; Baker 2007; Alpert 2015). Although the Catholic Church's post-Independence influence has waned in recent decades (Fuller 2004; Scally 2021), a religious sensibility continues to pervade Irish society and television (McCarthy 2021; Free 2021, 6). The "shine a light" events and the torches in Croke Park evoke the Catholic ritual of lighting a candle for the dead. Discussing the growing

---

[3] "Machnamh" is Irish for "meditation, reflection, consideration and thought" (Higgins 2020).

significance of sport as institutionalized religion has declined in twenty-first century Ireland Tom Inglis (2014, 109) suggests that sport creates "a strong sense of bonding and belonging that is almost spiritual, even if it does not generate moral commitments." Yet the Bloody Sunday commemoration surely conveyed a "moral commitment" to honor the dead of 1920 and, by implication, 2020. Croke Park has previously been referred to in Irish media as a "battlefield" where sport's symbolic warfare was briefly drawn into actual warfare (Free 2013, 226). In 2020, "GAA exceptionalism," also suggested in the title of the mournful music composed by Colm Mac Con Iomaire for the Bloody Sunday commemoration, "More than a Game," depended not on sport as symbolic warfare, but on a cultural ritual imbricated with the enduring legacy of religion.

Concluding Remarks

The GAA had been widely lauded for its exemplary role in sustaining national morale during the Spring 2020 lockdown. Its clubs' local rootedness was a key factor in its members' contributions to charitable activities and community voluntarism (Crosson and Free 2021). The ensuing enforced "split season" between club and inter-county competitions had two major positive outcomes for the club game: it brought additional focus on these competitions at a national level (including increased national broadcast of games and the rapid development of streaming services), while convincing many members and administrators within the GAA of the benefit of a staggered approach to the association's competitions, as evident in the decision to adopt a "split-season" model for 2021. However, as apparently spontaneous local celebrations of club victories became minor scandals, GAA's local embeddedness presented additional challenges. In contrasting media discourses, local commentary (keen to defend the association and its members) diverged from national media outlets that linked club celebrations with rising Covid-19 infections.

Yet, as the Gaelic football, hurling, and camogie final stages concluded in December, there was general agreement in Irish sports media that the GAA had overcome any tarnished reputation resulting from club celebrations. In the most extreme instance of (self-acknowledged) "hyperbole" we found, proclaiming the GAA as a "gift that's not just for Christmas," Darragh McManus (2020) in the *Irish Independent* dismissed all criticism from "pinchfaced doomsayers," arguing that "not for the first time, the GAA has swooped in, superhero-style, and saved this nation" by "lift[ing] us from the slough of despond caused by Covid-19."

Apart from the coincidence in sporting outcomes and the Bloody Sunday commemoration, key factors in the overwhelmingly positive reception were surely the performances of the GAA's senior administrators and players in promoting Government messaging. Following the All-Ireland hurling final on December 13, in his televised speech in the stadium GAA President John Horan appealed "to all supporters to celebrate this victory in a sensible manner and not tarnish the work of these great players." Winning Limerick team captain Declan Hannon paid tribute to "the frontline staff who've worked so tirelessly during this pandemic," and noted the "respect that we have for you all in going out there each day to keep us safe." Acknowledging that "businesses have been closed, people have lost their jobs" and "loved ones have passed away this year who would really love to be here," he pleaded with supporters to "respect the guidelines. [...] I hope ye enjoy this evening at home with your loved ones." In a change to standard practice, none of the cups were taken to winning counties, so as to avoid a focal point for gathering. In a Newstalk podcast documentary series, "The Split Season" (December 22), Hannon was among a group of players whose experience of training and playing during the pandemic was tracked. He describes traveling home by train that evening with "a bit of craic [and] a bit of a sing-song" before returning "into our home houses, and that was it." The acceptance of collective discipline in sacrificing celebration following victory, and the exhorting of supporters to do likewise exemplified the modelling, the embodiment of an idealized Irish sporting "habitus" (Free 2018) with which the GAA is inextricably associated given the organization's dependence on voluntary labor, community rootedness and players with "day jobs" across every sector of society.

The inter-county championships thus ultimately involved a series of staged performances of national inclusivity that somewhat eclipsed the fractiousness and recriminations over local club celebrations in early Autumn in a year "like no other." The arguments for Gaelic games' special significance in each case were congruent, but the higher level of abstraction and symbolism afforded by the inter-county championships, their accessibility only as television spectacles, and the centrality of the Bloody Sunday commemoration generally overcame arguments against "GAA exceptionalism."

REFERENCES

Alpert, Rebecca T. 2015. *Religion and Sports: An Introduction and Case Studies.* New York: Columbia University Press.

Anon. 2020. "Hand of History Is Moving the Chess Pieces of Championship 2020." *Irish Examiner*, November 23. LexisNexis Academic.

Begley, Ian. 2020. "Ballyjamesduff Has Top Covid Rate in Country." *Irish Daily Mail* October 17, 2020.

Birrell, Susan. 1981. "Sport as Ritual: Interpretations from Durkheim to Goffman." *Social Forces*, 60 (2): 354-376.

Baker, William J. 2007. *Playing with God: Religion and Modern Sport.* Cambridge, MA: Harvard University Press.

Bogue, Declan. 2020a. "GAA is Back and Attempts to Play by the Covid-19 Rules; GAELIC GAMES." *Belfast Telegraph*, July 20, 2020.

Bogue, Declan. 2020b. "Cavan Supply Fairytale Finish to Provincial Campaign Like No Other." *Irish Examiner*, November 23, 2020. LexisNexis Academic.

Boyle, Donnchadh. 2020a. "Appliance of Science helps GAA Solve Covid Conundrum; From Streaming Matches Online to New Ticketing Systems, Technology is Allowing Association to Cope." *Irish Independent*, July 24, 2020.

——. 2020b. "Ghosts of Heroes Past Inspire Tipp and Cavan Successes." *Irish Independent*, November 24, 2020. LexisNexis Academic.

Brubaker, Rogers. 2020. "Paradoxes of Populism During the Pandemic." *Thesis Eleven*. DOI: 10.1177/0725513620970804

Byrne, Jason. 2020. "Hogan Heroes: Historic Repeat is the Perfect Tribute." *Irish Sun*, November 23, 2020. LexisNexis Academic.

Campbell, John. 2020. "County Game Given Green Light Despite Club Ban; Gaelic Games." *Belfast Telegraph*, October 6, p. 40.

Clifford, Michael. 2020. "GAA Doc's Uncertain Prognosis for Season." *Irish Daily Mail*, July 14, 2020.

Cronin, Mike. 1999. *Sport and Nationalism in Ireland: Gaelic Games, Soccer and Irish Identity Since 1884*. Dublin: Four Courts Press.

Crosson, Seán. 2020. "The Mediatisation of the GAA's Commemoration of the 1916 Rising: 'A New Ireland Rises'?" In *Sport, the Media and Ireland: Interdisciplinary Perspectives*, edited by Neil O'Boyle and Marcus Free, 93-109. Cork: Cork University Press.

Crosson, Seán and Marcus Free. 2021. "'This Too Shall Past': Gaelic Games, Irish Media, and the Covid-19 Lockdown in Ireland." In *Time Out: National Perspectives on Sport and the Covid-19 Lockdown*, edited by Jörg Krieger, April Henning, Lindsay Parks-Pieper, and Paul Dimeo, 289-306. Champaign, IL.: Common Ground.

De Breadun, Deaglan. 2018. "'Hand of History' Helped Sign Off on Peace Process." *Irish Times*, March 31, 2018. https://www.irishtimes.com/news/ireland/irish-news/hand-of-history-helped-sign-off-on-peace-process-1.3445899

Department of the Taoiseach. 2020a. "Statement on the Introduction of New Measures to Limit the Spread of COVID-19." August 18, 2020. https://www.gov.ie/en/publication/77b6d- statement-on-the-introduction-of-new-measures-to-limit-the-spread-of-covid-19/

Department of the Taoiseach. 2020b. "Cavan, Donegal and Monaghan Placed on Level 4 under Ireland's Plan for Living with Covid-19." October 14, 2020.

https://www.gov.ie/en/press-release/ccc85-cavan-donegal-and-monaghan-placed-on-level-4-under-irelands-plan-for-living-with-covid-19/#:~:text=Placing%20Cavan%2C%20Donegal%20and%20Monaghan,25%20mourners)%20should%20take%20place.

Doughty Street Chambers. 2016. *Report on the Concentration of Media Ownership in Ireland*. London: Doughty Street Chambers, https://cdn.thejournal.ie/media/2016/10/media-ownership-report-oct-2016.pdf.

Duffy, Joe. 2015. *Children of the Rising: The Untold Story of the Young Lives Lost During 1916*. Dublin: Hachette.

Editorial. 2020a. "Cavan Day A Great Showcase for County," *The Anglo-Celt*, October 1, 2020.

——. 2020b. "We are in the Last Chance Saloon." *The Anglo-Celt*, October 8, 2020.

——. 2020c. "We Must Change our Habits." *The Anglo-Celt*, October 22, 2020.

Enright, Seamus. 2020. "Six New Cases in Cavan in Just One Day." *The Anglo-Celt*, August 6, 2020.

———. 2020b. "'Everyone Has to Up Their Game' County Board." *The Anglo-Celt*, October 15, 2020.

———. 2020c. "Warning Over Covid Mental Recovery." *The Anglo-Celt*, October 22, 2020.

Executive Office, The. 2020. "Executive Tightens Restrictions to Curb Covid-19." October 14, https://www.executiveoffice-ni.gov.uk/news/executive-tightens-restrictions-curb-covid-19

Farrell, Sinead. 2020. "GAA Suspends All Club Games with Immediate Effect Until Further Notice." *The 42*, October 5, 2020. https://www.the42.ie/gaa-cancel-club-activity-5223953-Oct2020/

Ferriter, Diarmuid and Susannah Riordan. 2017. *Years of Turbulence: The Irish Revolution and Its Aftermath*. Dublin: University College Dublin Press.

Fitzpatrick, Paul. 2020a. "This is Morally Wrong." *The Anglo-Celt*, August 27, 2020.

———. 2020b. "The Nanny State is Well and Truly in Charge Now." *The Anglo-Celt*, September 17, 2020.

Fogarty, John. 2020. "History Smiling on Tipperary." *Irish Examiner*, November 24, 2020. LexisNexis Academic.

———. 2020. "Tipperary Make Hope and History Rhyme." *Irish Examiner*, November 23, 2020. LexisNexis Academic.

Foley, Michael. 2020. *The Bloodied Field: Croke Park, 21 November 1920*. Dublin: O'Brien Press.

Fairclough, Norman. 2010. *Critical Discourse Analysis: The Critical Study of Language*. Abingdon: Routledge.

Free, Marcus. 2013. "Diaspora and Rootedness, Amateurism and Professionalism in Media Discourses of Irish Soccer and Rugby in the 1990s and 2000s." *Éire-Ireland*, 48 (1-2): 211-229.

———. 2018. "'Smart, Clued-in Guys': Irish Rugby Players as Celebrities in Post-Celtic Tiger Irish Media." *International Journal of Media and Cultural Politics*, 14 (2): 215-232.

———. 2021. "Introduction to the Special Issue: Contemporary Irish Television." *Television and New Media* 22 (1): 1-9.

Fuller, Louise. 2004. *Irish Catholicism since 1950: The Undoing of a Culture*. Dublin: Gill & Macmillan.

GAA. 2020a. "Covid-19 Update Safe Return to Gaelic Games." *gaa.ie*, June 5, 2020. https://www.gaa.ie/news/covid-19-update-safe-return-to-gaelic-games/

———. 2020b. "NHSC Guidelines on Return of Spectators to GAA Club Games." *gaa.ie*, July 10, 2020. https://www.gaa.ie/news/nhsc-guidelines-on-return-of-spectators-to-gaa-club-games/

Gallagher, Mark. 2020. "A to Z of a Sporting Year Like No Other." *Irish Daily Mail,* December 28, 2020. LexisNexis Academic.

Heaney, Seamus. 1990. *The Cure at Troy: Sophocles' Philoctetes*. London: Faber and Faber.

Higgins, Michael D. 2020. "It is Time to Reflect on the Painful Events of 100 Years Ago in Ireland." *Irish Times*, December 12, 2020. LexisNexis Academic.

Hughes, Craig. 2020. "Household Visits Ban." *Irish Daily Mail*, October 15, 2020.

Inglis, Tom. 2014. *Meanings of Life in Contemporary Ireland: Webs of Significance*. Basingstoke: Palgrave Macmillan.

Keys, Colm. 2020a. "Cavan Seize Their Chance to Complete Remarkable Symmetry." *Irish Independent*, November 23, 2020. LexisNexis Academic.

———. 2020b. "State Must Make Call on Championship Green Light." *Irish Independent,* October 16, 2020. LexisNexis Academic.

———. 2020c. "Can Hope and History Rhyme for Tipperary on Emotional Day?" *Irish Independent*, November 21, 2020. LexisNexis Academic.

Lally, Conor, Ronan McGreevy and Conor Pope. 2021. "Large Garda Presence Sustained in Dublin for Anti-lockdown Protests." *Irish Times*, March 17, 2020. https://www.irishtimes.com/news/crime-and-law/large-garda-presence-sustained-in-dublin-for-anti-lockdown-protests-1.4512885.

Lanigan, Philip. 2020a. "Time Penalty; Kildare, Laois, Offaly Could be Hit by Longer Lockdown." *Irish Daily Mail*, August 12, 2020.

———. 2020b. "Gaa Set to Ratify Plan for Split Season; Costello Cleared to Face Cavan as Red Card is Rescinded." *Irish Daily Mail*, November 28, 2020.

———. 2020c. "A Winter Made for TV; Lockdown Piles Pressure on Broadcasters to Cover More Matches." *Irish Daily Mail*, October 24, 2020.

Lynch, Suzanne. 2020. "Biden warns US-UK Trade Deal Will Not Happen If Belfast Agreement Undermined." *Irish Times*, October 18, 2020. LexisNexis Academic.

Luney, Graham. 2020. "Green Light for Cup Final Fans as Supporters Return to Grounds; IRISH CUP; Reds and United Await Verdict on Appeals Against Cup Suspensions." *Belfast Telegraph*, July 24, 2020.

Martin, Val. 2020 "Is Covid-19 Test Reliable." *The Anglo-Celt*, October 1, 2020.

McCarney, Damian. 2020a. "Game on as Demand Soars for Tickets." *The Anglo Celt*, July 30, 2020.

———. 2020b. "Matches Rescheduled Over COVID Concerns." *The Anglo Celt*, August 6, 2020.

McCarthy, Anna. 2021. "The Angelus: Devotional Television, Changing Times." *Television and New Media* 22 (1): 12-31.

McDonagh, Marese. 2020. "GAA Activity Blamed or Cavan Surge." *The Irish Times*, October 15, 2020.

McGrath, Shane. 2020. "Championship Enters Realms of Wishful Thinking as Virus Takes Hold Again." *Irish Daily Mail*, October 15, 2020. LexisNexis Academic.

McManus, Darragh. 2020. "Why the GAA is Not Just a Gift for Christmas." *Irish Independent*, December 5, 2020. LexisNexis Academic.

Moran, Seán. 2020a. "Smooth Return to Action Pleases Provincial Bosses; Return-To-Play Protocols Followed Diligently in All Four Provinces According to Officials." *The Irish Times*, July 21, 2020.

———. 2020b. "The 12 Days Of 2020: How Pandemic Helped GAA to Solve Fixtures Conundrum." *The Irish Times*, December 23, 2020.

———. 2020c. "History Repeating Itself Is No Rare GAA Occurrence." *The Irish Times,* November 25, 2020. LexisNexis Academic.

———. 2020d. "Fixtures Like No Other for Year Like No Other." *The Irish Times*, June 27, 2020. LexisNexis Academic.

———. 2021. "Losses of EUR34m. As Pandemic Takes Its Toll." *Irish Times*, February 17, 2020. LexisNexis Academic.

O'Connell, Jennifer. 2020. "GAA Exceptionalism Wins in a Pandemic." *Irish Times*, November 28, 2020. https://www.irishtimes.com/opinion/jennifer-o-connell-gaa-exceptionalism-wins-in-a-pandemic-1.4421374.

O'Connor, Wayne. 2020. "Outbreaks Linked To GAA, Communions and Schools All Part of Mid-West's Rising Caseload." *Sunday Independent*, October 18, 2020.

O'Halloran, Marie. 2021. "Protest Marks End of Mother and Baby Homes Commission's Term." *The Irish Times*, February 27, 2020. https://www.irishtimes.com/news/social-affairs/protest-marks-end-of-mother-and-baby-homes-commission-s-term-1.4497274

O'Regan, Eilish. 2020. "Covid Blame Game: Pool of Suspects for Virus Spread Just Keeps Growing." *Irish Independent*, October 16, 2020.

Roche, Frank. 2020. "Limit of 200 Fans is a Joke, Says Breffni Boss Graham." *Irish Independent*, July 22, 2020.

RTÉ News. 2020. "Tough Decisions Ahead but Meaningful Chrismas Possible Taoiseach." November 19, 2020. https://www.rte.ie/news/coronavirus/2020/1119/1179089-virus-reopening-christmas/

Ryan, Larry. 2020. "Tipperary in Raptures After Weekend of Historic Parallels." *Irish Examiner*, November 23, 2020. Lexis Nexis Academic.

Scally, Derek. 2021. *The Best Catholics in the World: The Irish, the Church and the End of a Special Relationship*. Dublin: Sandycove.

Chapter 3

A League of their Own: Male Privileges in Australian Rugby League During Covid-19

Jim McKay and Karen Brooks

In this chapter, we first provide a general context of how responses to the pandemic amplified extant gender injustices in Australia. We then use a case-study of "Project Apollo," an endeavor that enabled the Australian National Rugby League (NRL) to resume competition quickly (Carter, Steiner, and McLaughlin 2015; Jensen 2020; Yin 2017). Finally, we argue that the masculine matrix of cultural, economic, and political practices that sustained Project Apollo exemplify pervasive structures of male privilege, not only in sport, but in Australian society as well.

The Australian Response to Covid-19

Though the initial response to Covid-19 by Australian authorities was highly successful in suppressing the virus when compared to most other countries, it also reflected the global pattern of reinforcing and exacerbating longstanding social inequities (O'Sullivan, Rahamathulla, and Pawar 2020). This included decisions made by sport officials when, during the pandemic, they privileged male sports, especially at the professional level. A prominent feature of this preferential treatment was male sports receiving expedited resumption–long before other public institutions or entertainments were deemed either essential or safe (Pavlidis and Rowe 2021; Rowe 2020). This favoritism was arguably most prominent in the NRL receiving speedy permission to restart.

It is vital to understand that justifications by the NRL for special treatment was directly and indirectly facilitated by an array of agents. These included Australian Prime Minister Scott Morrison, senior state and federal authorities, players, fans, and self-interested sections of the media, despite numerous breaches of Covid-19 protocols by players. The Australian response to Covid-19 began with Morrison emulating other populist strongmen leaders by misrepresenting the pandemic as a war Australians would win if they came together (Daley 2020;

Lohmeyer and Taylor 2020; McCormack 2020). This theme became pervasive in everyday life with reassurances from political and other public figures, as well as social media memes stating, "We're all in this together."

It was no surprise that Morrison omitted gender in his pleas for national solidarity. Since becoming Prime Minister in August 2018, Morrison has failed a litany of leadership tests that have been attributed to his conspicuous lack of empathy (Hewson 2021). He has repeatedly and willfully ignored women's interests and concerns, especially in relation to violence against women (Zwica 2021). He also leads a party with a history of not only misogyny but more recently, employing staff accused of rape and other gross sexual misconduct in and beyond Parliament House (Murphy 2021a).

It's in this context that Morrison's economic policies contained the masculine bias in governance and policymaking, which has had disproportionately negative effects on women during Covid-19 (Smith et al. 2021). For example, his budget in October 2020 largely neglected female-dominated sectors like arts, recreation, hospitality, and healthcare. It also failed to address child care substantively, an issue largely navigated by women (Dixon and Hodgson 2020; Stewart 2020).

The deleterious effects of these and other retrograde policies were exposed in separate studies by two independent think tanks in March 2021. A report by *Per Capita* revealed that because Australia is one of the few developed nations without targets, gender equality has increasingly declined and ranked forty-fourth on the World Economic Forum's Global Gender Gap Index (Dawson, Kovac, and Lewis 2021). On International Women's Day 2021, the *Grattan Institute* reported that women suffered a "triple-whammy" during Covid-19 that worsened their lifetime economic disadvantage: women lost more work than men; took on more unpaid work; and were less likely to receive government support (Wood, Griffiths, and Crowley 2021). The political response to Covid-19 overwhelmingly favored men in Australia, with Morrison's budget directly supporting male-dominated industries, such as defense, construction, mining, and manufacturing.

Male Privileges and Female Disadvantages in Sport

It is imperative to situate these systemic female disadvantages in the context of everyday male privileges (Dowd 2008). Privileges are socially bestowed on people who belong to powerful groups. This is an inherently moral situation because people must decide how to use their social advantages. Some believe they have a duty to use a privileged position responsibly, like furthering social justice, while others use it to obtain unearned advantages. An example of the links between privileges, power, and morality is public condemnation of people who have used their positions to flout lockdown guidelines and/or get vaccinated before they are eligible. Male privileges are evident in everyday interactions, as well as in social relations at the global level (Pease 2010). However, these privileges are neither monolithic nor uncontested, because they intersect with institutional disadvantages, such as disability, race, ethnicity, social class, and sexualities (Messerschmidt 2018).

Sport is a microcosm of these entrenched and inequitable gender structures. Sportsmen are so indulged they often develop what's referred to as "spoiled athlete syndrome" (Leonard 2017), while sportswomen are still treated like second-class citizens (Adelson and Dinich 2020). One overt example is the Australian women's national basketball team flying to the London Olympics in economy seats while the men traveled in business class (AFP 2012). Women generally have unequal access to recreation and sport (Hargreaves and Anderson 2016), are systemically subjected to sexual assaults (Reichart, Smith, and Pegoraro 2020), receive meager and sexist media coverage (Cooky et al. 2021; Wenner 2021), and are underrepresented in leadership positions (Pape 2019). Though women's sports have become increasingly professional, many athletes are still paid far less than their male counterparts, cannot afford to play full-time, and must combine sport with other obligations, such as part and full-time work and caring for children and aged family members (Pavlidis and Rowe 2021).

These sexist structures converge with other systemic advantages and disadvantages, such as prejudice and discrimination against nonwhite male and female athletes (Nauright and Wiggins 2016) and those who identify as LGBTQIA (Newell 2020). There are also hierarchies of masculinities and disadvantages in sports injuries, and illnesses are often attributable to men emulating conventional but damaging ideals of masculinity (Young 2019).

It is within this multilayered context of gender politics—on and off field—we now explain a blatant example of male privilege in Australia during Covid-19: the NRL restart.

The Hypermasculine World of Rugby League

From its first organized season in Australia in 1908 until the 1980s, Rugby League, or simply "League," was played mainly in the two east coast states: New South Wales (NSW) and Queensland. The NRL was formed in 1998 and now has sixteen teams: ten in NSW, three in Queensland and one each in Melbourne, Canberra, and Auckland, New Zealand. The Women's Premiership was founded in 2018, with three Australian and one New Zealand teams that were affiliated with existing NRL men's clubs. The Australian Rugby League Commission (ARLC) was created in 2012 to administer the sport in Australia and internationally. The ARLC has six male and two female executives and all NRL clubs are chaired by men.

League is a violent, hypermasculine sport. It is constantly described with war metaphors, and has earned players nicknames like "Raging Bull," "The Axe," and "Mad Dog." It has been instrumental in validating Anglo-Celtic male versions of Australian nationalism, though significant numbers of Indigenous and Pacific

Islander players have recently entered the NRL (Parry 2020). League used to be called the "Opera of the Proletariat" because of its close connections with working class life (Moore 2000). It is now hyped as the "Greatest Game of All" due to its position in the lucrative, global media-sport complex (Wenner 2021). Male players earn huge salaries and endorsements, garner celebrity status (and all the concomitant interest in off-field relationships and their personal lives this attracts), and their (female) partners often bask in reflected glory and achieve a degree of fame as well. Consequently, League manifests the tendency of other sports to produce myriad scandals (Rowe and Palmer 2022). Transgressions in the NRL have included players' use of performance enhancing drugs, drunken sprees, close links with alcohol and betting companies, and accusations of sexual harassment, abuse, and domestic violence (Kinsella 2019; Knox 2021).

The most scathing criticisms have related to officials' failure to act convincingly in repeated cases of sexual assault (Hytner 2021; Knox 2020d). After a spate of sexual assault charges against various players during the 2019 off-season, Professor Catharine Lumby, who worked with the NRL pro bono for over a decade to prevent binge drinking and sexual assault, said player behavior was in "a crisis," and a small number of players were "education-proof" (Kontominas and Jonson 2019).

Similar to American football (Spencer and Limperos, 2020), sexual assaults by NRL players are framed by the male-dominated media in ways that exonerate perpetrators, cast doubts on accusers, and highlight individual men's failings rather than male structures of power (Packard Hill and Fuller 2018). When cases proceed to court, players have the privilege of "narrative immunity" (Waterhouse-Watson 2019) and "himpathy"— "inappropriate and disproportionate sympathy powerful men often enjoy in cases of sexual assault, intimate partner violence, homicide and other misogynistic behavior" (Manne 2018). One journalist said League was "the sport with the most odious reputation in Australia for the appalling behaviour of its footballers" (Mark 2021), while another called it one of the "most scandal-ridden professional competitions in the world" (Kane 2021). Despite this notoriety or perhaps because of it, League has maintained loyalty from its principally male fans through large live and TV audiences.

Exercising Male Privilege During Covid-19

Morrison, often dubbed "Scotty from Marketing," is a former advertising and marketing executive with a carefully orchestrated persona that is designed to depict him as a man of the people—what Australians call a "good bloke" (New Matilda 2020; Spargo-Ryan 2021). Demonstrating a love of sport is a ubiquitous aspect of this facade. A former Rugby Union player turned ardent League supporter, he often poses for photo-ops wearing the scarf and/or baseball cap of the NRL team in his electorate. After the World Health Organization (WHO) labeled Covid-19 a pandemic on March 11, 2020, Morrison displayed his incorrigibly populist side and strong allegiance to League. He recklessly told Australians to keep calm and carry on by following his intention to attend a match, along with projected crowds in the tens of thousands, the coming weekend (Jericho 2020).

However, he quickly backtracked due to Australia's federal system. State Premiers and the Prime Minister take advice from their respective chief medical officers (CMO) about protection and response strategies, but each state is responsible for enforcing rules, which differ in each jurisdiction, about physically distancing, wearing masks, and crossing state borders. After the federal CMO advised banning gatherings of more than 500 people, Morrison then announced he would not be attending the match, and suggested non-essential crowds exceeding 500 people should be prohibited nationwide. With a combination of luck, healthy fear, and civic duty, an overwhelming majority of Australians responded positively to the subsequent emergency restrictions by making safe decisions, like avoiding even small groups, physically distancing, isolating, and wearing masks. Medical experts nominated this striking display of political civility as major reason why Australia had one of the world's lowest case fatality rates from Covid-19 in its early stages (Duckett and Stobart 2020).

In contrast, ARLC Chairman Peter V'landys immediately sought preferential treatment. V'landys is a man who believes "If you don't spill blood for your organization, you're not doing your job" (Blaine 2020, 32). He is one of the most powerful and strongly-connected people in Australia, with *The Australian Financial Review* ranking him sixth in the "Cultural" category of its annual "Power List" in 2020. In addition to chairing the ARLC, V'landys is CEO of Racing NSW, the regulating body for thoroughbred racing that receives millions annually from Sydney's two main dailies to print its form guides. In 2014 V'landys was made a Member of the Order of Australia for services to horseracing. One of his best-known transactions was obtaining AU$234 million in government assistance for the horseracing industry in the aftermath of an equine influenza in 2007. V'landys adroitly performs a hybrid style of masculinity. He portrays himself as an everyman—a working class Greek migrant who learned valuable life lessons from playing League in his youth (Blaine 2020). He also blends elements of the archetypal strongman, showman, and heroic corporate male leader (Anderson and Warren 2011; Greenwald 2017; Hidalgo-Tenorio and Benítez-Castro 2021).

After becoming ARLC chairman in late 2019, V'landys discovered that the NRL was in dire financial straits, a situation that escalated with the onset of the pandemic. He faced the same predicament as all sports organizations worldwide that had overleveraged their media contracts (Rowe 2020). In this case, the NRL faced losing a multibillion-dollar TV deal if one of its broadcasters activated a clause it did not have to pay for games that were canceled. At a media conference shortly after the WHO declared Covid-19 a pandemic, V'landys asked the NRL to be included in Morrison's $AU17 billion stimulus package on the basis that League was vital to the national economy. He also claimed "Australia without rugby league is not Australia. We need the game to go to keep people's spirits up" (Read 2020a). V'landys also expressed concern about the players who stood to lose money if the season didn't proceed, suggesting,

> The last resort for us is to go to the players and ask them for a pay cut they've got mortgages and made commitments on the money they believe they're going to get we don't want to hurt any player financially or make them unviable (Chisholm 2020a).

In both cases, V'landys was tone-deaf in presuming footballers were somehow exceptions to millions of other Australians with these exact problems.

V'landys' appeal failed and the NRL completed its second round of games in empty stadiums with players and referees under strict biosecurity rules, while TV viewers watched "fake" League, with virtual audio crowd noise simulators and cardboard cutouts of spectators (Knox 2020c). It took until March 23 for NRL officials to follow all other sports in Australia, and most sports around the world, and suspend play rather than risk more financial and reputational damage by competing under such strict health regulations. Epidemiologist Dr. Hassam Vally welcomed this move, arguing that "This [Covid-19] is bigger than sport right now, we've all got to make some really hard sacrifices for the benefit of the whole community" (ABC News 2020a). However, V'landys was undeterred by being refused a bailout, halting play, and having to abide by public health rules. Leveraging male privilege, he therefore sought another way to obtain special treatment.

Project Apollo

Despite asking the government for financial support, in late March V'landys used ARLC funds to give every club a AU$2.5 million rescue package, a decision that likely saved the NRL from collapsing. However, the NRL innovations committee understood that more needed to be done to avoid falling off a fiscal cliff. Inspired by the Apollo 11 moon landing, the NRL established Project Apollo to explore options for restarting in May. According to V'landys, this was "in the best interests of our clubs, our players, our stakeholders and importantly our fans. There's a lot of people that will be happy with the decision to get the competition running again" (ABC News 2020b). New South Wales health minister, Brad Hazzard, and Australia's CMO, who said they were not consulted over this, raised concerns. Hazzard pointed out that "I don't think they (the NRL) are a law unto themselves they're part of society and they have a part -as we have all done to support not only safety for themselves but for all of us," (Guardian Sport 2020). V'landys responded with realpolitik. He insisted that matches were permissible under NSW public health orders and had also received authority to relaunch the competition from NSW Police Commissioner Mick Fuller, who was in charge of State Emergency Operations. V'landy's rationale was that "We've got to go back to some sort of normality at some point in time. We just can't be like this for the rest of our lives" (Barrett 2020). He later added, "the risk is minimal to zero, why shouldn't we restart? Why are we going to rob our fans and players because of scaremongering and alarmist rhetoric?" (Chisholm 2020b). While NSW Premier, Gladys Berejiklian, and Hazzard were circumspect about the return date, Deputy Premier John Barilaro was effusive, stating that "You measure risk versus the economic uplift, the social uplift, the mental wellbeing uplift there's no doubt that the NRL is the tonic we need to get through this virus," (SBS News 2020). The description of the restart as a "tonic" underscores the privileged status of the sport.

However, the federal CMO called the May timeline "premature" and the federal sports minister said it was a "bit ambitious" (AAP 2020b). The federal Deputy CMO hedged his bet, saying he preferred a blanket regulation but understood that sport was "a major part of the Australian psyche" (AAP 2020a). Morrison admired the NRL's determination: "I like that they're planning to try and get the show back on the road at least in some form. I like they've got an ambitious date." But he also stated a reboot would be subject to expert health advice and there would be no "special set of arrangements" (McGowan 2020).

In spite of these reservations, as well as the crippling social and business restrictions still in place across the country, V'landy's announced in late April the season would restart on May 28. It was, he said, "a landmark day for rugby league" and "a great outcome for our players, fans, partners and stakeholders" (ABC News 2020c). V'landys said players had "a responsibility to the game and community," and the interim NRL's CEO, in order to justify the restart, invoked the myth that its players were "role models" (Newton and Gotterson 2020). Ironically, the same day the restart was announced and V'landys put forward the athletes as role models, three players were fined and suspended for breaching physical distancing rules on a camping trip, where they rode dirt bikes and fired guns (ABC News 2020d). In a separate incident, another player was fined and suspended for partying with a group of young women. After examining TikTok videos, NRL officials found he had lied about his whereabouts and issued another fine and suspension, while police fined him AU$1,000 (Fox Sports 2020a). One journalist called the saga a "self-administered knockout punch" (Knox 2020b).

Despite these issues, the seeking of preferential treatment continued. Morrison stated during a radio interview that he hoped the Australian Border Force (ABF) would soon approve an application for an international travel exemption for the New Zealand Warriors (Snape and Mark 2020). At this time, all overseas travelers were banned from entering Australia and most Australians could not even travel interstate, let alone overseas. Nevertheless, the ABF allowed the Warriors to fly to NSW and establish a quarantine camp. Similarly, Premier of Queensland Annastacia Palaszczuk gave permission to the NRL's three teams based there to resume training and travel interstate (Brisbane City Council, Tourism and Events Queensland, and the NSW Government are NRL partners), though Queensland's borders remained closed to native Australians. The State of Victoria's only NRL team, Melbourne Storm, was unable to train at home because of strict emergency rules, so it received permission to temporarily move 330-kilometers north across the border to the NSW regional city of Albury, until restrictions were relaxed on May 11.

V'landys also signed an indispensable TV deal at the last minute. Though this was for an undisclosed discounted rate, it ensured NRL games would be broadcast on *Fox Sport* until the 2027 season and Nine Network for two more years thus, to some degree, shoring up the NRL's faltering finances. That he could do accomplish this during such tenuous times again illustrates the privilege and centrality of the League in Australia. The championship game was played on October 25, when a safe limit of 37,300 spectators were allowed into the stadium.

Male Privilege, Rugby League, and Populist Politics

Some individuals criticized the conduct of NRL officials and players. One sportswriter likened the initial request for financial assistance to "selfish panic merchants who have stripped supermarket shelves" (Wilson, C. 2020). Another journalist speculated the NRL had risked reputational damage by "putting pragmatism ahead of humanity" with its restart (Knox 2020a). According to one commentator, the behavior of the four players mentioned above who breached physical distancing rules on a camping trip, was "dumb, arrogant and reeked of self-entitlement" (Wilson, J. 2020). V'landys was also unflatteringly called "as pleasant as a nasal swab" (Webster 2020b), "a street-fighting bulldog" (Walsh and Stensholt 2020), and "a belligerent populist" (Tedeschi 2020). However, these criticisms had no impact on a group that exploited extensive networks of male privileges and harnessed populist sentiments about League.

In addition to receiving crucial financial support from male-dominated TV networks, the NRL was backed by the print and electronic media, in which men also have most of the power and influence. In his sociological overview of sport and Covid-19, Rowe (2020, 4) found that the media focused more on men's restarts than on women's, non-elite, and grassroots genres. Women's sport was pushed even further to the margins in Australia, with Project Apollo dominating media coverage, not just in sport, but as a lead news item due to the series of transgressions by players we documented above (Carter 2021). Indeed, NRL players were still making headlines in July 2021 over a succession of Covid-19 breaches, which prompted Queensland's CMO to warn she was on the verge of revoking exemptions for the NRL (ABC News 2021).

As mentioned, pay-TV channel Fox Sport is one of the NRL's TV major broadcasters. Far right-wing media baron Rupert Murdoch has a 65% stake in this company, and also owns Australia's top-selling tabloids that are published by his company *News Corp*. Consequently, it is unsurprising that predominantly male editors, writers, and commentators in Murdoch's empire were among the NRL's most steadfast advocates. On April 24, an editorial titled "Time That Premier Backed the NRL" appeared in Murdoch's daily in Brisbane, the *Courier Mail*. It called for Queensland's border to be opened for interstate NRL games, because "rugby league is the lifeblood of Queensland." The article also used a favorite gendered phrase of libertarians who want governments to play a minimal role in peoples' lives: "We're the Sunshine State, not the Nanny State" (Courier Mail 2020a).

In the lead up to the May 28 relaunch, V'landys was acclaimed on the front pages of Murdoch tabloids in Brisbane and Sydney with headlines like "How NRL Was Saved" (*Courier Mail* 2020b). One sportswriter wrote two acclamatory articles about V'landys for Murdoch's national newspaper, *The Australian*. In one he stated V'landys' heroic leadership meant rugby league had "blazed a trail for other Australian sports and sports around the world" (Read 2020b). This was followed by a feature article typical of the mostly male writers who lauded V'Landys with a self-explanatory title: "The man with the iron will" (Read 2020c).

A detailed and admiring account of V'landys' extensive economic, political, and cultural clout similarly appeared in a two-part interview in the *Courier Mail*. The first disclosed how an NRL club chairman with links to U.K. finance brokers and another with a connection to the NSW Premier facilitated the May 28 restart (Rothfield 2020a). The second explained how V'landys assembled a team of biosecurity, infectious diseases, and decontamination experts, used a network of lobbyists, and was supported by NSW Police Commissioner "from day one." The movers and shakers included a popular Sydney radio "shock jock" and league commentator, and the CEO of Murdoch's reactionary *Sky News Australia*, who has "a direct line to the PM and all senior politicians in Canberra." According to V'landys, "There were a lot of politicians who helped us. You can have a great relationship but you've still got to be able to prosecute the argument. They believed in us" (Rothfield 2020b). V'landys' disclosure was rare insight into the breadth and depth of male privilege across economic, political, and cultural institutions in Australia.

Moreover, personal attacks on V'landys only served to galvanize his predominantly male loyalists who derived pleasure from his tactics (Stuckey 2017). To the League faithful he was a "messiah" (Lockyer 2020) and a "godsend" (Encarnation 2020). He was re-elected as ARLC chairman in February 2021 and received overwhelming support for his leadership in a poll of all club chairs (Chammas 2021).

Admiration for V'landys extended well beyond the NRL. Richard Colbeck, the federal Minister for Youth and Sport said, "At the height of the sporting crisis of 2020, Peter V'landys stepped out ahead of the pack, set a mark to reboot the NRL season and effectively dared anyone to pull him back - nobody did" (Marshall, 2020, 19). Pru Goward, a former conservative federal Minister for Women, touted his authentic and militaristic mien as a "model for fearless leadership" (Goward 2020).

These endorsements of someone who sought and gained preferential treatment for a specifically male sport exemplifies how in the populist zeitgeist emotional connections with leaders have more cachet than whether or not leaders' statements are accurate (Lewandowsky 2020).

NSW Police Commissioner Fuller, also was a key NRL backer. One of V'landys' League associates credited Fuller's permission in April for the NRL to restart in 2020 with "virtually saving the NRL from financial disaster" (Holmes 2021). After the 2020 season concluded, V'landys floated the idea of appointing Fuller to the ARLC board on the basis he could help to help to repair the NRL's "bad-boy image" and ensure players were not associating with criminals—a curious acknowledgment given that the NRL constantly touts it players as role models. Fuller said he was well suited to the position and he had the imprimatur of NSW Police Minister David Elliott. These men were so conceited they never considered a perceived conflict of interest in, or legal ramifications of, the appointment, and hastily dropped the plan after being informed by government officials that it was illegal for a serving police commissioner to receive payment for another job (Webster 2021).

Fans and sponsors of the NRL have remained loyal through a raft of scandals and were mainly unconcerned about V'landys' aggressive conduct at the height of Covid-19 restrictions in Australia. Indeed, they reacted with a typical blend of amnesia and euphoria to the restart (Lenskyj 2002). V'landys was lionized in the pregame TV show and the media the next day (ABC News 2020f) and broadcasters were elated the match set viewing records (Fox Sports 2020b).

Conclusion:
Project Apollo as a Microcosm of Male Privilege

Leaders often use sport as an exemplar of the inherent fairness of liberal democracies with metaphors like "a level playing field." Our analysis suggests a more nuanced analogy: sport is, indeed a "part of society" but, as such, contains deep structural inequalities that both reflect and shape *who* gets the privilege to play in the first place and *whose* forms of sport are most valued.

In the case of the NRL, a tiny number of men were indulged by a network of powerful people according to the fallacy of special pleading: "offering an argument though evidence is lacking or even contrary" (Davis 2020). This support included a dedicated biosecurity infectious diseases and decontamination team, exemptions from high-level authorities, and backing from politicians, fans, and self-interested media and entertainment industries. The NRL also received AU$11.5 million in payments to which it and the men's Australian Football League (AFL) were entitled under the federal government's scheme to support eligible businesses, which offset what V'landys called a "modest" AU$24.7 million loss and left the NRL "financially secure" (Guardian Sport 2021; Stensholt 2021). Though players in netball, the nation's most popular female sport, also received subsidies, they were still highly stressed during the 2020 and 2021 seasons for reasons mentioned earlier about the multiple constraints sportswomen face, including paltry media coverage (Carter 2021).

A main feature of pandemic discourses is how leaders and the media have distorted the crisis with banalities about "sacrifices" and "heroes" (Barnett 2020; Lohmeyer and Taylor 2020; McCormack 2020). Project Apollo epitomized this pattern with V'landys and his supporters invoking fictions about the sacrifices and contributions of League. V'landys repeatedly said, "We are all in this together," but only with reference to the NRL, such as praising the "significant sacrifices" players made to restart competition (ABC News 2020e). These were, in fact, lifestyle *choices* made by a minuscule number of well-paid, privileged men, while millions of Australian men and women were practicing self-leadership, making real sacrifices and enduring a multitude of financial, psychological, and social hardships. League was also credited with providing a vital "lifeblood" or "tonic" for the metaphysical "national psyche." Australians negated such shibboleths and V'landys' absurd claim League was indispensable to the nation by carrying on without it. Though Project Apollo was technically permissible, it was contrary to the moral civility displayed by most citizens. It is hard to conceive of another group of Australians being systematically supported to engage in a similar non-essential and potentially dangerous activity as the NRL was.

Instead of supporting the "national side" during Covid-19, the men of League defiantly demonstrated "We're not all in this together." Their action is a telling vignette of wider structures of male privileges in Australia, and also indicative of why tens of thousands of women across Australia took to the streets on March 15, 2021, to support *March4Justice,* a nation-wide protest against Morrison's inaction on a series of allegations of rape, sexual abuse, and harassment (Murphy 2021b). The event was precipitated by a claim by a young member of government staff she had been raped close to Morrison's office (Murphy 2021c). Shortly after the protests, Morrison, who failed to support/address the protestors, though he was invited to do so, inflamed the situation by referencing events in Myanmar in a parliamentary speech, saying, "Not far from here such marches, even now, are being met with bullets" (Priestley 2021). He also said he was "too busy" to attend the march, but a few days later went to an AFL match with his Treasurer. A week later, he shook hands and had a beer in the locker room with members of a winning NRL team (Hislop 2021). Tahleya Eggers, the team's sports scientist and sole woman in the room, did not join the fraternal celebration. Instead, she observed from the periphery and posted a widely retweeted message that crystallized Morrison's unwillingness, or perhaps incapacity, to pay more than lip service to sexism, misogyny, and violence against women and, succinctly demonstrated the preferential treatment of men and sport: "I will not respect a man who has the time to shake hands of men who have won a football match but is "too busy" to attend the March for Justice."

References

AAP 2020a. "NRL Insists It Has Green Light to Restart as NSW Government Again Calls Move into Question." *The Guardian*, April 11, 2020. https://www.theguardian.com/sport/2020/apr/11/nrl-insists-it-has-green-light-to-restart-as-nsw-government-again-calls-move-into-question.

---2020b. "NRL Return Plan 'A Bit Ambitious' Says Federal Sport Minister." *The Guardian*, April 13, 2020. https://www.theguardian.com/sport/2020/apr/13/nrl-season-2020-return-date.

ABC News. 2020a. "NRL Announces Suspension of 2020 Season Due to Coronavirus Pandemic." *ABC News*, March 23, 2020. https://www.abc.net.au/news/2020-03-23/nrl-announces-suspension-of-2020-season-due-to-coronavirus/12082158.

---. 2020b. "NRL Plans for May 28 Return Amid Coronavirus as Nine Network Accuses League of 'Mismanagement'." *ABC News*, April 9, 2020: https://www.abc.net.au/news/2020-04-09/coronavirus-nrl-set-to-resume-2020-season-on-may-28/12136700.

---. 2020c. "NRL Announces 20-round Season, Grand Final to be Played on October 2." *ABC News*, April 28, 2020. https://www.abc.net.au/news/2020-04-28/coronavirus-nrl-to-conduct-20-round-season/12194624.

---. 2020d. "Latrell Mitchell, Josh Addo-Carr Charged with Firearms Offences, NRL Hands Out Hefty Fines." *ABC News*, April 28, 2020; https://www.abc.net.au/news/2020-04-28/nrl-fines-players-for-breaking-coronavirus-restrictions/12193882

---. 2020e. "NRL Strikes New pay Deal with Players as May 28 Restart Takes Shape After Coronavirus Shutdown." *ABC News*, May 5, 2020e: https://www.abc.net.au/news/2020-05-05/coronavirus-nrl-strike-pay-deal-with-players/12216940

---. 2020f. "NRL Season Returns After Coronavirus Shutdown as Parramatta Beats Brisbane 34-6." *ABC News*, May 29, 2020; https://www.abc.net.au/news/2020-05-28/coronavirus-nrl-parramatta-eels-beat-brisbane-broncos/12297720

---. 2021. "NRL Players on Notice as Jeannette Young Says She's Close to Booting the League out of Queensland." *ABC News*, July 23, 2021. https://www.abc.net.au/news/2021-07-23/jeannette-young-close-to-booting-nrl-out-of-state/100317618

Adelson, Andrea, and Heather Dinich. 2021. "NCAA Women's Tournament 2021: Inside an Overdue Reckoning Over Inequity in Basketball." *ESPN*, April 3, 2021. https://www.espn.com.au/womens-college-basketball/story/_/id/31182950/ncaa-women-tournament-2021-overdue-reckoning-inequity-basketball.

AFP. 2012. "Double Standards: Australian Women's Basketball Team Fly Economy as Men Travel BusinessClass." *The Journal.ie*, July 20, 2012; https://www.the42.ie/double-standards-australian-womens-basketball-team-fly-economy-as-men-travel-business-class-526993-Jul2012/.

Anderson, Alistair R., and Lorraine Warren. 2011. "The Entrepreneur as Hero and Jester: Enacting the Entrepreneurial Discourse." *International Small Business Journal* 29 (6): 589-609.

Barnett, Michael. 2020. "COVID-19 and the Sacrificial International Order." *International Organization*, December, E128–E47. https://doi.org/10.1017/S002081832000034X.

Barrett, Chris. 2020. "'We Could Do It Tomorrow if We Wanted': V'landys Hits Back as May Return Queried." *The Sydney Morning Herald*, April 10, 2020. https://www.smh.com.au/sport/nrl/we-could-do-it-tomorrow-if-we-wanted-v-landys-hits-back-as-may-return-queried-20200410-p54iy5.html.

Blaine, Lech. 2020. "The Art of Class War." *The Monthly*, August 1, 2020, 30-42.

Carter, Brittany, 2021. "Netball Vents Its Frustration with Footballers Breaking the Rules." *ABC News*, July 7, 2021. https://www.abc.net.au/news/2021-07-07/womens-sport-handle-covid-pandemic-better-than-mens/100272170.

Carter, Cynthia, Linda Steiner, and Lisa McLaughlin, eds. 2015. *The Routledge Companion to Media & Gender*. Abingdon: Routledge.

Chammas, Michael, 2021. "Clubs Back Head Office, But Early Debut a No-Joe." *The Sydney Morning Herald*, March 8, 2021. 43.

Chisholm, Ed. 2020a. "Coronavirus: Players at Risk of Losing Millions as Part Of 'Act of God' Clause as NRL Braces for Financial Catastrophe." *Sporting News*, March 15, 2020. https://www.sportingnews.com/au/league/news/coronavirus-players-at-risk-of-losing-millions-as-part-of-act-of-god-clause-as-nrl-braces-for-financial-catastrophe/11i1su28vqrv2196ssugh4qh2w.

---. 2020b. "Peter V'landys Hits Out at 'Scaremongering' Critics of May 28th Restart as D-day is Declared with Broadcasters." *Sporting News*, April 24, 2020. https://www.sportingnews.com/au/league/news/peter-vlandys-hits-out-at-scaremongering-critics-of-may-28th-restart-as-d-day-is-declared-with-broadcasters/1moi6jq8puyd514cvzq9avsf1e.

Cooky, Cheryl, LaToya D. Council, Maria A. Mears, and Michael A. Messner. 2021. "One and Done: The Long Eclipse of Women's Televised Sports, 1989–2019." *Communication & Sport*, March 24, 2021. https://doi.org/10.1177/21674795211003524.

Courier Mail. 2020a. "Time That Premier Backed the NRL." *Courier Mail*, April 24, 2020, 70.

---. 2020b. "How NRL Was Saved." *Courier Mail*, May 22, 2020, 1.

Daley, Paul. 2020. "Politicians, Take Note This Anzac Day: Coronavirus is a Pandemic. It is Not a War." *The Guardian*, April 25, 2020. https://www.theguardian.com/commentisfree/2020/apr/25/politicians-take-note-this-anzac-day-coronavirus-is-a-pandemic-it-is-not-a-war.

Davis, Glyn. 2020. "Special Pleading: Free Speech and Australian Universities." *The Conversation*, December 4, 2020. https://theconversation.com/special-pleading-free-speech-and-australian-universities-108170.

Dawson, Emma, Tanja Kovac, and Abigail Lewis 2021. "Measure For Measure. Gender Equality in Australia." *Per Capita*, March 3, 2021. https://percapita.org.au/wp-content/uploads/2020/03/MfM_summary_FINAL.pdf.

Dixon, Janine, and Helen Hodgson. 2020. "Modelling Finds Investing in Childcare and Aged Care Almost Pays for Itself." *The Conversation*, October 19, 2020. https://theconversation.com/modelling-finds-nvesting-in-childcare-and-aged-care-almost-pays-for-itself-148097.

Dowd, Nancy E. 2008. "Masculinities and Feminist Legal Theory." *Wisconsin Journal of Law, Gender & Society* 23 (2): 201-248.

Duckett, Stephen, and Anika Stobart. 2020. "4 Ways Australia's Coronavirus Response Was a Triumph, and 4 Ways it Fell Short." *The Conversation*, June 4, 2020. https://theconversation.com/4-ways-australias-coronavirus-response-was-a-triumph-and-4-ways-it-fell-short-139845.

Encarnation, Matt. 2020. "Club Boss Says Peter V'landys Arrival Was a 'Godsend' For NRL." *foxsports.com*, April 4, 2020. https://www.foxsports.com.au/nrl/nrl-premiership/club-boss-says-peter-vlandys-arrival-was-a-godsend-for-nrl/news-story/f04700a8a7f2cf9fb5d6848605c01e97.

Fox Sports. 2020a. "Ivan Cleary Breaks Silence on Nathan's 'Embarrassment' Over TikTok Fine." *foxsports.com.au*, May 14, 2020; https://www.foxsports.com.au/nrl/nrl-premiership/teams/panthers/nrl-2020-nathan-cleary-tiktok-penrith-panthers-ivan-cleary-fine-punishment-reaction/news-story/6420ac80ae7fe1ef9f4c4ffc8820e269.

---. 2020b. "Ratings Records Smashed as Million-plus Audience Feasts on NRL's Blockbuster Return." *foxsports.com.au*, May 29, 2020. https://www.foxsports.com.au/nrl/nrl-premiership/nrl-2020-broncos-vs-eels-roosters-vs-rabbitohs-storm-vs-raiders-round-3-tv-ratings-broadcast-deal/news-story/85e3a692055bc1c85a7614e3b9e6f4d8.

Goward, Pru. 2020. "A Model for Fearless Leadership in a Crisis? Hint: He Steers Two Major Sports." *WAtoday*, May 13, 2020. https://www.watoday.com.au/national/a-model-for-fearless-leadership-in-a-crisis-hint-he-steers-two-major-sports-20200513-p54sho.html.

Greenwald, Michael. 2017. "How the 'Greatest Showman' Paved the Way for Donald Trump." *The Conversation*, December 11, 2017. https://theconversation.com/how-the-greatest-showman-paved-the-way-for-donald-trump-85212.

Guardian Sport 2020. "NRL 'Not a Law unto Themselves' Says Australias Deputy Chief Medical Officer." *The Guardian*, April 10, 2020. https://www.theguardian.com/sport/2020/apr/10/nrl-restart-date-paul-kelly-brad-hazzard.

---. 2021. "NRL Says Clubs Financially Secure Despite Covid Pandemic Losses." *The Guardian*, February 26, 2021.https://www.theguardian.com/sport/2021/feb/26/nrl-says-clubs-financially-secure-despite-covid-pandemic-losses.

Hargreaves, Jennifer, and Eric Anderson, eds. 2016. *Handbook of Sport, Gender, And Sexuality*. London: Routledge.

Hewson, John. (2021). "Why Scott Morrison Can't Tell the Truth." *The Saturday Paper*, July 31, 2021, 7.

Hidalgo-Tenorio, Encarnación, and Miguel-Ángel Benítez-Castro. 2021. "Trump's Populist Discourse and Affective Politics, Or on How to Move 'The People' Through Emotion." *Globalisation, Societies and Education*, https://doi.org/10.1080/14767724.2020.1861540

Hislop, Madeline. 2021. "Tahleya Eggers' Reaction to Scott Morrison at the Footy Symbolises Every Woman in Australia Right Now." *Women's Agenda*, March 29, 2021. https://womensagenda.com.au/latest/tahleya-eggers-reaction-to-scott-morrison-at-the-footy-symbolises-every-woman-in-australia-right-now/.

Holmes, Tracey. 2021. "NSW Police Commissioner Mick Fuller's Appointment to the ARLC Has Been Praised by Some, But Also Raises Eyebrows." *ABC News*, February 20, 2021. https://www.abc.net.au/news/2021-02-20/police-commissioner-mick-fuller-proposed-role-at-arlc/13172870.

Hytner, Mike. 2021. "Former NRL Gender Adviser Catharine Lumby Expresses Concern Over League Leadership." *The Guardian*, April 23, 2021. https://www.theguardian.com/sport/2021/apr/23/former-nrl-gender-adviser-catharine-lumby-expresses-concern-over-league-leadership.

Jensen, Klaus Bruhn. 2020. *A Handbook of Media and Communication Research: Qualitative and Quantitative Methodologies* (third edition). London: Routledge.

Jericho, Greg. 2020. "Coronavirus is First a Health Problem, Second an Economic One." *The Guardian*, March 14, 2020. https://www.theguardian.com/commentisfree/2020/mar/14/coronavirus-is-first-a-health-problem-second-an-economic-one.

Kane, Darren, 2021. "ARLC's Move for Fuller Doomed Before It Began, But Not Because of the Money." *The Sydney Morning Herald*, February 27, 2021, 46-47.

Kinsella, Luke. 2019. "The 66 Scandals in Four Years That Have Rocked the NRL." *news.com.au*, February 8, 2019. https://www.news.com.au/sport/nrl/the-66-scandals-in-four-years-that-have-rocked-the-nrl/news-story/61bc26cdb901a29fa70defc8c.

Knox, Malcolm. 2020a. "Coronavirus: NRL as Essential Exercise? The Game Might Want to Look Outside Itself." *stuff.co.nz*, April 3, 2020.

https://www.stuff.co.nz/sport/opinion/120811970/coronavirus-nrl-as-essential-exercise-the-game-might-want-to-look-outside-itself.

---. 2020b. "How Can the NRL Slam Wayward Stars? They Are its Ultimate Ambassadors." *Brisbane Times*, May 1, 2020; https://www.brisbanetimes.com.au/sport/nrl/how-can-the-nrl-slam-wayward-stars-they-are-its-ultimate-ambassadors-20200501-p54oxa.html7ba01b5.

---. 2020c. "Echoes of Umberto as V'landys Waves Wand to Give People What They Want." *WAtoday*, May 22, 2020. https://www.watoday.com.au/sport/nrl/echoes-of-umberto-as-v-landys-waves-wand-to-give-people-what-they-want-20200529-p54xmd.html.

---. 2020d. "Beyond the NRL Rape Trials, the Game Still Fails to Tackle Misogyny." *The Sydney Morning Herald*, December 5, 2020, 32-33.

---. 2021. "Crown Case Begs question of Just What Sponsors NRL Clubs Would Refuse." *The Sydney Morning Herald*, February 12, 2021.https://www.smh.com.au/sport/nrl/crown-case-begs-question-of-just-what-sponsors-nrl-clubs-would-refuse-20210212-p571zd.html.

Kontominas, Belinda, and Andrea Jonson. 2019. "NRL Gender Adviser Catharine Lumby Says Some Rugby League Players are 'Education-proof'" *ABC News*, March 8, 2019. https://www.abc.net.au/news/2019-03-08/nrl-gender-adviser-says-some-players-are-education-proof/10881190.

Lenskyj, Helen. 2002. *Best Olympics Ever? The Social Impacts of Sydney 2000*. Albany: State University of New York Press.

Leonard, David J. 2017. *Playing While White: Privilege and Power on And Off the Field*. Seattle: University of Washington Press.

Lewandowsky, Stephan. 2020. "Why People Vote for Politicians They Know Are Liars." *The Conversation*, December 19, 2020. https://theconversation.com/why-people-vote-for-politicians-they-know-are-liars-128953.

Lockyer, Darren. 2020. "League Finds Messiah. Passionate V'landys Rescues the Game in Its Darkest Hour." *Courier Mail*, May 23, 2020, 93.

Lohmeyer, Ben A., and Nik Taylor. 2020. "War, Heroes and Sacrifice Masking Neoliberal Violence During the COVID-19 Pandemic." *Critical Sociology*, November 29, 2020. https://doi.org/10.1177/0896920520975824.

Manne, Kate. 2018. "Brett Kavanaugh and America's 'Himpathy' Reckoning." *The New York Times*, September 26, 2018. https://www.nytimes.com/2018/09/26/opinion/brett-kavanaugh-hearing-himpathy.html.

Mark, David. 2021. "What Australia's Politicians Could Learn from Rugby League." *ABC News*, March 27, 2021. https://www.abc.net.au/news/2021-03-27/what-australias-politicians-could-learn-from-rugby-league/100031490.

Marshall, Konrad, "40 Australians Who Mattered in 2020, Sport." *Good Weekend*, November 2, 2020, 19.

McCormack, Lisa. 2020. "Marking Time in Lockdown: Heroization and Ritualization in the UK During the Coronavirus Pandemic." *American Journal of Cultural Sociology* 8: 324-351.

McGowan, Michael. 2020. "NRL Plan to Start Games by End of May is 'Ambitious' Scott Morrison Says." *The Guardian*, April 14, 2020. https://www.theguardian.com/sport/2020/apr/14/nrls-plan-to-start-games-by-end-of-may-is-ambitious-says-scott-morrison.

Messerschmidt, James W. 2018. *Hegemonic Masculinity: Formulation, Reformulation, and Amplification*, New York: Rowman & Littlefield.

Moore, Andrew. 2000. "Opera of the Proletariat: Rugby League, The Labour Movement and Working-Class Culture in New South Wales and Queensland." *Labour History*, 79: 57-70.

Murphy, Katharine. 2021a. "Canberra's Pale, Stale and Male Tribe is Missing the Moment - As It Did with Julia Gillard's Misogyny Speech." *The Guardian*, March 6, 2021. https://www.theguardian.com/australia-news/2021/mar/06/canberras-pale-stale-and-male-tribe-is-missing-the-moment-as-it-did-with-julia-gillards-misogyny-speech.

---. 2021b. "Voices Raised in Anger Are Echoing Throughout the Land But it Seems Morrison Still Can't Hear." *The Guardian*, March 15, 2021. https://www.theguardian.com/australia-news/2021/mar/15/voices-raised-in-anger-are-echoing-throughout-the-land-but-it-seems-morrison-still-cant-hear.

---. 2021c. "A Reported Rape of a Staffer Was Not Enough for Morrison to 'Get it' Now Women Are Tired of Waiting." *The Guardian,* March 23, 2021. https://www.theguardian.com/australia-news/2021/mar/23/a-reported-of-a-staffer-was-not-enough-for-morrison-to-get-it-now-women-are-tired-of-waiting.

Nauright, John, and David K. Wiggins, eds. 2016. *Routledge Handbook of Sport, Race and Ethnicity*. London: Routledge.

Newell, Beau. 2020. "Call to Action: Why LGBTQ Inclusion Must be Amplified in Australian Sport, During and Post-COVID19." *Pride in Sport*, May 28. https://www.prideinsport.com.au/call-to-action-why-lgbtq-inclusion-must-be-amplified-in-australian-sport-during-and-post-covid19/.

Newton, Alicia, and Greta Gotterson .2020. "Mitchell, Addo-Carr Fined $50,000; Cleary Fined $10,000 for Self-isolation Breaches." *NRL.com*, April, 28, 2020. https://www.NRL.com/news/2020/04/28/mitchell-addo-carr-fined-$50000-cleary-fined-$10000-for-self-isolation-breaches/.

New Matilda. 2020. "Scotty From Marketing Makes The Urban Dictionary: To Do A 'Scomo' Is To…?" *New Matilda*, January 17, 2020; https://newmatilda.com/2020/01/17/scotty-from-marketing-makes-the-urban-dictionary-to-do-a-scomo-is-to/

O'Sullivan, Dominic, Mubarak Rahamathulla, and Manohar Pawar. 2020. "The Impact and Implications of COVID-19: An Australian Perspective." *The International Journal of Community and Social Development* 2 (2): 134-151. July 1, 2020. https://journals.sagepub.com/doi/full/10.1177/2516602620937922.

Packard Hill, Esther, and Glen Fuller. 2018. "One for the Team: Domestic Violence Scandals and Reflexive Media Commentary by Rugby League Players in Australia." *Communication & Sport*, 6(1) 41-57. https://doi.org/10.1177/2167479516678419.

Pape, Madeleine. 2019. "Gender Segregation and Trajectories of Organizational Change: The Underrepresentation of Women in Sports Leadership." *Gender & Society*, 34 (1): 81-105.

Parry, Keith D. 2020. "The Formation of Heroes and The Myth of National Identity." *Sport in Society*, March 2, 2020; DOI: 10.1080/17430437.2020.1733531.

Pavlidis, Adele, and David Rowe. 2021. "The Sporting Bubble as Gilded Cage: Gendered Professional Sport in Pandemic Times and Beyond." *M/C Journal*, 24(1). https://doi.org/10.5204/mcj.2736.

Pease, Bob. 2010. *Undoing Privilege: Unearned Advantage in A Divided World*. London: Zed Books.

Priestley, Angela. 2021. "A 'Triumph' That Protesters Not 'Met with Bullets'? No, Scott Morrison." *Women's Agenda*, March 15, 2021. https://womensagenda.com.au/latest/a-triumph-that-protesters-not-met-with-bullets-no-scott-morrison/.

Read, Brent. 2020a. "Coronavirus: NRL to Play on Behind Closed Doors, ARL Boss Warns of Catastrophe." *The Australian*, March 15, 2020.

https://www.theaustralian.com.au/sport/nrl/coronavirus-nrl-to-play-on-behind-closed-doors-arl-boss-warns-of-catastrophe/news-story/a35cc93a48feb6c5a993eed7302a6555.

---. 2020b. "V'landys Provides a Leadership Lesson." *The Australian*, May 15, 2020. https://www.theaustralian.com.au/sport/nrl/vlandys-provides-a-leadership-lesson/news-story/7194b3402b0b79489812b6e9096f4f92.

---. 2020c. "The Man With the Iron Will." *The Weekend Australian*, May 23, 2020, 35.39.

Reichart Smith, Lauren and Ann Pegoraro. 2020. "Media Framing of Larry Nassar and the USA Gymnastics Child Sex Abuse Scandal." *Journal of Child Sexual Abuse*, 29 (4): 373-392.

Rothfield, Phil. 2020a. "From a Code Red to Alive and Kicking," *Courier Mail*, May 22, 2020, 4-5.

---. 2020b. "Top Dog Torn in League Rescue." *Courier Mail*, May 23. 2020, 28-29.

Rowe, David. 2020. "Subjecting Pandemic Sport to a Sociological Procedure." *Journal of Sociology* 56 (4): 704-713.

Rowe, David, and Catherine Palmer. 2022. "Sport, Scandal, and Social Morality." In *Oxford Handbook of Sport and Society*, edited by Lawrence Wenner, Oxford: Oxford University Press (forthcoming).

SBS News 2020. "NSW Deputy Premier Backs NRL as 'The Tonic We Need' To get Through Challenges of COVID-19." *SBS News*, April 4, 2020. https://www.sbs.com.au/news/nsw-deputy-premier-backs-nrl-as-the-tonic-we-need-to-get-through-challenges-of-covid-19.

Smith, Julia, Sara E Davies, Huiyun Feng, Connie C R Gan, Karen A Grépin, Sophie Harman, Asha Herten-Crabb, Rosemary Morgan, Nimisha Vandan, and Clare Wenham. 2021. "More Than a Public Health Crisis: A Feminist Political Economic Analysis of COVID-19." *Global Public Health*, March 11, 2021. DOI: 10.1080/17441692.2021.1896765.

Snape, Jack, and David Mark. 2020. "Coronavirus Obstacles Clearing for NRL to Resume Season on May 28 As Queensland Agrees to Return." *ABC News*, May 1, 2020. https://www.abc.net.au/news/2020-05-01/coronavirus-travel-ban-pm-says-no-clearance-for-nz-warriors-nrl/1220655.

Spargo-Ryan, Anna. 2021. "Blokes Will Be Blokes." *Meanjin*, Winter. https://meanjin.com.au/essays/blokes-will-be-blokes/.

Spencer, Elizabeth A., and Anthony M. Limperos. 2018. "ESPN's Coverage of Intimate Partner Violence in the National Football League." *Communication & Sport* 8 (1): 3-25.

Stensholt, John. 2021. "Covid Cost AFL and NRL Hundreds of Millions, Financial Accounts Reveal." *The Australian*, February 26, 2021. https://www.theaustralian.com.au/sport/covid-cost-afl-and-nrl-hundreds-of-millions-financial-accounts-reveal/news-story/fe839a21679bf14f6235dcf7c206667e.

Stewart, Miranda. 2020. "Blink and You'll Miss It: What the Budget Did for Working Mums." *The Conversation*, October 28, 2020. https://theconversation.com/blink-and-youll-miss-it-what-the-budget-did-for-working-mums-148264.

Stuckey, Mary E. 2017. "American Elections and the Rhetoric of Political Change: Hyperbole, Anger, and Hope in U.S. Politics." *Rhetoric and Public Affairs* 20 (4): 667-694.

Tedeschi, Nick. 2020. "Bulldozer Tactics See NRL Win Australia's Race to Return First." *The Guardian*, May 25, 2020. https://www.theguardian.com/sport/2020/may/26/bulldozer-tactics-see-nrl-win-australias-race-to-return-first.

Turner, Brook. 2020. "The 10 Most Culturally Powerful People in Australia in 2020." *The Australian Financial Review Magazine the Power Issue*, October 2020; https://www.afr.com/work-and-careers/leaders/the-10-most-culturally-powerful-people-in-australia-in-2020-20200716-p55cru.

Walsh, Courtney. 2021. "AFL boss McLachlan determined to invest further to grow women's game." *The Australian*. March 12, 2021. https://www.theaustralian.com.au/sport/afl/afl-boss-mclachlan-determined-to-invest-further-to-grow-womens-game/news-story/a6e7b243597d909a025e1440e97011e8.

Waterhouse-Watson, Deb. 2019. *Football and Sexual Crime, From the Courtroom to the Newsroom*. Cham: Palgrave Macmillan.

Webster, Andrew. 2020a "V'landys' Tone-deaf Cash Grab in the Middle of Coronavirus Crisis." *Head Topics*, March 15, 2020. https://headtopics.com/au/v-landys-tone-deaf-cash-grab-in-the-middle-of-coronavirus-crisis-11876463.

---. 2020b. "Peter V'landys is Becoming as Pleasant as a Nasal Swab for AFL." *Head Topics*, May 5, 2020. https://headtopics.com/au/peter-v-landys-is-becoming-as-pleasant-as-a-nasal-swab-for-afl-12831884.

---. 2021. "The Mick Fuller Fiasco is an Embarrassment for the NRL And V'landys." *The Sydney Morning Herald*, February 22, 2021, 33.

Wenner, Lawrence. 2021. "Media, Sports, and Society." In *Research Handbook on Sports and Society*, edited by Elizabeth Pike, 111-126. Cheltenham: Elgar Publishing.

Wilson, Caroline. 2020. "'Panic merchant': AFL Columnist Caroline Wilson Slams ARL Chairman Peter V'landys Over Coronavirus 'Scaremongering'" *foxsports.com.au*, March 17, 2020. https://www.foxsports.com.au/nrl/nrl-premiership/nrl-2020-coronavirus-covid19-caroline-wilson-blasts-peter-vlandys-arlc-rugby-league/news-story/50c29cb71be84697a40d1b7adebb0893.

Wilson, Jim. 2020. "COVID-19 Rulebreakers Slammed Over 'Arrogant' Behaviour'". March 29, 2020. https://7news.com.au/sport/rugby-league/coronavirus-australia-nrls-covid-19-rulebreakers-slammed-over-arrogant-behaviour--c-1005137.

Wood, Danielle, Kate Griffiths, and Tom Crowley. 2021. *Women's Work: The impact of the COVID Crisis on Australian Women*. Grattan Institute, March 7, 2021. https://grattan.edu.au/report/womens-work/

Yin, Robert K. 2017. *Case Study Research and Applications: Design and Methods* (sixth edition). Los Angeles: Sage.

Young, Kevin. 2019. *Sport, Violence and Society* (second Edition). London: Routledge.

Zwica, Kristine. 2021. "Yes, Telling Women They Should Be Happy They're Not Being Shot At Is Bad. But This is the Moment The PM Really Took Women For Mugs." https://womensagenda.com.au/latest/yes-telling-women-they-should-be-happy-theyre-not-being-shot-at-is-bad-but-this-is-the-moment-the-pm-really-took-women-for-mugs/.

Chapter 4

One Big Family: Return to Play by MLS Referees Driven by Friendship and the Love for the Game

Yuya Kiuchi, Bill Dittmar, Scott Matteson

Introduction

Major League Soccer (MLS) suspended its regular season on March 12, 2020, following only having played games over two weekends in February and March. During the succeeding four-month hiatus, just like players and fans, referees were left uncertain about the status of the league. As one of the most experienced MLS referees Ismail Elfath commented, not knowing if the suspension was going to last for a week, a month, or even longer, "was worrisome." For full-time referees, their livelihoods were cut (Elfath 2021). Cory Richardson, an MLS assistant referee, concurred by stating that the period had "so many unknowns" but filled with rumors about when and how the league might start again (Richardson 2021). The chaotic nature of the period is reflected on the fact that Richardson first learned about the league's suspension on ESPN the day before he was supposed to leave for Toronto for a match, with another match scheduled in Salt Lake City the following week. As Richardson speculated what was to come, he received an email from Howard Webb, the General Manager of Professional Referees Organization (PRO), the organization in charge of training and assigning referees to MLS games, letting him know that the matches for the weekend had been canceled. The level of uncertainty, however, was understandable and widespread beyond the referee community, as the extent of the pandemic was still unknown.

While the referees lived in uncertainty, rumors and buzzes about the possible return to play began to surface after several weeks. Richardson remembers that referees talked to each other about any possible idea that the league might resume. Referees wondered if there would be Covid-19 tests, how often the tests might be required, who would pay for it, where the games would be, and if it at all was even feasible (Richardson 2021). Webb recalls that soon after the league's suspension, it became clear that resuming matches with the original schedule was not possible. In the meantime, the league started its effort to bring the match back by creating a bubble. Several options existed to host the possible bubble tournament including California, Texas, and Florida. In the end, by mid-May, Orlando, Florida, was selected as the host site for having a facility large enough to accommodate participating teams, staff, and officials, but the return-to-play date kept being pushed back. It was only in early June that MLS announced that the league would resume in the bubble established at the ESPN World Wide of Sports Complex in Disney World in Orlando on July 8. Twenty-six MLS teams were expected to arrive in Orlando on June 24 to prepare for the tournament-style event (Kay 2020).

While the time period leading up to the tournament, known as the MLS is Back Tournament, had a series of surprises and adjustments for all parties involved, from the referees' perspective, the event was a major success. Although not all referees were able to attend the event and those who attended agreed that being in the bubble and staying away from their families for weeks was not easy, they also enjoyed the strengthened camaraderie among themselves. Furthermore, referees' performance was of quality, even after several months of no officiating activities. Interviews with PRO staff and referees show that the success of both the tournament and refereeing was largely due to the strong sense of friendship, community, and cohesion among themselves. These factors kept the referees engaged and motivated during the suspension, enabling them to be ready for the tournament. Referees also helped each other while being away from home for up to five weeks, and truly expected the best from each other on the field during the tournament. Beyond technical and physical training, the intangible sense of connection amongst referees contributed to the successful event.

Information provided by PRO staff and referees are vital in understanding how they experienced the time period leading up to the resumption of the league. This study relies on interviews with two PRO staff members and four referees. Howard Webb and Mark Geiger both play management roles for PRO. The interviewed referees range from one of the most experienced referees to one of the newer referees. One of the interviewees decided against partaking in the tournament while three others joined. These interviews with referees illuminate how each experienced the suspension period, perceived the league's decision to play again, and decided to join, or not join, the event. Furthermore, one of the interviewees was a member of the labor negotiation team that represented all the referees to discuss the terms and conditions for the event with PRO.

Preparing for Return-to-Play

Once MLS decided to hold a bubble event, two major questions surfaced for PRO staff and referees. The first was how to make sure that the event would have enough referees. After all, while all MLS referees are fulltime referees, MLS assistant referees are not. Furthermore, the fulltime status did not mean that these referees were expected to be away from home for weeks at a time. Normally, referees travel for a few days at a time. The second question was about health and safety. Shorter than half a year into the pandemic world, information and knowledge about the risk of the disease was still very limited. To address both questions, PRO and its referees, along with relevant departments of MLS, worked closely to make decisions quickly to realize the event.

Negotiating with Referees

One of the major tasks for PRO was to ensure that it created an environment for referees to travel to and officiate at the event with heightened health and safety protocols. During the negotiation phase in early summer, Covid-19 was still new. The concerns MLS referees had when it came to returning to their sport were justified. Florida at the time had registered 269,811 Covid-19 cases with a national daily high of 15,300 new cases reported just prior to the beginning of the tournament (Tannenwald 2020), compounded by the understanding that the ability to test negative over the course of the first initial stages of infection was exceedingly high (Baxter 2020). Furthermore, testing was not perfect and only intended to detect markedly infected individuals (*ibid.*) provided additional cause for concern. PRO personnel were worried about the inevitable positive test results while the protocol for how the MLS was going to handle them was not initially made clear (Vejar 2020). To alleviate these concerns, MLS top staff consulted with national medical experts, epidemiologists, and a former surgeon general to ensure the safety and protection of all MLS personnel (Romero and Parry 2020).

For referees and even PRO staff, traveling to Orlando also meant possibly exposing themselves to Covid-19. Webb shared that the day after the league shut down, on March 13, he went back home to New Jersey. As he lived alone, he had no extended contact with people for fifteen weeks. But suddenly on the way to Orlando, he was exposed to the outside world (Webb 2021). Referees were aware of the high number of Covid-19 cases in Florida. To make matters worse, science was unclear as to what would happen if one person on a plane had Covid-19. Would everyone on the plane be at risk? The answer was not clear at the time. Getting out of his own bubble and getting to another bubble was "scary," Richardson (2021) shared.

As a part of PRO, MLS referees and assistant referees are represented by the Professional Soccer Referee Association (PSRA). PSRA serves as the referees' union and negotiates working terms and conditions, including match and relevant compensation, training requirements, logistics, and assessments. The original collective bargaining agreement (CBA) between PRO and PSRA understandably did not include any reference to a bubble-style event where referees would have to commit twenty-four hours of their day, seven days a week, for five to six weeks, possibly up to fifty days living and working in one place. Because referees would have to be tested to be approved to travel to Orlando, and quarantine for a certain period of time before they could officiate, organizers realized it was not worth having a referee in the bubble for just a week, only to be able to officiate one or two games. This meant that any referee who would agree to be in the bubble would have to commit to being there for at least a few weeks, if not longer. Therefore, as soon as the league decided to hold MLS is Back, the two parties had to come to the table to discuss and agree on a new set of terms and conditions (Geiger 2021; Webb 2021).

Katy Nesbitt, a PRO assistant referee, who would eventually be appointed to the final of the MLS is Back tournament, explained that one of the ways for her to deal with the uncertainty about health and safety was to be involved in the decision-making process of the return-to-play protocol. This is why she decided to be a part of PSRA's five-member negotiation team that negotiated the details of the tournament from the referees' perspectives, including logistics, as well as health and safety. Being a part of the committee helped her "[figure] out what the bubble [was] going to be like." She was able to learn what MLS's medical department was suggesting (Nesbitt 2021).

Discussing details on measures specific to a bubble tournament was particularly important because MLS was only second among major sport leagues, after the National Women's Soccer League, to have a bubble tournament in the U.S., and even in the world. The MLS's event predated that of the National Basketball Association, which held a similar bubble tournament at the same venue and used MLS's logistics as a model. Even outside the U.S., professional soccer leagues that had resumed their seasons, including Bundesliga in Germany, were playing in the market, or at various stadia without spectators, and not in a bubble. German referees traveled primarily by car while MLS referees were to fly (Geiger 2021). As Nesbitt planned to embark on this sphere of uncertainty, being an active member of the negotiation allowed her to help create a space where she could feel safe. Nesbitt (2021) commented that even though it did not necessarily ease her worry about uncertainties, it at least gave her a chance to know what was happening.

The work of Nesbitt and her colleagues were appreciated by other officials. Elfath (2021) commented that the new CBA included safety, testing, social distancing, compensation, rest time, and others, allowing him to not have too many concerns. Richardson (2021) also stated that having strict protocols and having to take multiple tests before heading into the bubble allowed him to feel safe. "If I didn't feel safe, I would not have been there," he said. PRO and PSRA worked to ensure that Nesbitt, Richardson, and their colleagues all felt safe working in Orlando.

Agreeing on the New CBA

After almost a month-long negotiation, PRO and PSRA created the framework with which they were able to find enough referees to cover all the games without having to invite anyone from the non-MLS referee list. Almost all MLS referees decided to travel to the event and enough assistant referees were able to attend. The fact that the quarantine period was shortened to only two days with additional testing helped with the number of officials able to attend. PRO and PSRA ended up agreeing that referees had to commit to stay in the bubble for at least twenty-one days.

While having enough referees was crucial, not having too many referees was also important. Under normal circumstances, an MLS match has four officials on the field, a video assistant referee (VAR), and an assistant video assistant referee (AVAR). While referees and assistant referees are certified to serve as VARs and/or AVARs, over twenty people officials who are registered as VARs or AVARs are not registered as referees or assistant referees. In other words, while any official registered as a referee may serve as a VAR, not all those registered as a VAR would be able to serve as a referee. To minimize the number of officials on site in the bubble, PRO decided to only invite officials registered as a referee or an assistant referee. These arrangements were needed because the supposed risk of transmission was significant. Geiger was acutely aware that referees could be a super-spreader of the virus not just among themselves but also to different teams. He continued that the biggest hurdle was to minimize risk and contact. He explained:

> How to keep everyone safe was obviously our number one priority. Every plan we put into place and every little detail centered around the referees safety. We were working with and coordinating with MLS Medical [Department] and using their expertise, guidance, and their recommendations to make the best situation for the referees. [Covid-19] was still so new at that point. Nobody knew how well or easily it was going to spread in the bubble and what the process was going to look like (Geiger 2021).

Webb (2021) also agreed that any referee who became infected could pose a "real threat to the continuation of the tournament." This was why the balance between having enough referees to hold the event and not having too many to increase the risk of exposure was important.

The new agreement between the two parties stated that referees on site would be put into one of three referee pods. Similarly, all the teams were assigned into one of six groups. To minimize the risk of transmission, referees in Pod 1 only officiated teams in Groups A and B; referees in Pod 2 only officiated teams in Groups C and D, and the same arrangement existed for referees in Pod 3. The exception was for the VAR and AVAR personnel because they did not interact with players. The pods were also in place beyond the field. Although referees were allowed to dine with someone from a different pod as long as appropriate social distancing was possible, they trained in pods. When they interacted with someone from another pod, for example during an instructional session, they had to wear a mask and maintain distance.

These agreements made between PRO and PSRA enabled many referees to feel safe, or at least safe enough, to travel to Florida. Elfath (2021) stated that he felt safe about the health and safety provisions put in place. He also knew what to expect upon arrival in Orlando, including the mandatory quarantine procedure.

Balancing Family and Soccer

Although PRO and PSRA created a comprehensive CBA, not all officials decided to travel to Orlando. For some referees, participating in the tournament appeared to pose extra risk because of their personal situation. Corey Parker (2021), a PRO assistant referee, shared that he and his wife had just welcomed a baby as the league shut down, making the possible consequence of infection even more heightened. Consequently, he decided not to join the MLS bubble. It was not an easy decision for him. On one level, he stayed home to take care of the baby as a parent. But on another level, even if he was able to be away from home, he had to be extra careful with a newborn in the house. Risk factors of the virus were still unknown. "I was terrified especially with a little one at home," Parker remembered. But Parker was not alone to have close family members to worry about. Rubiel Vasquez, another highly ranked PRO referee, also had a baby.

Even those without a baby had to consider the risk of traveling. Richardson (2021) shared his experience, stating that "I need to be sure that we would be safe, or as safe as possible. I also needed my wife's blessing." Nesbitt also shared how difficult it was, even after the MLS is Back event, when she heard about a team that she had recently officiated ended up having a positive case. She had to self-quarantine from her husband in their house. Even with utmost preparation, such risks were not completely eliminated. Nonetheless, both Nesbitt and Richardson decided to attend the event. Richardson (2021) remembers, "[my wife] noticed and said, 'hey, I have really liked having you here for the last four months, but I also know that you are not doing what you love to do.' Because of her acceptance and acknowledgment that this is what I enjoy and I want to do it, she gave me a go-ahead and off I went."

MLS is Back

Taking the Risk Seriously

PRO referees and staff took the risk of infection seriously as they traveled to and arrived in Orlando. Nesbitt, after being a part of the negotiation team, saw exactly what PRO and PSRA had agreed to implemented once she arrived in Orlando. Furthermore, "Everybody was incredibly safe, taking everything completely seriously the whole time" (Nesbitt 2021). Admitting feeling nervous on the way to Orlando, Webb, for example, was tested for Covid-19 not only before leaving for Florida but also after he arrived in Orlando. In total, he was tested thirty-one times for the tournament.

Despite the medical provisions in place, there were conflicting ideas about the feasibility of the tournament even after referees and teams started arriving in

Florida. A sense of doubt about the success of *MLS is Back* was present, especially after FC Dallas and Nashville SC withdrew because of positive Covid-19 tests (Tannenwald 2020). Although these two teams did not get infected in Orlando but rather brought the virus into the bubble, people wondered if the tournament would happen. Richardson remembers that he would not have been surprised if he had been told to pack up to fly home without having any games played (Richardson 2021).

However, once this initial uncertainty dissipated, referees felt safe. Upon arrival at the referee hotel, referees were immediately taken to the testing room. After the test, they were directly moved to their room where they had to stay until they received a negative positive test result. If the initial test came back positive, they would have to have two negative tests to be allowed outside their room. This meant anyone outside the room had their negative test result. Richardson remembers that the only time referees were allowed to not have a mask on was while eating and training. At all other times, a mask had to be worn. "I never saw anyone interacting with people they shouldn't. I never saw anyone not wearing a mask when they were supposed to," he recalls (Richardson 2021).

Successful Event

From the officiating quality perspective, MLS is Back was a success. Although it was rare for referees to not have officiated for as many months, they performed with quality. This was particularly noteworthy because usually, after an extended period of offseason, referees work on a few preseason matches that offer opportunities to "get rid of the rust and cobwebs" (Geiger 2021). Although multiple preseason games were originally scheduled, only one took place. This meant that when the games resumed in mid-July, the last game for the officials was back in February or March 2020. For those who did not have a game in the first two weeks, the last game was back in October or November 2019.

Geiger (2021) explained that the play was a little "sloppy" at the beginning but he was pleased with the referees' performance from the beginning. Webb (2021) also agreed that as play quality went up during the tournament, referee performance also further improved. Some assistant referees had some trouble with a delayed offside flag, a particular mechanic employed on a match with the VAR. Geiger, however, defended the assistant referees by stating that the delayed offside flag was a relatively new concept that had some learning curve, and had little to do with the pandemic-related suspension of play. Once certain adjustments were made, "everything looked pretty good for the rest of the tournament" (Geiger 2021).

One of the factors that helped with the quality of officiating was the tournament environment. Normally, referees would arrive at the match site a day before the game. They have a game and travel back home the same day or the day after. They repeat this routine week after a week. However, when they were in the bubble environment, "all you are doing is thinking, eating, or breathing soccer."

Geiger explained, "So it's not like you have your daily life to worry about. You're constantly around other referees. You're constantly talking about the game. You will have debriefs every three days or four days." Education was consistent and frequent. Referees did not have to wait a week or two for a debrief on the phone. It was immediate and in-person. Ultimately, this positively impacted the accuracy of decisions.

Referees Come Back Together

Although referees' excellence was in itself noteworthy and the bubble environment was instrumental for it, both staff and referees agreed on the importance of the sense of community that the referees had as a significant contributor to the success. For those PRO referees who are not FIFA referees, they rarely, if ever, have an opportunity to be in such a tournament environment. As noted above, refereeing during a regular season involves countless numbers of two-to-three-day trips. At the FIFA level, however, a referee is at an event for weeks at a time, if not over a month. Webb (2021) explained that the bubble was very similar to the World Cup. However, being immersed in refereeing for twenty-four hours a day could be daunting. Geiger (2021) was aware that while some referees with international tournament experiences knew what to expect to be at a tournament for several weeks, most did not. It meant more soccer-related exposure than normal, but also sometimes struggling to fill up a day.

Fortunately, referees were "with like-minded people" with "the same passion for the game, passion on the same aspect of the game." They would talk about the game over meals, watch games together (Webb 2021). Elfath, one of the most experienced referees in PRO, commented,

> We looked at each other as a family, and [said] that we were going to support each other through this. For those who are missing home or worried about the risk of COVID or worried about back-to-back matches that are at higher frequency than normal, we stuck together. We had a great support from PRO. For us, we got through it just by embracing that we were a team. We were going to succeed together. That carried itself to the training sessions, carried itself to the feedback sessions, and carried itself to the relaxation and fun aspects that we did in the shared meal room as much as possible (Elfath 2021).

Elfath agreed that if twenty-four hours were filled with soccer for weeks, life in the bubble would get "stressful." This is why "[the referees] helped each other unplug." He continued, "For many it was the first time it was just soccer for three to five weeks. Usually at most, it is three to five days. It could be hard to get in the routine, sometimes to forget about soccer" (*ibid.*). This is where experienced referees like Elfath helped less experienced referees establish a routine, relax, and be successful while being away from home for weeks.

Nesbitt (2021) remembers, "Everybody was so excited. Everybody was so happy to have the game back. It became a family. Everybody wanted the best for each other." She characterized that the atmosphere in the bubble was positive and PRO staff ensured that the atmosphere stayed as such. Richardson (2021) also characterized the camaraderie very positively by saying that being with other referees was "one of the coolest things." Referees were able to interact with each other outside of soccer, having meals together, training together, going to a game room to play poker or volleyball, going to a swimming pool, and being friends. Even preseason camps for which all referees travel and stay in one location is no more than several days in length. "Super glad we did it," says Richardson (2021). Nesbitt and Richardson were not alone. Webb (2021), one of the few staff members who traveled to Orlando, commented that it was an "exceptionally enjoyable and successful experience," adding that it was "one of the most enjoyable few weeks" that he had ever spent after he joined PRO. Elfath (2021) also stated that the referee hotel had a "great atmosphere" similar to tournaments except for medical provisions.

The sense of camaraderie did not only exist in the bubble. Parker, who decided to stay at home, continued to communicate with referees in Orlando to learn how things were going. He remembers that he even sent wine to some of his closer referee friends. To reflect on his experience watching the games from home, he said, "I wanted to be a part of the team, even though I was not there in person, so I could celebrate for them. I was texting them. I was watching as many games as I could." Webb also reached out to him multiple times, allowing him to "feel I was a part of the team" (Parker 2021).

Conclusion

A significant reason why referees were successful at MLS is Back was because of the strong sense of community among them. While the sense of community undoubtedly strengthened in Orlando, it was not formed in the bubble. It was something that the referees had developed and cherished for a long time. The friendship, community, and continued biweekly virtual training by PRO kept referees engaged while the league was in suspension. It was also facilitated by the agreement that the referee association had negotiated with PRO not just for their own safety but the safety of their colleagues, and created a positive environment in Florida.

Of course, friendship and camaraderie alone would not have realized the quality of officiating that MLS is Back experienced. It was also coupled with each referee's professionalism. Once the referees learned about the league suspension in March, they asked themselves, "How do I cope? How do I fill the gap? How do I stay physically and mentally connected to the game?" (Elfath 2021). Recognizing that physical fitness could disappear rather quickly without appropriate training, PRO's sport science team provided referees with various information and training methods to help them remain fit (Webb 2021). Elfath appreciated their input, commenting that they had more than enough information for him to remain in shape.

Richardson also commented that because gyms were closed, many referees had to improvise. Despite the closures, the training stipend that the referees received from PRO continued so that they could buy or rent gym equipment. Some also put books in a suitcase and used as weights (Richardson 2021). Nesbitt (2021), a resident of Philadelphia, also remembers that she had to be creative. Because buses were not running, she became "the crazy girl doing sprints" on the streets of Philadelphia. But her neighbors started cheering her up during her training.

Between early March and early July 2020, when there were no games, referees remained connected with each other. Richardson (2021) characterized the referee world as "very big but very small." He continued, "Everybody talks. [Talking with other referees] lets you feel like you haven't lost touch. Every time you talk to them, we say, 'we will get through this.'" Sometimes the conversation was about speculating where the bubble tournament would be held. As Richardson characterized, there was "a constant circle of 'this is what I heard.'" But it allowed him to say, "you haven't lost your brothers and sisters" (*ibid.*).

Some referees were also engaged beyond the PRO referee community. For example, many referees decided to make short videos of themselves juggling with a toilet paper rolls during the toilet paper shortage. Elfath (2021) reflected on his experience by stating that the league suspension was "a great opportunity to leverage my platform to help those that were hit harder by the stoppage than me. We organized community fundraisers to help local youth referees that were relying on that income, or local coaches that were relying on that income, also to help local amateur soccer organizations." He invited guests such as retired MLS player Landon Donovan and asked for donations. It was a way for him to be connected not just with other referees but also to the game in general.

Elfath and Nesbitt also admitted that a referee's life can be very lonely. Once referees were in Orlando, "Everybody was so excited. Everybody was so happy to have the game back. It became a family. Everybody wanted the best for each other" (Nesbitt 2021). It was not just among referees that the sense of community was made. Nesbitt commented that PRO staff made a "positive atmosphere" for them. Even back in March, Webb's immediate reaction to the league suspension was to "[focus] on "just staying in touch, and not just sharing information about officiating. Just staying in touch like a human being, being a part of a big family." He ended up sharing information with the staff and referees every day (Webb 2021).

Strong friendships among referees and quality officiating at the return to play event was the best that the event could ask for still in the middle of the pandemic. PRO staff and referees unequivocally agreed that their love for the game enabled the success to take place. Those who share the love for the same part of the same sport with the same goal, as much as they are competitive with each other, supported each other as one big community before, during, after the return to play. Because of the love for officiating, referees remained engaged and trained professionally.

Elfath (2021) positively reflected the experience of "just seeing the ball rolling again, blowing the whistle, [and] being with the colleague.". Richardson (2021) also missed the game. "Being away from the game for four months, something that we love to do. When you step away, you get an itch. You want to get back out there. You want to do it. You want to scratch that itch," said Richardson. About the first match at MLS is Back, he commented "Man it felt really good to put the flag up again. He's offside! I've got it!"

After the tournament, the referees looked forward to being able to spend even more time with their friends. Richardson says, "The game is fun. You get the itch and you want to scratch it. But you have just as much if not more fun hanging out with everybody after the game is over, relaxed. Whether you are going to go for a beer or whatever. It is a family. This is the best way I know to describe it. You go to battle together every game. And then once you get through the battle, you just want to hang out. You want to tell stories and see how the other refs' games are going. We are one big family."

REFERENCES

Asikci, Emre. 2020. "Major League Soccer Unlikely to Return by Mid-May." *Anadolu Agency*, April 14, 2020. https://www.aa.com.tr/en/sports/us-major-league-soccer-unlikely-to-return-by-mid-may/1804862.

Baum, Adam, and Shelby Dermer. 2020. "Major League Soccer to Restart with Tournament Similar to World Cup Format." *USA Today*, June 10, 2020. https://www.usatoday.com/story/sports/soccer/2020/06/10/mls-restart-season-tournament-similar-world-cup-format/5332583002/.

Baxter, Kevin. 2020. "Another Player Tests Positive for Coronavirus in MLS Orlando Bubble." *Los Angeles Times*, June 10, 2020. https://www.latimes.com/sports/soccer/story/2020-07-10/sporting-kc-player-tests-positive-coronavirus-mls-orlando-bubble.

BioReference Laboratories. 2020. "Major League Soccer Chooses OPKO Health's BioReference Laboratories to Provide COVID-19 Testing for Players and Employees." July 9, 2020. https://www.bioreference.com/major-league-soccer-chooses-opko-healths-bioreference-laboratories-to-provide-covid-19-testing-for-players-and-employees/

Elfath, Ismail. 2021. Interview with authors, April 7, 2021.

Geiger, Mark. 2021. Interview with authors, March 23, 2021.

Kay, Alex. 2020. "MLS Is Back Tournament 2020: Schedule, Start Date, Odds, News on Soccer Season Returning." *Forbes*, July 16, 2020. https://www.forbes.com/sites/alexkay/2020/06/16/mls-is-back-tournament-2020-schedule-start-date-odds-news-on-soccer-season-returning/?sh=678b36813687

Kiuchi, Yuya, Bill Dittmar, and Scott Matterson. 2020. "A Unique and Special Solution for a Unique and Special Time: Training Professional Football Referees Virtually." In Time Out: Global

Perspectives on Sport and the Covid-19 Lockdown, edited by Jörg Krieger, April Henning, Lindsay Pieper, and Paul Dimeo, 183-194. Champaign, IL: Common Ground Research Networks.

Nesbitt, Katy. 2021. Interview with authors, April 8, 2021.

Parker, Corey. 2021. Interview with authors, April 8, 2021.

Richardson, Cory. 2021. Interview with authors, April 9, 2021.

Romero, Iliana Limon, and Roy Parry. 2020. "Is It Still Safe for NBA, MLS to Come to Orlando?" *Orlando Sentinel*, June 20, 2020. https://www.orlandosentinel.com/coronavirus/os-sp-coronavirus-nba-mls-orlando-20200620-5n5pvzg3tfgd5lnvdhbdgjwimi-story.html.

Tannenwald, Jonathan. 2020. "MLS Tournament at Disney World in Trouble as COVID-19 Tests Force Game Postponement." *Philadelphia Inquirer*, July 13, 2020. https://www.inquirer.com/soccer/coronavirus-covid-19-orlando-mls-dc-united-toronto-fc-20200712.html.

Vejar, Alex. 2020. "RSL Players Express Doubts about Orlando 'Bubble' Scenario Proposed by MLS." *The Salt Lake Tribune*, May 15, 2020. https://www.sltrib.com/sports/rsl/2020/05/15/rsl-players-express/.

Webb, Howard. 2021. Interview with authors, April 14, 2021.

Part Two

The Olympic Movement

Chapter 5

Restart, Ready or Not? The Tokyo 2020 Olympic Games

Helen Jefferson Lenskyj

Introduction

News of Covid-19 first circulated around the globe in November 2019, and a few short months later, the virus had become a household word. Olympic industry officials were aware of its existence, but maintained a position of denial long after it was ethical or prudent to do so. On March 23, in the face of indisputable evidence that proceeding with Tokyo 2020 was neither feasible nor safe, the International Olympic Committee (IOC) announced the decision to postpone the event to July 23, 2021. Between January and April, 2020, IOC pronouncements on the issue had progressed through a series of stages: denial, anger, bargaining, and acceptance. Reflecting longstanding Olympic industry hubris, a face-saving self-congratulatory stage became evident soon after the postponement, as IOC media releases praised the organization for prioritizing athletes' safety over all other concerns (Lenskyj 2021).

The following discussion will document and analyze developments between May 1, 2020, and June 30, 2021, demonstrating how the self-congratulatory stage continued almost unabated, in the face of overwhelming proof that the "post-Corona world" predicted by the IOC had not materialized (IOC 2020g). Official Olympic News items on <olympic.org> and mainstream media reports of press conferences and interviews with Olympic personnel illustrate chronic problems of inflated claims, misdirection, and contradictory messages. Throughout 2020 and into the first six months of 2021, IOC president Thomas Bach and John Coates, chair of the IOC Coordination Commission for Tokyo 2020, were the most prominent spokesmen on Tokyo-related topics. Most of Bach's statements appear to have been carefully curated by the IOC media department, while another veteran IOC member, Richard Pound, was a favorite source for international journalists, always ready with a spontaneous and often controversial sound byte.

Olympic Industry Rhetoric

The predictable idealistic rhetoric continued as various Olympic boosters invoked Olympic values, characterizing a successful Tokyo 2020 (in 2021) as "the light at the end of this dark tunnel" with the potential to "heal a post-coronavirus world" (Kidd 2020). The 'end of the tunnel' cliché was first used by Bach in his March 2020 letter to athletes (Letter from president 2020), and constantly repeated (e.g., IOC 2020c). As #CounterOlympics, CON, observed in a May 2021 Twitter post, "the only light is the gleam in the eyes of the #IOC at the profits they will make" (CON 2021).

Invoking the support of "higher authorities" was another repeat tactic. In March 2020, Olympic News reported on what it called "an extraordinary statement" from G20 leaders in support of the postponement and the "symbol of human resilience" that Japan displayed (IOC 2020d). Again in June 2021, Olympic News celebrated the fact that G7 leaders had reiterated their support for "holding [Tokyo 2020]. in a safe and secure manner as a symbol of global unity in overcoming COVID-19," even though this mild endorsement appeared tacked on to the end of a more powerful statement promoting G7's "Shared Agenda for Global Action" (IOC 2021d).

If events of 2021 have a déjà-vu quality, it's because we have been here before. In mid-February 2020, Coates stated that, based on advice from the WHO, "there's no case for any contingency planning or cancelling the Games or moving the Games. There's no Plan B" (Wade and Yamaguchi 2020). Less than a year later, in January 2021, Bach echoed the same "no Plan B" assertion, while Pound, more realistically, pointed out that "it's got to be 2021 or it's not going to happen" (Powers 2021).

After the initial postponement announcement, the Olympic industry faced the monumental task of selling this unprecedented program change and its wide-ranging consequences to sports organizations, sponsors, spectators, and athletes. Given its access to a formidable public relations machine, the IOC presented these outcomes in the most positive light. Specifically, it proclaimed, the new "Tokyo model," discussed below, would be smaller, simpler, and cheaper, while the athletes would continue to be faster, higher, and stronger. The Tokyo model was designed to "maximize cost savings and increase efficiencies" through "optimizations and simplifications." The new Olympic-lite formula would shape the 2021 event and could even influence the planning of future Olympics, according to Olympic News (IOC 2020g). It seemed as if the promoters assumed that the Olympic goose-bumps effect would override more rational, evidence-based risk assessments. Having had more than 120 years of experience in winning hearts and minds through idealistic rhetoric, it is not surprising to see that they were, to some extent, successful.

As the months passed, the powers attributed to Tokyo 2020 became even more extreme. The event will be "a safe manifestation of peace, solidarity and resilience of humankind in overcoming the pandemic" and Tokyo will be "the best-prepared Olympic city," Bach pronounced at a March 2021 IOC session (Reuters 2021). Japanese organizers and politicians repeated this refrain until it was impossible for them to do so and simultaneously maintain any credibility in the eyes of the Japanese population. For his part, Pound succeeded in stealing Bach's and Coates' thunder in 2021, as he had done in 2020. While Bach and Coates were refusing to countenance any talk of postponement or cancellation, Pound gave a date in mid-June as the deadline for an IOC decision either way. Contradictorily, in the weeks before, he had been supporting the official position (Powers 2021).

One of the few weaknesses in this united front occurred in January 2021, when a Times (UK) journalist, citing a "senior member of the ruling coalition," reported a private consensus within the Japanese government that the Olympics would have to be canceled. They were looking for a "face-saving way" to announce the cancellation while possibly securing 2032 instead, according to the article (Parry 2021). Unsurprisingly, the official response was swift, labelling the story 'categorically untrue' (Ingle and McCurry 2021).

Yet, by June, one Olympic official was publicly criticizing the IOC for ignoring widespread public opposition. In an opinion piece in the Kyodo News, Japanese Olympic Committee member Kaori Yamaguchi stated that Tokyo had been "cornered" into proceeding, with the IOC appearing "to think it could steamroll over the wishes of the Japanese public," as surveys showed that up to 80% wanted Tokyo 2020 postponed or canceled. Most forceful of her comments was the statement that "'The power of sports' is of little comfort to people worried about the medical situation and their future lives" (Yamaguchi 2021).

Athletes' Resistance

In 2020, a few frustrated athletes challenged the IOC's relentless and unrealistic optimism. Hayley Wickenheiser, a member of the IOC Athletes' Commission (retired athletes), called for postponement (Prewitt 2020). Her intervention was not well received, as reflected in a speedy rebuke from the IOC "that stated 'what a pity' it was that I spoke out without asking the IOC first" (Morgan 2020). Her rebuttal was unequivocal: "I didn't know free speech had to go through the IOC" (Heroux 2020). Similarly, another Athletes Commission member who published a critique of a different Olympic-related issue was subjected to an unsuccessful attempt at censorship on the part of an IOC member (Personal communication 2021). In fact, active Olympic athletes are in many instances contractually bound by their international federation's Code of Ethics to refrain from making 'adverse comments' on executive decisions (e.g., FINA 2017, C6), and it is significant that the IOC expects even retired athletes to 'ask permission' to speak out. Clearly, members of the IOC, the self-appointed "supreme authority for world sport," feel entitled, by virtue of that authority, to intervene in the lives of individual athletes, active and retired.

As the July start date approached, IOC restrictions on athletes' free speech did not stop a small number of professional golfers and tennis players from expressing doubts that the Olympics could proceed safely. These included Rafael Nadal, Dustin Johnson, Adam Scott, and others. Significantly, celebrity athletes had less to lose in terms of money and reputation by publicly criticizing the IOC than their less powerful semi-professional counterparts, whose only route to elite competition and accompanying sponsorship rewards is through the Olympics.

In March 2021, Wickenheiser, having graduated as a medical doctor, once again called on the IOC to cancel the Olympics, stating unequivocally "It shouldn't be the IOC making that call. That should be the experienced doctors people with no skin in the game and nothing to gain or lose from this" (Heroux 2021). Presumably in the interest of "balance" (or because the company is Canada's official Olympic broadcaster) this Canadian Broadcasting Corporation report also gave airtime to Olympic industry spokesman David Shoemaker, CEO of the Canadian Olympic Committee. Predictably, he offered the usual idealistic rhetoric: "We believe these Games are important both for the athletes who will fulfil their dreams and the fans at home who will be inspired when they need it most" (Heroux 2021a). As Wickenheiser had pointed out in 2020, such sentiments were "insensitive and irresponsible." Shoemaker's suggestion that the tens of thousands of Canadians dealing with disease and death merely needed a diversion to 'be inspired' and forget their suffering was equally insensitive.

The "Tokyo Model"

In September 2020, the IOC and the TOC, in typical self-congratulatory mode, announced the new "Tokyo model fit for a post-corona world" (IOC 2020g). There was no evidence that this "post-corona world" would materialize by July 23, 2021, the proposed start date. Nor was there evidence that the Tokyo model and its safety measures were even close to adequate in the face of the global pandemic, by then experiencing its second wave. At the time of writing, less than a month before the proposed start date, there is no sign that the pandemic is under control in Japan or elsewhere, the distribution of vaccines is vastly unequal across countries, and Japan's own vaccination rate is dangerously low at about 5%. The notion of a level playing field, already challenged by Olympic critics in relation to areas such as training opportunities and government financial support for athletes, has no credibility in a corona or so-called 'post-corona' world.

As late as December 2020, details of the model remained disturbingly vague. Safety measures would include reduced numbers of personnel and spectators, limits on the time spent in Tokyo, and streamlined transport services. On the issue of athletes' health, general countermeasures would be adopted. A December interim report stated that athletes and support staff would not need to quarantine, but would be required to have negative test results prior to arrival. The now-routine rules concerning mask-wearing, social distancing, hand sanitizing and ventilation would apply. Vaccination (if available) would not be mandatory, but Bach urged athletes to act responsibly by getting it (IOC 2020h)

The first of three editions of the much-touted Playbooks were eventually released to the public in February, followed by versions 2 and 3 in April and June (e.g., IOC 2021e). The February versions, now deleted from <olympic.org> were customized for specific audiences Athletes and Officials, International Federations, Media, and so on but the first 50+ pages were very similar. For example an identical one-page statement of platitudes about safety and health was provided for every target group, but "signed" by a different Olympic industry official in each case. Kirsty Carpenter, chair of the Athletes Commission, appeared to be sending her personal message to athletes, while Christian Voigt, IOC Vice President of Marketing Development, sent his words of wisdom to the media. Updated rules in version 2 included daily Covid-19 testing and the appointment of Covid-19 liaison officers.

World Players Association was quick to respond with detailed critiques of the countermeasures presented in the Playbooks. It identified seven principles, including fully protecting athletes, providing effective testing, tracing, isolation, treatment and PPE, and ensuring safe accommodation, travel, distance, dining and ventilation. On all of these criteria, the Playbooks demonstrated major shortcomings. The Playbooks not only failed to provide full protection for athletes, but introduced a mandatory waiver absolving the IOC of any responsibility for athletes who contract Covid-19 (Global Union 2021).

Yahoo Sports obtained a copy of the waiver, which stated in part that that the athlete agreed to participate at their own risk "including any impact serious bodily harm or even death raised by the potential exposure to COVID-19 and other infectious diseases or extreme heat conditions" Although officials claimed that this kind of waiver was routine for participants in mega-events, the *Yahoo* journalist noted that no references to disease or heat appeared in the 2016 Rio Olympics athlete entry form (Bushnell 2021).

The Vaccination Question

In January 2021, Pound proposed that Olympic athletes should get vaccinated ahead of others, to ensure that the Olympics could proceed. He predicted that there would not be "any kind of a public outcry" from Canadians if the 300 to 400 members of Canada's national team were to receive the vaccine ahead of others (CBC 2021). Expanding on the theme, Pound suggested that all countries might consider prioritizing athletes to enable "a worldwide success in the face of a worldwide pandemic" ("Pound thinks" 2021). Despite the fact that a state of emergency had been announced for the Tokyo region the same week, he claimed that "the youth of the world, gathered in peaceful international competition, will contribute significantly to everyone's morale" (Pound et al. 2021a).

In January 2021, I emailed a contact at the *Toronto Star's* editorial department, pitching an opinion piece co-authored with my colleague, epidemiologist Dr. Ray Deonandan, on this issue of prioritizing athletes' vaccinations. I was told that the editors considered the question "too toxic" to address, and it was suggested that we contribute to the *Saturday Debate* on a different question: "Can the Tokyo Olympics still happen this summer?" Pound agreed to write the Yes argument (Pound et al. 2021a).

In surprising news on May 5, the IOC announced a deal with Pfizer and BioNTech, with the companies agreeing to donate vaccines for 11,000 athletes. A plan to vaccinate at least 60% of Paralympians was already in place. There was no special vaccine provision for non-athletes, including about 5000 technical officials and coaches, and 20,000 media, as well as 4000 organizing committee workers and up to 60,000 volunteers. By June 2, however, it was reported that about 10,000 volunteers, including doctors, had withdrawn, a trend that started with an earlier scandal involving the OC president's "sexist comments" controversy and continued as Covid-19 numbers increased (NHK World Japan 2021).

Details of the Pfizer deal included the condition that vaccinations would proceed "in accordance with each country's vaccination guidelines and consistent with local regulations" and that these doses would be "in addition to existing quotas and planned deliveries around the world" (IOC 2021a). It appeared that this wording was a futile attempt to counter accusations of queue-jumping. At the same time, on a global scale, critics were calling out countries that were practicing "vaccine apartheid" by hoarding supplies, while Africa, India and other emerging countries lacked not only vaccines but also basic medical supplies and protective equipment. It was an empty gesture to offer vaccines to athletes in countries where the logistics of transporting, storing and administering doses were insurmountable.

By May, the *Toronto Star's* editorial position was less cautious, and my pitch for a second co-authored opinion piece was readily accepted, with the *Saturday Debate* of May 15 addressing the question "Should Olympic athletes get priority to COVID-19 vaccines?" (Pound et al. 2021b).

The notion that athletes were more deserving of the vaccine than other, more vulnerable populations was both cruel and offensive, as were the rationales offered by Olympic boosters. The sick and dying, it was implied, simply needed a diversion, a sport mega-event as a "morale-booster." Critics, ranging from veteran journalists to community activists, pointed out that the Olympic industry's main motivation involved the financial stakes for sponsors and broadcasters, with a canceled Olympics threatening their hefty profits, as well as shaking the foundations of the insurance industry. As they noted, any humanitarian concern for the alleged uplifting impact of the television spectacle was hypocritical. A successful Tokyo 2020 would not serve as a symbol that the world had "conquered the virus." For that to happen, an equitable global vaccination plan was essential.

As events unfolded, the Olympic industry's well-made plans kept toppling like dominoes. First, it was rumored that there would be no international visitors, a restriction that was finally made public in March 2021. Also in March, the torch relay route was changed due to outbreaks in some regions, and spectators were banned. By May 11 there were more than five route changes to avoid crowds, and about forty towns that were to host international teams withdrew their offers. Despite the ban on international tourists, the predicted number of approved visitors who are not athletes is cause for concern: about 80,000 officials, journalists and support staff ("We need" 2021). July marked the announcement that Japanese spectators would also be banned from Tokyo venues.

By April, the IOC's and OC's demands for hospital beds and medical personnel were met with outrage, as doctors, nurses, and their supporters pointed to the growing numbers of Covid-19 patients throughout Tokyo and neighboring prefectures. The governors of Ibaraki and Chiba rejected the requests, stating that they would not allot hospital beds for athletes or others working at the Olympics (Kyodo News 2021). Asked about these responses at a May 12 press conference, Hashimoto asserted that the OC would be able to "create a situation where people do not have to get medical care," presumably referring to the "bubble." By May 20, as reality slowly prevailed, Bach announced that the IOC would provide medical staff to make up for the shortfall of 3,000 shortfall, but this top-down solution did not address the issue of hospital beds, ventilators, and support staff.

Coates, along with Bach and Pound, claimed that the success of several events in April and May amply demonstrated the effectiveness of the 'bubble' approach. Although only 700 athletes took part in four separate test events, Coates asserted that an Olympic bubble would be equally safe (IOC 2021c). There was a major flaw in his logic: The obvious discrepancy between bubbles no larger than 350 athletes associated with a single test event, and the 11,000 athletes in the Olympic bubble that would be in place over 16 days in July/August, as well the 4,000 athletes in Paralympic bubble in August/September.

Meanwhile, Bach's much-touted official visit to Hiroshima and Tokyo, scheduled to begin on May 17, was canceled because of the extended state of emergency in Tokyo, Osaka, and eight other prefectures. Instead, he would arrive in July, shortly before the opening ceremony. It is expected that the state of emergency will end on June 20 in most prefectures, with Tokyo and Osaka maintaining some restrictions.

Warnings from Science and Medicine

In May 2020, with the IOC issuing optimistic announcements about 2021 planning, and Japan's Olympic minister Seiko Hashimoto denying that a vaccine was a precondition for holding the event, some mainstream media were reporting more realistic predictions. Japanese experts in science and medicine, supported by their international counterparts, raised doubts about the containment of the virus one year hence, the challenge of testing and quarantining 15,000 athletes and their support entourages from 200 countries, and the uncertainty about vaccine development and global distribution (Du and Huang 2020).

It may seem reasonable to expect the World Health Organization (WHO) to take a more proactive role in relation to Tokyo 2020 after more than a year's experience dealing with the global pandemic, but this was not the case. In February 2020, WHO chief of emergencies Dr. Mike Ryan had claimed that the organization only offered "technical advice" and that it was "not the role of the WHO to call off or not call off any event" (Wade and Yamaguchi 2020). His 2021 statements were similarly non-committal. At a May 2021 media conference, he praised the 'tremendous amount of work done on the Playbooks', the organizers' "very, very systematic risk management approach" and the "highly competent" Japanese officials. On the question of cancellation, he stated "…it is not whether we will have [the] Olympics or not; it is how those individual risks are being managed" (IOC 2021c). Since the WHO was a key member of the All-Partners Task Force responsible for developing the countermeasures, including the Playbooks, Ryan, as an insider, adopted the same kind of self-congratulatory rhetoric that had begun in 2020, as reflected in the title of the May 10 Olympic News item: "WHO: 'IOC, organizers and Japanese government working extremely hard to ensure risks are well managed'." Of course, Olympic News routinely put the best spin on any development, regardless of its merits.

In a June New England Journal of Medicine (NEJM) article, Sparrow et al. used the World Players' critique (adapted with permission) to demonstrate "the urgent need for a risk-management approach." The authors concluded that "cancelling the Games may be the safest option" but went on to repeat the clichés popularized by Olympic industry boosters, calling the games "one of the few events that could connect us at a time of global disconnect" (Sparrow at al. 2021). Presumably their fence-setting was an attempt to avoid the public backlash that may have followed an explicit call for cancellation. More forcefully, they called on the WHO to convene its Emergency Committee, as it had done prior to the 2016 Rio Olympics when faced with the threat of the Zika virus.

In a subsequent opinion piece published in *The Hill*, two of the NEJM co-authors, Lisa Brosseau and Annie Sparrow, identified the many shortcomings of the final Playbooks, specifically their failure to recognize that aerosol inhalation is probably the most important mode of transmission of the virus. Instead, the Playbooks continued to focus on droplet and contact transmission, and the listed countermeasures were not customized to deal with risks to athletes in contact sports, or risks experienced by transportation, restaurant and other workers (Brosseau and Sparrow 2021). The recommendation for good ventilation opening a window every 30 minutes seems laughable in the context of the so-called Olympic bubble.

Also in June, *The Lancet* published an editorial titled "We need a global conversation on the 2020 Olympic Games." After listing the numerous threats posed by Covid-19, this editorial, like NEJM's, repeated the usual rhetoric: the Olympics' potential to "provide a worldwide morale boost, and promote unity." More constructively, it called for communication involving the WHO, the European Centre for Disease Prevention and Control, the US Centre for Disease Control, noting that these organizations have been "largely silent" on the question of cancellation (n. a. 2021).

A June editorial in the *International Journal of Infectious Diseases* was unequivocal, predicting a "perfect storm with every conceivable variant" carried by up to 100,000 visitors, and calling for mandatory vaccination of all those involved (Peterson et al. 2021)

The *British Journal of Sports Medicine* also published an editorial in June, proposing an athlete-centered approach: "athlete as community" instead of the dominant "athlete as commodity" lens. They identified a "disproportionate focus on the health protection of individual athletes" in the strategies used by mega-event organizers, and a failure to recognize that they are part of much wider communities. Therefore, they conclude that postponement or cancellation is necessary; "any other course of action would be contrary to public health measures" (Mann et al. 2021).

Cancellation?

The host city contract (HCC) makes it clear that the IOC is the only party with the power to postpone or cancel the event, and that the host city waives any right to damages. The HCC has a weak force majeure (FM) clause that covers "a state of war, civil disorder, boycott, embargo or belligerence [or] 'if the IOC has reasonable grounds to believe, in its sole discretion, that the safety of participants would be seriously threatened or jeopardized for any reason whatsoever" (HCC 2013, 72, emphasis added). It goes on to state that, if the IOC terminates the contract, "the city, the NOC [national Olympic committee] and the OCOG [organizing committee for the Olympic Games] hereby waive any claim and right to damages, or other compensation or remedy" (HCC 2013, 73). As one legal source explained, unless the FM clause includes language such as plague, epidemic, or pandemic, courts may not consider Covid-19 as an FM "especially where the only impact was to render an obligation more expensive to perform" (Outerbridge et al. 2020). A unilateral cancellation on the part of Tokyo and Japan would leave them liable for damages as well as the lost revenue in broadcast fees and sponsors.

From another perspective, the IOC would be unlikely to take the unpopular stance of forcing Tokyo to hold the event, a move that would potentially discourage any other city from bidding for future games and irreparably damage the brand.

Conclusion

Anti-Olympic and Olympic watchdog organizations both inside and outside of Japan were tireless in their monitoring and critiquing of all these developments. They were particularly vigilant as the July start date approached, with the IOC barely acknowledging the significant risk that the pandemic posed to all those involved. A petition calling for cancellation was launched at <change.org> in May. It generated tens of thousands of signatures within a few days, and by mid-June had reached about 427,000. In June, the Asian Japanese Women's Resource Centre called for global feminist solidarity in support of its statement opposing Tokyo 2020.

At the time of writing, there are three possible outcomes to the situation that the IOC now faces: Tokyo 2020 will proceed as planned, with opening ceremonies on July 23, 2021, or will be postponed again for a short period, or will be canceled. Other remote possibilities that observers have put forward include postponing Tokyo until 2024 and moving Paris and Los Angeles to 2028 and 2032 respectively. More recently, however, the IOC unilaterally named Brisbane as host of the 2032 games, so that option is ruled out. Until the current cycle, which began in 1992, both summer and winter games were held in the same year, so option one, which would see the Beijing 2022 Winter Games in February, and Tokyo 2020 Summer Olympics in July 2022, is not unprecedented.

Although the financial implications of the postponement or cancellation scenarios are significant for all concerned, with the Japanese government carrying the heaviest load, they are arguably less serious that a decision to stay the course for July 2021. At the time of writing, the majority view within Japan, as well as among medical personnel and informed critics, is that a July 2021 start date poses an unacceptably high health risk to Japanese residents, Olympic athletes and their entourages, and, most significantly, has the potential to become a super-spreader event with serious global repercussions. Despite global calls for cancellation, there is little doubt that the Olympic industry will continue to treat athletes as commodity, and to ignore any advice that does not meet their agenda.

REFERENCES

Brosseau, Lisa, and Annie Sparrow. 2021. "How the IOC can avoid." *The Hill*, June 16, 2021. https://thehill.com/opinion/healthcare/558794-how-the-ioc-can-avoid-a-covid-19-superspreader-olympics.

Bushnell, Henry. 2021. "Olympians must sign waiver." *Yahoo Sports,* May 28, 2021. ca.sports.yahoo.com/news/olympics-covid-waiver-tokyo-athletes-202234569.html.

CBC. 2021. "Olympic athletes should get priority." *CBC*, January 6, 2021. cbc.ca/sports/Olympics/dick-point-oic-athltes-vaccine-tokyo-olympics-1.5863205.

Counterolympics. 2021. Twitter, March 21, 2021. twitter.com/counterolympics/status/13957544060674621 46?s=21

Du, Lisa, and Grace Huang. 2020. "Tokyo Olympics unlikely to happen in 2021." *BNN Bloomberg*, May 1, 2020. bnnbloomberg.ca/tokyo-olympics-unlikely-to-happen-in-2021-virus-experts-warn-1.1430069.

FINA. 2017. "FINA Code of Ethics. "resources.fina.org/fina/document/2021/01/12/c9057283-1c4e-442e-807e-f88c982c7275/logo_fina_code_of_ethics_as_approved_by_the_ec_on_22.07 2017_final_0.pdf.

Global Union. 2021. "IOC must urgently guarantee world class athletes." *Uniglobal* uniglobalunion.org/news/ioc-must-urgently-guarantee-world-class-covid-19-protections-tokyo-olympics.

Heroux, Devin. 2020. "With sport, medicine worlds colliding." *CBC*, March 27, 2020. cbc.ca/sports/olympics/hayley-wickenheiser-had-to-speak-out-for-olympic-postponement-1.5512175.

———. 2021. "Hayley Wickenheiser again sounds alarm." *CBC*, April 23, 2021. cbc.ca/sports/olympics/Olympics-hayley-wickenheiser-again-sounds-alarm-saying wrong-people-making-decisions-on-games-1.5999462.

Ingle, Sean, and Justin McCurry. 2021. "Japan dismisses 'categorically untruestories'." *The Guardian*, January 22, 2021. guardian.com/sport/2021/jan/22/Tokyo-olympics-covid-putting-real-pressure-on-japan-says-australian-pm-amid-cancellation-rumours?CMP=Share_iOSAPP_Other.

IOC. 2020a. "Host City Contract." 2020games.metro.tokyo.lg.jp/hostcitycontract-EN.pdf.

———. 2020b. "Letter from President." *Olympic News*, March 22, 2020. olympic.org/athlete365/voice/22-march-letter-president-thomas-bach-athletes/.

———. 2020c. "IOC President: The Olympic flame." *Olympic News*, March 24, 2020.olympic.org/news/ioc-president-the-olympic-flame-can-become-the-light-at-the-end-of-this-dark-tunnel.

———. 2020d. "IOC thanks G20 leaders." *Olympic News*, March 27, 2020. olympic.org/news/ioc-thanks-g20-leaders-for-their-support-for-the-olympic-games-tokyo-2020

———. 2020e. "President Bach writes to Olympic movement." *Olympic News*, April 29, 2020. olympic.org/news/ioc-president-bach-writes-to-olympic-movement-olympism-and-corona.

———. 2020f. "IOC and Tokyo agree on measures." *Olympic News*, September 25, 2020. IOC olympics.com/ioc/news/ioc-and-tokyo-2020-agree-on-measures-to-deliver-games-fit-for-a-post-corona-world.

———. 2020g. "Tokyo 2020 organizers." *Olympic News,* December 2, 2020. olympics.org/en/news/tokyo-2020-covid-countermeasures-interim-report.

———. 2021a. "IOC welcomes Pfizer and Biotech's donation." *Olympic News*, May 6, 2021. IOC olympics.com/ioc/news/ioc-welcomes-pfizer-and-biontech-s-donation-of-vaccines-to-teams-heading-for-the-olympic-and-paralympic-games-tokyo-2020.

———. 2021b. "WHO: 'IOC, organizers and Japanese government'." *Olympic News*, May 10, 2021. olympics.com/ioc/news/who-ioc-organisers-and-japanese-government-working-extremely-hard-to-ensure-risks-are-well-managed-at-olympic-games-tokyo-2020.

———. 2021c. "Four test events in Japan." *Olympic News*, May 12, 2021. olympics.com/ioc/news/four-test-events-in-japan-conducted-safely-and-securely-with-participation-of-overseas-athletes.

———. 2021d. "G7 leaders reiterate support." *Olympic News*, June 14, 2021. olympics.com/ioc/news/g7-leaders-reiterate-support-for-the-olympic-and-paralympic-games-tokyo-2020.

———. 2021e. "Playbook: Athletes and Officials." IOC, June 15, 2021. stillmed.olympics.com/media/Documents/Olympic-Games/Tokyo-2020/Playbooks?The-Playbook-Athletes-and-Officials-V3.pdf.

Kidd, Bruce. 2020. "How the rescheduled Tokyo Olympics." *University of Toronto News*, March 27, 2020. utoronto.ca/news/how-rescheduled-tokyo-olympics-could-heal-post-coronavirus-world-u-t-s-bruce-kidd.

Kyodo News, 2021. "Governors refuse to allot hospital beds." *Kyodo News*, May 13, 2021. english.kyodonews.net/news/2021/05/7c9c086fcb08-governors-refuse-to-allot-hospital-beds-for-covid-infected-olympians.html.

Lenskyj, Helen. 2021. "Let the Games begin." In *Time Out. Global Perspectives on Sport and the Covid-19 Lockdown*, edited by Jörg Krieger, April Henning, Lindsay Parks Pieper, and Paul Dimeo, 15-27. Champaign IL: Common Ground.

Mann, Robert, Bryan Clift, Jules Boykoff, and Sheree Baker. 2021. "Athletes as community; athletes in community: covid-19, sporting mega-events and athlete health protection." *British Journal of Sports Medicine* 54 (18): 1071-72.

Morgan, Liam. 2020. "Olympian Wickenheiser reveals." *Inside the Games*, April 12, 2020. insidethegames.biz/articles/1093067/hayley-wickenheiser-ppe-opc-canada.

n.a. 2021. "Editorial: We need a global conversation". *The Lancet* 397:10291, 2225.

NHK World Japan. 2020. "10,000 people withdraw" *NHK World Japan*, June 2, 2021. nhk.or.jp/nhkworld/en/news/20210602_29/.

Outerbridge, David, Jessica R. Lumiere, Steven Slavens, and Nic Wall. 2020. "COVID-19 and force majeure clauses." *Torys LLP*, March 11, 2020. torys.com/insights/publications/2020/03/covid-19-and-force-majeure-clauses.

Parry, Richard Lloyd. 2021. "Japan looks for a way out." *The Times*, January 21, 2021. thetimes.co.uk/article/japan-looks-for-a-way-out-of-tokyo-olympics-because-of-virus-lf868xfnd.

Personal Communication. 2021. Anonymous Athletes Commission member. May 4, 2021.

Peterson, Eskild et al. 2021. "Mandatory immunization against SARS-CoV-2 of athletes, companions and supporters for the Tokyo Olympics." *International Journal of Infectious Diseases* 108:156-8.

Pound, Richard, Valerié Grand'Maison, Lee Robinson-Hill, and Helen Jefferson Lenskyj. 2021. "Should Olympic athletes get priority to COVID-19 vaccines?" *Toronto Star*, May 15, 2021. thestar.com/opinion/contributors/the-saturday-debate/2021/05/15/the-saturday-debate-should-olympic-athletes-get-priority-to-covid-19-vaccines.html.

Pound, Richard, Helen Jefferson Lenskyj, and Raywat Deonandan. 2021. "Can the Tokyo Olympics still happen this summer?" *Toronto Star*, January 23, 2021. thestar.com/opinion/contributors/the-saturday-debate/2021/01/23/the-saturday-debate-can-the-tokyo-olympics-still-happen-this-summer.html.

Powers, John. 2021. "The IOC insists there's 'no Plan B'." *Boston Globe*, January 27, 2021. bostonglobe.com/2021/01/27/sports/hopes-tokyo-olympics-still flickering-doubts-growing-louder/?event=event25.

Prewitt, Alex. 2020. "How Hayley Wickenheiser is using her unique platform." *Sports Illustrated*, April 11, 2020. si.com/olympics/2020/04/11/hayley-wickenheiser-ice-hockey-medical-school-doctor-coronavirus.

Reuters. 2021. "Safe Tokyo Games." *Reuters*, March 10, 2021. reuters.com/article/us-olympics-ioc-idUSKBN2B20TC.

Sparrow, Annie, Lisa M. Brosseau, Robert J. Harrison, and Michael T. Osterholm. 2021. "Protecting Olympic Participants from Covid-19 The Urgent Need for a Risk-Management Approach." *New England Journal of Medicine* nejm.org/doi/full/10.1056/NEJMp2108567.

Wade, Stephen, and Mari Yamaguchi. 2020. "No 'Plan B' for Olympics." *AP News*, February 14, 2020. apnews.com/936a921979a504cb9d4056dc44b2830a.

Yamaguchi, Kaori. 2021. "Tokyo Olympics have no meaning." *Kyodo News*, June 4, 2021. english.kyodonews.net/news/2021/06/6c03987c339c-opinion-tokyo-olympics-have-no-meaning-if-dialogue-is-abandoned.html.

Chapter 6

Lessons from Covid-19: The Organized Sport and its Responses to Climate Change

Tim Sperber

The Impacts of Covid-19 on Sport as a Forerunner for Future Climate Challenges

Mankind's relations with the environment has traditionally been discussed within different societal epochs, however, the global warming and subsequently changing climate was first internationally recognized at the 1992 Earth Summit in Rio de Janeiro (Mosley 2010). There, the first multilateral environmental treaties were discussed to recognize that there are increasing problems due to climate change (United Nations Framework Convention on Climate Change 1992). Both the emissions of Greenhouse-Gases (GHG) as an accelerator and the impacts of a changing climate were acknowledged as the most relevant issue of human behavior. While there must be differentiated between climate and weather, extreme weather phenomena such as floods, droughts and thunderstorms are very likely to occur more often and be more severe (IPCC 2021). Effects of a changing climate have impacted sport organizations already in various spheres: Playing surfaces turn dusty, playing seasons change, schedules of sports events are affected, and extreme weather affects sporting performance as well as the opportunity to enjoy sport, as an athlete or as a fan (Askew and Bowker 2018; Orr 2020; Goggins et al. n.d.).

Due to natural disasters several mass sport events had to be canceled such as the New York marathon 2012 after hurricane Sandy or matches of the Rugby World Cup 2019 in Japan due to the typhoon Hagibis (Smith et al. 2016; Melnick 2012; Reuters 2019). Furthermore, heat waves have caused relocations of running events like the marathon of the 2020 Tokyo Summer Olympic Games to Hokkaido province in the north of Japan (Ando and Tarrant 2019). Subsequently, sport as a relevant societal field is affected as well and has for instance developed the Sports for Climate Action Framework to mitigate its GHG (United Nations Climate Change Global Climate Action 2018). Until today the impacts of extreme weather phenomena have been timely and geographically limited. Nonetheless sport organizations, event organizers and sport infrastructure developer must consider that due to the impacts of a changing climate the provision of sport will be affected.

During the worldwide pandemic caused by Covid-19, when organized sport was barely possible, the downstream effects were tremendous. The implemented Covid-19 regulations to mitigate the spread of the disease illustrates for the first time the vulnerability of the globalized world and how it affected the sport system at its core. Sport events were widely postponed and canceled at every level. Due to lockdowns people were not allowed to exercise outdoors and different strategies to combat the pandemic also have led to a variety of short- and long-term impacts on sport (Krieger et al. 2021a; 2021b; Ramagole et al. 2020).

Whilst the appearance of Covid-19 came quickly, climate scientists have been calling for action for years. However, in comparison to Covid-19, there is both time to mitigate the effects of global warming and to prepare for the impacts. Investigating the recent history supports organized sport's ability to learn from the pandemic. The following research question shall guide the following analysis: What can organized sport learn from the impacts of the Covid-19 pandemic on sport in the face of a changing climate?

Therefore, this chapter analyzes impacts of Covid-19 on organized sport based on a literature review including academic papers, guidelines of sport organizations, government policies, and media publications. The snowballing method has been applied to find relevant literature and considers publications from March 2020 until September 2021. In the first step, the literature review aims to find impacts on the organized sport which caused challenges and resulted in opportunities to make the organized sport system more resilient. Furthermore, the analysis intents to illustrate weaknesses caused by the impacts of Covid-19 which have been barely tackled and could expose vulnerability in future crisis. In the second step, the findings are applied to likely impacts caused by climate change. The goal is to discuss in how far countermeasures during Covid-19 supported the organized sport to be more resilient and which adequate steps have to be taken in the face of a climate crisis. Both profit-oriented clubs in league systems and non-profit community sport clubs as well as multi-sport confederations and sport federations are considered. The scope of the analysis is limited by the impacts and respective countermeasure which can be lessons in the face of a changing climate.

Whilst extreme weather phenomena have been challenging sport organizations and event organizers sporadically, the global Covid-19 lockdown had downstream effects on various stakeholders within the organized sport. When reviewing the academic literature, media publications, and policy documents, three dimensions were found to illustrate analogies between Covid-19 and a changing climate: Financial implications, management/governance, and social aspects. The research dimensions explore connections in the sporting landscape of various sports as well as of different sport organizations within the organized sport system.

The overall aim of organizations has been always to maintain its operations. In the case of sport organizations this could be the execution of small and big sport events as well as the provision of training and physical activity. If under special circumstances this core of sporting opportunities cannot be provided, downstream effects are likely to occur. The analysis provides the basis to discuss future challenges for organized sport due to a changing climate including more frequent cancellations of sport events, competitions, and match days due to extreme weather phenomena.

Subsequently the discussion links the lessons and reactions during Covid-19 to prevent existential threats to individual sport organizations in the future caused by climate change. This learning approach aims to raise awareness that organized sport should note the experiences from the Covid-19 pandemic to mitigate climate change impacts on sport. Bringing the discourse of climate change into the discussion on how to rebuild the sporting environment more resilient and sustainable after the lockdown shall expand the literature in regard to Covid-19 and sport as well as sport ecology.

In the following section the concepts of vulnerability, robustness, and resilience set the conceptual frame to respond adequately to future challenges. The knowledge is essential to understand how sport organizations can build capacity to combat future crisis such as the climate crisis.

Vulnerability, Robustness and Resilience in Sport

Since robustness, resilience and vulnerability are of interest both in a pandemic and in a changing climate this section elaborates on the different concepts which have been used in the sporting context. The concepts are important to understand which cause and effect relationship external influences have on an organization. Within the sports context, governmental legislation, and superior sport organizations regulations are as important as societal and environmental factors. During Covid-19 especially governmental legislation to mitigate the spreading of the virus exposed the vulnerability of sport clubs.

Vulnerability can be defined as "the conditions determined by physical, social, economic, and environmental factors or processes, which increase the susceptibility of a community to the impact of hazards" (United Nations International Strategy for Disaster Reduction 2005, 1). Subsequently, reducing and managing challenges is important to resist exposures, maintain or restart an organizations' operation.

Hoeijmakers and Van der Roest (2021) stated that robustness is the amount of internal and external influences a system can resist to maintain functioning and in this regard provide sport opportunities. Robustness focuses on the maintenance during the crisis. Resilience goes a step beyond since it takes the "capacity for learning from past disasters for better future protection and to improve risk reduction measures" into account (United Nations International Strategy for

Disaster Reduction 2005, 4). Subsequently, the aim is to learn from this crisis in the face of a changing climate.

In the research area of sport ecology vulnerability, robustness, and resilience are considered when analysing extreme weather phenomena and natural disasters. Wicker et al. (2013, 513) argue a sport club is "resilient when it has the capability to mobilize a variety of resources (resourcefulness), to substitute missing resources (redundancy) in a timely manner (rapidity), and to be able to continue operating in crisis (robustness)." Human and financial resources are in this respect both needed and interlinked. Furthermore, knowledge imparted through licenses and certificates of the respective sports confederations plays a crucial role. A higher degree of these characteristics subsequently leads to a better recovery process.

Since natural disasters are likely to become more frequent and severe the importance of these concepts has been increased, raising awareness for such frameworks to help the sport sector make the sport system more resilient after the impacts of Covid-19 (World Economic Forum 2021; European Commission 2021; IPCC 2021). The impacts of Covid-19 on the organized sport system found in the literature review are elaborated in the following three sections. The lessons learned during the Covid-19 crisis shall benefit event organizers, policy makers, sport administrators, elite athletes, and sport organizations in the face of a changing climate within the financial, management and governance, as well as social dimension.

Financial Implications

First, it should be noted that due to globally implemented lockdowns, physical distancing and closed boarders, sport providers varying from mega-sport event organizers to community sport clubs could not carry out their core business. Different national strategies and temporal delays affected sport organizations, leagues and athletes unequally. The subsequent examples illustrate financial implications on organized sport.

Revenue losses for professional sports due to cancellations and postponements of mega sport events like the Olympic Games and gamedays of professional leagues occurred through compensation fees for sponsors and a lack of income due to fans (Drewes, Daumann, and Follert 2020; Macnaughtan 2020). Since broadcasting rights contribute to the majority of revenue of the large sport events and leagues, a restart of the UEFA Champions League, Premier League, Bundesliga and the major leagues in the USA came without fans in the stadia to decrease the losses (Hall 2020). The Organizing Committee of the Olympic Games (OCOG) in Tokyo estimated additional costs of US$ 1.6 billion for postponing the Olympic Games to 2021 (Owen 2020).

Long-term management tools like insurance altered the financial impact due to the unexpected pandemic. The organizers of the Wimbledon Tennis Grand

Slam for instance were insured for pandemic diseases and had minimal financial losses. Furthermore, the estimated event's surplus of £40 million for 2020 which flows back to the Lawn Tennis Association to promote tennis within the UK could be secured (Mitchell 2020). In comparison the German ice hockey league had to cancel the playoffs in 2020 due to financially uncertain times. (DEL Redaktion 2020). This led to a cumulated €20 million decrease in turnover for leagues' clubs in the 2019/20 season (Tripcke 2021).

Sport events play a crucial role within organized sport; however, smaller federations and clubs could barely carry out competitions and championships since increasing costs of mandatory hygiene concepts made it less profitable without spectators (Deutscher Olympischer Sportbund [DOSB] 2020). Smaller federations and clubs have less broadcasting time and generate a high proportion of revenue by engaging with their fan community mostly during competitions or match days. Ice hockey and handball in Germany as well as rugby in the USA are national examples where leagues faced financial trouble (Drewes, Daumann, and Follert 2020; Ehrlich et al. 2021). On an international level, amongst others World Athletics, World Rowing and the International Swimming Federation were granted financial support by the IOC (Lord 2020).

Covid-19 illustrated that sport organizations were scarcely prepared to react to crisis situations. While profit-oriented sport organization might have taken these risks into account, smaller clubs and federations did not have the financial resources to evaluate the risk and pay additional contingency insurances as a preventive measure. The unequal financial implications are both valid for professional sport within countries but also between sport with professional structures and those with merely volunteer commitment. During Covid-19, professional sport had been considered as an occupation and subsequently matches and competitions were eventually allowed by governmental authorities. Especially football leagues in Europe, Africa and South America, professional Cricket in India as well as the "Big Four" in America resumed shortly after the announcements (Vickery 2020; Chingoma 2021; Majumdar and Naha 2020). Although competitions took barely place, Olympic athletes resumed training to prepare for the postponed 2020 Tokyo Summer Olympic Games. However, grassroots sport, semi-professional, and professional niche sport organizations suffered increasingly from recurring lockdowns.

Because the core product bringing sport to both the members and fans - could not be provided, membership figures as well as match day revenues decreased (Singh Aulakh 2021; Hoeijmakers and Van der Roest 2021; Duckworth 2021). To counter such imbalance, the German football league set up a fund to support both struggling football clubs and clubs organized within the German umbrella organization (Ebert 2020). The IOC raised its Olympic Solidarity budget and pointed out the importance of sport in the aftermath of Covid-19, furthermore the IOC supported various IFs and athletes directly (International Olympic Committee 2020; Lord 2020). Since the financial aid was not sufficient or sport organizations were not eligible, the financial support was facilitated by various governments especially in global north countries like Germany, England and Australia (Sport England 2020; Bundesverwaltungsamt n.d.; Sport and Recreation Victoria 2021).

Furthermore, professional football clubs in England advised their players to take a pay cut to demonstrate solidarity with the non-playing staff which was furloughed (MacInnes 2020). While the income gap in Germany between athletes of different sports has been evident also before Covid-19 it became more precarious (Breuer et al. 2018). A survey on German individual athletes in Olympic and Paralympic sports indicates a 25% decline of income due to less appearance fees, prize purses and sponsors. In total, the research accumulates for 2020 a loss of income of around €6 million for the German athletes (Stiftung Deutsche Sporthilfe 2020).

Summing up the financial implications for organized sport due to Covid-19 supports the existing literature that fostering diverse revenue streams supports organizational capacity to maintain its operation (Filo, Cuskelly, and Wicker 2015). This is applicable to both semi-professional sport depending on the matchday income and for professional leagues depending heavily on broadcasting revenues. Furthermore, financial solidarity within organized sport helped troubled sport organizations to build back their sport offers. Meanwhile, Cooper and Alderman (2020) argue that one lesson for local networks or sport organizations with similar interests could be the idea to set up funds in flourishing economic times to use the money either for reconstruction after a crisis or to invest comprehensively in adaption or transformation. This would make the sporting communities financially more autonomous and could improve resilience after a crisis.

Learning from Covid-19 suggests that even if budgets are planned tightly, investments in insurances, solidarity funds and local assets might help moderating financial impacts also in the face of a changing climate.

Management & Governance

While direct financial support can be considered as resource, Covid-19 has proven that voluntary work was essential for the survival of smaller clubs. Since small clubs rely mainly on the commitment of volunteers and barely employ staff, they have generally lower expenses. Furthermore, small clubs have seldomly own sport venues which must be maintained (Feiler and Breuer 2021). Subsequently, smaller clubs were able to moderate the revenue losses better than bigger clubs with fewer volunteers and club-owned properties (Hoeijmakers and Van der Roest 2021; Feiler and Breuer 2021). Underlining the value of voluntary work in sport clubs and offering educational programmes could be a pathway to build more resilient sport clubs. Strengthening knowledge transfers within the organized sport system is valid for both clubs on the local level and professional clubs at the national and international level. Subsequently, implementing strategies to foster education and volunteer work within sport organization proved to be a viable tool to be less vulnerable and more robust to external influences (Nowy et al. 2015).

The impact of the pandemic was unforeseeable for most sporting actors. Confederations, policy makers and league organizers barely took this risk into account and subsequently had to adopt rapidly to the situation. Lobbying to restart their core business was carried out simultaneously when implementing practical guidelines to mitigate the spread of Covid-19 during the restart (Duckworth 2021; Horky 2020; Reiter 2020; Ramagole et al. 2020). Academia, medical associations, and sport organizations worked out concepts to restart the sport according to the regional legal regulations (Toresdahl and Asif 2020; Mann et al. 2020; Castagna et al. 2020). From a management perspective sport organizations could learn that a quick, unsophisticated implementation of the hygiene measures had been possible and could be fostered in regard to climate protection and climate adaption in the same way.

However, Covid-19 measures could be carried out in professional sport entities, while grassroots sport clubs could barely adopt to legal regulations and were not granted exemptions. In Germany for instance, professional sport had already implemented league schedules while amateur sport organizations were hardly allowed to compete and train until June 2021. Just then a campaign joined by the two largest German sport organizations lobbied for grassroot sport within organized sport (Deutscher Fußball-Bund e.V. (DFB) 2021).

As governance can be defined as processes of interaction within and between organizations, the organized sport system provides the framework with its norms, regulations and power structures (Byers et al. 2021). Although national and regional figures of Covid-19 cases and countermeasures have led to varying impacts on organized sport, guidelines and playbooks by international and national sport organizations distributed top-down perspectives for leisure sport and competitive sport to return to training as well as events. The role of federations has been both lobbying for the interests of sport organizations and transferring information to its members. Since the sport organizations were quick in their decision-making processes, the question arises whether sport organizations are able to adopt to a changing climate comparably fast (Byers et al. 2021).

From a governance perspective it is also interesting to take the power struggles during Covid-19 into consideration. In the beginning of the pandemic Canadian and Australian athletes and the respective NOCs threatened the IOC with a boycott if the IOC did not postpone the Olympic Games in Tokyo (Mann et al. 2020). Athletes have increasingly claimed power within the sporting society and it is very likely that due to a changing climate and high temperatures during sport events athletes will influence schedules and locations incrementally (Seltmann 2021; Smith et al. 2016). Providing an ideal sporting environment for elite athletes is a necessity to display high performances and should be in the interest of both athletes and sport administrators (Smith et al. 2016). Learning in this respect from Covid-19 includes taking the needs and demands of athletes and NOCs into consideration when awarding mega-sport events.

One lesson from Covid-19 is that long-term planning and management will be an organization's advantage to overcome future hazards. Implementing risk assessment as well as crisis and disaster management tools now can be considered as a chance and as a valuable investment for the future to build organizational capacity (Miles and Shipway 2020; Orr and Inoue 2018). Moreover, sport policy makers should improve the flow of information to reach out to members more rapidly and to implement preventive measures ahead of potential crisis situations. Subsequently, threats caused by impacts of a changing climate could be prevented and rapidly circumvented.

Social Aspects

When considering the social aspects within the organized sport system, two topics shall be highlighted: Firstly, the social interaction concerning fans and secondly the increasing inequalities within the sport system.

For smaller clubs and niche sports, fans play a financial role as consumers; however, they are also part of the sporting product since they create a vibrant atmosphere. This product is then more attractive to broadcasters and transmits emotions, group cohesion and joy (Drewes, Daumann, and Follert 2020). The social aspects of watching and experiencing sport have also been a crucial argument for policy makers to support mega-sport events. Sport events have been missing the atmosphere of a stadium since the return of professional sport without fans during Covid-19.

Intriguingly, interactive, creative broadcasting opportunities were made up such as live applications and screens which project the fans from their couch into the stadium. Majumdar and Naha (2020) argue that live interactions engage fandom differently, can flatten hierarchy and provide the opportunity for diaspora fans to engage from their living room. While the interaction both amid fans and between fans and athletes was affected due to Covid-19, research indicates that athletes played an important function as role models.

During the pandemic athletes advocated for social distancing and governmental regulations and engaged their fanbase to work out at home (Leng and Phua 2020). However, there have been also cases of athletes not behaving accordingly to Covid-19 regulation which caused individual sanctions such an Olympic athlete who was asked to leave the Olympic village (Morgan 2021). Athletes are generally considered as trustful agents when it comes to health measures, since they are perceived as fit and healthy (Behnoosh et al. 2017; Leng and Phua 2020). With this in mind, sport organizations should integrate athletes not only in their marketing activities but also in strategies to promote a sustainable lifestyle.

The impacts of Covid-19 on sport led to increasing inequalities in various spheres. In the sport for development context organizations had difficulties both connecting with young participants and maintaining their operations due to budget cuts (Singh Aulakh 2021). Furthermore, the pandemic highlighted unequal financial and training opportunities for athletes around the globe in preparation for international competitions since countries and NOCs handled the pandemic differently (Mann et al. 2020; Evans et al. 2020).

Covid-19 displays an inequality between elite, semi-professional, and grassroots sport. While elite athletes were quickly allowed to return to sport and maintain it, grassroots sport clubs were not (Evans et al. 2020; Drewes, Daumann, and Follert 2020; Bowes, Lomax, and Piasecki 2020). Moreover, elite sport organizations used Covid-19 testing capacity, which could be used in other societal sectors as well. Gender inequality increased especially in organized sport since women acknowledged a resource shift by sport organizations to male athletes (Bowes, Lomax, and Piasecki 2020; Rowe 2020) whereas informal physical activity did not reveal gender specific differences due to Covid-19 (Mccarthy, Potts, and Fisher 2021).

Moreover, social inequality within organized sport is evident between age groups. Physical distancing and staying at home appeals hindered physical activity for various age groups. Although young people could merely use online classes provided by athletes, clubs or apps to stay fit, physical activity rates have dropped and sedentary behavior as well as screentime increased (Xiang, Zhang, and Kuwaharab 2020). Physical activity data from the UK revealed that people aged sixty-five and older remained comparably active to younger age groups since they pursued more self-organized sport (Mccarthy, Potts, and Fisher 2021). Data from Germany indicated that, especially due to closed facilities, physical activity rates decreased and increasingly older age groups have been affected (Mutz and Gerke 2020).

Besides younger and older age groups, athletes with special needs have lacked the sporting opportunities provided by sport organizations (Evans et al. 2020; Fitzgerald, Stride, and Drury 2020). Since physical activity and sport supports these vulnerable groups in terms of personal development and health aspects, organized sport must support these groups particularly during future climate change related challenges. Covid-19 proved that concepts to provide safe spaces and exchange to fit the needs of the sport participants helped sport organizations to provide sport opportunities after lockdown (Rowe 2020).

Learning from Covid-19 means identifying risks for the various social groups and protecting these vulnerable groups by building an inclusive sport system with equal resource allocation and barrier-free sport facilities (Rowe 2020). From a systematic point of view this requires showing solidarity from well earning sport organizations by redistributing money into the sport system to eliminate sporting inequalities.

Interestingly, Covid-19 illustrated that informal sport can substitute for organized sport (Mccarthy, Potts, and Fisher 2021). This should be taken into consideration when implementing initiatives and long-term funds to increase the robustness and resilience of the organized sport system to allocate the resources efficiently. Within the Global Norths' context, financial support such as the EU

Erasmus+ funding and green sport initiatives are developed to strengthen physical activity, social cohesion and volunteerism (European Commission 2021).

Since Covid-19 uncovered the different regional and national handlings, which caused disparate impacts on organized sport, holistic approaches and regional characteristics should be considered when imagining climate change related impacts. Furthermore, sport policy makers should consider organized sport in countries of the Global South to bridge a gap between all sporting actors to minimize social inequities.

Discussion

Impacts on organized sport due to Covid-19 uncovered valuable insights in how far sport organizations, fans and athletes are affected by a crisis. The analysis on financial implications, management and governance as well as social aspects teaches which countermeasures are effective to overcome a crisis situation and in which cases prevention could have played a crucial role. Therefore, the discussion relates to the three dimensions and illustrates improvements which should be considered in the face of climate change.

Integration of Risk Assessment

From a financial point of view, contingency insurance has proved to be an adequate tool to mitigate the financial losses during Covid-19. Therefore, funds and insurance should be implemented to lessen the financial impact of extreme weather phenomena. Although just recently was announced that the FIFA World Cup Qatar 2022 had been insured for $900 million, it will be interesting whether more events will be insured in the future (Owen 2021). Smaller federations and sport organizations might not have the resources to calculate the risk and afford an insurance both for future pandemics and climate change impacts.

Furthermore, it will be interesting whether insurance companies specialize on the sport sector or if they pull out of this business since it is too risky and not economically.

While insurances might alter financial threats in the face of a changing climate, sport organizations should carefully evaluate their specific risks and in how far they might be impacted. Tools like the Climate Vulnerability of Sport Organizations (CVSO) framework must be disaggregated individually for the different needs of sport (Orr and Inoue 2018). Since the CVSO is hardly accessible for practitioners, information and tools for risk assessment should be easily available and provided by federations. Furthermore, the knowledge transfer to the respective sport organizations could then take place via workshops or online courses.

While some ISGBs such as the IOC, FIFA and World Athletics publish sustainability strategies and foster sustainability agendas including GHG emission reports for mega-sport event, smaller organizations have rarely adopted them since they are on a voluntary base and often associated with additional costs (Ross and Leopkey 2017). As they could save money both short-term and long-term through smart electricity and water savings policymakers should aim to foster an intrinsic motivation of sport organizations on every level to implement sustainable measures (Dingle and Stewart 2018).

Nonetheless, Covid-19 hygiene regulations were mandatory to organize events and one must mention that legal regulations in the field of sustainability are not yet binding for sport organization. However, it could be a precondition by federations for event organizers to implement, for instance, the ISO 20121 requirements focusing on sustainable sport events even on a local and regional level if they want to host specific competitions (International Organization for Standardization (ISO) 2012).

Foster Digitalization

Since fans contribute to a large extent to the sports' carbon footprint, the absence of fans during Covid-19 had a positive impact on environmental aspects (Triantafyllidis 2020; Cooper and Alderman 2020). Less consumption and travel should be therefore fostered to build a more sustainable sporting environment (Mastromartino et al. 2020).

Covid-19 showcased that clubs and federations which depend mostly on match day revenues were more vulnerable. Therefor sport organizations should aim to diversify their revenue streams. Clubs and federations who generate out of scale revenue through ticket sales, merchandise, and food and beverages during matchdays or competitions should think about alternatives. Digital formats of their sport product could engage fans which cannot attend the sport event in person. Digital solutions proved to integrate diaspora fans and partly dismantled social inequities during Covid-19 and could therefore be a tool to mitigate GHG of sport events (Majumdar and Naha 2020). These preventive measures to diversify income are in line with Wicker, Filo, and Cuskelly (2013) to build more resilient sport organizations.

However, it is questionable whether digital fan possibilities can transfer the same values and emotions. Targeting a better flow of information in a top-down approach and implementing innovative ideas by sport governing bodies could increase awareness.

More digital opportunities could also take place during decision-making processes of International Sport Governing Bodies (ISGB)s. During Covid-19 meetings and congresses took place virtually which both saved money and travel related GHG. For instance FIFA's expenses for its annual congress and committees decreased from just under €22.3 million in 2019 to €3.65 million in 2020 (Fédération Internationale de Football Association (FIFA) 2021). Generally, this could be a lesson to govern sport organizations more virtually on an international but also local level. Due to less travel, an organization can save travel expenses and reduce its carbon footprint.

Investments in Inclusive, Carbon Neutral Infrastructure

The costs for adaption during Covid-19 were immense, like the postponement of the Olympic Games, and strategic investments should be fostered to both mitigate GHG and to adapt to region specific weather hazards. Financial solidarity within organized sport aided various sport organizations during Covid-19 and solidarity could also be a solution to modernize sport venues to make them more robust to climate hazards (Dingle and Stewart 2018). While it is questionable whether profit-oriented leagues and clubs see a benefit of a diverse sporting landscape, advantages for winter and summer outdoor sport organization working together in mountainous regions are obvious.

Nonetheless, infrastructure should be built climate neutral or positive and provide ideal conditions to practise sport during extreme weather periods and after natural disasters. Air conditioning during warm seasons, heat during cold weather as well as water reservoirs in outdoor venues must be taken into consideration. This does not only save money in the long run but also ensures sporting opportunities even if, for instance, water is short in specific areas (Dingle and Stewart 2018). Subsequently, these investments decrease the financial burden for organized sport after extreme weather events. Functioning sport infrastructure not only leads to the ability to provide sport but also the chance to be used as safe spaces after natural disasters by providing shelter for local residents and conversely mitigate the spread of diseases (Kellison and Orr 2020).

These preventive measures make sport organization less dependent on financial support from governments. In Germany for instance the regional multi-sport confederations addressed the chancellor to support the reconstruction of sport infrastructure after major flooding in July 2021 (Ammon, Klett, and Bärnwick 2021). Researchers have illustrated that less dependency on one organizations' stakeholder strengthens organizational resilience and accelerates the process to return to its normal operation (Filo, Cuskelly, and Wicker 2015; Wicker, Filo, and Cuskelly 2013).

Promoting Education for Volunteers and Employees

Not only by showing how financial investments in infrastructure play a crucial role, Covid-19 illustrated that volunteers had an important role to maintain the sport organizations capacity (Hoeijmakers and Van der Roest 2021). Subsequently, investments in workshops of employees and volunteers and educational campaigns to promote sustainability could strengthen organizational capacity.

While physical distancing and hand hygiene were promoted in sport facilities through posts, it could be signs which draw attention on a resourceful use of water or shutting of the lights when leaving the facility. Since smaller sport organizations often lack resources to develop innovative ideas and concepts, it is necessary to receive concrete advice from the higher institution. Specific needs for various sports were individually adopted by their respective federations and according to regional legislation. This principle of guidance and adjustment should be applied for sustainability measures and adaptive policies as well. Subsequently, a broad understanding in how far a changing climate will impact sport can be achieved and adequate tools can be provided to both employees and volunteers in clubs.

Strengthening Athletes' Involvement

Covid-19 showcased the lack of integration of athletes' opinion for instance when postponing the Olympic Games. The IOC was pressured to take a stand weeks earlier than announced and buckled to the demands of athletes and NOCs (Zirin and Boykoff 2020). Generally, the shift of power relations towards athletes is likely to increase especially if the condition to compete in elite sport events could harm the athletes (Seltmann 2021). The Olympic women football final 2021 was postponed after the Canadian and Swedish teams refused to play in the heat (Rainbird 2021). In the face of climate change incorporating the athletes in the decision-making processes to award mega-sport events is significant when considering extreme temperatures during summer and in winter.

Although Covid-19 illustrated that not every athlete can be considered as a role model, reaching some of them and using their multiplier effects proved to be effective to promote Covid-19 measures. The same applies to the promotion of sustainable practises, athletes should act responsibly as a role model. While some athletes have been calling for climate action and already initiated projects in Australia, UK, USA or Germany, one has to raise the question in how far this is just greenwashing (The Cool Down 2021; Sports for Future e.V. 2021). Raising awareness and promoting a sustainable lifestyle is the first step to build a greener sport system. Nonetheless, the trend towards more international sport events in shorter intervals is very likely to return when travel restriction due to Covid-19 are lifted and elite athletes barely have the chance to change the entire system.

Reinforce Sporting Solidarity

The impacts of Covid-19 uncovered especially a social dimension. Since the most vulnerable groups were impacted severely, it is very likely that women, elderly, children and persons with special needs or pre-existing illnesses are also impacted mostly in the face of a raising temperatures and impacts due to a changing climate (Evans et al. 2020). Organized sport should take adequate steps to safeguard sport opportunities for these groups. Generally, it is a societal question how many financial and human resources shall be provided by governments, ISGBs, and smaller sport organizations to foster a diverse sporting landscape.

Increasing costs for water and electricity bills due to changing climate conditions might lead to raising inequalities between elite and grassroot sport as well as between elite sport. Since some elitist sport can afford preventive and adaptive measures and ask consultants to help them transform, niche and poorer sport clubs fall by the wayside. Covid-19 has displayed the unequal opportunities within organized sport to cope with the crisis. Although solidarity is a good starting point individual programmes are only a drop in the bucket and collective climate action has to be fostered.

Overall, one can state that raising awareness on climate change and sustainability in sport is necessary to avoid the impacts of a sudden crisis. Since climate scientists have been calling for action in the past three decades, sport policy makers, sport practitioners and sport scientists should deal with this issue more intensively to prevent likewise impacts as due to Covid-19. Transnational projects like As Sustainable as Possible (ASAP) by various NOCs, Sport and Sustainability International (SandSI) or the Green Sport Alliance help put a spotlight on this issue in sport. Aligning programmes and initiatives by sharing knowledge, experiences, resources, and multiplier effects could help the organized sport in its entirety since stable networks promote organizational resilience of sport organizations (Wicker, Filo, and Cuskelly 2013).

Conclusion

To summarize, Covid-19 impacted organized sport differently depending on regional differences, national legislation, and countermeasures, however, this crisis state is also possible in the face of climate change. Therefore, a pathway to a more equal, inclusive, and resilient sport system should be fostered to respond adequately.

In general, the ISGBs played an important role during the pandemic by publishing managerial guidelines to return to sporting competitions. Looking at the impacts of the Covid-19 pandemic, one can summarize that sport organizations must build organizational capacity to attenuate the impacts of climate change on sport. Developing resilient sport organizations should be fostered and can support event organizers not only in a pending climate crisis, but also when a political crisis occurs in host countries.

Sport administrators proved that they are able to respond quickly to new situations such as games without fans. By integrating fans in live interactions during the lockdown, GHG emissions due to less spectators' transportation nearly vanished, but so did personal social interaction. While they found ways to cope with less fans, organizations should take the opportunity to integrate sustainability strategies concerning their fans. Since the financial and social aspects of fandom are important, no fans in stadiums and only digital fandom could harm the idea of a peaceful get-together through sport (Casper, McCullough, and Pfahl 2020). Therefore, sport organizations have to find climate friendly business models to provide the same social experience however with a better climate footprint and should foster educational programmes for fans to support the environmentally friendly transformation. Although sport and affiliated GHG might only emit a small proportion of global GHG this transformation is necessary to limit the global warming to 1.5 degrees to prevent even more natural hazards (IPCC 2021).

Moreover, organized sport can act as a role model and according to the UN Sustainability Development Goals (SDGs) sport administrators should seek for intersectional approaches. Covid-19 has shown that a holistic approach is vital to ensure the provision of sport. Moreover, future research should investigate the status quo of awareness, climate protection and adaptation with a regional focus and illustrate how far organized sport is prepared to provide sport in a crisis.

Digitalisation in sport proved to be especially helpful during the crisis like contact tracing or the integration of diaspora fans. In how far digital solutions might help the sport movement to become more resilient and robust needs to be further investigated.

Concluding remarks shall be given to sociological aspects focusing on the inequality for different sport participants. Although certain solidarity funds like the Olympic Solidarity programme aim to provide equal opportunities, discourse has barely taken place when talking about influences of climate change. Both IFs, NOCs and athletes from the Global South have been widely neglected in the discussion but they are affected severely by a changing climate. Special solidarity funds could support an environmentally friendly and inclusive transformation process and integrating athletes as role models could help promote climate change action.

In general, learning effects should result both in organizational and political changes as well as in more conscious individual behavior. Sport policy makers should foster preventive measures, adaption, and long-term strategic decisions to provide sport for all societal groups within changing climatic conditions. Obligatory measures proved to be supportive for sport organizations during the Covid-19 restart, so why not implement compulsory sustainability guidelines introduced by leagues or IFs?

While this analysis focuses on selective learnings for the organized sport system, the informal sport sector, sport for development sector and gym operators were not considered. However, future studies could integrate these dimensions within the sporting society to provide a more holistic picture concerning impacts of Covid-19 in the face of a changing climate. Exchanging globally to learn from each other during the pandemic and in terms of climate change will help organized sport to provide its core business in the future: Connecting people to enjoy social interaction, stay active and live healthy.

REFERENCES

Ammon, Jörg, Stefan Klett, and Wolfgang Bärnwick. 2021. "Brief an Bundeskanzlerin Dr. Angela Merkel Vom 21. Juli 2021: Wiederaufbau von Vereinseigenen Sportstätten Nach Der Hochwasserkatastrophe."

Ando, Ritsuko, and Jack Tarrant. 2019. "IOC Plan to Move Tokyo Olympic Marathon to Hokkaido Due to Heat Concerns." Reuters. August 16, 2019. https://www.reuters.com/article/us-olympics-2020-marathon-idUSKBN1WV1DA.

Askew, Ashley E., and J. M. Bowker. 2018. "Impacts of Climate Change on Outdoor Recreation Participation: Outlook to 2060." *The Journal of Park and Recreation Administration* 36: 97–120. https://doi.org/10.18666/jpra-2018-v36-i2-8316.

Behnoosh, Shima, Michael Naylor, and Geoff Dickson. 2017. "Promoting Sport and Physical Activity Participation: The Impact of Endorser Expertise and Recognisability." *Managing Sport and Leisure* 22 (3): 214–33. https://doi.org/10.1080/23750472.2018.1424024.

Bowes, Ali, Lucy Lomax, and Jessica Piasecki. 2020. "The Impact of the COVID-19 Lockdown on Elite Sportswomen." *Managing Sport and Leisure*. https://doi.org/10.1080/23750472.2020.1825988.

Breuer, Christoph, Pamela Wicker, Sören Dallmeyer, and Michael Ilgner. 2018. "Die Lebenssituation von Spitzen-Sportlern Und-Sportlerinnen in Deutschland." Bonn. https://www.sporthilfe.de/fileadmin/pdf/Studien/Breuer_et_al._2018_Lebenssituation_Spitzensportler.pdf.

Bundesverwaltungsamt. n.d. "Corona-Überbrückungshilfen Des Bundes Für Den Profisport." Accessed July 30, 2021. https://www.bva.bund.de/DE/Services/Unternehmen-Verbaende/Compliance-Recht/Coronahilfen_Profisport/coronahilfen_profisport_node.html.

Byers, Terri, Khevyn-Lynn Gormley, Mathieu Winand, Christos Anagnostopoulos, Remi Richard, and Simone Digennaro. 2021. "COVID-19 Impacts on Sport Governance and Management: A Global, Critical Realist Perspective." *Managing Sport and Leisure*. https://doi.org/10.1080/23750472.2020.1867002.

Casper, Jonathan M., Brian P. McCullough, and Michael E. Pfahl. 2020. "Examining Environmental Fan Engagement Initiatives through Values and Norms with Intercollegiate Sport Fans." *Sport Management Review* 23 (2): 348–60. https://doi.org/10.1016/j.smr.2019.03.005.

Castagna, Carlo, Mario Bizzini, Alejo Perez Leguizamon, Angelo Pizzi, Riccardo Torquati, and Susana Póvoas. 2020. "Considerations and Best Practices for Elite Football Officials Return to Play after COVID-19 Confinement." *Managing Sport and Leisure* 0 (0): 1–8. https://doi.org/10.1080/23750472.2020.1783841.

Chingoma, Grace. 2021. "Covid-19: African Football Struggle." *The Herald*. July 21, 2021. https://www.herald.co.zw/covid-19-african-football-struggle/.

Cooper, J. A., and Derek H. Alderman. 2020. "Cancelling March Madness Exposes Opportunities for a More Sustainable Sports Tourism Economy." *Tourism Geographies* 22 (3): 525–35. https://doi.org/10.1080/14616688.2020.1759135.

Deutscher Fußball-Bund e.V. (DFB). 2021. "DFB Und DOSB Starten Petition Für Amateursport." DFB News. May 12, 2021. https://www.dfb.de/news/detail/dfb-und-dosb-starten-petition-fuer-amateursport-227332/.

Dingle, Greg William, and Bob Stewart. 2018. "Playing the Climate Game: Climate Change Impacts, Resilience and Adaptation in the Climate-Dependent Sport Sector." *Managing Sport and Leisure* 23 (4–6): 293–314. https://doi.org/10.1080/23750472.2018.1527715.

Drewes, Michael, Frank Daumann, and Florian Follert. 2020. "Exploring the Sports Economic Impact of COVID-19 on Professional Soccer." *Soccer & Society*, August. https://doi.org/10.1080/14660970.2020.1802256.

Duckworth, Austin. 2021. "Gegenpressing: The Bundesliga's Tactical Response to the Covid-19 Lockdown." In *Time Out: Global Perspectives on Sport and the Covid-19 Lockdown,* edited by Jörg Krieger, April Henning, Lindsay Parks Pieper, and Paul Dimeo, 29–40. Champaign, IL: Common Ground Research Networks.

Ebert, Michael. 2020. "Solidaritätsfonds Der Vier Champions-League-Klubs Wirft Fragen Auf." *Kicker.* April 1, 2020.

https://www.kicker.de/solidaritaetsfonds_der_vier_champions_league_klubs_wirft_fragen_auf-773239/artikel.

Ehrlich, Justin Andrew, Shankar Ghimire, Maroula Khraiche, and Mian Farrukh Raza. 2021. "COVID-19 Countermeasures, Sporting Events, and the Financial Impacts to the North American Leagues." *Managerial Finance* 47 (6): 887–95. https://doi.org/10.1108/MF-05-2020-0275.

European Commission. 2021. "Erasmus+: EU Programme for Education, Training, Youth and Sport." 2021. https://ec.europa.eu/programmes/erasmus-plus/node_en.

Evans, Adam B., Joanna Blackwell, Paddy Dolan, Josef Fahlén, Remco Hoekman, Verena Lenneis, Gareth McNarry, Maureen Smith, and Laura Wilcock. 2020. "Sport in the Face of the COVID-19 Pandemic: Towards an Agenda for Research in the Sociology of Sport." *European Journal for Sport and Society* 17 (2): 85–95. https://doi.org/10.1080/16138171.2020.1765100.

Fédération Internationale de Football Association (FIFA). 2021. "2020 Financial Statements: Consolidated Financial Statements, Notes, Report to the FIFA Congress." Zurich.

Feiler, Svenja, and Christoph Breuer. 2021. "Perceived Threats through COVID-19 and the Role of Organizational Capacity: Findings from Non-Profit Sports Clubs." *Sustainability* 13 (6937). https://doi.org/10.3390/su13126937.

Filo, Kevin, Graham Cuskelly, and Pamela Wicker. 2015. "Resource Utilisation and Power Relations of Community Sport Clubs in the Aftermath of Natural Disasters." *Sport Management Review* 18 (4): 555–69. https://doi.org/10.1016/j.smr.2015.01.002.

Fitzgerald, Hayley, Annette Stride, and Scarlett Drury. 2020. "COVID-19, Lockdown and (Disability) Sport." *Managing Sport and Leisure,* 1–8. https://doi.org/10.1080/23750472.2020.1776950.

Goggins, Dom, Clara Goldsmith, Caroline Grogan, Jessica Marsh, and Bronwen Smith-Thomas. n.d. "Game Changer: How Climate Change Is Impacting Sports in the UK."

Hall, Stefan. 2020. "This Is How Coronavirus Is Affecting Sports." World Economic Forum COVID Action Platform. April 9, 2020.

https://www.weforum.org/agenda/2020/04/sports-covid19-coronavirus-excersise-specators-media-coverage/.

Hoeijmakers, Resie, and Jan-Willem Van der Roest. 2021. "The Impact of the Covid-19 Crisis and the Robustness of Dutch Sport Clubs." In *Time Out: Global Perspectives on*

Sport and the Covid-19 Lockdown, edited by Jörg Krieger, April Henning, Lindsay Parks Pieper, and Paul Dimeo, 189–202. Champaign, IL: Common Ground Research Networks.

Horky, Thomas. 2020. "No Sports, No Spectators-No Media, No Money? The Importance of Spectators and Broadcasting for Professional Sports during COVID-19." *Soccer & Society* 22 (1–2): 96–102. https://doi.org/10.1080/14660970.2020.1790358.

International Olympic Committee. 2020. "IOC Increases Olympic Solidarity Fund by 16 per Cent Overall and by 25 per Cent for Direct Athlete Support Programmes Olympic News." Olympic News. November 11, 2020. https://www.olympic.org/news/ioc-increases-olympic-solidarity-fund-by-16-per-cent-overall-and-by-25-per-cent-for-direct-athlete-support-programmes.

IPCC. 2021. *IPCC, 2021: Climate Change 2021: The Physical Science Basis. Contribution of Working Group I to the Sixth Assessment Report of the Intergovernmental Panel on Climate Change*. Edited by Masson-Delmotte, P. Zhai, V., A. Pirani, S. L. Connors, C. Péan, S. Berger, N. Caud, et al. Cambridge Scholars Publishing. https://doi.org/10.1080/03736245.2010.480842.

Kellison, Timothy, and Madeleine Orr. 2020. "Climate Vulnerability as a Catalyst for Early Stadium Replacement." *International Journal of Sports Marketing and Sponsorship*, no. September. https://doi.org/10.1108/IJSMS-04-2020-0076.

Krieger, Jörg, April Henning, Lindsay Parks Pieper, and Paul Dimeo. 2021a. *Time Out: Global Perspectives on Sport and the Covid-19 Lockdown*. Edited by Jörg Krieger, April Henning, Lindsay Parks Pieper, and Paul Dimeo. Champaign, IL: Common Ground Research Networks.

———. 2021b. Time Out: National Perspectives on Sport and the Covid-19 Lockdown. Edited by Jörg Krieger, April Henning, Lindsay Parks Pieper, and Paul Dimeo. Champaign, IL: Common Ground Research Networks.

Leng, Ho Keat, and Yi Xian Philip Phua. 2020. "Athletes as Role Models during the COVID-19 Pandemic." *Managing Sport and Leisure*, 1–15. https://doi.org/10.1080/23750472.2020.1762330.

Lord, Craig. 2020. "FINA Among International Federations That Have Received COVID-19 'Hardship' Loans from IOC Funding Package." Swimming World News. July 15, 2020. https://www.swimmingworldmagazine.com/news/fina-among-international-federations-that-have-received-covid-19-hardship-loans-from-ioc-funding-package/.

MacInnes, Paul. 2020. "Premier League Players and Pay Cuts: The Key Questions Answered." *The Guardian*. April 6, 2020. https://www.theguardian.com/football/2020/apr/06/premier-league-players-and-pay-cuts-key-questions-answered-coronavirus.

Macnaughtan, Helen. 2020. "Japan, the Olympics and the COVID-19 Pandemic." *East Asia Forum*, June 23, 2020. https://www.eastasiaforum.org/2020/06/23/japan-the-olympics-and-the-covid-19-pandemic/.

Majumdar, Boria, and Souvik Naha. 2020. "Live Sport during the COVID-19 Crisis: Fans as Creative Broadcasters." *Sport in Society* 23 (7): 1091–99. https://doi.org/10.1080/17430437.2020.1776972.

Mann, Robert H., Bryan C. Clift, Jules Boykoff, and Sheree Bekker. 2020. "Athletes as Community; Athletes in Community: Covid-19, Sporting Mega-Events and Athlete Health Protection." *British Journal of Sports Medicine* 0: 1–2. https://doi.org/10.1136/bjsports-2020-102433.

Mastromartino, Brandon, Walker J Ross, Henry Wear, and Michael L Naraine. 2020. "Thinking Outside the 'Box': A Discussion of Sports Fans,

Teams, and the Environment in the Context of COVID-19." *Sport in Society* 23 (11): 1707–23. https://doi.org/10.1080/17430437.2020.1804108.

Mccarthy, Hannah, Henry W W Potts, and Abigail Fisher. 2021. "Physical Activity Behavior Before, During, and After COVID-19 Restrictions: Longitudinal Smartphone-Tracking Study of Adults in the United Kingdom." *Journal of Medical Internet Research* 23 (2). https://doi.org/10.2196/23701.

Melnick, Meredith. 2012. "New York Marathon Canceled in Wake of Hurricane Sandy." *HuffPost*, February 11, 2012. https://www.huffpost.com/entry/new-york-marathon-canceled-sandy_n_2067241?guccounter=1&guce_referrer=aHR0cHM6Ly93d3cuZWNvc2lhLm9yZy8&guce_referrer_sig=AQAAAK7pXoyj2k9lRFWTi-OhnIWRniDFA10Ae2hGcpiLIA5EbTDAyFPOeXBMqQO0mV0lHm79ENyaW-CL3WUX-QQ4wHxesINUFMgx4Vk-.

Miles, Lee, and Richard Shipway. 2020. "Exploring the COVID-19 Pandemic as a Catalyst for Stimulating Future Research Agendas for Managing Crises and Disasters at International Sport Events." *Event Management* 24 (4): 537–52. https://doi.org/10.3727/152599519X15506259856688.

Mitchell, Kevin. 2020. "Wimbledon Chief Says Tennis May Not Return until 2021 Due to Coronavirus." *The Guardian*. April 2, 2020. https://www.theguardian.com/sport/2020/apr/02/wimbledon-chief-says-tennis-may-not-return-until-2021-due-to-coronavirus.

Morgan, Liam. 2021. "Two Georgian Judoka Ordered to Leave Tokyo 2020 for Breaking COVID-19 Rules." *Inside the Games*. July 31, 2021. https://www.insidethegames.biz/articles/1111027/tokyo-2020-olympics-breaking-covid-rules.

Mosley, Stephen. 2010. *The Environment in World History*. 1st ed. Abingdon, Oxon: Routledge. https://doi.org/10.4324/9780203859537.

Mutz, Michael, and Markus Gerke. 2020. "Sport and Exercise in Times of Self-Quarantine: How Germans Changed Their Behavior at the Beginning of the Covid-19 Pandemic." *International Review for the Sociology of Sport*, 1–12. https://doi.org/10.1177/1012690220934335.

Nowy, Tobias, Pamela Wicker, Svenja Feiler, and Christoph Breuer. 2015. "Organizational Performance of Nonprofit and For-Profit Sport Organizations." *European Sport Management Quarterly* 15 (2): 155–75. https://doi.org/10.1080/16184742.2014.995691.

Orr, Madeleine. 2020. "On the Potential Impacts of Climate Change on Baseball and Cross-Country Skiing." *Managing Sport and Leisure* 25 (4): 307–20. https://doi.org/10.1080/23750472.2020.1723436.

Orr, Madeleine, and Yuhei Inoue. 2018. "Sport versus Climate: Introducing the Climate Vulnerability of Sport Organizations Framework." *Sport Management Review*.

Owen, David. 2020. "Covid's Cost to Sport." Inside the Games. 2020.

———. 2021. "FIFA Insures 2022 World Cup for $900m." *Inside World Football*. March 22, 2021. http://www.insideworldfootball.com/2021/03/22/fifa-insures-2022-world-cup-900m/.

Rainbird, Daniel. 2021. "Tokyo Olympics 2021: Canada-Sweden Soccer Final Rescheduled Due to Heat." Yahoo! Sports. August 5, 2021. https://ca.sports.yahoo.com/news/tokyo-olympics-2021-canada-sweden-olympic-womens-soccer-final-rescheduled-due-to-extreme-heat-121416307.html?guccounter=1&guce_referrer=aHR0cHM6Ly93d3cuZWNvc2lhLm9yZy8&guce_referrer_sig=AQAAABVmb3s6n8E2dxmkTQNSklxmTdueZj5CN4iJOn5blXraRgz-y6_TL5DJ8o4ecQfsxlJE_-zf-ia_Ti9_agqGa31Tj2tgWHt8tZbDC4rNcZ0oFzQNzdEUoZkCyqE07Y5INO7AOtBlozLF3hwsnXo-HdXx4JttI-AUexRsExkDhVkl.

Ramagole, Dimakatso, Dina Christa Janse van Rensburg, Lervason Pillay, Pierre Viviers, Phathokuhle Zondi, and Jon Patricios. 2020. "Implications of COVID-19 for Resumption of Sport in South Africa: A South African Sports Medicine Association (SASMA) Position Statement." *South African Journal of Sports Medicine* 32 (1): 1–6. https://doi.org/10.17159/2078-516x/2020/v32i1a8454.

Redaktion, DEL. 2020. "Deutsche Eishockey Liga Beendet Saison Vorzeitig." March 10, 2020. https://www.penny-del.org/news/deutsche-eishockey-liga-beendet-saison-vorzeitig/11283.

Reiter, Martin. 2020. "Adapting Sports Entertainment to the Lockdown: World Wrestling Entertainment, the Modification of Performance Practices, and the Logic of Capitalism during the Covid-19 Pandemic." In *Time Out: National Perspectives on Sport and the Covid-19 Lockdown*, edited by Jörg Krieger, April Henning, Lindsay Parks Pieper, and Paul Dimeo, 95–108. Champaign, IL: Common Ground Research Networks.

Reuters. 2019. "Rugby World Cup Matches Canceled Due to Approaching Typhoon Hagibis." *The Guardian*. October 10, 2019. https://www.theguardian.com/global/video/2019/oct/10/rugby-world-cup-matches-canceled-due-to-approaching-typhoon-hagibis-video.

Rowe, David. 2020. "Subjecting Pandemic Sport to a Sociological Procedure." *Journal of Sociology* 56 (4): 704–13. https://doi.org/10.1177/1440783320941284.

Seltmann, Maximilian. 2021. "Disrupting Institutional Reproduction? How Olympic Athletes Challenge the Stability of the Olympic Movement." *De Gruyter*. https://doi.org/https://doi.org/10.1515/sug-2021-0002.

Singh Aulakh, Balbir. 2021. "Impact and Implications of Covid-19 and Lockdown on India's Sports Ecosystem." In *Time Out: Global Perspectives on Sport and the Covid-19 Lockdown*, edited by Jörg Krieger, April Henning, Lindsay Parks Pieper, and Paul Dimeo, 153–68. Champaign, IL: Common Ground Research Networks.

Smith, Kirk R., Alistair Woodward, Bruno Lemke, Matthias Otto, Cindy J. Chang, Anna A. Mance, John Balmes, and Tord Kjellstrom. 2016. "The Last Summer Olympics? Climate Change, Health, and Work Outdoors." *The Lancet* 388 (10045): 642–44. https://doi.org/10.1016/S0140-6736(16)31335-6.

Sport and Recreation Victoria. 2021. "Community Sport Sector Short-Term Survival Package." April 21, 2021. https://sport.vic.gov.au/grants-and-funding/our-grants/community-sport-sector-coronavirus-covid-19-short-term-survival-package.

Sport England. 2020. "£195 Million Package to Help Sport and Physical Activity through Coronavirus." March 31, 2020. https://www.sportengland.org/news/195-million-package-help-sport-and-physical-activity-through-coronavirus.

Sports for Future e.V. 2021. "Ruderwald." 2021. https://sports4trees.com/ruderwald/.

Stiftung Deutsche Sporthilfe. 2020. "Studie: Deutschlands Spitzenathleten Fehlen Rund 6 Mio. Euro Corona-Bedingt in 2020." 2020. https://www.sporthilfe.de/ueber-uns/medien/pressemitteilungen/studie-deutschlands-spitzenathleten-fehlen-rund-6-mio-euro-corona-bedingt-in-2020.

The Cool Down. 2021. "The Cool Down." 2021. https://www.thecooldown.com.au/.

Toresdahl, Brett G, and Irfan M Asif. 2020. "Coronavirus Disease 2019 (COVID-19): Considerations for the Competitive Athlete." *Sports Health* 12 (3): 221–24. https://doi.org/10.1177/1941738120918876.

Triantafyllidis, Stavros. 2020. "Environmental Change, the Sport Industry, and Covid-19." In *Sport and the Pandemic: Perspectives on Covid-19's Impact on the Sport*, edited by Paul M. Pedersen, Brody J. Ruihley, and Bo Li, 24–32. Abingdon, Oxon: Routledge.

Tripcke, Gernot. 2021. "Eishockey-Start: DEL-Chef Über Zuschauer-Rückkehr Und Impfquote." Berliner Morgenpost. September 7, 2021. https://www.morgenpost.de/sport/article233251665/Eishockey-Start-DEL-Chef-ueber-Zuschauer-Rueckkehr-und-Impfquote.html.

United Nations Climate Change Global Climate Action. 2018. "Sports for Climate Action Framework."

United Nations Framework Convention on Climate Change. 1992. "United Nations Framework Convention on Climate Change."

United Nations International Strategy for Disaster Reduction. 2005. "Hyogo Framework for Action 2005–2015: Building the Resilience of Nations and Communities to Disasters." In *World Conference on Disaster Reduction*. Kobe/Hyogo, Japan. https://doi.org/10.1007/978-1-4020-4399-4_180.

Vickery, Tim. 2020. "South American Football Battles to Get Going Again after Coronavirus." *ESPN*. 2020. https://www.espn.com/soccer/paraguayan-primera-division/story/4107227/south-american-football-battles-to-get-going-again-after-coronavirus.

Wicker, Pamela, Kevin Filo, and Graham Cuskelly. 2013. "Organizational Resilience of Community Sport Clubs Impacted by Natural Disasters." *Journal of Sport Management* 27 (6): 510–25. https://doi.org/10.1123/jsm.27.6.510.

World Economic Forum. 2021. *The Global Risks Report 2021: 16th Edition*. 16th ed. Geneva: World Economic Forum.

Xiang, Mi, Zhiruo Zhang, and Keisuke Kuwaharab. 2020. "Impact of COVID-19 Pandemic on Children and Adolescents' Lifestyle Behavior Larger than Expected." *Progress in Cardiovascular Diseases* 63 (2020): 531–32. https://doi.org/https://doi.org/10.1016/j.pcad.2020.04.013.

Zirin, Dave, and Jules Boykoff. 2020. "The Olympics Teeter on the Brink: An Upsurge of Athletes and Federations Is Forcing the IOC to Consider Postponement of This Summer's Games." *The Nation*. March 23, 2020. https://www.thenation.com/article/world/2020-olympics-coronavirus-cancel/.

Chapter 7

The Modern Olympic Games in a Post-Pandemic World

Jeffrey O. Segrave

Introduction

> *The Ural peaks by it were scaled*
> *And every bar and barrier failed*
> *To turn it from its way.*
> *Slowly and surely on it came,*
> *Heralded by its awful fame,*
> *Increasing by the day.*
> (Winston Churchill, *The Influenza*, 1890)

Winston Churchill was only fifteen years old when he penned these words about the influenza pandemic that ravaged Europe in the late nineteenth century. Over a century later, his words remain hauntingly true. As it spread across the globe during the early months of 2020, the Covid-19 pandemic left devastation in its wake—businesses were closed, curfews imposed, families isolated, schools shut, and lives lost. Among the casualties of the pandemic were live events, movie releases, and productions of all sorts. Fairs and festivals, concerts and conferences, parades and galas, were canceled, postponed, or re-scheduled. Sporting events also fell prey to the pandemic: the NBA suspended its season on March 11, the English Premier League on March 13, and the NCAA's March Madness on the same day. Numerous other sports events were canceled, including the New York and Boston Marathons, Wimbledon, and the Little League World Series. On March 24, the Olympics followed suit. In a joint statement, the International Olympic Committee (IOC) and the Tokyo Organizing Committee for the Olympic Games announced that the 2020 Summer Olympics and Paralympics would be re-scheduled to a date "beyond 2020 but not later than summer 2021," adding that the Games could "stand as a beacon of hope to the world during these troubling times" and the flame as "the light at the end of the tunnel in which the world finds itself at present" ("Joint Statement" 2020).

As Churchill's words suggest, plagues and pandemic are not new. In the opening verses of Homer's *Illiad,* the Greek armies are ravaged by pestilence—

divine retribution directed against their vain and inglorious King Agamemnon. Perhaps, more well known are the bubonic plague of the fourteenth century—Black Death, as it was called—and the post-World War I Spanish flu. In more recent, years, the world has wrestled with outbreaks of SARS, MERS, avian flu, swine flu, Ebola, and Zika. Somewhat presciently, Bill Gates (2015) noted in a TED Talk that "if anything kills over 10 million people in the next few decades, it's most likely to be a highly infectious virus." While the death toll from Covid-19 currently falls well short of Gates's ghastly prediction, the Covid-19 pandemic, like the 9/11 attacks, the Asian financial collapse, and the global financial crisis of the early twenty-first century, serves as yet another asymmetric shock wave that tears at the fabric of the established social, political, and economic order. If the success of the past century has been the construction of an international system more committed to creating and sustaining a just, peaceful, and prosperous world, then the failure of the present has been the faltering inability of the institutions of the liberal international order to respond to the global pandemic threat in a concerted and efficient way. Great-power politics are taking on an increasingly zero-sum logic; countries, as Thomas Hobbes (2005) put it, "are in the state and posture of Gladiators; having their weapons pointing, and their eyes fixed on one another" (96-97). The Covid debate reminds us that the challenges of maintaining a peaceful and flourishing world in the face of fraying international relations is a formidable task. We are facing what author Philip Bobbitt (2020) calls a "crisis of change," a crisis "that underlines all the others because it is converting those other challenges into existential crises of governance" (57). We need organizations and systems, the Lebanese-American scholar Nassim Nicholas Taleb (2012) argues, that are "antifragile," which mitigate against global chaos and mistrust, institutions, like the resilient Olympic Movement of the past 150 years that has actively embraced and, for the most part, delivered a pacifist internationalism.

The purpose of this paper is to conjecture on the delivery and role of the Olympic Games in a post-Covid world. More specifically, I address two primary questions: First, how can the Olympics fulfill their ambitions in a post-Covid world? What changes does the IOC need to make in response to the global Covid-19 pandemic? Second, what will the role of the Olympic Games be in a post-pandemic environment? How can the Games best contribute to a world fractured by geopolitical and ideological divisions? In order to answer these questions, I will locate my theorizing within the context of the work of cultural commentators who have addressed what can be learned from the Covid-19 pandemic, specifically international affairs scholars such as Philip Bobbit, Hal Brands, Francis Gavin, Lawrence Summers, Laine Rutkow, and Fareed Zakaria. Ultimately, I argue that while the Olympics are neither the panacea for the political tensions nor the health threats that will likely haunt the post-pandemic era, their enduring international resilience, stature, and networking potential could well be a model for international reconciliation as well as a buffer against future pandemics.

The Post-Covid World

For I dipt into the future, far as the human eye could see,
Saw the Vision of the world, and all the wonder that would be,
Saw the heavens fill with commerce, argosies of magic sails,
Pilots of the purple twilight, dropping down with costly bales.
Heard the heavens fill with shouting, there rain'd a ghastly dew
From the nations' airy navies grappling in the central blue.
Far along the world-wide whisper of the south-wind rushing warm,
With the standards of the peoples plunging thro' the thunder-storm.
Till the war-drum throbb'd no longer, and the battle-flags were furl'd
In the Parliament of man, the Federation of the World.
There the common sense of most shall hold a fretful realm in awe,
And the kindly earth shall slumber, lapt in universal law.
*(*Alfred Lord Tennyson, Locksley Hall, 1835*)*

In order to muse on the way in which the Olympics can achieve their goals in a post-pandemic world, I need to define what I mean by a post-Covid world. This paper is not about a post-pandemic world because the virus is behind us—far from it—but because we have crossed a critical threshold of awareness; we now know what a pandemic looks and feels like and we have witnessed the massive devastation it can cause in terms of human life, unemployment, poverty, and isolation. Clearly, we are still in the throes of Covid-19 and, even if it is eradicated, new outbreaks and new variants are almost certain to occur in the near future. With this new-found knowledge, we now live in a new era: the post-pandemic world (Zaharia 2020, 2-3).

Also, in order to consider what the role of the Games might be in a post-Covid era, it is necessary to understand the impact that Covid-19 will have on what has become known as the liberal international order, an order of which the Olympics have become a conspicuous and significant part during their recent history. And, by the international liberal order, I mean the politico-economic framework established by the U.S. after World War II that has been marked by openness in trade, international institutions like the United Nations (UN), rules and norms that regulate and normalize international conduct, and interconnections that facilitate cooperative solutions to common problems (Zaharia, 2020, 209).

At this point, of course, no one knows precisely what the impact of the pandemic on the liberal global order will be. It is hard to know how long the pandemic will last and how much damage it will inflict. It is possible to imagine a future in which a vaccine will become widely and readily available, nationwide lockdowns will be lifted, governments will emerge largely unscathed, and the existing system will survive intact. It is equally plausible, however, to imagine an alternative, and less encouraging, scenario in which Covid-19 leaves a shock wave every bit as devastating and lethal as World War I and World War II. In geo-political and geo-economic terms, the political scientist Francis Fukuyama (2020) posits two extreme outcomes from the Covid-19 debacle—a rising fascism or a rebirth of liberal democracy. Unfortunately, however, as international political science scholars Hal Brands, Peter Feaver, and William Inboden (2020) note, "the bulk of informed opinion leans towards a maximalist—and deeply pessimistic—appraisal" (298). International affairs theorist G. John Ikenberry (2020), in fact, goes so far as to say that Covid-19 will bring about no less than "the end of the liberal world order." Other observers argue that, in the face of an ineffectual, cooperative response to the health crisis, we will see a shift in the global ideological balance away from democracy and towards autocracy and dictatorship; that the health crisis may be America's "Suez moment" and hasten China's ascendancy, ushering in Cold War 2.0.; that it will facilitate a high level of populism and anti-globalization sentiment among key political elites, or, to put it another way it will hasten the impetus to de-globalize; and that it will require a profound international effort to even begin to construct an effective health and fitness bulwark against future pandemics (Applebaum 2020; Ash 2020; Bader 2018; Campbell and Doshi 2020; Rudd 2020; Rutkow 2020).

Whatever its enduring effects, Covid-19 already qualifies as the greatest shock to the established international liberal system since the 2007-2009 financial crisis. When it comes to the institutions of the liberal order, Covid-19 has revealed deep-seated flaws and failings within numerous preeminent international bodies, including the World Health Organization, the World Trade Organization, the European Union, and the G7 (McTague 2020; Pickering and Trivedi 2020). The economist and former Director of the National Economic Council Lawrence Summers (2020) suggests that Covid-19 will prove to be a hinge event in modern history, a moment that will forever and inextricably alter the course of history. American diplomat Richard Haass (2002) avers that it will not so much reshape history as accelerate it, exacerbating the already splintered social, political, and economic infrastructure of the liberal international order. Although not inevitable, the negative scenario haunts the predictions of nearly every analyst of global politics in one form or another; hence, the need for an institution like the Olympic Games to try to fulfill its goals and seek redress to the deteriorating international social, political, and health environment.

The Olympics in a Post-Covid World

> ……. *all things stedfastnes doe hate*
> *And changed be: yet being rightly wayd,*
> *They are not changed from their first estate.*
> *But by their change their being doe dilate:*
> *And turning to themselues at length againe,*
> *Doe worke their owne perfection so by fate:*
> *Then ouer the Change doth not rule and raigne.*
> *But they raigne ouer change, and doe their states mantaine.*
> (Edmund Spenser, *Two Cantos of Mutabilitie,* 1609)

If, as the *Olympic Charter* notes, the "goal of Olympism is to place sport at the service of the harmonious development of humankind, with a view to promoting a peaceful society concerned with the preservation of human dignity" (IOC 2020a, 11), then in order to accomplish its fundamental mission, the IOC must adhere to its commitment to change, specifically as reified in the Olympic Agenda 2020 and the Olympic Agenda 2020+5. The Olympic Agenda 2020 (IOC 2020b) is an interrelated set of forty detailed recommendations that were accepted by the IOC in 2014 as a strategic roadmap to safeguard Olympic values and strengthen sport in society. The Olympic Agenda 2020+5 (IOC 2021) is a further set of fifteen recommendations adopted by the IOC in 2021 as a way to confront the far-reaching social, financial, economic, and political consequences of the coronavirus pandemic. In particular, the Olympic Movement must seek to maximize its influence in the realms of politics and diplomacy, economic and racial inequalities, health and fitness, the environment, human rights and education.

Politics and Diplomacy

First, it is crucial that the IOC not only sustain but intensify its pacifist internationalist agenda. No other international organization captures the public imagination or commands the global media airways more than the Olympics; no other global ritual pays homage to intercultural amity and understanding in the same way that the Olympics do. Fraying international relations have been exacerbated by the pandemic. The world is fracturing rather than converging, becoming increasingly divided along geopolitical and ideological lines, even as it requires cooperation among them. Even a committed globalist like France's President Emmanuel Macron (2020) laments his "dependency on other countries" and has announced his new post-pandemic goal of achieving independence for France. U.S. President Joe Biden's "Buy America" plan personifies the same political introvertism and isolationism. The result, as numerous political commentators conclude, will be a rise in regionalism and the rollback of the benefits associated with globalization, including a reversal in the free flow of goods, services, money, and people, all of which has transformed the world in positive ways over the past four decades (Schake 2020). The challenge for the future, as the Canadian academic Ronald Daniels (2020) recognizes, lays in the difficult, ongoing work of sustaining internationalist projects and global institutions that "forge partnerships and lay the foundation to address the tendency toward fragmentation" (ix). Not only does the Olympic Movement represent one of the best examples of internationalism—both the Olympic and Paralympic Games represent what political commentator Fareed Zakaria (2020) calls "factories of assimilation and amalgamation" (143)—but, despite geopolitical roiling throughout the course of the twentieth century, particularly two World Wars and the Cold War, not to mention incidents of internal corruption, financial impropriety, and overt nationalism, often bordering on outright chauvinism, the Games still stand as one arena in the world where nations can gather in peace with the avowed intension to spread a global pacifist message.

Recent developments have furthered the global pacifist reach of the Olympic Movement in the form of Youth Olympic Games, which represent a significant expansion of internationalism into new cities and countries. In 2026, the Youth Olympic Games will be held in Dakar, Senegal, the first time that Olympic competition will be held on the African continent. Of no little importance in spreading intercultural understanding and communication is the recent program initiated by the IOC called Athlete365, a multi-lingual one-stop-shop and dedicated platform that allows athletes the opportunity to connect and support one another. The program offers specially designed programs and resources in six languages, which to date, has attracted more than 100,000 Olympians and elite-level athletes. But, nowhere, of course, is the goal of international cooperation more in evidence than in the recently forged partnership between the IOC and the UN. "Olympic principles are United Nations principles," Secretary General of the UN, Ban Ki-Moon states (2009); both organizations embrace the unifying and conciliative promise of international sport as a way to foster dialogue, peace, and development.

Of all the political tensions that tear at the prospects of international peace—a tension that the Olympics have often of late found themselves at the epicenter of—the mounting economic and political confrontation between the U.S. and China is perhaps the most trenchant (Mahbubani 2020; Palmer 2021). As numerous political commentators note, we are witnessing the rise of a new global super-power and the threat, if not reality, of "a new Cold War" (Ash 2020; Bader 2018). Never before in history has an emerging power ascended so quickly and on so many different fronts, from the technological to the military to the economic (Allison 2020). A hard-edged realpolitik has returned in the form of an intensifying great-power rivalry between China and the U.S. for world hegemony. Rather than sharing the burden of global leadership in a time of health crisis, Washington and Beijing have turned their animus on each other. Despite the deep structural interdependencies in economies, the current fiction showcases how easily domestic policy and decision making in both countries can destabilize and exacerbate a relationship that has been growing ever more fragile in recent years. Nor are the prospects for mitigating the tension particularly promising. While the web of international organizations comprised of alliances like NATO, economic backstops including the IMF and World Bank, political forums such as the UN, and judicial bodies like the International Court of Justice and the International Criminal Court may well have enabled an unprecedented period of collective growth and security, they were never designed to deal with the transnational complexities of an interconnected world. Covid-19 has exposed them, as global affairs scholar John Lipsky (2020) argues, as "useless in coping with global treats that pit states against each other" (59). But, as Summers (2020) asserts, we must find a way to live in a post-Covid world "where security depends more on exceeding a threshold of co-operation with allies and adversaries alike than on maintaining balance of power" and the establishment of a productive and predictable U.S.-China relationship will be the *sine qua non* for strengthening the institutions of global governance and intercultural amity. The Olympic Games are one way to seek détente.

Not surprisingly, numerous organizations and critics have called for a boycott of the 2022 Beijing Olympic Winter Games, most on the basis of human rights violations. Most notably, a group of more than 180 primarily regional organizations have formed a coalition in support of Uighurs in Xinjiang, as well as self-determination in Tibet, Taiwan, and Hong Kong. But, governments and political figures have conspicuously eschewed calls for boycotts of late, partly on the grounds that boycotts have proven to be what anthropologist Susan Brownell (2021) calls "epic failures" that harm athletes and treat them as political pawns, and partly in recognition of the fact that boycotts can actually strengthen anti-democratic sentiments and practices in totalitarian states. Even U.S. Senators Mitt Romney's and Ted Cruz's recent critique of China's record on human rights falls short of calling for a boycott of the Games—Romney (2021) advocates an "economic and diplomatic boycott" and Cruz challenges the IOC to move the Games out of Beijing (quoted in Roche 2021)—both seemingly recognizing, as Brownell (2021) argues, that engagement—political, social, critical and individual, especially athlete interactions—rather than boycott enhances the promise of the Games and mitigates discriminatory practices and racism.

Consequently, while numerous commentators have critiqued the recent allocation of the Games to the totalitarian regimes of Russia and China (Lenskyj, 2014; Wagg and Andrews, 2012)—not without reason, given, for example, the Nazification of the Games in 1936 or the violation of human rights in the face of both the 2008 Beijing and 2016 Rio Games—the Olympics Movement remains to this day, as it has always been, a relevant, even if indirect, force for promoting peace and international amity between nation states and assuaging bigotry and prejudice. Never, perhaps, will its diplomatic and ideological leavening power be of more importance than it will be as the world confronts the negative deglobalizing and politically destabilizing consequences of Covid-19 and the emergent confrontation between China and the U.S. Despite its failure, the recent joint bid by North and South Korea to host the 2032 Olympics serves as a palliative to east-west tensions. As *New York Times* reporter Victor Mather (2018) puts it, "the mere idea that the Koreans might bid together suggests the Olympics remain a powerful incentive to keep the countries, which are technically at war more than six decades on from the Korean War, talking about peace." The IOC may not be what President Thomas Bach calls "a super-world government where the IOC can solve or even address issues for which not the UN Security Council, no G7, no G20 has solutions" (2020), but it is one of a variety of influential NGOs that can positively impact global affairs by easing political hostilities and cultivating intercultural exchange.

Economic and Racial Inequalities

Second, the IOC can only champion the "fundamental equality of all people" (IOC 2020b) and "encourage and support the development of sport for all" (IOC 2020a, 17) if it continues to foster programs that seek redress to the debilitating wealth disparities and racial inequalities and injustices that have been exposed by the Covid-19 pandemic. Such inequalities not only define the internal realities of an individual county—economist John Kenneth Galbraith (1958) once wrote that America was demarcated by "private opulence and public squalor" (189)—but, more importantly, inequalities that create a divide between continents, regions, and nations. As Zakaria (2020) notes, the pandemic is the "great unequalizer" (151) and the decline in global economic equality sustained by progress in China, India, and other developing economies in Asia, Africa, and South America will likely be erased and "we will return to a world of great and widening global inequality" (151). Various studies indicate that the pandemic will push between 70 and 430 million people back into extreme poverty over the next few years (Mahler 2020; Sumner, Hoy, and Ortiz-Juarez 2020). In short, the most essential inequality—between the richest and poorest countries—is now growing again at an alarmingly rapid rate (Zakaria 2020, 154). IMG Chief Kristalina Georgieva states that "in the flight to safety a lot of capital has left the emerging economies, the developing world; nearly $90 trillion has flown out way more than during the global financial crisis" (World Health Organization 2020).

If the Olympics and Paralympics are to seek equality, the IOC must continue to financially support sport on a global basis—as the Olympic Agenda 2020 (IOC 2020b) and the Olympic Agenda 2020+5 (IOC 2021) mandate, and as the IOC's March 2021 remote Session reports ("Tokyo 2020" 2021)—by investing in sport programs in underprivileged communities, reducing the cost of the bidding process, maximizing the use of existing facilities and temporary and demountable venues for the Games, subsidizing the cost of hosting the Games, enforcing the principle of sustainability in planning and staging the Games, establishing a viable framework for the Olympic program, and, in general, reducing the cost of organizing and delivering the Games. If the Games are to truly remain celebrations of our global community, then the IOC must also continue to ensure equal opportunity and access for athletes from all nations by sustaining, if not enhancing, its budget allocation, especially to Olympic Solidarity, but also to aid package programs, which, while more marginal, are still committed to promoting access. These include programs such as the Sport for Hope program, the Olympafrica model, and Olympic scholarships, not to mention programs—such as the IOC Refugee Olympic Team—that reach out not only to refugees but other populations impacted by displacement. Furthermore, nowhere is the athletic model for inclusion and acceptance more on display than in the Paralympics and Special Olympics (Shriver 2021). Strengthening relationships with organizations that manage and promote sport for athletes with different abilities must remain an essential dimension of any progressive Olympic agenda.

Health and Fitness

Nowhere, of course, have resource inequalities been more openly exposed by the pandemic than in the arena of health. "The difference between rich and poor countries will likely be accentuated as the world divides in two," writes Zakaria (2020), "places with health-care systems and places without them" (154); what writer Susan Sontag (1978) poignantly calls the "kingdom of the well" and the "kingdom of the sick." In other words, disease exacerbates inequalities and access to sport and fitness programs must be a national and, indeed, international and Olympic response to the ravages of Covid-19. As numerous health policy and management scholars argue, no country or organization at this point can mitigate a global catastrophic health threat on its own; public health systems must be viewed as interconnected entities, both within countries and organizations and across international borders, and must also be supplemented and augmented by transnational organizations dedicated to public health and welfare (Gilbert 2020; Kahn, Mastroianni, and Venkatapuram 2020; Rutkow 2020). As Zakaria (2020) asserts, "you cannot defeat a global disease with local responses" (28).

In order to mitigate the unjust social choreography of global pandemics the Olympic Movement must significantly increase resources to the development of sport and fitness programs. The immediate responses to Covid-19 will be antiviral therapies, vaccine development and deployment, contact tracing, and mass immunity, but the long-term responses must also include attention to regimes of sport and physical and mental health. As the IOC intones, "We have an interest and a responsibility to get the couch potatoes off the couch. Only children playing sport can be future athletes. Only children playing sport can enjoy the educational and health values of sport" (IOC 2020b). During the 2021-2024 Olympiad, the IOC has laudably increased its budget allocation to support athletes and National Olympic Committees from $311 million to $590 million, as well as an additional aid package of $150 million during the pandemic, much of which has been directed to programs that foster grass-roots athletics and inject sport and fitness programs into school curricula. Or, to put it another way, as much as it can, the IOC needs to support sport development in the same way that it supports elite sport. Furthermore, as the IOC has recently recognized, it must also strengthen its partnership with UNESCO to include sport and its values in school curricula.

The Environment

Perhaps of equal importance is the IOC's commitment to sustainability, especially in the context of the environment, as a factor in ongoing mitigation against pandemics and in its efforts to enhance health worldwide. This is especially imperative as we come to realize that new viruses emerge on a regular basis as humans increasingly encroach on animal ecosystems that were once undisturbed. Mega-sport sites continue to contribute to the destruction of natural habitats. In the case of the Olympics, the construction of facilities, most notably in Albertville, Nagano, Sochi and Rio, negatively impacted the natural environment in ways that were both underestimated and irreversible. Even though the IOC has declared the environment, alongside sport and education, to be the third dimension of the Olympic Movement, the challenge still remains how to balance the requirements of modern sport, especially with its totemistic valuation of space, as well as the economic and political aspirations of a community, with the need to protect the beauty and health of the natural and human environment.

Furthermore, mega-events, like the Olympics, continue to accelerate rapid global travel and tourism, hence potentially incubating and spreading disease. "In the coming months and years," Rutkow (2020) argues, "as countries shift from the COVID-19 emergency response to the recovery process, the world must reconsider and perhaps fundamentally shift its approach to protecting and promoting the health of populations" (93). The role of the Olympic and Paralympic Games Movements is crucial in the promotion of health and fitness through the spread of sport programs. Public health remains what Rutkow (2020) calls" an invisible discipline within international affairs" (94) and hence a crucial focus of attention in the conduct of the Olympic reform agenda.

Human Rights

Furthermore, the IOC can only realize its ambitions to promote diversity, non-discrimination, solidarity, and tolerance within global efforts on the basis of its commitment to and advocacy for human rights. As a significant contributor to the NGO-ization of global society, and in keeping with its alliance with the UN and the UN's Universal Declaration of Human Rights, the Olympic Games offer the opportunity to leverage both governments and sponsors in the name of human rights. Beginning in 2018, the IOC now requires organizing committees to obtain certification from the International Standards Organization whose standards of event sustainability management systems are oriented to social justice. Equally progressive, the IOC, in 2017, added provisions about human rights to the host city contract, effective for the first time in the organization of the 2024 Paris Games, recognizing that "The Games offer an opportunity to further strengthen the purpose of Olympism and the positive values promoted by the Olympic and Paralympic Games in very tangible ways" (Brownell 2021). Finally, the IOC has entered into formal agreements or directly worked with several organizations, including the International Labor Organization (ILO) and the Building and Wood Workers' International, in order to promote social justice and contribute to the welfare of migrant workers, eliminate poverty and child labor, enhance labor conditions, and safeguard against the displacement of local populations. Most recently, in preparation for the 2022 Beijing Winter Games and in light of China's record on human rights, the IOC has appealed to the ILO, a UN body, to help negotiate a settlement on behalf of more than a million Muslims detained in reeducation camps in western China ("IOC's Bach" 2019).

Education

Ultimately, the future success of the Olympic Movement and its ability to realize its global pacifist ambitions remains in the hands of its educational programs, including the cultural Olympiads. One of the primary goals of the IOC is "to encourage and support initiatives blending sport with culture and education" (IOC 2020a, 17), a lofty goal but one that bespeaks of engagement and encounter and one that will require the IOC to enter into or strengthen its relationships with NGOs, intergovernmental organizations and agencies, and arts organizations. Fruitful planned initiatives include the inauguration of an Olympic Laurel award for outstanding contributions to promote Olympism, the development of Olympic Houses to cultivate public dialogue, the establishment of an Olympic Museum on the move program, and the creation of an artist-in-residence program.

Conclusion

None of this is to say that the IOC should not continue its efforts to foster gender equality, advocate for non-discrimination on sexual orientation, protect and honor clean athletes, reinforce athletes' rights and responsibilities, encourage the development of virtual sports, or further blend sport and culture—recommendations all central to the Olympic Agenda 2020 and the Olympic Agenda 2020+5. But, in the face of the Covid-19 pandemic, the Olympics are best positioned to fulfill their ambitions and rise to the challenge of redeeming a post-Covid world by doubling their efforts to ensure the spread of sport as a bulwark against disease and by operating as a powerful model and component of the liberal international order that promises, even as it remains under siege, global cooperation and prosperity.

It is, of course, entirely feasible that the liberal order possesses a higher degree of resilience than many observers suggest. It is wholly possible that the pandemic will lead not to de-globalization but to re-globalization along established geo-political lines, that there will be no dramatic, adverse shifts in the global balance of power, especially with regard to relations between the U.S. and China, that the liberal order will not only hold but be revitalized, and that the pandemic will lead to the demise of autocracy and popularism rather than democracy and internationalism (Brands, Feaver, and Imboden 2020, 297-315). No matter what the geo-political scenario though, we can be certain that global public health efforts will demand greater attention as a geopolitical security challenge than ever before. The end of any pandemic is ever an asymptote, "never disappearing but rather fading to the point where its signal is lost in the noise of the normal" (Greene and Vargha 2020, 36), such that, if there is perhaps any one arena in which the IOC and Paralympic organizations need to exert their structural and cultural power in order to fulfill their goal of what modern Olympic Games founder Pierre de Coubertin (2000) called "moral betterment and social peace, as well as physical development" (537), it is to invest in efforts to buttress long-term programs that mitigate against ill-health and poor levels of fitness, most especially in cultures and communities negatively and differentially impacted by global health crises.

As the worst of the Covid-19 pandemic passes, we will no doubt emerge, as the author Katherine Anne Porter (1939) puts it, into the "dead cold light of tomorrow" (264). Historically, efforts to construct effective international arrangements and agreements typically emerge in the aftermath of war, crisis, and turmoil. How in a world perched precipitously between competition and cooperation—competition between the world's leading powers and the need for a zero-sum cooperation between them—we will be able to maintain a credible balance will be one of the great challenges for the post-pandemic era (Brands and Gavin 2020), a challenge for which the Olympics are, in both practice and principle, ideally suited. In other words, the Olympic and Paralympic Movements have a salient role to play in the mitigation of future pandemics and can serve as a salve for the global political roiling and the roll back of globalization that appears to threaten the very international harmony that the Olympics have always strived to create.

REFERENCES

Applebaum, Anne. 2020. "The People in Charge See an Opportunity." *The Atlantic*, March 23, 2020. https://www.theatlantic.com/ideas/archive/2020/03/when-disease-comes-leaders-grab-more-power/608560/

Ash, Timothy Garton. 2020. "The U.S. and China Are Entering a New Cold War: Where Does That Leave the Rest of Us?" *The Guardian*, June 20, 2020. https://www.theguardian.com/commentisfree/2020/jun/20/us-china-cold-war-liberal-de.

Bach, Richard. 2020. "IOC President Bach Writes to Olympic Movement: Olympism and Corona." *TAGS Olympic News, IOC News*, April 29, 2000. https://www.olympic.org/news/ioc-president-bach-writes-to-olympic-movement-olympism-corona.

Bader, Jeffrey. 2018. *U.S.-China Relations: Is It Time to End the Engagement?* Washington, D.C..: Brookings Institute, September 2018. https://www.brookings.edu/wp-content/uploads/2018/09/FP_20180925_us_china_relations.pdf.

Bobbitt, Philip. 2020. Future Scenarios: "We Are All Failed States, Now." In *COVID-19 and World Order: The Future of Conflict, Competition, and Cooperation*, edited by Hal Brands and Francis J. Gavin, 56-71. Baltimore: Johns Hopkins Press.

Brands, Hal, Feaver, Peter, and William Imboden. 2020. "Maybe It Won't Be So Bad: A Modestly Optimistic Take on COVID and World Order." In *COVID-19 and World Order: The Future of Conflict, Competition, and Cooperation*, edited by Hal Brands and Francis J. Gavin, 297-315. Baltimore: Johns Hopkins Press.

Brands, Hal, and Francis J. Gavin. 2020. "COVID-19 and World Order." In *COVID-19 and World Order: The Future of Conflict, Competition, and Cooperation*, edited by Hal Brands and Francis J. Gavin, 2-20. Baltimore: Johns Hopkins Press.

Brownell, Susan. 2021. "Olympic Games, China and Human Rights." Keynote speech delivered at Culture COVID Controversy: Tokyo 2020 Beijing 2022: An Olympic Symposium, Massachusetts Institute of Technology, Boston, Massachusetts, May 5, 2021.

Campbell, Kurt M., and Rush Doshi. 2020. "The Coronavirus Could Reshape Global Order." *Foreign Affairs*, March 18, 2020. https://www.cnas.org/publications/commentary/the-coronavirus-could-reshape-global-order.

Coubertin, Pierre de. 2000. *Olympism: Selected Writings*. Edited by Norbert Müller. Lausanne: International Olympic Committee.

Daniels, Ronald J. 2020. "Foreword." In *COVID-19 and World Order: The Future of Conflict, Competition, and Cooperation*, edited by Hal Brands and Francis J. Gavin, ix-xii. Baltimore: Johns Hopkins Press.

Fukuyama, Francis. 2020. "The Pandemic and Political Order." *Foreign Affairs*, July/August, 2020. https://www.foreignaffairs.com/articles/world/2020-06-09/pandemic-and-policial-order.

Galbraith, John Kenneth. 1958. *The Affluent Society*. Boston: Houghton Mifflin.

Gates, Bill. 2015. "The Next Outbreak? We're Not Ready." TED2015. https://www.ted.com/talks/bill_gates_the_next_outbreak_we_re_not_ready/transcript?language=en.

Gilbert, Gwendolyn L. 2020. "SARS, MERS, and COVID-19—New Threats: Old Lessons." *International Journal of Epidemiology* 49 (3): 726-728.

Greene, Jeremy A., and Dora Vargha. 2020. "Ends of Epidemics." In *COVID-19 and World Order: The Future of Conflict, Competition*, and Cooperation, edited by Hal Brands and Francis J. Gavin, 23-39. Baltimore: Johns Hopkins Press.

Haass, Richard. 2020. "The Pandemic Will Accelerate History Rather Than Reshape It." *Foreign Affairs*, April 7, 2020. https://www.foreignaffairs.com/articles/united-states/2020-04-07/pandemic-will-accelerate-history-rather-reshape-it.

Hobbes, Thomas. (2005) [1651]. *Leviathan*. Edited by A. P. Martinich. Toronto: Broadview Press.

Ikenberry, G. John. 2020. "The Next Liberal Order." *Foreign Affairs*, July/August 2020. https://www.foreignaffairs.com/articles/united-states/2020-06-09/next-liberal-order.

International Olympic Committee. 2020a. *Olympic Charter*. Lausanne: International Olympic Committee. https://olympics.com/ioc/olympic-charter.

---. 2020b. "Olympic Agenda 2020: 20 + 20 Recommendations." Lausanne: International Olympic Committee. https://olympics.com/ioc/olympic-agenda-2020.

---. 2021. "Olympic Agenda 2020+5: 15 Recommendations." Lausanne: International Olympic Committee. https://olympics.com/ioc/news/ioc-session-approves-olympic-agenda-2020-5-as-the-strategic-roadmap-to-2025.

"IOC's Bach Asked to Intervene in Tokyo Olympic Labor Dispute." *USA Today*, November 22, 2019. http://www.usatoday.com/story/sports/olympics/2019/11/22/iocs-bach-asked-to-intervene-in-tokyo-olympic-labor dispute.html

"Joint Statement from the International Olympic Committee and the Tokyo 2020 Organizing Committee," March 24, 2020. https://olympics.com/ioc/news/joint-statement-from-the-international-olympic-committee-and-the-tokyo-2020-organising-committee

Kahn, Jeffrey P., Mastroianni, Anna C., and Sridhar Venkatapuram. 2020. "Bioethics in a Post-CIVID World: Time for Future-Facing Global Health Ethics." In *COVID-19 and World Order: The Future of Conflict, Competition, and Cooperation*, edited by Hal Brands and Francis J. Gavin, 114-134. Baltimore: Johns Hopkins Press.

Ki-Moon, Ban. 2009. Keynote address delivered at the 2009 Olympic Congress, Copenhagen Denmark, October 3, 2029. https://www.un.org/sg/en/content/sg/speeches/2009-10-03/keynote-address-xiii-olympic-congress.

Lenskyj, Helen Jefferson. 2014. *Sexual Diversity and the Sochi 2014 Olympics: No More Rainbows*. London: Palgrave.

Lipsky, John. 2020. "Prospects for the United States' Post-COVID-19 Policies: Strengthening the G20 Leaders Process." In *COVID-19 and World Order: The Future of Conflict, Competition, and Cooperation*, edited by Hal Brands and Francis J. Gavin, 204-222. Baltimore: Johns Hopkins Press.

Macron, Emmanuel. 2020. "Addresse aux Français." June 14, 2020. https://www.elysee.fr/emmanuel-macron/2020/06/14/adresse-aux-francais-14-juin-2020.

Mahbubani, Kishore. 2020. "How China Could Win Over the Post-Coronavirus World and Leave the U.S. Behind." *Marketwatch*, April 18, 2020. https://www.marketwatch.com/story/how-china-could-win-over-the-post-coronavirus-world-and-leave-the-us-behind-2020-04-14.

Mahler, Daniel Gerszon. 2020. *World Bank*, June 8, 2020. https://blogs.worldbank.org/opendata/updated-estimates-impact-covid-19-global-poverty.

Mather, Victor. 2018. "North and South Korea Plan to Jointly Bid on 2032 Summer Olympics." *New York Times*, September 19, 2018. https://www.nytimes.com/2018/09/19/sports/olympics/north-south-korea-olympics.html.

McTague, Tom. 2020. "The Pandemic's Geopolitical Aftershocks Are Coming." *The Atlantic*, May 18, 2020. https://theatlantic.com/international/archive/2020/05/coronavirus-pandemic-second-wave-geopolitics-instability/611668/.

Palmer, Alex. 2021. "The Man Behind China's Aggressive New Voice." *New York Times Magazine*, July 7, 2021. https://www.nytimes.com/2021/07/07/magazine/china-diplomacy-twitter-zhao-lijian.html.

Pickering, Thomas, and Atman Trivedi. 2020. "The International Order Didn't Fail the Pandemic Alone." *Foreign Affairs*, May 14, 2020. https://www.foreignaffairs.com/articles/world/2020-05-14/international-order-didnt-fail-pandemic-alone

Porter, Katherine Anne. 1939. *Pale Horse, Pale Rider*. New York: The Modern Library.

Roche, Lisa Riley. 2021. "Mitt Romney Calls for Economic, Diplomatic Boycott of Beijing Olympics." *Deseret News*, March 15, 2021. https://www.deseret.com/utah2021/3/15/22331714/mitt-romney-calls-for-economic-diplomatic-boycott-of-beijing-olympics.html.

Romney, Mitt. 2021. "The Right Way to Boycott the Beijing Olympics." *New York Times*, March 15, 2021. https://www.nytimes.com/2021/03/15/opinion/politics/beijing-olympics-mitt-romney.html.

Rudd, Kevin. 2020. "The Coming Post-COVID Anarchy." *Foreign Affairs*, May 6, 2020. https://connections-qj.org/article/coming-post-covid-anarchy-pandemic-bodes-ill-both-american-and-chinese-power-and-global.

Rutkow, Lainie. 2020. "Origins of the COVID-19 Pandemic and the Path Forward: A Global Public Health Policy Perspective." In *COVID-19 and World Order: The Future of Conflict, Competition, and Cooperation*, edited by Hal Brands and Francis J. Gavin, 93-113. Baltimore: Johns Hopkins Press.

Schake, Kori. 2021. "Building a More Globalized Order." In *COVID-19 and World Order: The Future of Conflict, Competition, and Cooperation*, edited by Hal Brands and Francis J. Gavin, 331-347. Baltimore: Johns Hopkins Press.

Shriver, Timothy. 2021. "The COVID-19 Pandemic Highlights Why Equal Access to Healthcare Is Imperative." *Washington Post*, January 18, 2021. https://www.specialolympics.org/stories/news/the-covid-19-pandemic-highlights-why-equal-access-to-healthcare-is-imperative.

Sontag, Susan. 1978. "Illness as Metaphor." *New York Review of Books*, January 26, 1978. https://www.nybooks.com/articles/1978/01/26/illness-as-metaphor.

Summers, Lawrence. 2020. "Covid-19 Looks Like a Hinge in History." *Financial Times*, May 14, 2020. htttps://www.ft.com/content/de643ae8-9527-11ea-899a-f62a20d54625

Sumner, Andy, Hoy, Chris, and Eduardo Ortiz-Juarez. 2020. "Estimates of the Impact of COVID-19 on Global Poverty." *WIDER Working Paper 2020/43*. Helsinki: UNU-WIDER. https://wider.unu.edu/publication/estimates-impact-covid-19-global-poverty.

Taleb, Nassim Nicholas. 2012. *Antifragile: Things That Gain from Disorder*. New York: Random House.

"Tokyo 2020 Should Become a Manifestation of Human Resilience." 2021. *Journal of Olympic History*, 29 (1): 3-6.

Wagg, Simon, and David Andrews eds. 2012. *East Plays West: Sport and the Cold War*. London: Routledge.

World Health Organization. 2020. COVID-19 Virtual Press Conference, April 3, 2020. https://www.who.int/docs/default-source/documents/covid-19-virtual-press-conference-transcript-3-april-2020.pdf?sfvrsn=43e2f2f3_6.

Zakaria, Fareed. 2020. *Ten Lessons for a Post-Pandemic World*. New York: W. W. Norton.

Chapter 8

Is the Olympic Values Education Programme (OVEP) Relevant in a Post-Covid-19 World?

Hilla Davidov

Introduction

In facing the current Covid-19 pandemic, social dynamics have been challenged by governmental restrictions around the world. The experience of being limited by sanitary containment complemented by the onslaught of the pandemic has been dramatic for, among others, individuals who are used to sporting activities. The pandemic forced individuals and whole societies into altered lifestyles and patterns. Social interaction became increasingly digitized and educational management models were equally affected. As such, this study looks at Israel and how social isolation restrictions have caused its education system to adopt distance learning and, as a result, the use of new learning technologies as compulsory tools in the classroom.

Prior to the Covid-19 pandemic, most physical education (PE) classes were held outdoors or in sports halls. The inherent nature of PE requires movement, close proximity, and activity in groups or teams. Thus, PE programs as they are currently constituted and delivered in schools do not allow for incorporating restrictive social distancing measures. Therefore, and in order to be compliant, PE faces many challenges. However, this also creates opportunity for innovation in the field, which is especially salient for curriculum development.

For example, the Olympic Values Education Programme (OVEP) curriculum incorporates characteristics of current PE pedagogy and has potential for use in schools. However, the program needs to be responsive to events such as the Covid-19 pandemic and the new social reality that includes online learning. It is an inspiring challenge for Olympic Education to address the changes caused by the pandemic in sport settings. Therefore, it is beneficial to analyze how PE in general and Olympic Education in particular, can remain relevant in the post-

Covide-19 future and contribute to the Olympic Agenda 2020,[1] as well as the UN global education agenda.[2]

Background and Aims

Towards the end of February 2020, Covid-19 broke out in Israel. In March and early April 2020, schools were closed and teaching took place remotely. During April and until the end of the school year, schools were gradually reopened but with restrictions as directed by the Ministry of Health. In preparation for the start of the next school year in September 2020, the Ministry of Education was preparing for an adapted format for teaching and learning in schools, a format that combined distance learning with in person instruction. Moreover, it was clear that the situation was dynamic and there was a possibility that schools would once again have to close their gates in accordance with the state of the epidemic and health guidelines (Ratner et al. 2020, 3).

A potential positive outcome of the pandemic has been greater access to online educational platforms for participants where these facilities exist. In the majority of schools, lectures have been rapidly converted from face-to-face to online, using several platforms such as Zoom, Skype, and Google Meet (Chatziralli et al. 2021, 1464).

Specific guidelines were published for PE teachers that emphasized the opportunity of this crisis to deepen and enrich students with PE knowledge; sports sciences and training principles; increase awareness of the importance of engaging in physical activity; and teach nutrition and impart values through physical activity and various sports games. It was noted that the constraint of distance learning created an opportunity for innovative learning in which students are active partners and independent learners who develop personal responsibility and ability, and thus outlined a significant way to implement the overarching goal of PE - active and healthy lifestyle management (Israel Ministry of Education 2020, 1).

Using new technologies in PE classes can improve their quality, enriching students' experiences by generating enjoyable experiences with the ultimate goal of producing habits of physical sports practice that will last a lifetime. This research area has great potential for sports practice because it can help teachers improve the quality of PE classes by presenting practical experiences and new ways of using these technologies in the classroom, as well as collecting reports of the benefits technologies present for students and establishing guidelines and

---

[1] Olympic Agenda 2020 is a set of forty detailed recommendations with the overarching goal to safeguard the Olympic values and strengthen the role of sport in society.
[2] Ambitions for education are essentially captured in Sustainable Development Goal 4 (SDG 4) of the 2030 Agenda, which aims to "ensure inclusive and equitable quality education and promote lifelong learning opportunities for all" by 2030.

advice for their use in the classroom. This may encourage more PE teachers to introduce these technologies, as well as to ensure they are used correctly by PE teachers to generate the expected benefits (Calabuig-Moreno et al. 2020, 20).

The aim of this study is to provide recommendations for improving PE teachers' preparedness for moving to online learning based on experiences during the Covid-19 pandemic. This study seeks to understand how teachers of different experience levels coped with and adapted to the move to online learning during Covid-19. Further, it examines the role and importance of teaching values through PE from the teachers' perspectives. Finally, aims to show how OVEP may be adapted to meet both challenges faced during Covid-19 and support the delivery of values-based education during both emergency and non-emergency periods. The findings may support teachers and decision-makers in Israel in making informed decisions towards the transition to distance learning, plan basic materials to help revitalize online PE classes in the future, and keep Olympic education relevant in a post Covid-19 world.

Olympic Values Education Programme (OVEP)

The Olympic Movement spreads the fundamental principles of Olympism through universal and permanent activity. According to the founder of the modern Olympics, Pierre de Coubertin, the modern Olympic Games should be more than an event taking every four years. Coubertin regarded the Olympic Games as a framework for promoting the deeper significance of Olympic ideas and their educational possibilities (Wassong 2006, 222). His views remain significant for Olympism, especially his view of sport as a way of life and its role in building a structural sports component into children's education. The goal of the Olympic Movement is to contribute to building a peaceful and better world by educating youth through sport practiced in the Olympic spirit, which requires mutual understanding with a spirit of friendship, solidarity, and fair play (IOC 2020, 11, 15).

Olympism is not without its critiques. Some have exposed the mythology surrounding idealistic Olympic education by focusing on the generally unquestioned value of Olympism as a key tool in character-building and moral education (Lenskyj 2012, 265). For some, it is difficult to imagine how an educational initiative that has its roots in a corrupt system - the Olympic industry would be considered capable of imparting moral lessons of any kind (Lenskyj 2012, 266). Strong concerns have also been expressed with regards to the overarching stakeholder hierarchies that enable Olympic organizers to capitalize on school spaces, the use of Olympic education as a proxy that legitimizes corporate stakeholders' educational presence, the privileging of an immutable Western-values model, and the inherent bias towards pro-sport and pro-Olympic perspectives (Lenskyj 2012, 265).

OVEP, however, is a series of learning resources created by the International Olympic Committee (IOC 2017, 10). Its original purpose was to provide an education resource for developing nations who lacked the funding or human resources to develop their own Olympism-based education materials (Binder 2012, 295). Taking into account the IOC's social responsibility and the focus on sport as a vehicle to deliver the message, OVEP was developed to further the IOC's global youth strategy. Olympic sport traditions and their values are used as the backdrop for the IOC's values-based teaching and learning opportunities. OVEP integrates sport and physical activity within a cultural and educational framework, and is in line with the United Nations General Assembly declaration of the Decade of Education for Sustainable Development (DESD 2005-2014) (U.S. Sports Academy 2011, 2). Today, Olympic education programs are implemented in many countries around the world. How it is integrated within education varies from country to country but are delivered, in most cases, through PE (Georgiadis 2010, 6715). OVEP has been delivered in fifty-seven countries, though not all of them using the full program and some are counted even if only using an OVEP demonstration.

The challenge of using sport and physical activity to provide a context for learning about life is how to realize these aims. The legacy of Olympic education, particularly at the elementary and middle school age level could serve as a bridge between the striving for excellence by elite athletes and the dreams of young children jumping over a school bench (Binder 2010, 16). OVEP uses the context of Olympic sports and core principles of Olympism to encourage participation in values-based learning and to assume the responsibilities of good citizenship (IOC 2021).

Physical activity and sport have significant benefits for health, well-being and youth development. Sport can be a tool for outcomes such as peace, holistic education, and social development. Recognizing the potential of sport as an educational and communication tool, OVEP was designed to inspire and allow young people to experience life/humanistic values such as excellence, respect, and friendship (IOC 2018, 1).

Distance Learning and Use of Technology in PE Due to Covid-19

Throughout the Covid-19 pandemic, many people found themselves in quarantines and working and studying from home (Bergdahl and Nouri 2020, 1). Many governments around the world temporarily closed educational institutions in an attempt to contain the spread of the virus, implementing a shift into distance learning. By April 22, 2020, 172 countries (as of February 28, 2021) had made country-wide decisions to close schools, impacting 1,484,712,787 learners (UNESCO 2021).

Many countries have reconsidered technology-based teaching, in which online platforms have a major role for teaching in every field of study. It is critical for the educational sector to have preparedness plans to ensure safe and functional education in times of crisis, especially where distancing measures may be required. Therefore, decision makers should plan accordingly (Klaiman et al. 2011, 10) and consider the how PE activities can be appropriately carried out in the future (Savagpun 2020, 35).

In many studies preceding Covid-19, the possibility of online classes was examined as a part of future education, in that online classes can provide highly efficient and diverse elective classes to self-directed students. PE centers on physical activity and is clearly distinct from general knowledge-based subjects. Therefore, online PE classes require special preparation and operation. Currently, as in-person school attendance and online classes are occurring in tandem around the world, there is a need to examine whether online PE classes are being held and conveying the values of PE appropriately (Hyun-Chul and Wi-Young 2020, 2). Teachers need to know how to operate and lead their students, while also not to be left behind by technology that is embedded in other fields of knowledge (Zaltsman 2017, 39). Therefore, an expansion and planning of technology-based teaching will be necessary following Covid-19.

Addressing Different Learning Situations through Tailored Pedagogy

There is a need to adapt pedagogical approaches to various constraints and conditions. This research is focused on the blended learning approach. This approach may provide solutions to a number of different learning situations, including routine mode (without special restrictions), emergency mode (when significant constraints exist and adjustments are required), and intermediate mode (when partial restrictions are in order). Understanding various learning situations will make it possible to plan the blended learning processes that are tailored, quality-oriented and maintain an educational continuum.

In defining the blended learning approach, there is a need to define three learning approaches and the differences between them: distance learning (physical/geographic distance between the learner and teacher), online learning (learning that takes place partially or entirely via the Internet), and blended learning (mixture of face to face and online learning).

There are interactions between the three learning approaches: Distance learning and online learning can be a component of blended learning; online learning can be a component of distance learning (Tsviran and Morgenstern 2020, 15).

Methodology

Study Participants

Survey participants were 197 PE teachers in Israel, drawn from those were participating in an "Optimal distance learning" seminar, as well as PE teachers recruited through social media. Participation was based on voluntary self-selection. All study participants were required to provide informed consent before participating and all survey responses were anonymized. The average age was 43.644 years, with a range of 23 to 65 years, with 67.5% female and 32.5% male participants. Table 1.1 shows the teaching experience in years and the average age related to teaching years. Table 1.2 shows school level and Table 1.3 shows school sector.

Table 1.1: Teaching experience in years and average age

Years	Teachers	%	Average age
1-4	21	10.7	32.14
5-10	45	22.8	36.48
11-15	37	18.8	40.43
16-20	19	9.6	44.157
21-25	30	15.2	48.06
26-30	25	12.7	53.44
30+	20	10.2	58.4

Source: Author

Table 1.2: School Level

School level	Teachers	%
Elementary	114	57.9
Middle	34	17.3
High school	49	24.9

Source: Author

Table 1.3: School Sector

School level	Teachers	%
Elementary	114	57.9
Middle	34	17.3
High school	49	24.9

Source: Author

Study Design

An online questionnaire was used consisting of thirty-eight questions grouped into five main sections: 1) Demographics, 2) PE teachers' readiness for delivering distance learning, 3) teachers' perceived coping, 4) adaptation to change (using ADAPTA-10 [Pérez-Fuentes et al. 2020 1-12], and 5) familiarity and use of OVEP before and during the Covid-19. There was one question regarding the PE teachers' level of satisfaction with distance learning in PE classes and an additional open question for any other remarks.

Results

PE Teachers' Readiness for Delivering Distance Learning

In this section, the teachers were asked whether before or during Covid-19, they participated in training regarding distance learning and / or operating technological tools. Before Covid-19, seventy-three teachers (37.06%) participated and one hundred and twenty-four (62.94%) did not participate. During Covid-19 one hundred and sixty-six teachers (84.26%) participated and thirty-one (15.74%) did not participate, as shown in Figure 1.

The teachers were asked whether before Covid-19 they had been exposed to digital tools for distance learning. Forty-four (22.3%) responded not at all, seventy-seven (39.1%) to a small extent, fifty-nine (29.9%) moderate extent, and only seventeen (8.6%) were to large extent, as shown in Figure 2. The teachers were asked if they thought the use of technological tools improves the quality of teaching in PE. Six (3%) responded not at all, thirty-three (16.8%) small extent, seventy-two (36.5%) moderate extent and only eighty-six (43.7%) were large extent, as shown in Figure 3.

were asked if they thought the use of technological tools improves the quality of teaching in PE. Six (3%) responded not at all, thirty-three (16.8%) small extent, seventy-two (36.5%) moderate extent and only eighty-six (43.7%) were large extent, as shown in Figure 3.

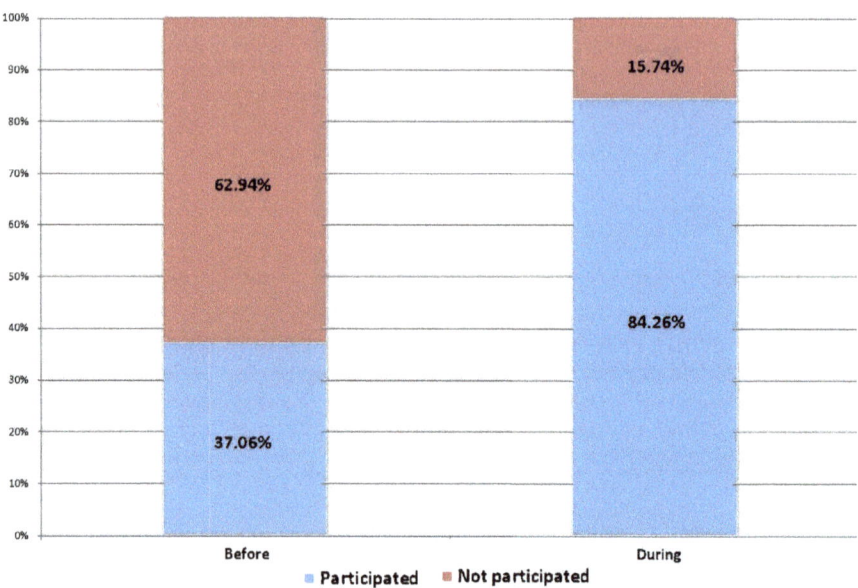

Figure 1: Distance learning and/or operating technological tools training Before and During Covid-19
Source: Author

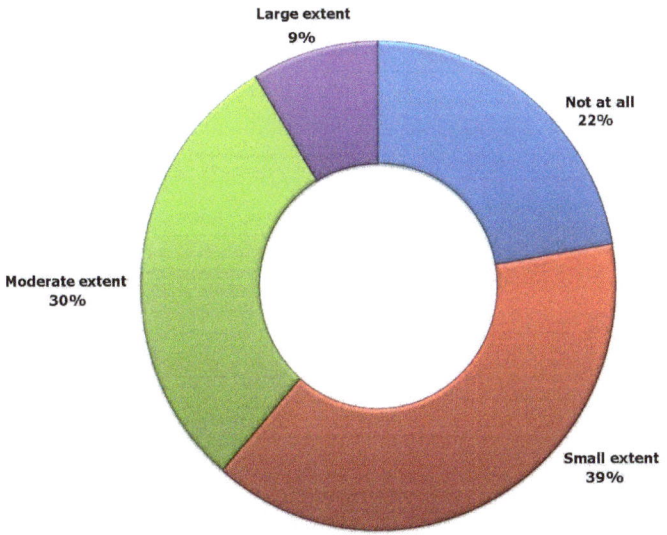

Figure 2: Exposure to digital tools for distance learning before Covid-19
Source: Author

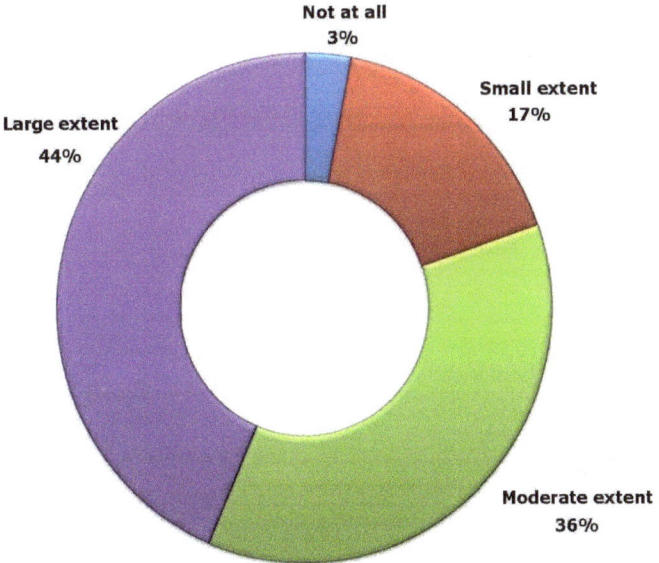

Figure 3: Technological tools improves the quality of teaching in physical education.
Source: Author

Teacher's Perceived Coping

In this section the teachers were asked to rate their perceived coping with the transition to distance learning. Factor analysis was used in order to have a data reduction (dimension reduction factor), by finding what unites the eighteen statements. In this way, it was possible to analyze on the dimension level (not on an individual statement level). By using a Correlation Matrix four factors explained 58.992% of the variance, as shown in table 1.4.

Table 1.4: Principal component analysis Rotation Method Varimax with Kaiser Normalization

Student-Teacher interaction (17.664%) Reliability Cronbach's Alpha 0.791		Teacher's Adaptation (14.565%) Reliability Cronbach's Alpha 0.797		Teaching methods (14.202%) Reliability Cronbach's Alpha 0.731		Class Management (12.560%) Reliability Cronbach's Alpha 0.720	
9	0.691						
4	0.677						
5	0.608						
2	0.567						
7	0.563						
16	0.547						
		18	0.782				
		15	0.762				
		17	0.682				
		14	0.595				
				1	0.757		
				3	0.575		
				8	0.520		
				6	0.507		
						12	0.763
						11	0.600
						13	0.585
						10	0.567

Source: Author

Adaptation to Change, ADAPTA-10

The Adaptation to Change Questionnaire, ADAPTA-10, is a short instrument that enables finding out the individual's ability to adjust to new demands based on two dimensions: emotional (items 1-5) and cognitive-behavioral (items 6-10). The mean of all items in each dimension was: emotion=3.735, with reliability Cronbach's Alpha 0.774; and cognitive-behavioral=3.868, with reliability Cronbach's Alpha 0.855. Pearson's correlations were computed among two dimensions: emotional and cognitive-behavioral of the adaptation to change (ADAPTA-10) and four factors of the teachers' perceived coping (student-teacher interaction, teachers' adaptation, teaching methods and class management), as shown in Table 1.5. No significant correlation was found between the two dimensions, emotional and cognitive-behavioral [$r (197) = .04$, $p=.58$], which indicates they are independent of each other. A significant correlation was found between the emotion dimension and the student-teacher interaction, teachers' adaptation, and class management. A strong correlation was found between the four factors between themselves. That is, the defined factors are independent and the correlation between them is significant. For example between teachers' adaptation and student-teacher interaction [$r (197) = .534$, $p < .001$]; and teaching methods [$r (197) = .540$, $p < .001$] and class management [$r (197) = .506$, $p < .001$]. Also between student-teacher interaction and teaching methods [$r (197) = .663$, $p < .001$]; and student-teacher interaction and class management [$r (197) = .597$, $p < .001$].

Table 1.5: Pearson correlation between Adaptation to change and Teacher's perceived coping.

Variable	Cognition	Student-Teacher interaction	Teacher's Adaptation	Teaching methods	Class Management
Emotional ADAPTA	0.040	.222*	.291**	.134	.151*
Cognitive ADAPTA	-	-.065	-.009	.017	-.040
Student-Teacher interaction	-	-	.534**	.663**	.597**
Teacher's Adaptation	-	-	-	.540**	.506**
Teaching methods	-	-	-	-	.555**
Class Management	-	-	-	-	-

Correlation is significant at the 0.01 level (2-tailed).
Correlation is significant at the 0.05 level (2-tailed).

Source: Author

Familiarity and Use of OVEP

In this section the teachers were asked about their familiarity with OVEP, its use, and their insights regarding its efficiency. Eighty (40.6%) teachers were not familiar at all with the Olympism project (OVEP), sixty-two (31.5%) knew little about the program, thirty-eight (19.3%) knew somewhat, and only seventeen (8.6%) knew a lot about the program. One hundred forty (71.1%) teachers reported that they were using a lot of sport to teach values and life skills; forty-three (21.8%) somewhat, thirteen (6.6%) little, and only one (0.5%) not at all. Fifty-three (26.9%) teachers reported that during Covid-19 they were able to teach a lot values and life skill, although it was by distance learning. Eighty-one (41.1%) responded somewhat; fifty-one (25.9%) a little, and twelve (6.1%) not at all. One hundred fifty-two (77.2%) teachers thought using sport as a tool for teaching values and life skills was significant in a post-Covid-19 world. Thirty (15.2%) responded somewhat, fourteen (7.1%) a little, and only one (0.5%) not at all. Regarding the statement "Teaching values and life skills in PE classes is equally effective in distance learning," forty-three (21.8%) teachers answered a lot, eighty-one (41.1%) somewhat, forty-eight (24.4%) a little, and twenty-five (12.7%) not at all, as shown in Figure 4.

One-way multiple comparison variance analysis was computed between teachers' experience and teacher's perceived coping, adaptation to change (ADAPTA-10), and familiarity and use of OVEP (statements 2-5), as shown in Table 1.6. The significance test indicated that there was variance between the groups. The Post Hoc Tukey's HSD (honestly significant difference) test indicated a variance between the senior teachers who had more years of experience and the teachers who were less experienced. The cognitive adaptation average was higher as teaching experience was lower. For example, with ten years teaching experience, the cognitive adaptation average was the highest, 4.04. It is shown that the emotional adaptation average was higher as teaching experience was higher too. For example, thirty or more years teaching experience the emotional adaptation average was the highest, 4.07. Looking at the teachers' perceived coping and teacher experience, the student-teacher interaction average and class management were higher among the up to ten years teaching experience group (3.06 and 3.06), while the teachers' adaptation average was higher among the thirty or more years teaching experience group (3.14). In teaching methods there was no difference among the teaching experience years. No significant difference was found between number of teaching experience years and the OVEP statements.

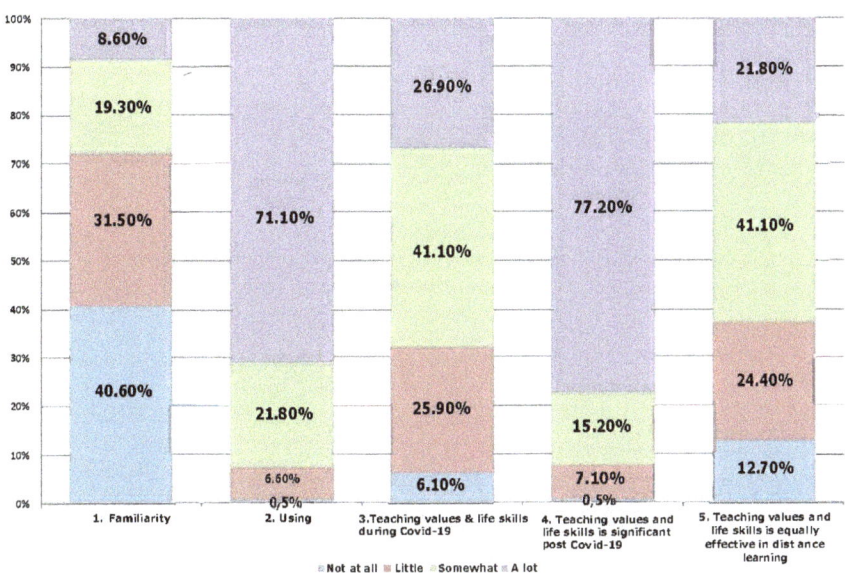

Figure 4: Teachers' familiarity with OVEP, use, and their insights regarding its efficiency
Source: Author

A significant correlation was found among teachers who reported "not at all," to their perceived coping of adaptation (Mean: 2.47) and teaching methods (Mean: 2.32), which were the lowest, as shown in table 1.7. A Spearman's correlation was run to determine the relationship with a Multiple Comparison between Teacher's perceived coping, adaptation to change (ADAPTA-10) and the questions regarding the familiarity and use of OVEP, as shown in Table 1.8.

Regarding the statement. "Teaching values and life skills in PE classes is equally effective in distance learning," there was a weak correlation between those who answered "not at all" and those who reported they did not use different teaching methods, such as digital tools (=.206, n=197, $p < .001$), and their adaptation to the changes (=.162, n=197, $p < .001$). There was a weak correlation between their OVEP statement "Using sport as a tool for teaching values and life skills is significant a lot in the post COVID world" and their cognitive adaptation (=.236, n=197, $p < .001$). There was a moderate correlation between those teachers who reported that during Covid-19 they had been able to teach a lot of values and life skill and the statement that teaching values and life skills in PE classes is equally effective in distance learning (= .407, n=197, $p < .001$).

PE Teachers' Level of Satisfaction with Distance Learning

Thirteen (6.6%) teachers were very satisfied with teaching in distance learning, while ninety-one (46.2%) were satisfied, forty-nine (24.9%) neither satisfied nor dissatisfied, and thirty-two (16.2%) somewhat dissatisfied, and twelve (6.1%) were very dissatisfied, as shown in Figure 5.

Table 1.6: Descriptive & Inferential Statistics regarding the research variables: Teachers' experience, teacher's perceived coping, adaptation to change (ADAPTA-10), and familiarity and use of OVEP

Teacher's experience	Mean				Sig
	Till 10 years 66 Teachers	Till 20 years 56 Teachers	Till 30 years 55 Teachers	30+ 20 Teachers	
Student-Teacher interaction	3.06 (Std. Deviation 0.87)	2.75 (Std. Deviation 0.71)	2.69 (Std. Deviation 0.73)	2.85 (Std. Deviation 0.81)	0.055
Teacher's Adaptation	2.95 (Std. Deviation 0.95)	2.71 (Std. Deviation 0.69)	2.86 (Std. Deviation 0.75)	3.14 (Std. Deviation 0.88)	0.183
Teaching methods	2.79 (Std. Deviation 0.84)	2.80 (Std. Deviation 0.70)	2.72 (Std. Deviation 0.79)	2.74 (Std. Deviation 0.83)	0.939
Class Management	3.06 (Std. Deviation 0.87)	2.75 (Std. Deviation 0.71)	2.69 (Std. Deviation 0.73)	2.85 (Std. Deviation 0.81)	0.055
Cognitive ADAPTA	4.04 (Std. Deviation 0.74)	3.91 (Std. Deviation 0.71)	3.77 (Std. Deviation 0.77)	3.47 (Std. Deviation 1.00)	0.025
Emotional ADAPTA	3.61 (Std. Deviation 0.89)	3.65 (Std. Deviation 0.84)	3.86 (Std. Deviation 0.66)	4.07 (Std. Deviation 0.67)	0.066
OVEP-Q2	2.64 (Std. Deviation 0.57)	2.55 (Std. Deviation 0.78)	2.73 (Std. Deviation 0.49)	2.60 (Std. Deviation 0.68)	0.539
OVEP-Q3	1.89 (Std. Deviation 0.90)	1.93 (Std. Deviation 0.89)	1.85 (Std. Deviation 0.87)	1.85 (Std. Deviation 0.81)	0.971
OVEP-Q4	2.70 (Std. Deviation 0.63)	2.73 (Std. Deviation 0.59)	2.65 (Std. Deviation 0.64)	2.65 (Std. Deviation 0.67)	0.915
OVEP-Q5	1.67 (Std. Deviation 1.01)	1.70 (Std. Deviation 0.95)	1.82 (Std. Deviation 0.94)	1.70 (Std. Deviation 0.73)	0.841

* Post Hoc =Tukey Btukey Alpha (0.05)

Source: Author

Table 1.7: The correlation between, teacher's perceived copings to their statement regarding the effectiveness in distance learning of teaching values and life skills in physical education classes.

Teacher's experience	OVEP - Statement no.5 Mean Teaching values and life skills in physical education classes is equally effective in distance learning.					Sig
	Not at all	Little	Somewhat	A lot	Total	
Student-Teacher interaction	2.65 (Std. Deviation 0.84)	2.74 (Std. Deviation 0.78)	2.91 (Std. Deviation 0.81)	2.95 (Std. Deviation 0.74)	2.85 (Std. Deviation 0.79)	0.297
Teacher's Adaptation	2.47 (Std. Deviation 0.70)	2.77 (Std. Deviation 0.82)	3.04 (Std. Deviation 0.79)	2.93 (Std. Deviation 0.87)	2.88 (Std. Deviation 0.82)	0.016
Teaching methods	2.32 (Std. Deviation 0.78)	2.72 (Std. Deviation 0.71)	2.82 (Std. Deviation 0.79)	2.97 (Std. Deviation 0.76)	2.77 (Std. Deviation 0.78)	0.008
Class Management	2.65 (Std. Deviation 0.84)	2.74 (Std. Deviation 0.78)	2.91 (Std. Deviation 0.81)	2.95 (Std. Deviation 0.74)	2.85 (Std. Deviation 0.79)	0.297
Cognitive ADAPTA	3.98 (Std. Deviation 0.55)	3.80 (Std. Deviation 0.78)	3.87 (Std. Deviation 0.79)	3.87 (Std. Deviation 0.88)	3.87 (Std. Deviation 0.78)	0.834
Emotional ADAPTA	3.62 (Std. Deviation 1.04)	3.54 (Std. Deviation 0.82)	3.82 (Std. Deviation 0.78)	3.86 (Std. Deviation 0.62)	3.74 (Std. Deviation 0.80)	0.143
No.	25	48	81	43	197	0.403

* The mean difference is significant at the 0.05 level.

Source: Author

Table 1.8: Spearman correlation between Adaptation to change and the familiarity and use of OVEP

	Age	PC interaction	PC Adaptation	PC Methods	PC Management	Adp cognition	Adp emotion	OVEP 3	OVEP 4	OVEP 5
Age Sig	1.000	-0.139	0.052	-0.093	-0.139	-.142*	.167*	0.010	0.015	0.033
		0.051	0.468	0.194	0.051	0.047	0.019	0.892	0.835	0.643
Student-Teacher interaction Sig.		1.000	.469**	.511**	1.000**	0.020	0.126	0.123	-0.094	0.126
		-	0.000	0.000		0.782	0.079	0.084	0.187	0.077
Teacher's Adaptation Sig.		-	1.000	.497**	.469**	0.005	.270**	0.054	-0.114	.162*
		-	-	0.000	0.000	0.940	0.000	0.452	0.112	0.023
Teaching methods Sig.		-	-	1.000	.511**	0.003	0.121	.163*	-0.139	.206**
		-	-	-	0.000	0.966	0.092	0.022	0.051	0.004
Class Management Sig.		-	-	-	1.000	0.020	0.126	0.123	-0.094	0.126
		-	-	-	-	0.782	0.079	0.084	0.187	0.077
Cognition Adaptation Sig.		-	-	-	-	1.000	0.102	0.031	.236**	-0.008
		-	-	-	-	-	0.155	0.663	0.001	0.912
Emotional Adaptation Sig.		-	-	-	-	-	1.000	0.100	0.012	0.106
		-	-	-	-	-	-	0.161	0.866	0.137
OVEP3: teachers who reported that during Covid-19 they have been able to teach a lot values and life skill Sig.		-	-	-	-	-	-	1.000	.194**	.407**
		-	-	-	-	-	-	-	0.006	0.000
OVEP4: Using sport as a tool for teaching values and life skills is significant a lot in the post Covid world Sig.		-	-	-	-	-	-	-	1.000	.155*
		-	-	-	-	-	-	-	-	0.029
OVEP5: teaching values and life skills in physical education classes is equally effective in distance learning Sig.		-	-	-	-	-	-	-	-	-
		-	-	-	-	-	-	-	-	-

*. Correlation is significant at the 0.05 level (2-tailed).
**. Correlation is significant at the 0.01 level (2-tailed)

Source: Author

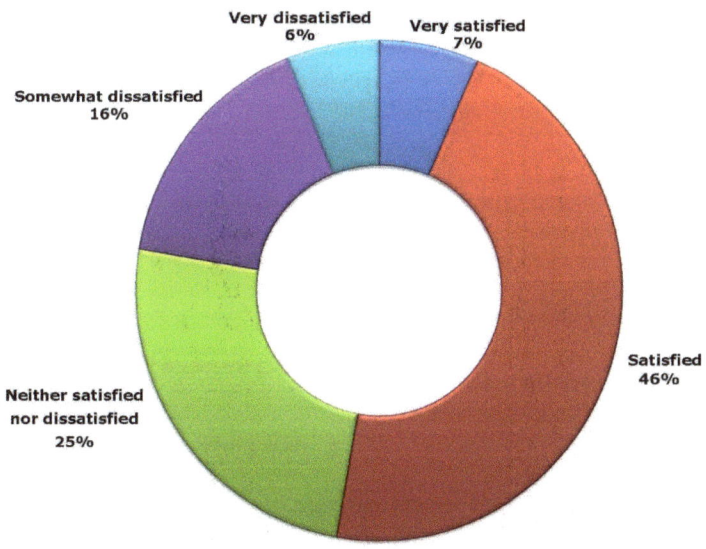

Figure 5: Teachers' level of satisfaction with distance learning
Source: Author

Discussion

More teachers were participating in distance learning and operating technological tools for training during Covid-19 compared with pre-pandemic times. This can be explained by the awareness and needs that were raised by the Covid-19 situation. Since schools were under lockdown, the only way to teach was through distance learning and the teachers' knowledge of technological tools was crucial.

The objective of this study was to find out if there was a correlation between the teachers' perceived coping with the two dimensions (emotional and cognitive-behavioral) measured by ADAPTA-10. Teacher's perceived coping was more positively correlated with the emotional than the cognitive-behavioral dimension. That is, those who had higher levels of emotional coping adapted quickly to changes and were more positive in their perceived ability to cope. It is possible that the events of Covid-19 were very emotional and therefore those who could cope better with the emotions made better adjustments to the situation in comparison to those who coped better cognitively.

The cognitive-behavioral adaptation average was higher as teaching experience was lower. That might be explained by better technological knowledge and familiarity using digital tools compared with senior teachers. The emotional adaptation average was higher as teaching experience was higher. Senior teachers with more years of experience may be more mentally mature, have a better understanding of systems, and may therefore be better able to adapt to changes emotionally compared to the less experienced teachers. Looking at the teacher's perceived coping and teacher experience, student-teacher interaction average and class management was higher among those with less teaching experience, and the teacher's adaptation average was higher among those with more teaching experience. In addition, it was also found that anyone who reported better interaction with students also reported better classroom management during the distance-learning period. Good interaction between teachers and students has a direct effect on the teachers' class management, which is crucial for success especially at time of change. When planning new methods for distance learning, there is a need to take into account different needs and skills according to the teachers' experience years.

The majority of the teachers were not familiar with OVEP. That could indicate that the project is on pause or there is a need to make more promotional efforts in order to improve awareness of OVEP among the PE teacher community. However, the majority of the teachers reported that they use sport as a tool for teaching values and life skills. During Covid-19 there was a downward trend of teaching values and life skills that can potentially be explained by the inherent nature of PE. It is a subject that requires learners to move and be quite close to each other, so the characteristics of this subject does not follow the social distancing measures (Savagpun 2020, 351). Still, the majority of teachers think that using sport as a tool for teaching values and life skills will be significant in the post Covid-19 world. That is why it is important to analyze how PE activities will be appropriate be in the future (Savagpun 2020, 35).

Those teachers who perceived themselves as not having the ability to adapt to changes and different teaching methods also expressed a lack of confidence in the efficiency of teaching values and life skills in PE classes through distance learning. It might be that those who have better cognitive adaptation skills for change are worse at coping with new teaching methods and understand the importance of using sport as a tool for teaching values and life skills. This group also reported no difference in the efficiency of teaching values and life skills in PE classes in distance learning.

The role of decision-makers is to provide tools for teachers to implement when they are required. There is a need to better understand PE's challenges, and to create innovative program tailored to needs in the field. The direct interaction between PE teachers and students is essential, and the lack of it during the Covid-19 crisis emphasized its value (Dunstan 2020). Therefore, future programs need to find creative ways to handle distance learning and develop pedagogical techniques that will overcome related obstacles. The transition to distance learning in PE requires an (not short) adjustment period. This indicates a crucial need for advance preparation of distance learning for teachers ahead of emergencies. It is important to cultivate and encourage teachers' positive attitudes towards the benefits of technological and digital tools so they will be confident in the opportunity to improving their teaching skills. In addition, future curricula should integrate synchronous distance learning routinely, even during normal periods, so that in emergency times the transition will be familiar and easier. Half of the teachers were satisfied with distance learning, which means they adapted to the new situation and even found its benefits. However, there is still a need for a studying process in order to improve satisfaction among the other half.

Conclusions

Covid-19 caused a sudden shift to education by forcing teaching and learning online. This sudden change also changed the experience of PE for both teachers and learners. This study examined the difficulties of running online PE classes in the context of Covid-19 and aimed to use survey findings to develop an efficient operation plan to address these, with a focus on OVEP. Changes in strategic learning methods are needed to understand online PE characteristics and thereby better communicate the value of PE (Hyun-Chul and Wi-Young 2020, 1). As teachers want to deliver values-based education and OVEP is already available, it needs to be made accessible for online use and delivery. In the "new normal" lifestyle, in which society becomes more digitalized, educational management models are also affected. Many countries have started to reconsider technology-based teaching, in which online platforms will take a major role for teaching quality in every field of study. The pandemic shifted attention to virtual learning capabilities and will likely result in the development and expansion of e-learning ideas, software, and infrastructure. Disruption to PE is inevitable around the world and arrangements need to be made whereby teachers and students can continue developing skills and values through sport. In this context, blended learning approaches may not only effectively address the education dilemma during the pandemic, but also lay the foundation for teaching opportunities in the future (Chatziralli et al. 2021, 1463-4).

The main findings indicate that the teachers faced some challenges, such as pedagogical, technical, and communicative with learners. Based on these, the following recommendations are presented in order to help overcome these challenges in the future. Firstly, special training is needed for PE teachers to understand the characteristics of online PE and thus better communicate the added value of PE as a tool for teaching values. Secondly, there is need to cultivate blended learning expertise through routine sharing of online PE classes (not only during crises). In addition, there is a need to change the evaluation strategy in order to encourage active learner participation. Thirdly, there is significant need to take into account the differences between more and less experienced teachers with reference to the different characteristics in their ability to adapt to changes, both emotionally and cognitively.

Although The PE teachers are not very familiar with OVEP, most of them reported that values-based education is important and that they are using sport as a tool for teaching values and life skills. Most teachers had not received training for distance learning and digital tools in the pre-Covid-19 world. The pandemic forced them to get training quickly in order to adapt to the new situation and most of them understand the need and importance of this training. Blended learning that mixes the strengths of the two methods–face to face and online learning–is one of the main recommendations, especially for PE in Israel. If the education system is moving towards a hybrid model, OVEP can be a useful tool. Children will continue to face challenges and PE can help them to meet those challenges with tools to better understand their own internal experiences, empowering them to skillfully and confidently respond to the changing world around them. Further, in the event of a future emergency the transition will be easier and more manageable for both teachers and students. The post-Covid-19 world will need sport education to contribute to this effort. Therefore, training in advance for PE teachers is necessary. As such, The IOC should actually structure OVEP, adapted for online learning and make it more available and accessible to harness its positive potential. OVEP, then, needs to be adapted and relevant in the post-Covid-19 world with the transition to distance PE learning.

Acknowledgements

I would like to thank Prof. Stephan Wassong, Prof. Gershon Tenenbaum, Dr. Michal Arnon, Dr. April Henning, Dr. Michal Zaltsman, and Renana Neidman for their support and comments.

REFERENCES

Azizan, Farahiza Zaihan. 2010. "Blended Learning in Higher Education Institution in Malaysia". In *proceedings of Regional Conference on Knowledge Integration in ICT*, 454-465.

http://library.oum.edu.my/oumlib/sites/default/files/file_attachments/odl-resources/4334/blended-learning.pdf

Bergdahl, Nina, and Jalal Nouri. 2020. "Covid-19 and Crisis-Prompted Distance Education in Sweden." *Technology, Knowledge and Learning* 26 (September): 443-59. https://doi.org/10.1007/s10758-020-09470-6

Binder, Deanna L. 2010. "Teaching Olympism in Schools: Olympic Education as a Focus on Values Education." University lectures on the Olympics. Bellaterra: Centre d'Estudis Olímpics (UAB). *International Chair in Olympism* (IOC-UAB). 1-17.
https://ddd.uab.cat/pub/worpap/2010/181092/binder_eng.pdf

Binder, Deanna L. 2012. "Olympic Values Education: Evolution of Pedagogy". *Educational Review* 64 (3), 275-302. http://dx.doi.org/10.1080/00131911.2012.676539

Calabuig-Moreno, Ferran, Maria H. González-Serrano, Javier Fombona, and Marta García-Tascón. 2020. "The Emergence of Technology in Physical Education: A General Bibliometric Analysis with a Focus on Virtual and Augmented Reality." *Sustainability* 12 (7): 2728. https://doi.org/10.3390/su12072728

Chatziralli, Irini, Camila V. Ventura, Sara Touhami, Rhianon Reynolds, Marco Nassisi, Tamir Weinberg, Kaivon Pakzad-Vaezi et al. 2021. "Transforming Ophthalmic Education into Virtual Learning During COVID-19 Pandemic: A Global Perspective." *Eye* 35: 1459-1466. https://doi.org/10.1038/s41433-020-1080-0

Dunstan, Alan. 2020. "The Future of Physical Education after Covid-19." Accessed February 28, 2021. https://alanrjdunstan.medium.com/the-future-of-physical-education-after-covid-19-ab602f0d0579

Georgiadis, Konstantinos. 2010. "The Implementation of Olympic Education Programs at World Level." Procedia *Social and Behavioral Sciences* 2 (5): 6711-6718. https://doi.org/10.1016/j.sbspro.2010.05.017

Hyun-Chul, Jeong, and So Wi-Young. 2020. "Difficulties of Online Physical Education Classes in Middle and High School and an Efficient Operation Plan to Address Them." *International Journal of Environmental Research and Public Health* 17 (19): 7279. https://doi.org/10.3390/ijerph17197279

IOC. 2017. The Fundamentals of Olympic Values Education. A Sport-Based Programme. International Olympic Committee. Olympic Foundation for Culture and Heritage. Lausanne, Switzerland. https://stillmed.olympics.com/media/Document%20Library/OlympicOrg/IOC/What- We-Do/Promote-Olympism/Olympic-Values-Education-Programme/Toolkit/The-Fundamentals/English.pdf?la=en&hash

——. 2018. Factsheet Olympic Values Education Programme (OVEP) update- February 2018. Lausanne, Switzerland.
https://stillmed.olympic.org/media/Document%20Library/OlympicOrg/Factsheets-Reference-Documents/OVEP/Factsheet-Olympic-Values-Education-Programme-OVEP-January-2018.pdf

——. 2020. Olympic Charter. International Olympic Committee. Lausanne, Switzerland. https://stillmed.olympics.com/media/Document%20Library/OlympicOrg/General/EN-Olympic-Charter.pdf?_ga=2.218989149.572676143.1628844386-140693061.1619979508

——. 2021. "Olympic Values Education Programme." Accessed February 25, 2021. https://www.olympic.org/olympic-values-and-education-program

Israel Ministry of Education. National Supervision of Physical Education. 2020. "General Guidelines for Teaching Physical Education In the Shadow of the Corona Crisis." Tel-Aviv, Israel. https://meyda.education.gov.il/files/Mazkirut_Pedagogit/hinuchgufani/Guidelines%20for%20Teaching%20Physical%20Education%20tspa.pdf

Klaiman, Tamar, John D. Kraemer, and Michael A. Stoto. 2011. "Variability in School Closure Decisions in Response to 2009 H1N1: A Qualitative Systems Improvement Analysis." *BMC Public Health* 11 (73): 1-10. https://doi.org/10.1186/1471-2458-11-73

Lenskyj, Helen Jefferson. 2012. "Olympic Education and Olympism: Still Colonizing Children's Minds." *Educational Review* 64 (3): 265-274. http://dx.doi.org/10.1080/00131911.2012.667389

Pérez-Fuentes, María Del Carmen, María del Mar Molero Jurado, África Martos Martínez, Elena Fernández-Martínez, Raquel Franco Valenzuela, Iván Herrera-Peco, Diana Jiménez-Rodríguez et al. 2020. "Design and Validation of the Adaptation to Change Questionnaire: New Realities in Times of COVID-19." *International Journal of Environmental Research and Public Health* 17 (15): 5612. https://doi.org/10.3390/ijerph17155612

Ratner, David, Glikman Hagit, Lifshtat Nurit, Raz Tal, and Levi Yoav. 2020. "Remote Teaching and Learning: Lessons from the Period of Quarantine Following the COVID-19-Teacher Survey." Israel ministry of education. Tel-Aviv, Israel. https://meyda.education.gov.il/files/Rama/Remote_learning_Teachers_Survey_202 0.pdf

Savagpun, Pufa. 2020. "The New Normal of Physical Education Classroom Model with the COVID-19 Revolution." *Journal of Education Naresuan University* 22 (3): 351-357. https://so06.tci-thaijo.org/index.php/edujournal_nu/article/view/242466

Tsviran, Liat, and Ofer Morgenstern. 2020. "Integrated Learning (Hybrid)." Review at the Request of the Israel Senior Division of Strategy and Planning, Ministry of Education: 1-89. Tel-Aviv, Israel. Accessed July 8, 2021.

U.S. Sports Academy. 2011. "Olympic Values Education Programme (OVEP) Progress Report: 2005-2010." *The Sport Journal*. February 7, 2011. https://thesportjournal.org/article/olympic-values-education-programme-ovep-progress-report-2005-2010

UNESCO. 2021. "COVID-19 Impact on Education: Global Monitoring of School Closures." Accessed February 28, 2021. https://en.unesco.org/covid19/educationresponse

Wassong, Stephan. 2006. "Olympic Education: Fundamentals, Success and Failures." Proceedings: *International Symposium for Olympic Research*: 220-229. https://link.gale.com/apps/doc/A176818725/AONE?u=anon~425a82e1&sid=googleScholar&xid=7e4ad9cf

Zaltsman, Michal. 2017. "Physical Education in the Technological Era." *Eye Contact Teachers' Organization Journal* 265 (1): 39.

Part Three

National Perspectives

Chapter 9

The Philippines: Restarting Sports in "Bubbles"

Severino R. Sarmenta Jr.

Introduction

As the Covid-19 pandemic continued, many sports leagues and tournaments around the globe restarted in mid-2020. Prompted mostly by financial and commercial reasons, most of which stemmed from the desire to avoid losing broadcast and online streaming income, these sports proceeded cautiously within the limitations of pandemic health protocols. Though fans who had missed games may have welcomed the return, others frowned upon the restart attempts. As one person noted in June 2020, sports still needed to take a back seat as "the competition endangers the players; accelerates the general spread of the virus; risks the players' exposing their parents, grandparents and other highly vulnerable friends and family members to the deadly virus; and sends the entirely wrong message to fans around the world that sports competition can be safely resumed. It can't. Not yet" ("Editorial" 2020).

Popular sports that attracted large crowds and involved huge numbers of players, officials, and personnel were undoubtedly potential spreaders of the virus. However, as more testing became available and some cities started to contain the spread, sports in different parts of the world managed to resume. Resumptions oftentimes occurred without familiar crowds and with increased health and safety protocols in place to detect infected participants. For example, patrons and fans were initially prohibited from CPBL baseball games in Taiwan and Bundesliga football matches in Germany (Sun 2021; Duckworth 2021). The National Basketball Association (NBA) of the United States introduced a "bubble" format where teams, officials, and media housed together in one location, ferried to common practice areas, participated in empty playing venues, and underwent regular testing to detect infections. Like many sport leaders around the world, Filipino sports officials were also eager to stage a comeback in any viable form and looked to the NBA bubble as a model.

The bubble format option allowed four Philippine sports leagues to resume tournaments by October 2020. The Philippine experience contrasted largely to other Asian countries that slowly managed to resume sports tournaments without, or with limited, audiences not in contained bubble formats. Through interviews with key individuals who helped organize or participated in the Philippine sports recovery attempts, this essay provides an overview of the challenges of restarting sport in a contained setting and suggests that not all sports may be able to return to play without a bubble during the pandemic.

The Philippines Attempts to Resume a Shuttered Sports Schedule

In early 2020, Philippine professional, school, and recreational sports were scratched or postponed as the Covid-19 virus crept into the country and then slowly erupted into a pandemic. Among the Philippine sports that were canceled were the popular professional basketball games, collegiate and semi-professional volleyball leagues, professional and university football games, and national multi-sports events. Placed in jeopardy was the training of national athletes for the Tokyo Olympics and the 31st Southeast Asian Games scheduled for November 2021 in Vietnam.

The most prominent Philippine sports league derailed was the Philippine Basketball Association (PBA), as it was set to mark its forty-five-year anniversary. Men's basketball, introduced during the American occupation, remains the most popular sport in the country, owing perhaps to the national team's success in international tournaments, the sport's high media exposure, and the relatively easy access to playing courts for mostly male participants. The PBA season would have been marked by a year-round schedule of nationwide celebratory activities, but managed only to hold an opening day celebration and one game. The league closed on March 11, 2020, and for months it was uncertain when and how it would resume. PBA assistant coach Richard Del Rosario (2021) of the Ginebra team explained that, "initially, when the PBA canceled the games, nobody knew how serious the problem was. Then when months passed, there was no clear direction on when the league would re-start." The impact was also felt by the athletes. Von Pessumal (2021), a professional basketball player for the PBA San Miguel team, said that the inactivity of tournaments was hard to bear. He recalled that "it was a very difficult adjustment from a player's perspective. I am very dependent on certain routines to get me in game shape. Without having regular team practices, I had to find all kinds of ways to stay fit." Many teams and athletes whose tournaments or training sessions were scratched resorted to online or "Zoom" sessions done on video conferencing platforms.

The longing for Philippine sports entertainment was compounded by the gradual return of tournaments in other Asian countries that managed to limit the spread of the virus with stringent health safety protocols and by barring audiences from attendance. FIBA Asia columnist Enzo Flojo (2021) enumerated that several sports in Asia managed to return while the Philippines was still determining and charting its own recovery path. Aside from baseball in Taiwan, many basketball leagues, according to Flojo (2021), around Asia managed to restart: The Chinese Basketball Association (CBA), Korean B. League (KBL), B. League of Japan, P. League+, SBL of Taiwan, Australia's National Basketball League (NBL), Qatar's Amir Cup, Lebanon's FLB, and Iran's IBL. Flojo (2021) explained that for the countries that managed to restart some sports, "their health systems and structures haven't been overburdened, generally speaking, and this gives them the confidence to hold their leagues even if an outbreak arises from it."

Attempting to Restart

For the next six months as infection cases grew, various Philippine sports planned to resume but could not do so without government approval. An Inter-Agency Task Force on the Management of Emerging Infectious Diseases (IATF) was in charge of Philippine containment efforts and remained the sole body that could grant permission for businesses, public events, and sports to resume. With public health concerns as its priority, the IATF oversaw testing, hospital facilities, and the procurement of available vaccines, rendering sports resumption as a low priority concern.

With shelved tournaments and athlete training on hold, Philippine sports leagues were left to map out their own possible resumption, subject to IATF approval. PBA Coach Yeng Guiao expressed that it was up to the league to initiate its own restart since the government and other sectors had so many other concerns during the pandemic (Sports Page 2020). Sport leaders floated around suggestions based on the experience of other countries. The most notable came from PBA Assistant Coach Del Rosario as his plan provided a blueprint for the restart of the PBA, as well as for other leagues. "In my initial proposal I suggested some health protocols, tournament format and even made a mock schedule," Del Rosario (2021) explained, "When my proposal was put on the back burner because of perceived difficulties in its execution, I did more research. I studied protocols of different leagues around the world who were able to start their season amidst the pandemic. At that time there was no NBA Bubble yet." At that time, there was still no viable international peg or model on which to pattern Philippine sports restarts.

Other leagues and athletes also wanted to resume playing for various reasons. The province-based National Basketball League (NBL) needed only to finish its championship series. Philippine Football Federation (PFF) broadcast and production head Cedelf Tupas explained that the league had a title sponsor in Qatar Airways, which was only in its first season as a partner. The PFF wanted to honor this commitment. But there was also a desire to keep the sport in the public eye. "Football has been fighting for recognition and relevance in the Philippines for so many decades. The pandemic presented a unique opportunity for stakeholders to show their passion for the sport and competence. People within the community wanted to prove a point that we can pull off a league and come up with a strong sports entertainment product," Tupas (2021) pointed out. Unlike in other countries in Asia, like Indonesia and Malaysia, football does not have the same popular following as basketball in the Philippines. A football tournament, even in a bubble environment, could provide media with stories on the sport while other events were still on hold.

Organizers of the Chooks-to-Go 3-on-3 basketball tournament were also eager to resume in a bubble format. Anton Roxas (2021), broadcast commentator for the live streaming of the tournament resumption, explained "the original plan was to have three tournaments every season but because of the pandemic, only one tournament would take place in 2020 and it would happen in a bubble set-up inspired by the NBA. The bottom line was to make it happen no matter what in order to let the basketball fans in the Philippines know that 3-on-3 is a legitimate sport and that players can choose it as a profession in their careers." The goal to keep the game in the public eye was understandable as this relatively new version of basketball was gaining interest; it had previously been played in front of huge crowds in malls and other public venues. The sport would be also be included in the 2020 Tokyo Olympics for the first time and there was expectation that maybe a Philippine team could qualify for the Games.

Although not discussed publicly, the desire for most Philippine sports leagues to restart was prompted by the need to maintain a presence in public consciousness even during the health crisis. Almost all Philippine professional sports teams are owned by corporations and participate in tournaments to gain media exposure for brand names and products. Players and other team members of professional sports leagues continued to receive compensation even without playing, creating a dilemma for companies that did not gain media mileage that was otherwise significant when leagues were in play.

Resumption

According to *New York Times* writer Matthew Futterman (2020), sports restarts occurred if "work agreements with players could be negotiated and that public health authorities raised no objections." This is exactly what the four Philippine sports organizations that restarted managed to attain when they restarted in October and November 2020. The pandemic cases in the country continued to rise but there was some leniency allowed by the government to enable selected businesses to resume. Within this window, sports leaders proposed bubble set-ups for the restart of tournaments. Because the National Capital Region continued to have the highest number of infections, the four leagues proposed bubble venues in less populated, isolated communities.

The NBA bubble was already underway in July 2020 and arguably gave Philippine sports leagues a viable model on which to map their own versions. With NBA games and features shown daily on Philippine television and covered amply by social media, the U.S. league's bubble execution—the housing and accommodations, locked-in playing and living conditions, as well as health safety protocols—was readily available for Philippine sports to mirror. Del Rosario (2021) said "When the NBA started and I saw that they were implementing some of the points in my proposal, it gave me hope that we can do it as well."

Creating and maintaining the sports bubbles was not easy. *Sports Illustrated* reporter J.A. Adande (2020) put it succinctly that with such set-ups, "leagues were not just creating an environment. They were conducting medical and social experiments." The Philippines did not have a multi-venue facility like that used by the NBA where hotels were adjacent to practice and playing spaces. Thus, the Philippine bubbles departed from the NBA version: Two of the four leagues—the PBA and the Philippine Football Federation—housed their teams adjacent to playing venues while two others—the 3 on 3 tournament and the NBL—managed to find suitable venues that had playing venues in the same complex as dormitories and accommodations. The availability of bubble contexts to manage health safety protocols and limit the number of personnel involved was the only way leagues received government permission through the IATF to restart.

In time, four Philippine sports leagues got government permission through the IATF to resume in October 2020 in bubble formats. Though far from ideal as venues and health protocols offered distinct challenges, the success of the Philippine restarts depended on several key features.

1. Government Sanctions

The government wanted to prohibit public gatherings and sport was understandably disallowed from continuing. However, with a bubble set-up and health protocols in place, the government allowed certain events to resume. To date, only professional sports have been permitted in the Philippines. Sports columnist and analyst Mike Ochosa (2021) explained that the IATF consulted with another government agency, the Games and Amusement Board (GAB), which supervises professional sports in the Philippines. This made professional sports easier to regulate than amateur competitions, especially during the pandemic. There was no government agency that supervised collegiate sporting events, making that restart more difficult.

However, allowing only professional competitions to resume prevented high-profile women's sports from occurring in 2020. The Philippine Superliga and the Premier Volleyball League, two popular women's volleyball groups, did not receive permission to resume as they were not formally recognized as professional leagues, though players were generally known to receive allowances. In time, the PVL opted to turn professional and managed to get its own bubble tournament underway in July 2021 and a women's professional basketball league was also set to start in a bubble format in 2021. Government approval thus allowed some teams to restart in a bubble, while others remained sidelined.

2. Available "Bubble" Facilities

There are no facilities in the Philippines that closely approximate what was perhaps the ideal set-up of the NBA 2020 bubble. Most Philippine hotel resorts do not have basketball, football, or volleyball facilities for elite competition, nor the number of rooms needed to fully accommodate teams. In the PBA bubble, only twenty-five players and personnel were allowed per team, forcing them to limit coaches and utility personnel. Sports venues in close proximity to hotel accommodations had to follow strict health protocols.

Officials that managed to resume their sports in 2020 found facilities that enabled them to either house athletes within a compound or in accommodations adjacent to the sports venue. For example, the Chooks-to-Go 3-on-3 tournament organizers housed participants inside the Inspire Sports Academy in Calamba, Laguna, a province two and a half hours away from the National Capital Region. The National Basketball League version was at the Bren Guiao Sports Complex in Pampanga (a province about an hour and a half away from Manila), which had dormitories adjacent to the playing venue. The PBA bubble, also in Pampanga, held games and practices at the Angeles City University campus while housing participants at the Quest Hotel inside the Clark Airbase layout, the former United States military outlet. The PFL played games on the Philippine Football Federation training pitch in Carmona, Cavite, and housed participants in the Seda hotel in Laguna. Tupas (2021) explained that the Seda Hotel was not near the playing venue but it was the accommodations approved based on health safety protocols. Players were transported in buses and were not allowed to disembark until it was time for their matches (Perrine, 2021).

3. Government and Medically Approved Health Protocols

As mandated by the IATF, the bubble sports communities had to strictly observe health safety protocols. There were no spectators in attendance but the number of athletes and tournament personnel also created sizeable gatherings, a lure for the unpredictable virus that subsisted on human contact. The sports bubbles strictly adhered to the following measures:

Masking

People involved in all four tournaments adhered to mask wearing, except athletes in training and competition. Terrado (2021) pointed out that in the NBL bubble, "wearing of facemask(s) and face shields were strictly being implemented." Wearing facemasks proved important in helping halt the spread of the virus.

Physical Distancing

Physical or "social" distancing was a mandatory norm for all the bubble events that restarted Philippine tournaments. Terrado (2021) explained that in the National Basketball League, meals were done in batches to allow people to spread out while eating. In the Philippine Football League, stadium announcer Claudia Perrine (2021) related that aside from the constant tests, the non-bubble personnel were "not allowed to enter the pitch or go across to the other side of the field. I was also told to go home straight stay home and avoid any social gatherings." Distancing measures were strictly enforced.

Testing

The medical tests to detect infections were in place in all the four bubble tournaments. Jurado (2021) explained that for the 3-on-3 tournament he "took RT-PCR testing three days before the bubble, then antigen tests when I entered and left the bubble. The players also had it, with the addition of random tests every leg." Terrado (2021) had a similar experience in the NBL as participants "were tested before entering and leaving the bubble with two more tests also done while inside the bubble." Meralco assistant coach Ronnie Magsanoc of one of the PBA teams, pointed out that the bubble participants "had regular RT-PTR testing inside the hotel together with hotel staff that gave us convenience aside from peace of mind. The test results were relayed to the PBA and the 12- mother teams as soon as they were ready" (Magsanoc, 2021).

Other monitoring protocols were also set in place. In the PBA bubble, One Sports reporter Carlo Pamintuan (2021) explained that "we downloaded the Stay Safe app and checked in and out of venues to make sure that we weren't spending time elsewhere." PBA player Pessumal (2020) added, "We were required temperature checks and sanitization always upon entering or exiting facilities. Overall I think they were able to accomplish their tasks of having a safe bubble." In order to minimize the risk of spreading the virus inside the bubble, officials ensured all personnel underwent repeated testing.

Leadership

Setting up a sports bubble was like establishing a temporary community, with different personalities, responsibilities, needs, and concerns. The importance of cooperation and teamwork were givens for success but strong leadership by those in charge was even more indispensable with the health concerns at play.

Jurado (2021) revealed that "according to former 3-on-3 commissioner Eric Altamirano, there were a lot of fears going into this pandemic, whether the league could pull this bubble off. The team owners and the players trusted the league." This was concurred by Roxas (2021) who said, "I believe that one big reason the Chooks 3-on-3 bubble became successful was due to the planning and implementation of its commissioner (Altamirano)." In the PFL, Perrine (2021) disclosed: "Our commissioner Coco Torre really handled it well and in a very professional manner." The NBL likewise had leadership that made sure all participants followed the protocols. Terrado (2021) pointed out that, "Commissioner Edward Aquino was able to handle the bubble well. He ensured that everyone was following safety protocols inside through the help of the league staff. He assigned a safety officer to monitor the health of the players through temperature checks. He was also constantly coordination with the GAB representative in the bubble." In the best of circumstances, conducting a sports tournament has layers of challenges on a daily basis, even if plans and structures have already been implemented. The pandemic added a difficult layer of concern that had to be addressed to ensure the completion of the tournament and the safety of all participants.

4. The Support of Athletes/Players/Teams

In all of the sports bubbles during the pandemic, a key factor in their success was the agreement of the players and teams to enter the bubbles and abide by its rules so that tournaments could be played. On June 23, 2020, PBA commissioner Willie Marcial met with players prior to their entry into the bubble and gained their support (PBA Bubble 2020). Even when there was the detection of possible infections, the players remained supportive of the bubble's durability (Henson, 2021). In the PFL, Tupas (2021) said "(The) league met with team managers but also got inputs from key players like Stephan Schrock and Anton del Rosario who is also an owner of one of the clubs." For the NBL, league commissioner Edward Aquino consulted with teams and players via Zoom meetings before joining the bubble. Reaching out to gain the support of players proved helpful in the face of possible infections.

Though players were eager to enter bubbles in order to play, separation from families and regular life routines caused stress. Pessumal (2021) said, "Personally, I did not have a particularly hard time dealing being isolated in the bubble. I knew that this would be the safest way for me to be able to play basketball during a pandemic. Although, I know that some of my teammates that have kids had a difficult time." Isolation and separation were important considerations when planning for the bubble.

5. Health Emergency Plans and Contingencies

And yet even the best laid plans and strictest policies cannot completely deter a ruthless virus from attempting to pierce the sports bubbles. It was therefore necessary to have contingency plans in place. In both the PFL and PBA bubbles, some players and officials tested positive for the infection. Pamintuan (2020) reported that a PBA referee and a player had initially tested positive for infection, prompting the league to temporarily suspend play while additional testing was done. Subsequent tests were negative and the league managed to resume, although with a more rigid schedule with teams playing back-to-back game days.

The kick-off of the PFL was delayed a few days by a weather storm and when two players tested positive for infection. This alerted the local government unit that oversaw the tournament venue. However, the league commissioner Torre and chief medical officer Dr. Marc Castro assured the government that isolation procedures were undertaken. The league eventually managed to start after three days, implemented stricter health protocols, and completed its tournament without further infections (Del Carmen 2020).

6. Adjusting to the Training Guidelines

Before entering the PBA bubble, teams were allowed to practice, but only in small groups of three to five at a time, with only physical conditioning and shooting drills permissible. Pessumal (2020) pointed out that "our coaches had to be very creative with practice planning. Not only are we allowed a limited number of people per hour, we also were not permitted to have contact drills. Mostly, the drills we conducted were individual shooting drills." Even inside the bubble, conducting practices while having to wear face masks proved to be challenging. Magsanoc (2021) said that "One of the challenging tasks for coaches inside the bubble is adapting to wearing safety materials while running practices. (It was) hard to communicate at times and a bit taxing because of the masks and face shields we are wearing that leads to difficulty in breathing in certain instances." Scheduling, according to Del Rosario (2021), was also beyond the teams' control. "Since we were sharing facilities we had to adjust and shatter routines," he explained, "Change is always difficult and you will naturally encounter resistance, so we had to keep our team right-minded. We embraced the challenges of the bubble and focused on appreciating that we are able to play again and keep our jobs." Practice schedules in the PBA bubble were managed by the league and teams could only work within the prescribed training hours.

Despite the training limitations, the bubble format allowed athletes, teams, and even league personnel to concentrate on their assigned tasks. PBA Arena Announcer Sirjay De La Cruz (2021) pointed out that "(The) bubble environment is meant for an individual to concentrate on the task at hand. The players can solely focus on improving themselves and getting their bodies ready for the game while everything else will be taken care of, such as their food, place to stay, and other activities." With its housed-in environment, participants in the bubble were isolated from families and other concerns that they normally would attend to personally in a pre-pandemic environment. Teams had control over all schedules and movements within the bubble.

7. Sustaining the Sports Experience

Unlike in other Asian countries, at no point did the Philippine government allow public attendance at any of the events that occurred in sports bubbles in 2020. Letting in even limited audiences was still too risky. Thus, the role of print, broadcast, and online media was even more essential in creating a connection between fans and their team sports in the bubble format. Reporters from the organizations that held the broadcast rights also resided in the sports bubbles, as well as a limited number of other print and online media practitioners. They, too, had to follow strict health protocols. For example, One Sports interviewer Carlo Pamintuan adjusted his approaches, from reaching out to players while in their rooms to observing social distancing. Regular interviewing methods also had to be adjusted as "asking questions while wearing a mask and a face shield could be quite challenging and transcribing muffled quotes was also a nightmare" (Pamintuan 2021). In the PBA broadcasts, courtside reporters interviewed coaches and players from a distance. There were attempts to maintain the connection between fans and players from the isolated bubble venues. The availability of social media channels also helped keep tournaments in the public eye.

Is the bubble the only way?

The "bubble" format allowed for the restart of some Philippine sports, as live audiences continued to be prohibited. Tupas (2020) explained during the height of the pandemic, "while it minimizes health risks, the bubble format could prove to be very costly and unsustainable. But at the moment, it is deemed the safest and perhaps the only way that sports can resume." The bubble sports environment was at best a contingency measure as it placed athletes, officials, game personnel, and media in a restrictive community, but one that was unavoidable due to the need to keep people at a distance. It involved an enormous amount of finances as accommodation, food, training, and practice needs, as well as expenses for recreational facilities, had to be considered. Above all, the bubble format kept the fans away from the in-person sports experience, leaving them to follow teams and favorite players in mostly broadcast channels or social media.

The Covid-19 pandemic was far from over in 2021 and continued attempts to resume will encounter difficulties and hurdles. To date, the NBA did not return to the bubble format for its 2021 season and slowly allowed fans to return to venues. This may not be feasible in other countries that do not have the same vaccination pace as the United States. In the Philippines, the Premier Volleyball League (PVL) for women completed its own bubble tournament in Ilocos Norte, a province 200 kilometers north of Manila in July and August of 2021. The PBA started its 2021 season in July in Manila but had to bring games to a halt when the National Capital Region shifted its lockdown to a stricter quarantine level. The games resumed in an altered bubble format in September where more hotels were used to house players in Pampanga.

Departing from bubble formats will rely heavily on how the pandemic behaves and how countries respond to its continuing threat to public health. Many countries like the Philippines are still grappling with the pandemic while awaiting more vaccines to contain the spread of the virus and getting its sports program back on track without necessarily having to resort to a bubble in the future.

REFERENCES

Adande, J.A. (2021). "What We've Learned." *Sports Illustrated*, March 11. 2021. https://www.si.com/sports-illustrated/2021/03/11/sports-and-the-pandemic-what-weve-learned-daily-cover

Bustillos, Esteban. 2020. "Should Sports Make a Comeback During a Pandemic." *GBH News*, July 29, 2020. https://www.wgbh.org/news/local-news/2020/07/29/should-sports-be-making-their-comeback-during-a-pandemic

Del Carmen, Lorenzo. 2020. "Season of Uncertainty ends on a high for PFL." *Tiebreaker Times*, November 20, 2020. https://tiebreakertimes.com.ph/tbt/season-of-uncertainty-ends-on-a-high-for-pfl/197127?fbclid=IwAR32qkMPU53NVCR-ShmuZqyeKr0JcnwZYJZeuskXCEUEXHga8Utyt9V71bg

Duckworth, Austin. 2021. "Gegenpressing: The Bundesliga's Tactical Response to the Covid-19 Lockdown." In *Time Out: National Perspectives on Sport and the Covid 19 Lockdown*, edited by Jörg Krieger, April Henning, Lindsay Parks Pieper, and Paul Dimeo, 29-39. Champaign, Illinois. Common Ground Research Network.

De La Cruz, Sirjay. 2021. PBA Public Address Announcer. E-mail interview by the author. February 9, 2021.

Del Rosario, Richard. 2021. Ginebra San Miguel PBA Team Assistant Coach. E-mail interview by the author. April 19, 2021.

"Editorial: Shut Down Sports During Covid-19 Pandemic." *Mercury News*. June 25, 2020. https://www.mercurynews.com/2020/06/25/editorial-sports/

Flojo, Enzo. 2021. FIBA Asia Columnist. E-mail interview by author. March 8, 2021.

Futterman, M. 2020. "Why Major Sports Might Risk Comebacks During the Pandemic." New York Times, May 31, 2020. https://www.nytimes.com/2020/05/31/sports/coronavirus-sports-comeback-reopening.html?

Henson, J. 2021. "Another Bubble for PBA?" *Philippine Star Global*, April 5, 2021. https://www.philstar.com/sports/2021/04/04/2088678/another-bubble-pba/amp/

Jurado, Theodore P. 2020. "Chooks-to-Go 3x3 in Calamba a Big Success." *Journal Online*. October 31, 2020. https://journal.com.ph/sports/basketball/chooks-to-go-3x3-in-calamba-a-big-success/?fbclid=IwAR38u94iC12Tcg96jaa1Yk-3rpiMO8Y7B1QlUSD49-HlGtj6irVWEvnvHOQ.

---. 2021. People's Journal and People's Tonight Sportswriter. E-mail interview by author. March 30, 2021.

Magsanoc, Ronnie. 2021. Meralco Bolts PBA Team Assistant Coach. E-mail interview by author. February 20, 2021.

Ochosa, Mike. 2021. Sports Columnist and TV Analyst. Email interview by author. April 9, 2021.

Pamintuan, Carlo. 2020. "How the PBA Navigated through a Challenging Season." *ESPN5*, December 28, 2020. https://tv5.espn.com/basketball/pba/story/_/id/30542593/how-pba-navigated-challenging-philippine-cup-season-2020.

---. 2021. One Sports Reporter. E-mail interview by author. February 25, 2021.

PBA ON TV 5. PBA Bubble. https://facebook/com/watch/?y:990782371421790.

Perrine, Claudia. 2021. Football Stadium Announcer. E-mail interview by author. March 9, 2021.

Philippine Football Federation. Press Release. October 24, 2020.

Pessumal, Von. 2021. Player, San Miguel Beer PBA team. E-mail interview by author. April 4, 2021.

Roxas, Anton. 2021. Broadcast Commentator, Chooks-to-Go 3 on 3 tournament. E-mail interview by author. March 28, 2021.

Sports Page. 2021. TV 5. June 21, 2020.

Sun Yu-Kue, Daniel. 2021. "Baseball, CPBL and Taiwanese Nationalism in the time of Covid-19." In *Time Out: National Perspectives on Sport and the Covid 19 Lockdown*, edited by Jörg Krieger, April Henning, Lindsay Parks Pieper, and Paul Dimeo, 109-121. Champaign, Illinois. Common Ground Research Network.

Terrado, Reuben. 2021. Sportswriter Spin.ph and NBL Commentator. E-mail interviews by author. April 19, 2021 and April 30, 2021.

Tupas Cedelf, P. 2021. Broadcast and Production Head, Philippine Football Federation. E-mail interview by author, March 26, 2021.

Wojnaroski, Adrian. 2020. "NBA Approves 22-team format to finish season." *ESPN.com*, June 4, 2020. https://www.espn.com/nba/story/_/id/29267294/source-nba-approves-plan-return-orlando

Chapter 10

Fighting a Pandemic by Recommendations and Trust: Sports in Sweden during Covid-19

Johan R. Norberg, Karin Andersson, and Susanna Hedenborg

Introduction

Epidemics are always products of specific historical conditions, and they develop in specific societal contexts. Consequently, each society will experience a pandemic differently and every society has in some sense always prepared itself for this very pandemic (Sörlin 2020). Sweden is an illustrative example of this observation. Although Covid-19 is a global phenomenon, Sweden faced and fought the pandemic in a unique way (Kavaliunas et al. 2020). While most countries imposed severe restrictions on their citizens, the Swedish government chose to keep the society relatively open. Admittedly, the government decided on several restrictions to prevent travel abroad and large gatherings. A nationwide lockdown was, however, never enforced. Instead, companies, shops, and restaurants could remain open, and Swedish citizens were allowed to move freely within the country's borders. Sweden was distinct in that experts, rather than politicians, were put in charge of crisis management (Ludvigsson 2020). The Public Health Agency of Sweden, run by experts in epidemiology and public health, maintained a leading role in framing the Swedish policy response to the pandemic (Jonung 2020). Instead of prohibitions and repressive measures, Sweden fought the virus mainly with information and non-binding health recommendations. This "light touch" approach was motivated by the Public Health Agency with the argument that people who are "well-informed and motivated" will voluntarily follow given recommendations and that confidence in people's capacity to act responsibly is better than coercive measures (FHM 2020 a). Thus, from a governance perspective, Sweden chose a "soft" strategy to fight Covid-19 that was based on trust and responsibility rather than rules and prohibitions (Kavaliunas et al. 2020; Helsingen et al. 2020; Harring et al. 2021; Norberg et al. 2021).

In this chapter, we analyze how the Swedish policy response to Covid-19 was received within the fields of sports and physical activity. Employing trust as an analytical concept, we examine how the organized sports movement and citizens in general handled and reacted to the Swedish Public Health Agency's recommendations and guidelines. The text builds on our first analysis of Swedish sport during Covid-19, published in Time Out: National Perspectives on Sport and the Covid-19 Lockdown (Norberg et al. 2021).

Sources and Methodology

This study is based on a variety of quantitative and qualitative data. Information regarding the sports movement's sports policy efforts during the crisis has been obtained through interviews with two representatives of the Swedish Sports Confederation (SSC) and interviews with representatives of three national sports federations; the Swedish Judo Association, the Swedish Gymnastics Association, and the Swedish Orienteering Association. These interviews have been supplemented with public documents such as governmental regulations, recommendations from the Public Health Agency, and information derived from the SSC's website.

The perspective of local sports clubs has been examined by an online survey aimed at sports clubs in the region of Scania in the southern part of Sweden. The survey was conducted together with RF-SISU Skåne, (regional department for the SSC in the region of Scania) and was answered by 652 clubs, representing sixty-one sports distributed over all thirty-three municipalities in the region of Scania.

Data about individuals' reactions and attitudes towards Covid-19 has been obtained from the research project Voices from closed stadiums: The corona crisis as a potential vehicle for sports-development. In this project, the long and short-term consequences on sports and physical activity in Sweden caused by Covid-19 are studied by using both quantitative and qualitative data (Norberg et al. 2020; Andersson et al. 2021; Radmann and Svensson 2021). The "Voices"-project began in April 2020 with an extensive web survey concerning how the Covid-19 pandemic affected sports and exercise habits, as well as sports consumption in Sweden. At this point, 1,141 people have answered the questionnaire. The survey was followed up with qualitative in-depth interviews with ninety strategically selected respondents.

This study has been funded through grants from the *Swedish Research Council for Sport Science*.

Theoretical Perspectives on Trust and the Swedish Response to Covid-19

The Swedish Covid-19 strategy has caused immense international interest. Mainstream media as well as academia have debated the effectiveness of the Swedish strategy and speculated on why Sweden chose to go its own way (Esaiasson et al. 2020). Critics have claimed that the Swedish strategy was too liberal, relying on references to higher death rates in Sweden in comparison to Scandinavian neighboring countries. Others have marvelled at Sweden's capacity to maintain a relatively open society during the pandemic, and that Swedish citizens apparently are willing to comply with non-binding health recommendations (Kavaliuanas et al. 2020; Pierre 2020; Davies and Roeber 2021).

Yet, why did Sweden choose a "light touch" approach in the fight against Covid-19? According to the Swedish Public Health Agency, the strategy was designed as a balancing act between needing to minimize mortality and morbidity within the population, while simultaneously avoiding other negative consequences for Swedish society (FHM 2019). Additionally, societal costs of a lockdown would have been higher than if companies and schools could remain open, not least since healthcare professionals and other individuals with important societal functions would be forced to stay at home during a lockdown (Kavaliunas et al. 2020).

Others have added that the Swedish strategy is a consequence of certain elements in the Swedish legal system (Wenander 2021). According to economist Lars Jonung, the Swedish constitution does not give the government permission to declare a state of emergency in peacetime. As a result, the use of national lockdowns is practically prohibited (although local lockdowns are allowed under specific circumstances). Moreover, the Swedish constitution guarantees the independence of public agencies. Unlike many other democratic systems, it is not permitted for Swedish ministers of government to intervene in matters that are assigned to various public authorities. This is why Sweden, to a high degree, delegated to experts in the Public Health Agency to design the national Covid-19 strategy (Jonung 2020).

From a governance perspective, the Swedish Covid-19 strategy can be regarded as trust-based governance. This is a doctrine of governance that has gained increased interest in recent years, especially in research on public administration and the management of organizations (SOU 2018, 38). The interest of trust in governance can partly be understood as a backlash and criticism of the extensive bureaucratization, audits, and the market ideology that followed when New Public Management became a dominant doctrine of governance in the public sector (not least in Sweden). The research on trust-based governance is far from uniform, nevertheless, a common starting point is that the effectiveness of organizations and welfare programmes would increase if the actors that are expected to implement policies for instance, doctors, teachers, and social workers were given more autonomy and time to focus on their core activities rather than time-consuming administration (Bringselius 2018).

Trust can be defined in different ways. However, a common approach is to define trust as an actor's willingness to be vulnerable without the ability to monitor or control the other party (Vanneste and Yoo 2020; Bringselius 2018). Thus, at the core of trust-based governance is an assumption that those to whom the governance strategy is directed will comply without enforced sanctions. This justifies that the Swedish Covid-19 strategy based on non-binding health recommendations can be regarded as a form of trust-based governance.

Three Conditions for Trust-Based Governance

Research indicates that trust-based governance is more likely to work under specific circumstances. A first condition is compliance, meaning that the groups or actors addressed by the non-binding recommendations and other trust-based governance techniques, must voluntarily accept the aims of the policies. Consequently, it follows that trust-based governance has great potential to work in societies where citizens are inclined to orient themselves towards common, rather than personal, goals. (Ring and Van de Ven 1992). Conversely, in societies where democratic structures are weak, or where there is mutual distrust between citizens and authorities, it is less likely that citizens will accept and follow non-binding recommendations (Reicher and Stott 2020). Importantly, it should be emphasized that Sweden is known for high levels of civic trust, both between citizens and in the relationship between citizens and political decision-makers, authorities, and other societal institutions (Trädgårdh 2018; Rothstein 1998). Consequently, Sweden seems to be better suited than many other countries to employ trust-based governance strategies. Nevertheless, the empirical question remains: were the Public Health Agency's recommendations followed in the fields of sport and physical exercise?

A second condition is comprehensibility; governance based on recommendations or guidelines must always be interpreted and translated by the governed into actions in specific situations. In theories of management and public administration, this is often unproblematic. Governance strategies based on trust are usually applied in areas where the governed have competence to interpret situations and turn general principles into actions. For instance, doctors and teachers are examples of professions capable of making decisions based on general principles (Rothstein 1998; Gruber 1988). However, this professionalism cannot be expected of citizens who are supposed to understand and interpret authorities' guidelines to combat a virus during a pandemic. Thus, a further important question is: were the Swedish Public Health Agency's recommendations comprehensible with regard to sports and physical activity?

Finally, governance based on trust presupposes the governed to take personal responsibility for their actions. As an effect, the implementation of trust-based governance strategies can become a challenge for established hierarchies and power relations within specific policy areas, where sport is no exception. In Sweden, organized sport is based on a hierarchical and pyramidal chain of command where local clubs are expected to accept the authority of the national sports federations and the SSC. Therefore, the question arises: to what extent were power relations and hierarchies in Swedish sports affected when the national sports federations' authority and autonomy was challenged by general health recommendations addressed to all citizens? Who was now in charge?

Swedish Sport and The Fight of Covid-19: Compliance, Criticism and Confusion

The Virus Arrives, and Restrictions are Introduced

In Sweden, the onset and spread of the Covid-19 virus and its subsequent societal restrictions began in March 2020 when the virus reached Sweden. Although the Swedish government and the Public Health Agency did not enforce a national societal lockdown, several measures were taken to limit the spread of the virus.

Firstly, a number of bans were introduced. On March 11, the government announced a national ban on public gatherings of over 500 people until further notice (SFS 2020, 114). Two weeks later, on March 27, only gatherings of fifty people were allowed. (SFS 2020: 162). Thereafter, travel abroad was prohibited. Already on March 14, the Ministry of Foreign Affairs advised against non-essential travel to all countries. Three days later, the government banned non-essential travel into Sweden from countries outside the EU. At the end of March, visits to elderly care and hospitals were also prohibited. For restaurants and bars, only table service became allowed (Prop. 2019/20, 172).

Besides these prohibitive measures, the government and the Public Health Agency primarily met the pandemic by issuing regulations and general recommendations (FHM 2020b), i.e., guidelines that were legally non-binding but expected to be followed by citizens, companies, public authorities, and organizations (Wenander, 2020). Many of these recommendations were aimed directly at Swedish inhabitants. Under the heading "Keep your distance and take responsibility," all citizens were urged to maintain their hand hygiene and to keep distance from each other in places where people gather, such as shops, malls, and museums. Citizens were also advised to keep a distance when on public transport and to avoid rush hours. In addition, unnecessary travel should be avoided as well as larger social events such as parties and funerals. For companies, the recommendation was to let their employees, if possible, work from home and avoid travel. Furthermore, stores and department stores were recommended to limit the number of customers. In education, all upper-secondary schools and universities were advised to close to the public and to conduct remote teaching, while preschools and elementary schools were recommended to continue as normal (FHM 2020c).

The Pandemic's Effects on Swedish Sports

Covid-19 had several immediate effects on Swedish sports. For instance, the restrictions on international travel made it impossible for athletes to participate in international sporting events. Also, the ban on large gatherings necessitated large exercise events and public elite sports events to be canceled, postponed, or conducted without spectators (Norberg et al. 2020).

However, the intention of the Public Health Agency was not to hinder physical activity. In fact, sports and physical activity were deemed as positive and allowed to continue if conducted "safely." More precisely, all sporting activities that could exacerbate a spread of Covid-19 should be avoided, as should close contact between athletes. Exercise and sporting activities should, if possible, take place outdoors. As long as these guidelines were followed, sports clubs, gyms, fitness centers, and public baths could remain open (FHM 2020c).

The Public Health Agency's ambition to restrict but not ban physical activity limited the pandemics' negative effects on citizens' exercise habits and on organized youth sports. Our web survey and interviews with individuals about reactions and attitudes towards Covid-19 show that the informants (aged 16 and above), in general, decreased their participation in accustomed sport activities. Yet, overall, physical activity levels remained stable as many citizens changed their sport activities to outdoor venues and "friluftsliv." There were no gender differences in relation to the answers. There were, however, differences related to age and in relation to sport discipline. In particular, young adults and sport-supporters decreased their physical activity (Andersson et al., 2021).

For organized youth sports, the new restrictions made it impossible to organize matches, cups, and league games, while training was still allowed. Furthermore, the Public Health Agency's recommendation for outdoor activities coincided with a warmer spring climate. Hence, statistics from the SSC show that the total activity levels in Swedish youth sports decreased by a modest 8% during the spring of 2020. Not surprisingly, indoor sports were more affected than outdoor sports (Riksidrottsförbundet 2021a).

Compliance and Criticism: Sports in Sweden Reacts to the New Restrictions

How were the Covid-19 related restrictions received in the field of sport? Did individuals, clubs and sport federations comply with the Public Health Agency's recommendations despite the absence of sanctions? Judging from our empirical data, the pandemic and the subsequent societal restrictions were taken seriously by both individuals and sports organizations in Sweden. Admittedly, many of the respondents expressed disappointment and frustration concerning the inconvenience caused by the pandemic. At the same time, the restrictions were accepted as a necessity.

In our interviews with representatives of the sports federations we do not find signs of defiance or systematic attempts to circumvent the Public Health Agency's recommendations. The SSC and the national federations for judo and gymnastics all emphasized that their primary goal during the pandemic has been to follow the public health authority's restrictions and thereby limiting the spread of the virus. This position is clearly expressed in the following quote from a representative of the Swedish Gymnastics Association:

> We have done our best to avoid a further spread of the virus, meaning that we have been very strict in following the guidelines (representative of the Swedish Gymnastics Association).

Thus, a first result in this study is that the Swedish soft governance strategy has been effective in the field of sports and that compliance, but also trust, have been key words. As the statement above shows, the representative of the Swedish Gymnastics Association considered that compliance with the state's guidelines entailed less risk of contamination, which in turn shows that he does not question the state's authority nor its competence.

However, a high degree of acceptance in sports does not mean that the strategy has been appreciated. In our web-surveys and interviews concerning individuals' reactions and attitudes towards Covid-19, we find a lot of criticism. Many respondents state that they felt insecure and confused when they had to quit or alter their sporting habits; "why could some sporting competitions still continue and others not? Why was it ok to play soccer but not to bike?" (Simon, MTB enthusiast). Some complain about the lack of information, while others found the excess of information overwhelming; "one has been overloaded with information from the authorities mixed with peoples' opinions and sentiments" (Alexandra, gymnastics trainer). Some respondents chose a passive approach waiting for clarifications, while others chose to interpret the health recommendations on their own. Jacob, an older trainer in orienteering in the Swedish town Eskilstuna comments, "the hardest thing is not to know, one sits around waiting for guidelines and slowly one loses motivation" (Andersson et al. 2021).

Critical views also emerge in our interviews with sports organizations. The representatives of judo and gymnastics argue that there were too many health recommendations, which were hard to interpret. Sometimes they have even been perceived as inconsistent. As an example, the representatives of the Swedish Gymnastics Association told of frustration and conflict among their local clubs when some age groups were allowed to train but not others. Moreover, at times, gymnastics were not allowed at public sporting facilities but allowed to continue in commercial gyms and fitness centers.

> Since the commercial organizations have been allowed to remain open and not needed to limit their groups to eight people, I'm worried that lots of the adults

that turned to commercial alternatives will not return (representative of the Swedish Gymnastics Association).

In sum, the data reveals that the sports federation sometimes perceived the restrictions as both unfair and unreasonable still, the guidelines were defended in their contacts with their local clubs.

Among the local sports clubs, the criticism is not as strong. In our survey of the region of Scania, almost all clubs (95 %) stated that the pandemic had affected their activities. However, two out of three found the restrictions intelligible, while one third stated that the guidelines were unclear or difficult to adapt to their own sport activities. Importantly, clubs that stated to have a high trust in the competence of the SSC also considered the recommendations easier to interpret in comparison to clubs that did not state to have a high trust in the SSC (Andersson and Jansson 2021).

Who's in Charge? The Governance of Swedish Sport During Covid-19

In the SSC, extensive work was initiated to follow up on the pandemic's effects on Swedish sports, as well as to support national sports federations and local sport clubs. Above all, financial support to sport organizations for lost commercial revenue became a priority. On March 20, and in accordance with a petition from the SSC, the government announced that a special "Covid-19 grant" of SEK 500 million was to be allocated in between clubs and organizations that could prove "lost revenues because of the restriction of public events" (Regeringskansliet 2020 a). Later the same year, an additional SEK 1 billion was granted to mitigate the pandemic's economic effects on Swedish sports (Norberg et al. 2021)

Regarding governance within the organized sports movement, a complex picture emerges. On the one hand, it is evident that the SSC and the national sports federations gave the local clubs power and responsibility to comply with the Public Health Agency's guidelines and recommendations. The SSC and the national sports federations took the role of providing help to the local clubs by interpreting and spreading information about the restrictions. Yet, no systematic control of the sport club's compliance was carried out. Nor were sanctions imposed on clubs or training groups that violated the restrictions. In the words of a representative of the SSC:

> Our purpose has been twofold; firstly, to contribute to less contagion by ensuring that recommendations are followed, and secondly, to create to-the-point recommendations to allow as much sport as possible to continue (representative of the Swedish Sports Confederation).

On the other hand, our interviews also indicate that the national sports federations regarded the SSC as a superior sport's governing body with both responsibility and power. The SSC played an important role during the pandemic by representing the interests of the sports movement in contacts with the government and the Public Health Agency. Furthermore, the SSC designed and distributed the government's economic support. According to the Secretary General of The Swedish Judo Association, it was unthinkable for a national federation to develop an independent strategy for dealing with the pandemic. The SSC was expected to lead the way:

> We have always been careful to follow the Swedish Public Health Agency's recommendations and the SSC's interpretations. Even though we have medical expertise we have avoided making our own recommendations. However, we have always tried to translate the national recommendations so that they become comprehensible to those who practice judo (Secretary General, The Swedish Judo Federation).

Correspondingly, the representatives of the Gymnastics association point out that they had hoped for clearer directives from the SSC, more help in dealing with the pandemic, and a more sophisticated understanding of the pandemic's negative effects for an indoor sport such as gymnastics. In the words of a representative of the Swedish Gymnastics Federation:

> The recommendations have not been easy to interpret and have even been contradictory; when recommendations that concerned sport clubs were lifted, recommendations that concerned individuals were still intact, meaning we could still not conduct our training as we used to (representative of The Swedish Gymnastics Federation).

In essence, a combination of lacking communication and overly general recommendations caused irritation. The SSC were aware that the recommendations could appear obsolete for some sports disciplines. A representative of the SSC reflects:

> I think it has been most frustrating for those clubs that are not indoors, such as orienteering, motor-cross, and triathlon. How do you explain to a child that they are not allowed to put on their helmet, drive eight leaps, and then go home without talking or even seeing anyone? (Representative of the Swedish Sports Confederation).

This quote illustrates that SSC sympathized with the organizations. Yet, their main priority was to prevent a further spread of the virus. According to the SSC, their role and responsibility concerning organized sport was to support and to provide advice to member organizations a point they stressed during the interviews. In the end, clubs and sports federations ultimately decided on their own whether to cancel or to continue their activities.

Based on the conducted interviews, all representatives seem to agree that they made serious efforts to follow guidelines, however the respondents also point toward a lack of logic in the guidelines that they were supposed to interpret. When asked who they considered to be in charge of their situation, most voiced that the SSC were also rather following orders. Instead, the Public Health Agency was referred to as the institution with seemingly most power. Adding to this, an unmentioned aspect is that the development of the virus-spread per se necessarily also controlled the situation omnipresent.

A Summer of Relief and Cautious Optimism...

The summer of 2020 became a short period of relief and cautious optimism. Many Swedes considered the worst crisis to be over and expected that Swedish society would gradually transition back to normality during the upcoming fall.

Sport was no exception. While international competitions remained suspended, national leagues and championships were now initiated. This was partly possible due to the fact that the Public Health Agency´s regulations did not apply to "professional athletes." According to the Agency, their recommendations were never intended to ban entire professions. Thus, for people who performed sports as a livelihood, competitions were allowed, albeit without an audience (Riksidrottsförbundet 2021b). In mid-June, therefore, some of Sweden's most popular elite sports not least football and equestrian sports could restart.

A ban on gatherings of more than 50 people made public events impossible. It prohibited large exercising events for enthusiasts, such as the Stockholm marathon and further mass-participation competitions in orienteering and cycling. For the SSC, this also became a task with a high priority to solve. Accordingly, during the summer of 2020, the confederation began an unsolvable struggle to bring about exceptions in the Public Health Agency's general recommendations to enable sporting events with many participants scattered over large areas (Riksidrottsförbundet 2020). The Secretary General for Swedish Orienteering highlights that the recommendations were met with disappointment within orienteering clubs:

> The frustration has been enormous among the members who are older than 70, who were not allowed to join training, which is understandable—shouldn't it be a good thing to run in the forest? (Secretary General, The Swedish Orienteering Federation).

The Secretary General expressed understanding for the complexity of SSC´s tasks, however it becomes evident that she would want to see other aspects of sports prioritized:

> The SSC has had a huge challenge since they need to accommodate many sport disciplines, but the focus has been too strong on audience (i.e., supporting sports for lost commercial revenues), when one would think that the goal should rather be that people get out and get some exercise (Secretary General, The Swedish Orienteering Federation).

Clearly, the statement above illuminates a conflict between the sports movements' economic interests and different aspects of healthy practices. It underlines the view that, according to the Swedish Orienteering Federation, the overall purpose of the Public Health Agency should be to promote physical activity. Recommendations that discouraged participants aged older than seventy to join orienteering in the forest, would, seemingly, contradict that purpose. In turn, when taken to its extreme, this points toward a discussion concerning different aspects of health during this crisis: staying fit or staying clear of Covid-19.

...Followed by the Second Wave of Covid-19

As summer turned to fall, dark clouds emerged on the horizon. Already in September, the Public Health Agency reported an increased spread of the Covid-19 virus in sports teams and in connection to sports events, especially in ice hockey and in football (FHM 2020d). This was worrying news for Swedish sport. During the summer, the SSC had intensified its efforts to persuade the government and the Public Health Agency to gradually let the audiences return to the stands. Initially, the government reacted positively, but due to the increased spread of infection, all measures of this kind were postponed.

As the weather became colder, the number of infected and seriously ill citizens in Sweden increased. Thus, the Swedish Public Health Agency's recommendations remained intact: Swedes were urged to continue to avoid congestion and, if possible, work from home. Universities and colleges should remain closed, with all teaching conducted virtually.

At the end of 2020, new national restrictions were introduced, all at the initiative of the Public Health Agency. On November 20, the government decided to limit the number of people allowed at public gatherings from fifty to only eighty persons (Regeringskansliet 2020b). On December 3, lower and upper secondary schools were recommended to close for a month (Regeringskansliet 2020c). On December 18, all "unnecessary" activities run by the state, regions and municipalities were recommended to shut down until the end of January 2021 (Regeringskansliet 2020 d). The latter recommendation was primarily a way to persuade municipalities to close public premises such as swimming facilities, museums, and sports halls. Since much of the organized youth sport in Sweden is conducted in public facilities, the recommendation had a major effect in the form of closed halls and canceled sporting activities throughout the country. According to the Swedish Public Health Agency, however, outdoor training at public sports facilities was still permitted, provided that the agency's general guidelines were followed (FHM 2020e; Book et al. forthcoming).

Gradually Lifted Restrictions and Steps Toward a Restart for Swedish Sport

In the spring of 2021, Covid-19 restrictions began to be eased, with the result that sports activities could, slowly but surely, restart. On January 22, children up to the age of fifteen were allowed to exercise indoors (Riksidrottsförbundet 2021 c). In February, the age was raised to eighteen years (Riksidrottsförbundet 2021 d). For adults, however, public sports facilities remained closed. In addition, the ban on public gatherings exceeding eight participants remained. For most of the first half of 2021, the Health Agency maintained that adults should continue to exercise outdoors. For all age groups in the sports movement, the recommendation was to completely refrain from camps, matches, cups, and other competitions. Only professional athletes were exempt from the recommendations.

Beginning June 1, much awaited news arrived. The Public Health Agency announced that smaller cups, matches, and competitions could take place again. Moreover, the number of spectators at sports events increased to 500 people outdoors, while 150 athletes were allowed to participate in competitions on forest grounds, on water and on roads (Riksidrottsförbundet 2021e). Beginning July 1, the limits for audiences were raised further to 3,000 people with designated seating. At the same time, exercise races and similar competitions were allowed with up to 900 participants in the start and finishing areas (Riksidrottsförbundet 2021f).

Conclusion

In this chapter, we have analyzed how the Swedish policy response to Covid-19 was received within the fields of sports and physical activity. Employing trust as an analytical concept, we have examined how the organized sports movement and citizens in general handled and reacted to the national restrictions that followed the pandemic.

The Swedish strategy for fighting the pandemic was mainly based on information and non-binding recommendations rather than bans and regulations. It was built on trust in the citizens' own societal commitment and capacity to act responsibly. In the field of sport, the strategy gave rise to both criticism and confusion. Nevertheless, it was a strategy that was mainly accepted and put up with. National sports federations, local sports clubs, and individuals chose to trust the Swedish Public Health Agency's expertise and to comply with their recommendations.

An important overall explanation for why sports in Sweden chose to comply with non-binding health recommendations is the generally high level of civic trust among Swedish citizens. International studies show that Sweden, together with other Scandinavian countries, stands out with high levels of civic trust both between individuals and in citizens' attitudes towards public institutions (Trädgårdh 2018). Thus, trust has both been a prerequisite for the "light touch" Swedish Covid-19 strategy, as well as a key factor of the strategy's success, at least in sports.

Based on the respondent's shared experiences, trust in Swedish authorities remained high during the pandemic. For example, informants did not question that following the state's guidelines was the best way to minimize contagion, undeniably implying that respondents united behind the Swedish strategy, although some controversies arose. For instance, general guidelines proved problematic to employ to all sport-disciplines, causing some to question the logic of some recommendations (e.g., that people aged older than seventy should not participate in forest-orienteering). This sheds light on the complexity of creating recommendations that should apply to a big group of people, as well as to a broad understanding of health, both from a long- and short-term perspective.

However, if civic trust has been key in the Swedish fight against Covid-19, then one also needs to address how and to which extent the pandemic affected trust in Swedish society? Has frustration and stress during these extraordinary circumstances generated distrust between citizens' and swedes' relationship to politicians and authorities? Or, conversely, has the social contract in Sweden, alongside citizens' willingness to contribute to a common good, been strengthened? In our view, based on the data, the latter, and more positive scenario is more the likely answer. One could say that during Covid-19, the civic trust in Swedish society was put to the test and at least in the field of sports the test held up.

REFERENCES

Andersson, Karin, Alexander Jansson, Sara Karlén, and Jens Radmann. 2021. "Spatial transitions, levels of activity, and motivations to exercise during COVID-19: a literature review," Sport in Society, DOI: 10.1080/17430437.2021.2016702

Andersson, Karin, Anna Fabri, Peter Fredman, Susanna Hedenborg, Alexander Jansson, Sara Karlén, Jens Radmann, and Daniel Wolf-Watz. 2021. *Idrotten och friluftslivet under coronapandemin. Resultat från två undersökningar om coronapandemins effekter på idrott, fysisk aktivitet och friluftsliv*, Mistra Sport & Outdoors Rapport 2021:2.

Andersson, Karin, and Alexander Jansson. 2021. *Enkätresultat från RFSISU-Skånes verksamhetsuppföljning: kunskap bidrar till aktivt engagemang inom Skånebaserade idrottsföreningar*. Unpublished report. Malmö University.

Book, Karin, Susanna Hedenborg, and Karin Andersson. "New spatial practices in organised sport following COVID-19: the Swedish case." Sport in Society (2022): 1-16.

Bringselius, Louise. 2018. "Inledning". In *Styra och leda med tillit Forskning och praktik.*, Governement Offices of Sweden. SOU 2018:38.

Davies, Guy, and Bruno Roeber. 2021. "Sweden has avoided a COVID-19 lockdown so far: Has its strategy worked?" *ABC News*. February 28, 2021. https://abcnews.go.com/International/sweden-avoided-covid-19-lockdown-strategy-worked/story?id=76047258.

Esaiasson, Peter, Jacob Sohlberg, Marina Ghersetti, and Bengt Johansson. 2020. "How the coronavirus crisis affects citizen trust in institutions and in unknown others: Evidence from 'the Swedish experiment'." *European Journal of Political Research*. doi: 10.1111/1475-6765.12419.

FHM, Folkhälsomyndigheten. 2020 a. *Information om karantän*, 2020. Published on February 5. https://www.folkhalsomyndigheten.se/nyheter-och-press/nyhetsarkiv/2020/februari/information-om-karantan/.

———. 2020b. HSLF-FS 2020:12 *Gemensamma författningssamlingen avseende hälso- och sjukvård, socialtjänst, läkemedel, folkhälsa m.m.* Published on April 1. https://www.folkhalsomyndigheten.se/contentassets/a1350246356042fb9ff3c515129e8baf/hslf-fs-2020-12-allmanna-rad-om-allas-ansvar-covid-19-tf.pdf

———. 2020c. *Det här gäller för träningsmatcher*. Published on April 2. https://www.folkhalsomyndigheten.se/nyheter-och-press/nyhetsarkiv/2020/april/det-har-galler-for-traningsmatcher/

———. 2020d. Flera utbrott av covid-19 inom idrottslag och i samband med tävlingar. Published on September 22. https://www.folkhalsomyndigheten.se/nyheter-och-press/nyhetsarkiv/2020/september/flera-utbrott-av-covid-19-inom-idrottslag-och-i-samband-med-tavlingar/

———. 2020e. *Möjligt att fortsätta träna på utomhusanläggningar under vissa förutsättningar*. Published on December 22. https://www.folkhalsomyndigheten.se/nyheter-och-press/nyhetsarkiv/2020/december/mojligt-att-fortsatta-trana-pa-utomhusanlaggningar-under-vissa-forutsattningar/

Gruber, Judith E. 1988. *Controlling Bureaucracies. Dilemmas in Democratic Governance*. University of California Press: California.

Harring, Niklas, Sverker C. Jagers, and Åsa Löfgren. 2021. "COVID-19: Large-scale collective action, government intervention, and the importance of trust." *World Development* 138.

Helsingen, Lise M, Erle Refsum, Dagrun Kyte Gjøstein, Magnus Løberg, Michael Bretthauer, Mette Kalager1, and Louise Emilsson. 2020. "The COVID-19 pandemic in Norway and Sweden threats, trust, and impact on daily life: a comparative survey". BMC Public Health 20, 1597. https://doi.org/10.1186/s12889-020-09615-3.

Jonung, Lars. 2020. "Sweden's constitution decides its exceptional Covid-19 policy," in *VoxEU CEPR Research-based policy analysis and commentary from leading economists*. Published June 18. https://voxeu.org/article/sweden-s-constitution-decides-its-exceptional-covid-19-policy

Kavaliunas, Andrius, Pauline Ocaya, Jim Mumper, Isis Lindfeldt, and Mattias Kyhlstedt. 2020. "Swedish policy analysis for Covid-19." *Health Policy and Technology* 9(4): 598-612.

Ludvigsson, Jonas F. 2020. "The first eight months of Sweden's COVID‑19 strategy and the key actions and actors that were involved." *Acta Paediatr* 109: 2471. https://doi.org/10.1111/apa.15582

Norberg, Johan R., Daniel Svensson, Alexander Jansson, and Susanna Hedenborg. 2021. "The Impact of the Covid-19 Pandemic on Sport in Sweden". In: *Time Out: National Perspectives on Sport and the Covid-19 Lockdown*, edited by Jörg Krieger, April Henning, Lindsay Pieper and Paul Dimeo, 15-28. Common Ground Research Networks.

Pierre, Jon. 2020. "Nudges against pandemics: Sweden's COVID-19 containment strategy in perspective" in *Policy and Society*. Vol. 39: 3: States and COVID-19 Policy-Making.

Prop. 2019/20:172. *En ny lag om tillfälliga smittskyddsåtgärder på serveringsställen.* Socialdepartementet.

Regeringskansliet. 2020a. *En miljard kronor till kultur och idrott till följd av coronavirusets effekter.* Published on March 20. https://www.regeringen.se/pressmeddelanden/2020/03/en-miljard-kronor-till-kultur-och-idrott-till-foljd-av-coronavirusets-effekter/

———. 2020b. *Max åtta personer vid allmänna sammankomster och offentliga tillställningar.* Published on November 22. https://www.regeringen.se/pressmeddelanden/2020/11/max-atta-personer-vid-allmanna-sammankomster-och-offentliga-tillstallningar/

———. 2020c. *Digital pressträff med statsministern den 3 december 2020.* Published on December 3. https://www.regeringen.se/pressmeddelanden/2020/12/digital-presstraff-med-statsministern-3-december-2020/

———. 2020d. *Ytterligare nationella restriktioner för att hejda smittspridning.* Published on December 18. https://www.regeringen.se/artiklar/2020/12/ytterligare-nationella-restriktioner-for-att-hejda-smittspridning/

Reicher, Stephen and Clifford Stott. 2020." On order and disorder during the COVID‐19 pandemic ". *British Journal of Social Psychology*, 59, 702. https://doi.org/10.1111/bjso.12398

Riksidrottsförbundet. 2020. *RF ber finansministern om besked.* Published on August 20. https://www.rf.se/Nyheter/Allanyheter/RFberfinansministernombesked/

———. 2021a. *Färre unga idrottade under corona trend som oroar.* Published on March 16. https://www.rf.se/Nyheter/Allanyheter/farreungaidrottadeundercoronatrendsomoroar

———. 2021b. *Ett år med corona maj 2021.*

———. 2021c. *Träning för barn och ungdomar kan starta igen.* Published on January 21. https://www.rf.se/Nyheter/Allanyheter/traningforbarnochungdomarkanstartaigen

———. 2021d. *Nu får alla barn och unga träna.* Published on February 4. https://www.rf.se/Nyheter/Allanyheter/nufarallabarnochungatrana

———. 2021e. *Lättnader för idrotten från den 1 juni.* Published on May 12. https://www.rf.se/Nyheter/Allanyheter/lattnaderforidrottenfran1juni

———. 2021f. *Lättnader införs för motionslopp och publik.* Published on June 28. https://www.rf.se/Nyheter/Allanyheter/lattnaderinforsformotionsloppochpublik/

Ring, Peter Smith, and Andrew H. Van de Ven. 1992. "Structuring cooperative relationships between organizations." *Strategic Management Journal* 13(7): 483-498.

Rothstein, Bo. 1998. *Just institutions matter: The moral and political logic of the universal welfare state.* Cambridge: Cambridge University Press.

SFS 2020: 114. *Förordning (2020:114) om förbud mot att hålla allmänna sammankomster och offentliga tillställningar.*

SFS 2020: 162. *Förordning om ändring i förordningen (2020:114) om förbud mot att hålla allmänna sammankomster och offentliga tillställningar.*

SOU 2018:38. *Styra och leda med tillit Forskning och praktik*, Guvernement Offices of Sweden

Sörlin, Sverker. 2020. "Vi försöker gemensamt finna en väg där en väg aldrig funnits," *Dagens Nyheter*, Published April 5. https://www.dn.se/kultur-noje/sverker-sorlin-vi-forsoker-gemensamt-finna-en-vag-dar-en-vag-aldrig-funnits/

Trädgårdh, Lars. 2018. "Granskningssamhället i högtillitslandet Sverige," in SOU 2018:38. *Styra och leda med tillit Forskning och praktik*, Government Offices of Sweden.

Wenander, Henrik. 2021. "Sweden: Non-binding Rules against the Pandemic Formalism, Pragmatism and Some Legal Realism." *European Journal of Risk Regulation* 12(1): 127-142. DOI: https://doi.org/10.1017/err.2021.2

Chapter 11

Bring Back Our Sport: Power Play at the Resumption of Sport Activities in the Gambia

Pascal Mamudou Camara

Introduction

The Covid-19 pandemic and the quest for the resumption of sport has demonstrated the challenges of and opportunities for amateur sport in developing countries like the Gambia. This chapter intends to comparatively analyze the influence of sport stakeholders (football and school sports) on government regulations. The quest for resumption in the Gambia lays bare the relationship between sport and politics, and the different treatments accorded to different sports by government institutions. Organizational behavior literature stipulates that personality traits of individuals in leadership positions do overshadow or alters the organization's norms of cooperation with external entities even in Africa (Chatman 1989; Zoogah 2009). It is also imperative to understand the role influential individuals in sport organizations play through the lens of the Covid-19 pandemic and the pursuit for the resumption of sport activities.

Using radio interviews, newspaper articles, social media posts and official correspondence, this chapter explores the contributions of a diverse pool of sport stakeholders that negotiated the resumption of sport activities from March 2020 to January 2021. This period covers the beginning, peak and easing of measures during the first wave of Covid-19 in the country. The authenticity of official correspondence obtained through Facebook posts and personal contacts were corroborated by officials of the National Sports Council (NSC) and Secondary School Sports Association. Other correspondences which could not be accessed posed a limitation to the study as the available ones could not divulge conflicts of interests or other positions. The radio, television and newspaper contents of formally established outlets were obtained through the Heads of Sport Departments and the media outlets' online platforms.

Government's Position and Search for Reopening

The Gambia recorded its first Covid-19 case on March 18, 2020 and a day later the NSC issued a release suspending all sporting activities in the country. This decision followed the government's order to close the nation's borders (Standard 2020e). Subsequently, all sports and notably the Gambia Football Federation (GFF) accepted the authority and decision of the NSC: "all our planning is premised on government decision" (Confederation of African Football 2020b; Jarju 2020). The President of the Republic, Adama Barrow, used his constitutional powers and announced the first three-week long State of Public Emergency (SOPE) starting on March 17, 2020. Subsequent states of emergency came with stricter measures including night curfews from 10:00pm to 5:00am and markets only opened from 6:00am to 2:00pm (State House 2020b).

As early as April, individuals attempted to escape the SOPE and the restrictions through outdoor sport activities. Public sport spaces remained strictly closed but some private sport facilities, like gyms, continued operating behind closed doors (Standard 2020a). Residents along the coast played football at the beach for recreational purposes. Athletes organized training sessions either in isolation or in small groups. The NSC described the threat to its authority and the Presidential proclamation as "undesirable act of unscrupulous individuals and groups" (Standard 2020a). Sport organizations, like the Gambia Volleyball Association, remained compliant to the government orders by opting to engage its players and officials through WhatsApp groups and sharing technical and general knowledge information on the history of the sport (Jallow 2021).

Gym owners in particular received warnings to immediately cease operating for the "wellbeing of the people of the Gambia" and comply with the rules emanating from the "highest office of the Gambia" (ibid). The unregulated nature of gyms in the Gambia serves as the first challenge by groups on NSC as it provides an opportunity to defy the restrictions without violating them. Gyms in the Gambia could be classified into formal and informal. The formal ones are in rented enclosed spaces while the informal ones are just modern or homemade equipment in an open space inside a compound, similar to other African contexts (Draper et.al 2006). There are more informal gyms in the Gambia than there are formal ones due to the high cost and limited accessibility of formal ones. The mode of operation of the informal ones, which are sometimes free, is that it also serves as a hub for all the young boys in the neighborhood in the evenings.

By July 2020, the quest swelled to community level as there were rumors of some communities planning to host the annual summer community football competitions, called Nawettan (Camara and Seltmann 2018; Standard 2020d). The NSC again issued a warning to this effect but the GFF's announcement of the suspension of its Supper Nawettan, the climax of Nawettan, discouraged many communities from staging their preliminary tournaments (Standard 2020g). Though the release could be seen as asserting authority, there was little effect the release and the NSC in particular could have on the sport fraternity's surging quest for reopening. There are two major reasons for this: first, there is more direct funding of community sports by sports federations than NSC and would therefore command more coercive power than NSC; second, the weak government institutions mean that influential individuals in sport organizations yield more power and influence decisions at community level than NSC (Standard 2020b).

Followers of various sports, especially football and wrestling, formed the nucleus of collective institutional requests to reopen sport. Initially, the only available informal channels were social media and local radio stations. Some of the radio sport shows such as Lambaji on local wrestling, do host talk shows in the local languages and allow for listeners to call and contribute (West Coast Radio 2021). This served as one of the forums through which fans were able to channel their request to the government. Others took to social media to express their opinions and tag prominent local journalists and sports authorities. Commentators echoed statements such as "bring back our sport" and "if concerts and political gatherings are allowed why not sports" (Standard 2020f; Whats-On-Gambia 2021). This pressure on the media and officials obliged media houses and individual journalists to take the request to the next level. Interviews with sports officials only reechoed the request of the supporters of the different sports.

In a separate but equally influential development, the government received the second of two financial support grants from the International Monetary Fund of $21.3 million and World Bank of $30 million in October 2020. The funds were disbursed to sectors and families considered affected by the pandemic (International Monetary Fund 2020). Sectors such as the media, tourism, healthcare workers and "sex workers living with HIV AIDS" received financial packages (Ceesay 2020). The sport sector did not receive any such support though such request were sent to the NSC but no justification forwarded. This obliged the sports federations to publicly request government to allow sport to reopen or consider them in the support packages. The President of the Gambia Wrestling Association, Modou Faye Cham, directly laid bare the effect of the restrictions: "big contracts […] all bite the dust when Covid-19 hit the nation with the restrictions on public gathering" (Standard 2020c). He justified the request of the supporters emphasizing the specific nature of traditional wrestling in the Gambia as a sport that does not receive international subvention but depends on the surging number of combats, "the absence of activities effectively rendered both the association and its members broke and dysfunctional" (*ibid.*).

It is important to highlight that the general perception that "prayers" are more effective on the pandemic than the vaccines also played a role on the insistence of stakeholders for the reopening of sport (Afrobarometer 2021). Following direct demands from the sports associations and formal gyms requesting for reopening, the NSC assumed its intermediary role and invited sport associations separately "to assess the Covid-19 pandemic effect" (Standard 2020h). The Executive Director of the NSC, Marchel Mendy, assured the sport fraternity that "government authorities are working on the matter" as NSC has forwarded the concerns to the authorities (Standard 2020b). The requests were just being channeled through the NSC but it was common knowledge that the final decision lies with the Office of the President. Generally, officials of sports organizations avoid personal or organizational confrontation with the NSC as it sometimes employs its most effective power, to dissolve any sport organization in the country (Standard 2015).

By November 2020, the political play and reported corruption by government officials on the pandemic dwindled the fear of the virus and increased social interactions including the request for resumption of sport (Malagen 2021). The President of the Republic, Adama Barrow, embarked on the constitutionally sanctioned annual Meet the People Tour (State House 2020a). Commentators and opposition parties see this move as purely meant to gain political points at the expense of other parties because the measures would not be adhered to (Standard 2020i). The perception on the tour also prompted the music industry to start concerts. Other political parties also had their rallies. Some teams and athletes in some sports started training in groups, though it was not officially allowed: "even though it is not normal training, we will meet and play to ease out the stress" revealed a basketball coach (Singhateh 2021). Athletes of individual sports who depended on it for survival also made pronouncements. A traditional wrestler declared that his sport "died in the few months it has ceased to be active" (Standard 2020f). The activities in the political and musical scenes were comparatively branded as "unfair and nonsensical not to allow football, basketball, wrestling or other forms of sports to go ahead" (ibid.). These declarations prompted the government's negotiation with the public request to shift to a higher level. The Minister for Youth and Sport, Bakary Badjie, promised to follow up the matter with the Government Spokesperson and in Cabinet Meetings (meeting of the President and his ministers) since decisions on Covid-19 are discussed at that level (Badjie 2020). The decisions taken at Cabinet Meetings on reopening of sport in general are not divulged publicly though other decisions like reopening of markets were.

The Political Power of Football

The NSC was obliged to respond to allegations that it was deliberately hindering the resumption of sports in the country. Marchel Mendy confirmed that the NSC forwarded the requests for funding and reopening of sport to the "right" government institutions. Mendy emphasized that other than the NSC writing to the Ministry of Health, he exchanged phone calls and personally visited the Director of Health Services, Mustapha Bittaye and the Director of Health Promotion and Education, Modou Njie. These two individuals are the direct face of the government that updates the public on the daily situation of the pandemic in the country. The pronouncement by the NSC demonstrates how government institutions shift key responsibilities to one another in the face of uncertainty just to avoid public backlashes:

> He (Mustapha Bittaye) told me that they have lifted the restrictions on sports. I asked him since when, because I have not seen it written anywhere in the papers and my office has not received any correspondence to that respect. He showed me a document through WhatsApp but the letter was not signed. I told him that we (NSC) cannot rely on this because if we do, it will mean that it is not officially endorsed. I asked him for a signed one and he said, if I needed that, I will have to get it through another person. He gave me the number of someone at the Ministry of Justice, I called the person, who also referred me to the Gambia Public Printing Cooperation (GPPC) to get the said document. We got the document from the GPPC and reviewed it but there was nothing that showed that restrictions on sport have been lifted. We went back to the Ministry of Health and met the Director of Health Promotion and Education (Modou Njie) who informed us that he will talk to his Minister about it and they will draw the guidelines that will need to be adhered to in sport (Mendy 2020).

This also shows the pressure which the NSC was under from various stakeholders as it had to explore informal means to get their request granted. All the institutions resisted taking direct responsibility and publicly compromising the credibility of the government position. This is due to the fear of social mistrust, increased public criticism and the subsequent political implication for the Gambia government to lose votes (Jeng and Drammeh 2020).

Concurrently, pressure mounted from within the football circles which required the football federation to act or shift attention and responsibility to other entities. The Fédération Internationale de Football Association (FIFA) disbursed Covid Relief Funds to all member associations (FIFA 2020). Following a short silence by the GFF over the format of distribution of the $1.5 million ($1=51 Dalasi) grant coupled with non-activity at the time, some football stakeholders started complaining (Standard 2021b). With the support of home-based former footballers, some current footballers formed a WhatsApp group called "Gambian athletes are not slaves" and also used the media to criticize the federation on the management of the funds (Eyeafricatv, 2021). This is due to highly held belief that football officials live off funds from international federations meant for the welfare of athletes and development of the sport. Senior officials of the football federation met with some of the disgruntled players and settled the insurgence. A break-away faction of clubs and regional football organizations also raised a red flag on the manner in which the football federation intended to spend the first installment (Standard 2021b). The items the football federation intended to use the funds on, they argue, were already covered by the regular FIFA subventions and that there was no need to spend the Covid-19 funds meant for the football clubs on such items.

The lack of clear structural alignment by government institutions exposed by the pandemic also manifested in the football structure. The GFF held a meeting with players who wanted their share of the funds sent directly to them and not through the clubs. The clubs, on the other hand, argued that players were not members of the GFF. The disgruntled stakeholders' concerns were fanned off following a meeting of their representatives with officials of the football federation. To silence some of the unhappy footballers, some clubs announced direct redistribution of the funds to players and staff (ibid.). Other than the level of mistrust manifested, these episodes highlight how international sports bodies like FIFA lack absolute control over funds disbursed to member associations and therefore continues to breed corruption and administrative malpractices in the management of the funds (Chiweshe 2014).

With the surge in stakeholder pressure, the GFF on December 22, 2020 announced the annual Club Management Meeting for January 10 and the registration of players for the season from December 23 (GFF 2020). This announcement raised eyebrows as to the authority of the GFF to announce the formalities that precedes the league. The GFF also decided that the league would start in January. The First Vice President of the football federation, Ebou Faye, who commands great influence in Gambian football, shifts responsibility and the public pressure from the football house to central government through the NSC and the Ministry of Health: "we have given them all the measures and protocols that we will be putting in place" (Faye 2020). The media reported that the Ministry of Health was in the process of drawing up guidelines for the reopening of sports. Those in fact were guidelines drawn by the football federation and sent to the Ministry of Health to legitimize and formalize the commencement of the league. The Ministry of Health's silence and its satellite institutions over the guidelines plays best to safeguard the interest of the government in and outside the country.

The silence by the health authorities was taken as consent and no official communication was issued to support or condemn the actions of the football federation. Ebou Faye publicly dressed-up their actions by promising to put testing mechanisms and other protocols in place while clubs were tasked to protect their players and adhere to the measures (*ibid.*). Matches were neither declared as closed-door nor open to the fans and no testing centers were installed because the whole country had limited testing centers. Further ceremonial measures were announced such as players not being allowed to spit in the pitch and avoid handshakes during initial protocols (Manneh 2021). The football officials decided the order of priority in the reopening. Male first and second divisions would resume first while third division and female football to be decided on later. The justification put forward by the football federation when the issue was raised was "that is how it happens every year" (Faye 2021). Comparatively, similar activities in other countries like Senegal served as further justification from the football authorities as the Senegalese football league commenced almost two weeks earlier (Tellerreport 2021; The Point 2020; LSF 2020).

The resumption of the league and the silence of government institutions while the GFF violates state regulations demonstrates the political power of football in the country. Furthermore, the senior national team was to play a decisive Africa Cup of Nations qualifiers in March at home against Angola and a victory, which eventually happened, marked the nation's first qualification to the tournament (Confederation of African Football 2020a). There was a lot of enthusiasm built around this match by the general public which the government would not go against and the football federation exploited that opportunity. The silence of the whole government was to keep the votes of the youth. As the Gambia is a socially close-knit society, the dissatisfaction of a small group of the population easily spills over and the youth make up 60% of the population (Gbos 2013). Since the Gambian male youth is highly enthusiastic about football, deciding against the efforts of the football officials was tantamount to political suicide ahead of the December 2021 Presidential Elections. On the other hand, the government's public consent to reopening will jeopardize its geopolitical image and sense of responsibility especially before its international donors.

Government institutions were also being cautious into getting trapped in the political power play at the GFF by the personalities at the helm. Though the political affiliation of the President of the GFF, Lamin Kabba Bajo and Second Vice President, Ebou Faye is not publicly explicit, the former held various ministerial positions in the previous government while the latter holds considerable influence in Banjul and finished third in the 2018 Mayoral Elections (Manneh 2017). The First Vice President, Bakary K. Jammeh, and the Director of Finance, Kemo Ceesay are senior officials of a major opposition party. With the exception of the Secretary General, Lamin Jassey, the President of the Republic and his party does not enjoy open political support from the GFF (Standard 2021c). The presence of opposing political forces to the current regime at the football federation conditions a cautious approach to matters related to football.

It is important to highlight here that all the quests for reopening focused on the urban area. The regional governments and community football organizations had little or only peripheral engagement in the activities and only replicated what happened in Banjul. The centralization of government institutions and other mass initiatives in the urban areas is one of the effects of colonial urban settlements legacy sustained from decolonization to date (Salm and Falola 2005). This is because like other African countries, modern sport entered the Gambia through the sea port, colonial administrators and religious clerics all based in Banjul (Alegi 2010). The male first and second division leagues resumed on January 14 with fans and the football federation issued a public reminder that the Covid-19 measures were still in place throughout the whole country and admonished fans to adhere to them. This is as a result of the "huge interest" being built around the domestic football league by fans and the football federation experimenting with night matches (GFF 2021). In its quest to avoid possible future public blame, the football federation narrowed its scope to only the urban-centered national league though football activities had already taken cue in other parts of the country.

The resumption of the football leagues generated ripple effects in other sports whose officials had not declared the resumption of their leagues. Other sports such as volleyball and wrestling followed football by announcing the commencement of their leagues. Basketball had promised its clubs to start in October 2020 but had not made any announcement by January. This led to comparisons between sports and internal clamors for resumption: "the executive has to come and tell us what they are up to now since the *restrictions have been eased* (emphasis added) and the clubs have started training" demanded one of the Basketball coaches (Singhateh 2021).

Protecting Vulnerable Children, School Sports Must Wait

By late January 2021, the male football leagues, volleyball male and female leagues and wrestling bouts had already started. There were neither written guidelines from the Ministry of Health nor public objections to the resumption of the leagues. Other sports also started to pull their strings clamoring for the resumption of their activities. The Gambia Secondary School Sport Association (GSSSA) and the Gambia Primary School Sports Association (GPSSA) (from now on both referred to as school sports) planned nationwide school athletics championships (Inter-schools) from March 18 to 21, and February 18, 2021, respectively. All were denied resumption by the Ministry of Basic and Secondary Education (MOBSE). To avoid a possible public backlash on the decision, MOBSE leaned on the Office of the President who claimed that: "strict adherence to health guidelines cannot be guaranteed from the children" (Office of the President 2021c).

Contrary to football and other sports, the requests were channeled through MOBSE and not directly through the NSC. Though the NSC was established by an Act of Parliament in 2000 and entirely responsible for sport, MOBSE yields absolute control over schools (Standard 2015). Unlike other sport organizations, MOBSE solely funds the activities of both GSSSA and GPSSA. It therefore yields more control over them than the NSC though they are all registered under the NSC. This further demonstrates another weakness of the sport structure and lack of separations of powers between government institutions. Other than funding and policy guidelines, the regional division of the school championships are mirrored on MOBSE structures which has six regions and not the standard seven regional administrative divisions from the Ministry of Local Government and Lands or sport organization as employed by the NSC.

The NSC did not counter the position of MOBSE but rather assumed an intermediary role on the issue by addressing it before the National Assembly Select Committee on Youth and Sports. Marchel Mendy of the NSC justified the extent of his efforts for the resumption of school sports as well as his office's limitations on the final decision taken: "after our meeting, there were other meetings at higher levels that I was not privy to attend. It was in those meetings the decision to postpone or suspend Inter-school's athletics competition was upheld" (Secka 2021). Though the decision to suspend school sports did not emanate from the NSC, the decision affects its public image within the sport fraternity: "we do not want to be a catalyst of the spread of the virus in the schools, but if we suspend the competition, we may be challenged and we would not be able to defend our position" (*ibid.*). The National Assembly did not take any further step on the matter though it had several debates on the Covid-19 restrictions, measures and support to other sectors. This again highlights the value attached to sport organizations by state institutions.

Like football, the Secretary General of GSSSA, Lamin Jammeh, also leaned on the media to publicly challenge the logic of the authorities by comparing their situation to the normal school activities: "other activities are going on and those that participate in them are our very students, so here we are protecting them and they are being exposed in other social gathering" (Jammeh 2021). Comparatively, officials of football took to the media to clarify issues, inform on decisions and add pressure on the requests while officials of school sports yearn for public sympathy. Another teacher was quoted arguing that: "students have trained so hard for the competition, and for some of them, it would be their final chance to prove themselves to be scouted by government departments" to be subsequently employed and compete for them (Whats-On-Gambia 2021). The lack of influential figures within the administration of school sports, meant little influence over the decisions taken by the authorities.

The GSSSA wrote a petition to the MOBSE and the Office of the President but the Presidency replied that the suspension on school sports will be upheld because of "the potential danger that exposing our young and budding talents to Covid-19 could put them in harm's way" (Office of the President 2021b). Unlike the handling of the reopening of football, the Office of the President backed MOBSE by emphasizing school sport's inability to control the athletes within the stipulated guidelines. The main arguments raised by the Office of the President that there is no guarantee that all the athletes, officials and spectators will be subjected to tests before entering the venue; that enforcing the wearing of face masks by all remains a huge challenge; "government cannot take chances with the lives of our youth" and that there may not be enough law enforcement officers to ensure social distancing is adhered to in and around the venue were the same concerns raised by other political parties before the Presidential Tour (*ibid.*). The Office of the President shifted responsibility to the Ministry of Health by indicating that "suspension on all sporting activities are based on advice from the health authorities" and that authorities of school sport should liaise with the ministry (*ibid.*). This was only meant to shift attention and avoid further public pressure as the Ministry of Health does not have the powers to overturn an Executive Orders (Constitution 1997). The Office of the President also showed support to MOBSE by emphasizing the temporary suspension of school sports (Office of the President 2021a).

One of the schools, Bottrop, decided to challenge the authority of MOBSE by holding its Inter-house. The Inter-house is the in-school sports competition that precedes the inter-schools where the best athletes are identified in the different disciplines to represent the schools. MOBSE yielded its authority within the school system by demanding an explanation from the school administration as to why they defied the "Executive Orders" (MOBSE 2021). This also goes to show the level of control each of the government institutions has over their jurisdiction. While the NSC and its line ministry were not able to stop events but pressured to act on behalf of its stakeholders, MOBSE successfully exerted its powers over its jurisdiction, the school system. This is mainly because the institutional hierarchical structures in the education system are more formal while the autonomy of sport organizations compromises the powers of NSC and structures of the sport system.

The general lack of public enthusiasm on school sports outside the school system also meant little public support for their cause. Furthermore, school sports does not have a key community-linked event like the Nawettan, the influence of which could have other ramifications. Like the GFF, school sports officials also designed guidelines and sent to MOBSE. The officials further suggested a closed-door inter-school athletics championship and stream the events for public consumption online. The claim by the Office of the President for "protection" of the school-going children renders the public clamor for reopening of school sports less appealing as this is also a widely held opinion.

The decision to suspend school sports has direct effect on the Gambia Athletics Association (GAA). The school athletics championship is the basis of the GAA for scouting national athletes and preparing national teams. With the exception of athletics, other sports organizations have minimal engagements in the school system and the suspension of which does not affect their flagship activities. Following the announcement of the suspension of school sports, the President of the Gambia National Olympic Committee (GNOC) who also doubles as the President of GAA frowned at the decision: "it is unjustifiable to stop one sport and allow another to operate under the same rules" (Standard 2021a). This he did in his capacity as the President of GAA and not the GNOC. The GNOC remained silent in all issues surrounding reopening of sport demonstrating the peripheral role it plays in the relations between sport organizations and government institutions.

Conclusions

This chapter confirms the influence of powerful individuals on key decisions of institutions as highlighted in the literature. While the public pressure on institutions, informal structures and individual influence paved the way for football to force its way to reopen, the lack of instrumental individuals and formal organizational hierarchical structures denied school sports. The former's position had ripple effects on other sports like wrestling, volleyball and basketball, while the latter also had its adverse effect on athletics, which was not able to host events due to a lack of school championships.

Though the Ministry of Health is seen to be the overall authority with regards to directives on Covid-19, the reopening of sport in the country demonstrates lack of a centralized decision-making institution. As at the time of writing, the mandatory wearing of face masks in public places; maintenance of social distancing and the washing of hands, were the only measures maintained but hardly upheld in practice. While some sports were able to exploit the government's institutional weaknesses with individual influence and public pressure, others were short of exerting such pressure.

The power of the public pressure is eminent in changing government positions. The NSC was obliged to explore informal means to ease the pressure as the formal means were not yielding the desired results. To avoid blames, public institutions avoided taking a clear position on key responsibilities. The Ministry of Health never issued any official communication to declare the reopening of sport. Other organizations such as the National Assembly and GNOC all remained silent on the issue. With support from the Office of the President, MOBSE was able to directly inserted its powers on sport in the schools.

The direct supervisory role of MOBSE on school sports renders it less powerful, even with the mediation efforts of the NSC. The position and power of athletics as compared to wrestling and football is also demonstrated in the government's treatment of both issues with the same concern. Sports with a huge following and community appeal like football and its Nawettan can directly and successfully influence government positions. Government institutions treat sport as a rather informal sector that does not require great attention, ignoring its strong influence on society and that in turn serves as the perfect formula for sport officials to exploit and influence government decisions.

REFERENCES

Afrobarometer. 2021. "Gambians laud Covid-19 response but do not trust vaccines." *Afrobarometer*, July 13, 2021. https://afrobarometer.org/sites/default/files/press-release/The%20Gambia/news_release-gambians_laud_covid-19_response_but_do_not_trust_vaccines-afrobarometer-13april21.pdf.

Alegi, Peter. 2010. *African Soccerscapes. How a Continent Changed the World's Game*. Ohio: Ohio University Press.

Badjie, Bakary. 2020. "Exclusive interview with Hon. Mr. Bakary Badjie." *Star TV*, December, 2020. https://www.youtube.com/watch?v=V2dUkT1V0kg

Camara, Pascal Mamudou and Seltmann, Maximilian. 2018. "The Gambia." In *Sports Volunteering Around the Globe: Meaning and Understanding of Volunteering and its Societal Impact*, edited by Kirstin Hallmann and Sheranne Fairley, 93-102. Cham: Springer.

Ceesay, Mafuji. 2020. "Sex Workers to get Covid funds". *Standard*, December 2, 2020. https://standard.gm/sex-workers-to-get-covid-funds/

Chatman, Jennifer A. 1989. "Improving interactional organizational research: A model of person organization fit." *Academy of Management Review* 14 (3): 333-349.

Chiweshe, Manase Kudzai. 2014. "The problem with African football: Corruption and (under)development of the game on the continent." *African Sports Law and Business Bulletin* 2/2014: 27-33.

Confederation of African Football. 2020a. "Press Release. Total AFCON Cameroon 2021 Qualifier: CAF sets guidelines to strengthen the security system for upcoming matches." *Confederation of African Football*, February 6, 2020. https://www.cafonline.com/news-center/news/total-afcon-cameroon-2021-qualifiers-caf-sets-guidelines-to-strengthen-the-secur

———. 2020b. "Gambia cancels season due to Covid-19." *Confederation of African Football*, January 20, 2021. https://www.cafonline.com/news-center/covid-19/gambia-cancels-season-due-to-covid-19.

Constitution of the Republic of the Gambia of 1997, Article VI § Part.

Draper, Catherine E. et.al. 2006. "An inventory of the South African fitness industry." *South African Journal of Sports Medicine* 18 (3); 93-104.

Eyeafricatv. 2021. "Good Morining Africa, 12th March 2021." *Eyeafricatv*, July 13, 2021. https://www.facebook.com/eyeafricatv/videos/444414643542075.

Faye, Ebou. 2020. "Sports Bantaba." *Star TV*, December 12, 2020. https://www.facebook.com/183537458792972/videos/717103992328619.

Faye, Ebou. 2021. "Ebou Faye 1 st Vice President of Gambia Football Federation" interview by Sarjo Jammeh. *West Coast Radio*, January 11, 2021, Sports File.

FIFA. 2020. FIFA COVID-19 Relief Plan Stage 3 Regulations. *FIFA*, September 10, 2021. https://digitalhub.fifa.com/m/7cc3b437e346828c/original/rr6vyahcjzjzzo0aiebj-pdf.pdf

Gambia Bureau of Statistics. 2013. "Population and Housing Census, Spatial Distribution." *Gambia Bureau of Statistics*, March 20, 2021. https://www.gbosdata.org/downloads/census-2013-8

Gambia Football Federation. 2020. "GFF schedules club management meeting registration of players." *Gambia Football Federation*, March 23, 2021. https://gambiaff.org/gff-schedules-club-management-meeting-registration-of-players/

———. 2021. "Public Health Protocol to be Observed at League Matches." *Gambia Football Federation*, April 26, 2021. https://gambiaff.org/public-health-protocol-to-be-observed-at-leaguematches/?fbclid=IwAR2vDOAWxEAfurd2FStDnRbSEB1aoGVxujFTeYKuLrDmqu59JvCqngjMlg4

International Monetary Fund. 2020. "IMF Executive Board Completes First Review under the Extended Credit Facility Arrangement for The Gambia, and Approves US$28.8 Million Disbursement." *International Monetary Fund*, March 10, 2021. https://www.imf.org/en/News/Articles/2021/01/15/pr2112-the-gambia-imf-executiveboardcompletes-1st-review-under-ecf-approves-disbursement

Jallow, Bai Dodou. 2021. "Bai Dodou Jallow President of Gambia Volleyball Federation" interview by Hagie Drammeh. *West Coast Radio*. January 18, 2021, Sports File.

Jammeh, Lamin. 2021. "Lamin Jammeh Secretary General of Secondary School Sports Association" interview by Hagie Drammeh. *West Coast Radio*, January 25, 2021, Sports File.

Jarju, Omar. 2020. "Ebou Faye plan to crown Real de Banjul champions is premature." *Chronicle*, May 1, 2020. https://www.chronicle.gm/ebou-faye-plan-to-crown-real-de-banjul-champions-is-premature

Jeng, Amat and Drammeh, Ba-Samba. 2020. "Gambia´s main problem is not the new constitution." *Standard*. May 26, 2020. https://standard.gm/gambias-main-problem-is-not-the-new-constitution/

LSF. 2020. "Championnats nationauy 2020-2021: on prend les memes que la saison passée et l'on recommence." *LSF*, September 14, 2021. https://lsfp.sn/championnats-nationaux-2020-2021-on-prend-les-memes-que-la-saison-passee-et-lon-recommence/.

Malagen. 2021. "Profiting from Pandemic: Coronavirus test results for sale in Gambia." *Malagen*, July 12, 2021. https://www.malagen.gm/Video/VideoDetails/Covid-19--an-Outbreak-of-Bribery_13

Manneh, Alagie. 2017. "Ebou Faye Banjul mayoral aspirant." *Standard*. December 7, 2017. https://standard.gm/ebou-faye-banjul-moyoral-aspirant-2/

Manneh, Kalifa. 2021. "Kalifa Manneh former Head of Medical Department at Gambia Football Federation" interview by Hagie Drammeh, *West Coast Radio*, January 11, 2021, Sports File.

Mendy, Marchel. 2020. "Sports Bantaba 19/12/2020." *Star TV*, December 19, 2020. https://www.facebook.com/183537458792972/videos/3756532841076592

Ministry of Basic and Secondary Education. 2021. "Request for explanation." Letter to Director of Regional Education Office. January 2, 2021.

Ministry of Youth and Sports. 2010. *The National Sports Policy 2010-2019*. Banjul: Ministry of Youth and Sports.

Office of the President. 2021a. "Re: Temporal suspension of sports in School." Letter to Permanent Secretary Ministry of Basic and Secondary Education. January 27, 2021.

———. 2021b "Re: petition on temporal suspension on school sports." Letter to Secondary School Sports Association. February 15, 2021.

———. 2021c. "The 56 th Independence Anniversary Celebrations." Letter to all addressees. January 25, 2021.

Secka, Kebba. 2021. "NSC views suspension of Inter-Schools sports unfair treatment." *Foroyaa*, February 2, 2021. https://foroyaa.net/nsc-views-suspension-of-inter-schools-sports-unfair-treatment/.

Singhateh, Foday. 2021. "Foday Singhateh Coach of YMCA Basketball team" interview by Hagie Drammeh. *West Coast Radio*, January 25, 2021, Sports File.

Standard. 2015. "NSC scraps all but nine associations." *Standard,* July 12, 2021. https://standard.gm/nsc-scraps-all-but-nine-associations/.

———.2020a. "Sports Council vows to tackle violators of emergency orders." *Standard*, January 28, 2021. https://standard.gm/sports-council-vows-to-tackle-violators-of-emergecny-orders/.

———. Standard. 2020b "NSC warns restrictions on sports events not lifted." *Standard*, March 5, 2021. https://standard.gm/nsc-warns-restrictions-on-sports-events-not-lifted/.

———. 2020c. "Wrestling boss breaks silence from Covid-19 hibernation." *Standard*, March 5, 2021. https://standard.gm/wrestling-boss-breaks-silence-from-covid-19-hibernation/

———. 2020d. "Let us forgo Nawettans this year." *Standard*, January 28, 2021. https://standard.gm/let-us-forgo-nawettans-this-year/.

———. 2020e. "NSC suspends all sports events." *Standard*, January 22, 2021. https://standard.gm/nsc-suspends-all-sports-events/.

———. 2020f. "Political rallies allowed sports events still banned." *Standard*, January 22, 2021. https://standard.gm/political-rallies-allowed-sports-events-still-banned/.

———. 2020g. "Are back to sport protocols ready? wrestling and football fans yearn return of action." *Standard*, January 20, 2020. https://standard.gm/are-back-to-sport-protocols-ready-wrestling-and-football-fans-yearn-return-of-action/.

———. 2020h. "NSC meets sports associations, assess Covid-19 Pandemic effect." *Standard,* July 12, 2021. https://standard.gm/nsc-meets-sports-associations-assess-covid-19-pandemic-effect/

———. 2020i. "Meet the people tour it's for the people, use it for that." *Standard*, September 14, 2021. https://standard.gm/meet-the-people-tour-its-for-the-people-use-it-for-that/

———. 2021a. "GAA urges gov't to rescind ban on school sports." *Standard*, March 6, 2021. https://standard.gm/gaa-urges-govt-to-rescind-ban-on-school-sports/.

———. 2021b. "Stakeholders demand explanation from GFF query Covid-19 funds expenditure plan." *Standard*, February 4, 2021. https://standard.gm/stakeholders-demand-explanations-from-gff-query-covid-19-funds-expenditure-plan/.

———. 2021c. "GFF to decide fate of 2 staff politicians." *Standard*, May 12, 2021. https://standard.gm/gff-to-decide-fate-of-2-staff-politicians0/.

State House. 2020a. "President Adama Barrow begins Nationwide Tour." *State House*, April 12, 2021. https://www.statehouse.gm/president-adama-barrow-begins-nationwide-tour

———. 2020b. "President Barrow Lifts the State of Public Emergency." *State House*, April 12, 2021. https://www.statehouse.gm/president-barrow-lifts-state-public-emergency.

Salm, Steven J & Falola, Toying. 2005. *African Urban Space in Historical perspective*. New York: University of Rochester Press.

Tellereport. 2021. "In Senegal wrestlers can finally resume the fight." *Telereport*, July 12, 2021. https://www.tellerreport.com/news/2021-04-03-in-senegal--wrestlers-can-finally-resume-the-fight.r1t_To1UrO.html.

The Point. 2020. Barrow seeks Macky's help as covid-19 cases rurge in Gambia. *The Point*, September 15, 2021. https://thepoint.gm/africa/gambia/headlines/barrow-seeks-mackys-help-as-covid-19-cases-surge-in-gambia.

West Coast Radio. 2021. "Laamba-Ji." *West Coast Radio*, July 14, 2021. https://westcoast.gm/news/.

Whats-on-Gambia. 2020. "Inter-Schools Athletics Championship suspended due to coronavirus pandemic." *Whats-on-Gambia*, March 20, 2021. http://www.whatson-gambia.com/index.php/news/3088-inter-schools-athletics-championship-suspended-due-to-coronaviruspandemic?fbclid=IwAR0EZhuLDPvB6WyxZkWGfomKAlQ2qmdNzlQKkab86a1OkAIb02js90fUdE.

Zoogah, David B. 2009. "Cultural Value Orientation, Personality, and Motivational Determinants of Strategic Leadership in Africa." *International Journal of Leadership Studies* 4 (2): 202-222.

Chapter 12

What the Danish Covid-19 Lockdown and Re-Opening Can Teach Us About Sports Participation and How It Can Be Promoted

Jens Høyer-Kruse and Bjarne Ibsen

Introduction

The Covid-19 lockdown in the spring of 2020 and later again from the autumn of the same year changed for a large part of the population in Denmark both the opportunities for and the necessity of physical activity and movement. In their leisure time, many could not practice fitness, swimming, football and other sports because sports facilities, sports clubs and fitness centers had to close. For others, however, homework and study provided better time and opportunities for walking, running and cycling.

Covid-19 has serious health and social consequences, but it is also an unusual 'experiment' from which one can learn. Among other things, what significance more organized opportunities and structures for sports have on the population's level of physical movement activity, which can provide new knowledge about which factors are particularly important for the citizens' different ways of being physically active.

Based on a large questionnaire survey of Danes' physical movement habits in autumn 2020, this article will shed new light on whether and how the changes in everyday life as a result of Covid-19 had an impact on physical activity (PA) level. What factors may explain why some became less physically active while others became more active? And what can be learned from this to promote the PA of citizens in the future?

Method

More than one source was used to analyze the impacts of Covid-19 on the PA level and the Danish sport system. The primary data basis for the analysis is the answers of just over 143,000 respondents to a survey questionnaire about their movement habits, which also included questions regarding PA during Covid-19. The questionnaire is a part of the research project 'Moving Denmark a national study of how and why we move' which the authors of this article are responsible for in collaboration with colleagues from the University of Southern Denmark. The questionnaire was distributed in the fall of 2020 via the digital postbox 'e-Boks' which is linked to Danish personal registration numbers. The questionnaire was answered electronically by clicking on a link in the digital letter.

The questionnaire was answered by 40% of those who received the invitation to answer the questions. In order for the statistical analysis to be representative of the entire population, the data are 'weighted' in relation to gender, age and municipality size.

The questionnaire includes questions about movement habits and PA in four domains: at home, at work or education, during transportation, and in leisure time. Physical activities in leisure time include fourteen activity types: Walking, running, cycling, fitness, mental training, team ball games, other ball games (tennis, badminton, golf, etc.), gymnastics, dancing, activities in water, activities on water, outdoor activities, street sport activities and 'others sports'.

At the end of the questionnaire, the respondents were asked: *'Has Covid-19 affected how often you have been physically active in the last twelve months? Indicate if you have been more active, less active or if your activity level is unchanged in each of the areas below'*. The respondents were asked to respond to this regarding 1) practical work at home, 2) PA during work or study, 3) PA during transport (e.g., walking, cycling and running) and 4) PA in leisure time.

The statistical analyses are either descriptive or logistic regression. They include the abovementioned dependent variable on the degree of how the respondents were affected by Covid-19 in their leisure time, and a range of independent variables on gender, age, PA types, organizational settings and work situation.

A limitation of our survey primarily concerns recall bias, where our respondents might risk over- or underestimating their movement habits or Covid-19 consequences.

The following analyses are also based on information about the political and organizational changes during the Covid-19 crisis, which had an impact on citizens' opportunities to be physically active, as well as analyses of the number of members in voluntary sports clubs (VSCs) and participants in commercial fitness centers.

How Covid-19 Changed the Opportunities for Doing Sports and Being Physically Active in Denmark

Denmark was among the first countries in Europe to act resolutely against the virus by declaring a national lockdown and closing its borders (DR 2020). Furthermore, the Danish government banned large public gatherings, closed all unnecessary venues across its cities, heavily discouraged the use of public transportation and all manner of travel unless essential. Daycares, schools and universities were very quickly shut down and air travel was severely restricted. Administrative establishments and public places (non-essential stores, places of worship, cinemas, theaters, performance venues, etc.) were closed including sports facilities, VSCs and fitness centers. Outdoor recreational activities were not under any restrictions besides the ban on assemblies of more than ten people.

The Danish government and health authorities did not cooperate or consult with the organizations in the Danish sports sector during the different lockdown measures. However, in the gradual re-opening a wide assemblage of the organizations were included in a follow-op and dialogue group, primarily to be able to communicate directly and anticipate the consequences in the sector.

Most of these lockdown measures came into effect mid-March 2020. However, the swift response and the widespread lockdown quickly paid off and Denmark was one of the first European states to announce the gradual and controlled easing of restrictions. From mid-April, pre-schools and elementary schools welcomed back young children and a week later small stores and small businesses reopened to the public. Sport and recreational activities were included gradually in the following phases of the reopening (Covid-19 i Danmark 2021). This, however, did not mean a total normalization of participation in sport and recreational activities.

First of all, the ban on large assemblies were still in effect and was only very cautiously eased and later tightened again when the number of infected of Covid-19 started to rise in the autumn. A prerequisite for the reopening of the many indoor facilities was the compliance to the health authorities' guidelines including distance requirements, assembly size and hygiene in the facilities and during PA.

Despite the relatively rapid but gradual reopening of the society in Denmark, which also catered for sport, the continued assembly ceiling and guidelines for indoor sports meant that many events, tournaments, meetings, training courses and larger training sessions were canceled or prevented from being resumed fully.

Learnings from the Lockdown and Re-Opening

The results and analysis below are divided into three sections. The first part is an analysis of how the VSCs managed the lockdown and the gradual re-opening, and an analysis of the significance of the Covid-19-specific restrictions on organized sport for the level of PA, and how it may have affected the legitimacy of organized sport. The second section includes an analysis of the significance of the changes in the working lives of many adults for the level of PA as well as a discussion of how this knowledge can be used to promote PA. The last section is an analysis of the significance of a versatile movement repertoire for the changes in the level of PA under Covid-19, and a discussion of what we can learn from this knowledge.

Physical Activity During Covid-19 Challenges the Legitimacy of Organized Sport

The VSCs in Denmark have a strong position and legitimacy, based on strong historical roots and a significant public support, which was created in the middle of the twentieth century (Ibsen and Eichberg 2012). According to historical institutionalism (Stinchcombe 1965; Peters 2011), 'path dependence' is an important explanation for contemporary organizational structures, which can be difficult to change. When this happens, it is often in the context of major societal crises and changes where the path in question meets a 'crossroad'. The question is whether the Covid-19 crisis is such a 'crossroad' for VSCs in Denmark?

Organizations try to enhance their legitimacy by aligning their value systems with those of other organizations and the broader social system. This applies in particular to civil society organizations, such as national sports organizations (NSOs) like The Danish Sports Confederation (DIF) and DGI (a national organization for sport for all), which depend on the affiliation of citizens and the support of the public sector. The success of civil society organizations thus depends on the environment perceiving them as non-profit working for a larger cause than the organization's own existence (Dowling and Pfeffer 1975).

The political goodwill towards VSCs during Covid-19 is partly due to the generally great legitimacy of voluntary organizations and volunteers, and partly to the fact that the NSOs succeeded in creating a notion that the Covid-19 lockdown for organized sports and exercise had serious consequences for the health and well-being of children and adults. This concern was repeatedly expressed by NSOs in their arguments for allowing sports activities during lockdown and the gradual re-opening.

> I am afraid that the health and mental consequences of an almost real closure of club sports will be very, very serious. In connection with the spring's restrictions, we experienced that the Danes largely stopped exercising and became inactive when they lost the offers from club sports (Morten Mølholm Hansen, CEO of The Danish Sports Confederation, Fredericiaavisen.dk, October 23, 2020. Translated from Danish to English by the authors).

However, more studies in Denmark show that the alleged negative impact on the PA level of the population was exaggerated. A study of the impact of Covid-19 for health and working environment, conducted in autumn of 2020, shows no significant changes since 2019 in the PA level of the adult population and small changes in self-rated health (Møller et al. 2021).

Although many VSCs for long periods from mid-March 2020 to mid-May 2021 were prevented from conducting training and other activities, the VSCs lost very few members. A count of the total number of members in VSCs in Denmark shows that the number fell by 4% in 2020. The decline in membership occurred in most sports, but in some sports the number of members increased, especially outdoor activities (surfing / rafting, water skiing, golf, tennis, parkour, etc.) (DIF,

2021). These were all activities that were still possible to practice with no or very few obstacles.

Covid-19 apparently had a much greater negative impact on the commercial fitness centers. A study shows that the number of customers in the centers fell by 20% from February 2020 to February 2021 (DFHO 2021). In Denmark many practice fitness in VSCs (Ibsen 2020), but they lost only 6% of the members during the same period. This suggests that VSC-organized fitness was better at retaining membership than the commercial fitness center were. The reasons for this could be that it is often more expensive to be a member of a commercial center compared to a VSC-organized center and thus many wanted to save the cost of their membership in these. In relation with the reopening, the VSC-organized centers were also subject to fewer restrictions compared to the commercial centers (JP Finans 2021).

Our study on movement habits in Denmark which is described in the method section shows, that the PA level was unchanged or only slightly less or slightly greater than before Covid-19 for the vast majority of the adult population. The respondents were asked to answer whether they were less physically active, unchanged physically active or more physically active than before Covid-19 on four domains: at home, at work or education, during physical transport and in leisure time. The answers show relatively small changes in the level of PA. First, in all four domains a relatively small proportion of the respondents assessed that they were much less physically active (2% at home, 10% at work or education, 9% during physical transport and 11% in leisure time). Second, there was also a small proportion who became much more physically active (9% at home, 5% at work or education, 6% during physical transport and 8% in leisure time) (Figure 1). And some of these changes can of course be attributed to factors other than Covid-19. The results have much in common with the results of a similar study in Flanders, Belgium in 2020 (Constandt et al. 2020).

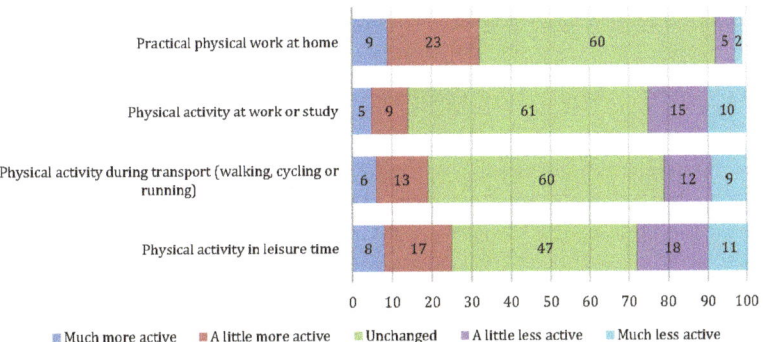

Figure 1: The assessment of the level of PA during Covid-19 (October / November 2020) in comparison with before Covid-19. Percentage of adult citizens (15 years and older) (N = 143,917). Source: Authors

Our study also shows that the changes in the level of PA in leisure time during Covid-19 depended on the types of exercise and sports activity the individual practiced. Figure 2 shows that people who regularly practice gymnastic, ball games, fitness and dance, i.e., activities that are largely practiced in an organized context and indoors reduced their PA level in leisure time more compared to people who practiced running, outdoor activities, walking/hiking and cycling, i.e., activities that are practiced outdoors and are predominantly self-organized. The same figure shows that citizens who practice PA in a VSC or in a commercial organization (fitness center, etc.) had reduced their level of PA under Covid-19 to a greater extent than citizens who practice self-organized physical movement activities.

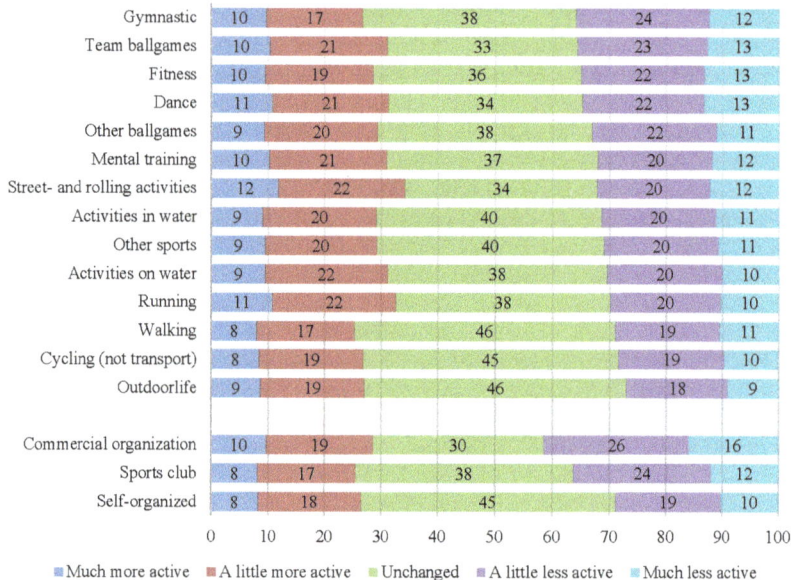

Figure 2: Proportion of adult citizens who in October and November 2020 answered that they were more or less physically active than before Covid-19 in leisure time, divided by what PA types they normally practice at least once a week and in what organizational contexts they practice activities (%) (N = 143,917). (Ibsen & Høyer-Kruse 2021).

However, the differences are small, and this is due to the fact that most people who practice organized indoor PA, also practice various forms of self-organized outdoor PA (Ibsen & Høyer-Kruse 2021). However, if we look at those who exclusively practice sports and exercise with a high degree of organization and facility dependence, the differences become clearer. A logistic regression analysis shows that the probability of being less physically active in leisure time compared to before Covid-19 was almost twice as large for the citizens who practice sports or other physical activities in a VSC or a fitness center in comparison with the citizens who are physically active in their free time on their own (see Table 1). And the probability of being less physically active was almost three times as high among citizens who exclusively practiced activities with a high degree of organization and facility dependence (fitness, team ball games, gymnastics, dance and water activities) than among citizens who exclusively practiced activities with a very low degree of organization and facility dependence (walking, running, cycling, water activities, outdoor activities and rolling and street activities), and twice as large as among citizens who practiced both types of activity (the table is not included). Covid-19 thus had significant consequences for the level of PA for those who only practice organized and facility-dependent sports and exercise activities. But this group makes up a small part of the adult population (7%).

Table 1: Results of binary multiple logistic regression analysis of the correlation between citizens' participation in PA types and their assessment of whether they were slightly or much less physically active when answering the questionnaire than before Corona (N =133,510).

	Exp(B)	Sig.
GENDER (reference: Male)		0,000
Female	1,208	0,000
AGE (reference: 15-19 years)		0,072
20-29 years	1,062	0,256
30-39 years	0,961	0,000
40-49 years	0,829	0,000
50-59 years	0,781	0,000
60-69 years	0,742	0,000
70-79 years	0,788	0,000
80 years and older	0,845	0,000
PA TYPES		
Walking at least once a week	0,794	0,000
Running at least once a week	0,635	0,000
Cycling at least once a week	0,868	0,000
Fitness at least once a week	1,463	0,000
Mental training at least once a week	0,954	0,007
Team ballgames at least once a week	1,368	0,000
Other ballgames at least once a week	1,024	0,295
Gymnastic at least once a week	1,216	0,000
Dance at least once a week	1,232	0,000
Activities in water at least once a week	1,187	0,000
Activities on water at least once a week	0,891	0,002
Outdoor life at least once a week	0,723	0,000

Street- and rolling activities at least once a week	0,929	0,194
Other sports at least once a week	0,865	0,000
ORGANIZATION		
Active in a VSC	1,657	0,000
Active in a commercial organization	1,815	0,000
Active in a 'leisure school for adults'	1,310	0,000
Active at work (sports etc.)	1,166	0,000
Active on their own / self-organized	1,014	0,408
WORK AND FLEXIBILITY (reference: outside labor market)		0,000
Work with no or low flexibility	0,824	0,000
Work with high flexibility	0,767	0,000
Constant	0,359	0,000

Source: Authors

Both the Covid-19 virus and the related lockdown had consequences for the health of many citizens, but the studies mentioned cannot confirm the expressed fear that many citizens would become much less physically active. The lockdown of a large part of organized sports and exercise in 2020 had relatively little impact on the population's PA level, because very few exclusively practice indoor sports and exercise, which were particularly affected by the Covid-19 restrictions, while the vast majority practice other forms of physical exercise, for which there were few obstacles to practice and for some could even be practiced to a greater degree than before Covid-19. This raises questions on how important organized sports are from a narrow health perspective.

Sport has always justified itself by the fact that it is healthy to do sport (Hansen 2017), but under Covid-19 it was almost only the importance of sport for health and well-being that sports organizations used as argument for allowing sports in VSCs. In an article on the closure of fitness centres during the Covid-19 pandemic in England, Chow (2021) claims that the requirement of the health authorities that physical exercise may only take place outdoors either alone or with members of the household clarified what the health authorities considered to be 'essential exercise' unlike other forms of more organized training, which the authorities consider to be 'inessential exercise' (Chow 2021). In a Danish context, sports organizations and public authorities regard VSC-based sports and exercise as 'essential exercise' which is given greater value than training in both commercial centres and self-organized activities because it is claimed that VSC sports better than other forms of exercise promote social relations, democratic learning and bodily 'education'. However, the arguments for re-opening VSCs in Denmark nevertheless concentrated on the narrow physical and health benefits of PA and to a small extent on the special qualities of sports and training in VSCs. Perhaps because the organizations assumed that politicians and public authorities considered the health benefits as the most essential of sports and exercise.

The health sector is based to a much greater extent on knowledge and evidence than sports and culture is, and therefore it is conceivable in the light of the experience of Covid-19 that the health system in future will focus more on other types of exercise and organizational settings of that than organized sport that can promote the population's PA. The sports organizations' one-sided focus on the health value of organized sports was a strength under Covid-19, but in the longer term it may weaken their legitimacy when research shows that the level of PA depends to a lesser extent on the organized offers of sports and exercise than has hitherto been assumed.

A Flexible Working Life Enhances a More Active Everyday Lifestyle

It characterizes modern life that work, family life and leisure are more integrated, and at the same time work and leisure activities take place at changing and sometimes overlapping times (Jensen 2009). Many workplaces allow their employees occasionally to work from home and to plan their work themselves. Research shows that it is of great importance for the way people practice sports and exercise (Pilgaard 2012). It is likely that Covid-19 has reinforced this development.

One of the big changes in the everyday life of adult Danes during Covid-19 was that many had to spend much more time at home than normal. Forty percent of the workforce in Denmark in 2020 occasionally or regularly worked at home, which was an increase from 28% the year before. Primarily in work areas where a large proportion of the employees have a higher education (finance, communication, public administration etc.), while homework to a small extent took place in construction, trade, transport, etc., which typically employs vocationally trained and unskilled workers (Hohnen 2020).

Although for some it was a big burden to work at home, especially if the work had to be combined with childcare, it also provided more time and flexible opportunities for many to practice a variety of movement activities. This was especially true for those who can plan for themselves when they work. Our study of the Danes' movement habits shows that people who can plan their work themselves increased their PA in their leisure time during Covid-19 to a greater extent than people who cannot plan their work themselves (Figure 3). This correlation is statistically significant when checked for the impact of other coincident variables on the level of PA under Covid-19.

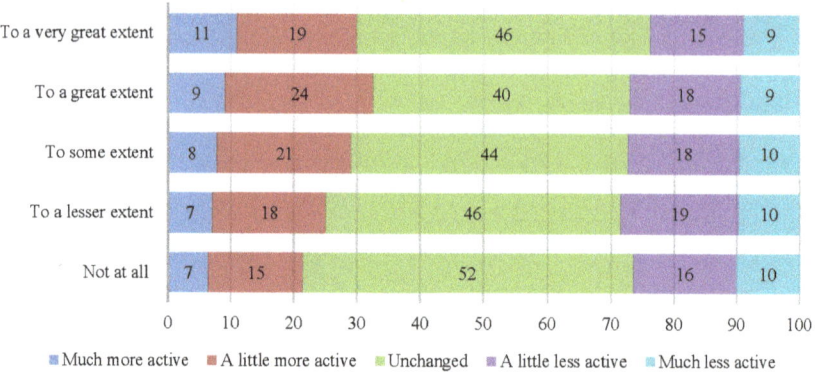

Figure 3: Proportion of citizens in the labor market who in October and November 2020 assessed that they were more or less physically active in leisure time than before Covid-19, divided by the 'extent they can plan when during a workday' (%) (N = 74,684). (Ibsen & Høyer-Kruse 2021).

For many years, attempts have been made without much success to promote PA in workplaces where work is not physically strenuous. It is this part of the workforce that has largely worked at home during Covid-19, and relatively many of them have increased their level of PA. This suggests that increased work flexibility, where employees can plan their work to a greater extent than one is used to (and whether they want to work from home), will have a positive impact on the PA level.

If a flexible everyday life, for example where ones work at alternating times, is to have a positive impact on sports participation and exercise, the individual must have the opportunity to exercise whenever and where they wish. This, however, is not possible in most indoor sports facilities and VSCs. Primarily because most facilities cannot be used individually at a time of your choice (except for most indoor swimming pools). However, a large study of Danish sports facilities shows that the capacity of these facilities is not utilized optimally, and many facilities are rarely used in the middle of the day (Høyer-Kruse et al. 2019). Better opportunities for the citizens themselves alone or with others to book a facility (e.g., to play badminton) would give them the opportunity to do sports at times that suit the individual best.

At the same time, the opportunity to practice different activities can be supported by inspiring outdoor activity facilities where people live. During Covid-19, new and inspiring hiking trails have been established in several places in Denmark, which appeal to both nature experiences and the desire to be physically active (DIF 2020). But also outdoor fitness equipment, parkour facilities, new tracks in forests for mountain biking as well as easier access to streams and coasts to activities in and on water, could promote PA. Such outdoor facilities have increasingly gained ground in Denmark, but it is still the provision of traditional sports facilities that makes up by far the largest share of the costs of new facilities for sports and physical exercise.

Versatile Movement Experiences Promote Physical Activity

Although for long periods it was not possible to go to the fitness center, play handball or go to the swimming pool, there were plenty of opportunities to be physically active either by increasing the activity level in activities you are familiar with, or start practicing activities not previously practiced. However, it depends on whether 'new' movement activities 'match' the individual's motives, preferences and movement experiences.

Inspired by Bourdieu's book 'The logic of practice' (1978, 1990), Engström, Redelius and Larsson argue that the culture of movement includes many different forms of movement and activity, each with its own logic. Participation in this practice e.g., playing football or doing fitness is related to the individual's habitus, as "a system of embodied habits and dispositions, taken-for-granted perceptions and preferences that will guide the individual in his or her ways of acting, thinking, perceiving and valuing things" (Engström et al. 2018).

The study of the Danes' movement habits suggests that the changes in the level of PA during Covid-19 were influenced by the individual's bodily habitus, i.e., the importance attached to PA as well as the movement experiences and movement repertoire. First, the study shows that the most motivated for exercising whatever the motive is maintained or increased their level of PA to a greater extent than the less motivated (Ibsen et al. 2021). Secondly, the study shows that citizens who practice many different types of activities over the course of a year increased their PA to a greater extent than citizens who practice few activities (Figure 4). While there is no difference in how many types of activities women and men practice, there is a significant correlation with age. The young are the most versatile while the oldest have a much more limited repertoire of activities. And citizens with a high level of education have a broader repertoire of activities than citizens with a short or no education.

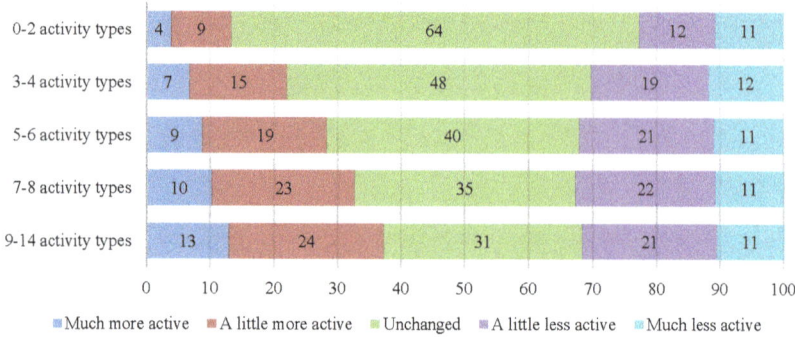

Figure 4: Proportion of citizens who in October and November 2020 assessed that they were more or less physically active in leisure time than before Covid-19, divided by the number of types of activities they have practiced in the last 12 months (%) (N = 143.201). (Ibsen & Høyer-Kruse 2021).

These results can be interpreted in such a way that versatile movement experiences and a broad movement repertoire means that one can switch to or increase the activity-frequency in other forms of movement when circumstances change. This could be physical or social circumstances, e.g., due to impaired physical skills, physical disability, changed living conditions (family with children or a new job) or major societal changes, such as the Covid-19 pandemic.

Versatile movement experiences and a wide repertoire of movements are achieved in many different settings: family, friends, day care institutions, schools and of course in the VSCs. In order to ensure that as few as possible become less active when beforementioned circumstances occur we as a society should encourage especially children and young people but also adults to adopt or cultivate versatile movement experiences across the different settings.

But the school's ability to give children and young people broad movement experiences are limited both by the teachers' professionalism and the school's facilities for sports and movement. In recent years, however, public schools in Denmark have been obliged to seek cooperation with the local community, including VSCs, and therefore many VSCs conduct events or teaching courses at schools in various sports activities (Ibsen & Levinsen 2019). It can help the children get a 'taste' and experience of different movement activities. The biggest challenge for VSCs is that the vast majority of clubs only provides one or few sports and therefore do not contribute to giving the children many movement experiences.

Conclusion

As the society in Denmark re-opens after lockdown, we are faced with a number of important insights after the Covid-19 'experiment'.

This chapter shows that the VSCs coped with the Covid-19 challenges surprisingly well both during the lockdown and the gradual reopening: the number of members fell only slightly; there was great political will to support the VSCs; coaches and volunteers were able to handle the many detailed requirements; and many VSCs showed great creativity with new and flexible training concepts e.g., online training. However, this strengthened legitimacy is challenged by the fact that the extensive restrictions on organized sports and exercise in both VSCs and commercial fitness centers had relatively little impact on the level of PA in the adult population. Although it seems that the VSC have strengthened their position in several ways during lockdown and reopening, it is conceivable that the NSOs claims that the lockdown of sports facilities and the activities of many VSCs was a threat to public health will change the legitimacy of VSCs in the long run.

Our analysis shows that the participants in organized sports and exercise had reduced their PA in leisure time to a greater extent than others, but this primarily applied to those who only practice that type of PA in leisure time. Those who also or exclusively practice self-organized sports and exercise had to a much lesser extent reduced their PA. However, Covid-19 also provided an opportunity to be more physically active, and this was especially true for the groups who, due to Covid-19, had to study or work at home.

Our analysis also shows that those who can plan their work themselves (with the opportunity to work at home) increased their PA to a greater extent than employees who are unable to do so. And this is especially true of employees with a higher education. The doctrine of Covid-19 is therefore that a greater freedom to plan one's own work will promote the level of PA. If the employers thus want to have or promote physically active employees, then a greater degree of freedom to plan working life will be one of the ways to do so.

The fact that so relatively many increased their level of PA is partly due to the fact that Covid-19 provided a better opportunity to practice many self-organized forms of PA. The analysis shows that those who have broad movement experiences, i.e., practicing many different forms of movement during a year, increased their level of PA to a much greater extent than those who practice few forms of movement. Based on this insight we, as a society, should strive for people to have a variety of movement experiences. For example, through greater collaboration between schools and VSCs, combinations of programs in different VSCs and that we as adults introduce our children and young people (and ourselves) to different activities.

The future will reveal whether the experiences from the Covid-19 experiment and what society and sport have learned from it will have consequences for the way sports and physical activities are practiced, organized and promoted in order to create a more physically active population.

REFERENCES

Bourdieu, Pierre. 1978. "Sport and social class". *Social Science Information*, 17(6), 819–840.

———. 1990. *The logic of practice*. Cambridge, MA: Polity Press.

Chow, Broderick D.V., 2021. "Swolecial Distancing: Gym Closures and the Quarantine Workout". In *Time Out Global Perspectives on Sport and the Covid-19 Lockdown* edited by Jörg Krieger, April Henning, Lindsay Parks Pieper, and Paul Dime. Illinois, 119-132: Common Ground.

Constandt, Bram, Thibaut, Erik, Bosscher, Veerle De, Scheerder, Jroen., Ricour, Margot, and Willem, Annick. 2020. "Exercising in Times of Lockdown: An Analysis of the Impact of COVID-19 on Levels and Patterns of Exercise among Adults in Belgium". *International Journal of Environmental Research and Public Health*. 2020 Jun 10;17(11):4144.

Covid-19 i Danmark. 2021. *Liste over politiske tiltag efter nedlukningen 11. marts 2020*. August 13, 2021. https://covid19danmark.dk/tiltag#liste-over-politiske-tiltag-efter-nedlukningen-11-marts-2020.

DFHO. 2021. *De økonomiske konsekvenser for fitnessbranchen. Notat til Folketingets Kulturudvalg.* Copenhagen: DFHO.

DIF. 2020. *Idræt i naturen oplever stort boost under corona*. November 15, 2020. https://www.dif.dk/da/bdfl/nyheder/nyheder/2020/11/20201115_idraet-s-i-s-naturen?

———. 2021. https://www.dif.dk/da/politik/vi-er/medlemstal.

DR. 2020. *Statsministeren: Danmarks grænser lukker fra klokken 12 i morgen*. March 13, 2020. https://www.dr.dk/nyheder/indland/statsministeren-danmarks-graenser-lukker-fra-klokken-12-i-morgen

Dowling, John and Pfeffer, Jeffrey. 1975. "Organizational Legitimacy: Social Values and Organizational Behavior". *Pacific Sociological Review* 18.1: 122–136.

Engström, Lars-Magnus, Redelius, Karin and Larsson, Håkon. 2018." Logics of practice movement culture: Lars-Magnus Engström's contribution to understanding participation in movement cultures". *Sport, Education and Society*, Volume 23, 2018 – Issue 9.

Hansen, Jørn. 2017. *Folkelig sundhed og foreningsservice?* Bredsten: DGI.

Hohnen, Marie. 2020. *40 pct. arbejdede hjemme under COVID-19-nedlukningen*. Denmark: Danmarks Statistik, 22. September 2020. https://www.dst.dk/da/Statistik/bagtal/2020/2020-09-22-40-pct-arbejde-hjemme-under-nedlukningen

Høyer-Kruse, Jens, Iversen, Evald Bundgaard, and Forsberg, Peter. 2017." Idrætsanlægs benyttelse og brugernes tilfredshed". *Movements, 2017:7*. Odense: Center for forskning i Idræt, Sundhed og Civilsamfund, University of Southern Denmark,

Ibsen, Bjarne. 2020. "Fitness in Denmark: A Unique Combination of the Commercial and Non-profit Sectors". In *The Rise and Size of the Fitness Industry in Europe* edited by Jeroen Scherder, Hanna Vehmas and Kobe Helse, 137 - 156. Palgrave Macmillan.

Ibsen, Bjarne and Eichberg, Henning. 2012. "Dansk idrætspolitik". *In Idrætspolitik i komparativ belysning – national og international* edited by Henning Eichberg. Odense: Syddansk Universitetsforlag.

Ibsen, Bjarne and Levinsen, Klaus. 2019." Collaboration between sports clubs and public institutions". *European Journal for Sport and Society*. Volume 16, 2019 – Issue 2: Social Roles os sport Organizations. Published online: 19 May 2019.

Ibsen, Bjarne, Høyer-Kruse, Jens, and Elmose-Østerlund, Karsten. 2021. *Danskernes bevægelsesvaner og motiver for bevægelse*. Report. Odense: Center for forskning i Idræt, Sundhed og Civilsamfund. University of Southern Denmark.

Ibsen, Bjarne and Høyer-Kruse, Jens. 2021." Coronas betydning for fysisk aktivitet og idrætsdeltagelse". Copenhagen: *Forum for Idræt. Forthcoming*.

Jensen, Anders Fogh. 2009. *Projektmennesket*. Århus: Aarhus Universitetsforlag.

JP Finans. 2021. *Fitnessleder er uforstående overfor forskellige regler om coronapas: »Det giver ingen mening«*. June 1, 2021. https://finans.dk/erhverv/ECE13009980/fitnessleder-er-uforstaaende-overfor-forskellige-regler-om-coronapas-det-giver-ingen-mening/

Møller, Sanne Pagh, Ekholm, Orla, and Thygesen, Lau Caspar. 2021. *Betydningen af Covid-19 krisen for mental sundhed, helbred og arbejdsmiljø*. Copenhagen: Statens Institut for Folkesundhed.

Peters, B. Guy. 2011. *Institutional Theory in Political Science. The New Institutionalism*. New York. Bloomsbury Publishing.

Pilgaard, Maja. 2012. *Flexible sports participation in late-modern everyday life An everyday life sociological analysis of the development, the variation and the character of leisure time sport and exercise among the Danish population*. Ph.d. thesis. Odense: Faculty of Health Sciences, University of Southern Denmark.

Stinchcombe, Arthur L. 1965. Social structure and organization. In Handbook of 92 organizations edited by J. G. March, IL: Skokie.

Part Four

Youth and Fitness Sport

Chapter 13

Covid-19 and The Shifting Role of Parent as Youth Sport Spectator

Jerry F. Reynolds and Matt Moore

Introduction

The Covid-19 pandemic spurred much change in the lives of citizens around the globe. Due to health concerns from millions of cases around the world and in the United States, individuals made significant life alterations to promote safety and well-being. One industry required to make notable modifications were youth sport organizations. Youth sport organizations modified their practices in order to hold competitions, interpersonal interactions, and sport activities. The role of parent spectators was an important factor in these decisions. Parent spectators attend to support their child(ren)'s activities, yet as a result of the pandemic 38% (n=3,936) of 10,359 surveyed were less willing to travel to their child's events (Pierce, Stas, Feller, and Knox 2020). Furthermore, 50% of parents had concerns about their children contracting Covid-19 through sport participation and 46% of parents worried about their own contraction of the virus (Solomon 2020). Parents with lower levels of concern believed the social and physical benefit of sport outweighed risks of the virus. While many sports organizations continued operations with modifications or temporary shut downs, there were several dimensions to consider with the biopsychosocial need to promote health and safety. The U.S. Center for Disease Control (CDC 2020) offered many recommendations to protect the safety of youth athletes. These included limited and/or managed spectator presence to best promote safety. Over the course of 2020, parent discomfort levels with attending events also increased from 42% in May 2020 to 76% in August (Pierce, Stas, Feller, and Knox 2020). To balance safety concerns and the ability of parents to view their children's sporting events, many youth sports organizations considered virtual (online) platforms.

Research on virtual spectating experiences of parents is novel. Within this chapter, the authors share their research that captured the virtual experience of youth sport spectators during the Covid-19 pandemic. This chapter documents the nature of parent virtual spectating. Virtual spectating experiences were brought to parents through streaming services and social media platforms (e.g., Facebook

Live and YouTube Live) that allowed viewing the game from off-site venues (e.g., home or work). Through a mixed methods research approach, the authors were able to capture retrospective parent reactions to their personal virtual spectating experience. Results from this exploratory study promote further understanding of both the spectator experience in a virtual context, as well as the psychosocial experience of parenting in modern youth sports, especially when physical presence was limited or restricted due to health concerns. Implications for future research and sport administration are discussed. The authors also generated a grounded theory statement.

Research has also documented the nature of interactions between parents and youth, but minimal research has focused on virtual spectating experiences of parents. Previous research on virtual spectating focused upon professional football (Weed 2007; 2008; 2020) and revealed the role of sport in creating social connections and bonds exterior to the game experience. In a similar way, youth sports are important in shaping family dynamics and interactions (Blom, Visek, and Harris 2013; Dorsch et al. 2015; Jeanfreau, Holden, and Esplin 2020; Trussell and Shaw 2012) and approximately 90% of U.S. children will participate in an organized sport by the age of 18 (Ryan-Dunn et al. 2016). Before delving into the virtual spectating experience, it is important to highlight the parent role as spectator. Parents as youth sport spectators can be assets and/or challenges to the family sport experience. Parental investment in youth sports is a cultural norm in the U.S., as approximately sixty million youth participate in organized sports annually (NCYS 2021). Many consider parents as the strongest influence on a youth's involvement and experience (Hellstedt 2005; Holt et al. 2008; Holt et al. 2009). Parents support their children in sports for the following reasons (1) the promotion of physical fitness, (2) the development of physical skills, (3) new social interactions, and (4) the acquisition of life skills, supplemental to those learned in school-based settings (Anderson-Butcher et al. 2012; Anderson-Butcher et al. 2016; Hedstrom and Gould 2004; HHS 2019). Youth sports are a $15 billion industry in the U.S. and are projected to increase to nearly $19 billion and $78 billion globally by 2026 (Intrado 2019).

Through spectator behaviors and feedback loops, parents engage child athletes, coaches, referees, and at times, other spectators (Dorsch et al. 2020). Parents may seek to reinforce their child's participation and performance through this form of communication. At times, parents can serve as advocates through expressing disagreement with officiating decisions or unsportsmanlike behavior. The youth sports environment is different from other family communication platforms, as there is a feedback loop encompassing communication, coordination, and maintenance of relationships among multiple adults and child athletes in one public space (Blom, Visek, and Harris 2013). There are also limited opportunities for the child to engage in this communication, as parent communication occurs while the child is in the midst of a competition or practice. Optimal involvement of parents requires understanding and enhancement of the child's experience through dually acknowledged goals that support both emotional well-being and require flexibility in parenting, concurrent with the athlete's age and level of competition (Dorsch et al. 2017).

The Covid-19 pandemic raised concerns about the long-term consequences on sports participation, as recent research estimated 30% of children who participated prior to the pandemic lack a desire to participate again (Aspen Institute 2021; Kelly, Erickson, Pierce, and Turnnidge 2020). This encouraged scholars to examine new approaches in research and evaluate factors within the sport system that promote or hinder engagement. Virtual sport spectating is one of these factors, as parental engagement is often key to a child's desire to play (Knight 2019).

Literature Review

Research on parenting practices in the youth sport domain focuses upon several themes (Dorsch et al 2021). Knight (2019) asserted most research concerning youth sport parents explored the influence of parental involvement on parental behaviors and the psychosocial outcomes and progression of athletes. The Covid-19 pandemic, which has challenged parents to balance the promotion of health and safety while simultaneously offering sports experiences to their children, presents a new variable for researchers to explore.

The grounded theory approach used in this study was an adaptation of earlier studies (Gray 2004; Omli and Lavoi 2009,) which sought to understand parenting challenges and the nuances, not just of multiple sport environments, but also the impact on family dynamics. There exists limited information regarding best practices for virtual spectating experiences. This study explored parenting experiences to aid in the development of a theory and future interventions to improve the overall spectating environment in virtual spaces. Furthermore, this research offers considerations for sports organizers to look at the overall psychosocial impact of virtual spectators on the family system.

Studies on Parent Spectating

Efforts to address concerns about the youth sport domain are not new. These efforts date back to the 1930s (Frankl 2007), as changes in the workplace and child labor laws increased leisure opportunities for children. Through parent focus groups, Wiersma and Fifer (2008) documented the positive and negative aspects of parental involvement in organized sports. Participants in their focus groups identified parental experiences as being simultaneously positive and challenging. Parents reported a mutual benefit of joy, stemming from watching their child acquire skills and have a positive sports experience. Parents also reported enjoying interactions with other adults and their families in a shared setting and building community connections. Documented challenges included cost burden (e.g., equipment, fees, transportation) and social pressure to invest more money and time, especially as competition transitioned from recreation to travel-based settings. Focus group participants also shared challenges in balancing family time (e.g., meals, multiple children) and unequal levels of commitment among parents. Providing appropriate emotional support and managing sometimes unfavorable reactions of parent spectators to their own child athletes was a stressor. Shields et al. (2005) found approximately 13% of parents got angry with children about their performance. Similar research found sport experiences youthful, fun, overly structured, competitive, and, at times, violent (Fields et al. 2007; Fiore 2003; Frankl 2007). Based on these findings, researchers encouraged the expansion of intervention research concerning parents in this domain (Harwood and Knight 2015, 2016; Knight 2019).

One study found 76% of parents reported feeling uncomfortable due to spectator behavior of others, while 82% of parents believed education in this setting was necessary, and 97% indicated youth sports organizations should develop parent behavioral standards (Bach, 2006). Harwood and colleagues (2019) used an online approach in working with tennis parents, discovering education improved parent ability to manage emotions, expectations, and promote healthy relationships. This study provides support for scholars to look more closely at the role of family in sport-based settings.

The level of involvement of parents is also nuanced. Hellstedt (1987) created three parent archetypes: overinvolved, moderately involved, and uninvolved. Overinvolved parents are deeply involved in the athletic careers of their children and behaviors, including creating conflict with coaches, officials, and put excessive pressure on their child to perform (Hellstedt, 1987; 2005; Dorsch et al. 2017). Moderately involved parents exhibit behaviors such as engaging children in the decision-making process concerning sports activities. Conversely, underinvolved parents exhibit apathy towards their child's sports experience and demonstrate a lack of investment that can be emotional, financial, or disengaged (Hellstedt, 2005; Fredricks and Eccles 2004; Dorsch et al 2017). Dorsch et al (2017) expanded the scope of these terms to include appropriately involved parents, described as emotionally and physically present, providing encouragement, acting appropriately towards all participants, being helpful, and having realistic expectations related to participation (Dorsch et al. 2017; Fredricks and Eccles 2004; Wuerth, Lee, and Alfermann 2004). Overinvolved parents micromanage their child's athletic activities by interfering with coaches and living vicariously through their child. Dorsch et al. (2017) expanded the on Hellstedt's studies (1987, 2005) to include extreme involvement. This is characterized by parents who focus strictly on outcomes related to perfectionism and/or the attainment of a college scholarship, and frequently embarrass their children. Stefansen, Smette, and Strandbu (2018) characterized the current generation of parents as one of having "deep involvement" across demographics. Such behaviors allow parents to connect with children and are increasingly viewed as part of the normal realities of engagement in the sport system (Fields, Collins, and Comstock 2007; Walters, Schluter, Stamp, and Thomson 2016). The nature of "deep involvement" is difficult to quantify, unpredictable, and unreliable (Block and Lesneskie 2018). Our study examined how parent emotions transferred across spectating modalities, offering insight into broader parent behavior that is connected to the current generation of youth athletes during Covid-19.

Method

Participants

To be eligible to participate in this study, participants had to be a current parent of a youth athlete (ages 8-18) and reside in the U.S. The parent had to have observed their child's sport events through a virtual platform and been willing to comment on their experience of virtual. The total sample size was 34 participants.

Demographic Characteristics of Virtual Spectating

Researchers recruited participants through social media and a digital university communication center. Researchers received responses from 18 (out of 50) states. Demographic characteristics, such as age, gender, and race were collected from the parent participants. The median age of all participants was 43.1 years (SD=6.56). The sample was predominantly female (n=93, 83%) and one participant identified as being non-binary. Indiana was the state of residence for more than half of the participants (64 of 112, 57%) and the second most represented state was Louisiana (n=19, 17%). The remaining 26% of participants represented 15 additional states. A summary of the participant demographics can be found in Table 1. Ninety-five of 112 (84.8%) reported being white or Caucasian, and seventeen participants classified themselves as African-American, Hispanic, or bi-racial. The most common sport settings were baseball (n=22), basketball (n=21), soccer (n=21), swimming (n=13), and softball (n=10).

Procedure

After our University Institutional Review Board granted approval, the research team posted recruitment information about the study on social media and multiple websites. Specifically, this included posting study information on Facebook, a University Communication Center, and two community-based sport Facebook pages. The recruitment information outlined the nature of the study, described the inclusion and exclusion criteria, and provided individuals with a link to the study survey. Informed consent was collected via the survey software prior to participation. Participation in the study was voluntary and anonymous.

Instrumentation

Parents provided demographic information about themselves (e.g., gender, age, race and/or ethnicity, and geographic location), their child (e.g., age, gender, and sport), and their child's sport setting (e.g., school, recreational, club, travel). Parents also answered a question about the virtual platform used for spectating. Following these demographic questions, parents read an open-ended prompt about their spectating experience. The prompt read:

> The past year and the COVID 19 pandemic presented challenges for families whose children participate in sports. One of the most notable challenges is the inability for parents to attend events in person. Instead, many parents had to watch their children virtually through various streaming platforms. Recall your experience as a virtual spectator over the past year (even if it was a one-time occurrence). Describe your experience with as much detail as possible. Feel free to include any thoughts regarding what you liked or disliked about the experience.

The open-ended question, which the research team developed to allow thick description of emotional experiences within the setting of youth sports (Gray 2004; Omli and LaVoi 2012), went through pilot testing with five parents not involved in the present study. This provided the research team an opportunity to evaluate the wording of the question and promote clarity. The 34 participants provided a total of 37 responses, as some parents chose to describe more than one instance of virtual spectating.

Data Analysis

Given the topic of virtual spectating is novel, this research employed an exploratory design. A grounded theory procedure (Oliver 2012; Oktay 2012; Pulla 2016), which involved the collection of data prior to formulating a theory "grounded in data" (Creswell 2003), guided the data analysis. The theory that emerges from a grounded theory process is different than typical theories in the social sciences in that it often does not include casual relationships between variables (Strauss and Corbin 1990). Grounded theory procedures are ideal for analyzing responses from a large (thirty or more) number of participants (Oliver 2012; Oktay 2012; Pulla 2016), especially when the phenomenon of interest is not well understood (Creswell 2003). Because our objective was to increase the understanding of a parent's experiences with virtual sport spectating, and no studies of this kind exist in the literature, grounded theory procedures were appropriate. Specifically, the research team followed these procedures for data analysis (Omli and LaVoi 2012):

1. The research team retrieved participant responses from a secure online database (Qualtrics).

2. Members of the research team read through all data multiple times, response by response, to become familiar with the virtual spectating experiences of parents.

3. Initial line-by-line coding involved looking at responses to interview questions independently of other responses. Members of the research team created a preliminary code for each unit of meaning (i.e., a sentence or paragraph used by a participant to describe a specific event); a total of six preliminary codes emerged. The research team triangulated these preliminary codes.

4. During the coding process, members of the research team grouped data themes with common properties into a single code, until a set of three themes that provided a comprehensive account of the data, while minimizing conceptual overlap among themes, emerged. The consolidation of data themes involved a constant comparative process, which is a hallmark of grounded theory (Oliver 2012; Oktay 2012; Pulla 2016). Throughout the constant comparative process, codes that emerged from participant responses were repeatedly compared to the raw data (e.g., responses from other parents) and researchers revised responses until the codes fit the data as perfectly as possible (Creswell 2003).

5. After assigning and testing codes through the constant comparative process, members of the research team found that the categories of behavior captured by individual codes could be organized into three higher-order themes.

6. After finalizing lower- and higher-order themes, the research team developed a theory to provide a holistic representation of the data. According to Creswell (2003), a grounded theory can "assume the form of a narrative statement, a visual picture, or a series of hypotheses or propositions" (56). For this study, a narrative statement was deemed to be the most meaningful summary of the data.

Trustworthiness of Findings

A grounded theory should include at least 20–30 participants (Creswell 2003). A total of 34 parents participated in this study, allowing the emergence of a theory grounded in the experiences of a large sample of informants. "The research team employed triangulation to ensure greater veracity of interpretations than would have been possible if a single investigator had developed the theory alone" (Omli and LaVoi 2012, 14). To establish greater trustworthiness of the findings, researchers engaged an additional individual with experience in qualitative methodology to review the themes. The interrater reliability rate of 92% was similar to previous grounded theory research involving athletics (Buman et al. 2008; Omli and LaVoi 2012).

Results

This section identifies various themes that emerged from the analysis of participant responses. The researchers trust they captured each participants' voice in the examples used to illustrate themes and to portray virtual spectating experiences. Researchers identified three themes: (1) enjoyable experiences, (2) negative experiences, and (3) concerns about the child. Researchers explored the meaning of each theme through quotes from participants. See Figure 1 for a summary of the themes and supporting quotes.

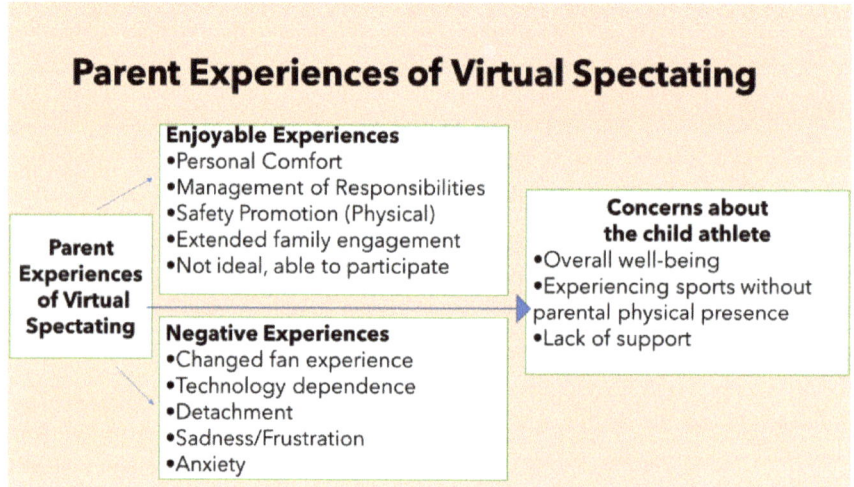

Figure 1: Parenting Experiences of Virtual Spectating

Enjoyable Experiences

Of those who participated in virtual spectating, participants (n=11) stated they enjoyed the experience. Enjoyable aspects included: reduction in cost for travel and admissions, avoiding crowds, spectating options for individuals at high-risk for Covid-19, and the inclusion of family and friends who might not get to watch otherwise. One participant responded, "I thought it was great. The experience was cost effective and I had no worries about crowds or other spectators." Two participants enjoyed watching from the comfort of their home writing, "I got to watch my son from the comfort of my own home. I could cook dinner while waiting for his next race." Another participant added, "It was nice to watch from the comfort of our home. It was great to watch them play and did not cost as much money or travel time." Many participants appreciated the option to watch virtually to protect spectators and to include individuals who would not typically get a chance to observe. For example, "I appreciated the option to watch virtually. It was great for higher risk spectators and grandparents." A second participant echoed this, "A big advantage was that family and grandparents from out of town were able to watch". A third participant shared, "I got to watch my niece. I had not seen her play before. We live far away and are thankful the school was willing to do this."

While many indicated they prefer watching a sporting event in person, several noted they were "100% content with the experience." One participant response provided a perfect summary, "Although there is nothing like in person sporting experiences and supporting/cheering on athletes, virtual was not bad considering the pandemic concerns. The broadcast made the experience possible for individuals to still be a part of the game."

Negative Experiences

Of those who participated in virtual spectating, participants (n=23) stated they had at least one negative experience. Negative aspects included: technical issues (n=11) and personal negative and undesired emotions (n=17). For technical issues, participants shared challenges with the streaming services which impacted their ability to enjoy the event and served as a source of frustration. One participant shared, "I tried watching my son play indoor basketball virtually and it was a disaster. Facebook had several glitches and it was a frustrating experience." Another participant reported, "There were significant technical difficulties, which included no sound and a lack of a clear picture." A third participant responded, "Virtual spectating was very difficult. It was hard to see who was swimming and what their times were." Other participants found the experience to be negative, but tried to make the most of it. For example, "The quality was not the best, but it was better than nothing." A second participant added, "It was difficult to follow due to poor video quality; however, just being able to see any part of the game let us remain grateful." Several parents indicated the technical challenges "eliminated the excitement and energy of the experience" and "technical challenges took away from the excitement and connection to the game." These responses raise a broader question about internet accessibility and access to necessary technology.

Several participants experienced negative and undesired personal emotions as a result of participating as a virtual spectator. These emotions included anxiety, heartbreak, devastation, sadness, and detachment. One participant disclosed, "I was devastated that we would only be able to watch on Facebook. I cried, my daughter cried, and we cried together. I was angry, but ultimately sad that I would be missing out." Another participant shared, "It was heartbreaking to not be able to watch my child and their teammates compete." A third participant stated, "I miss interacting with others and talking about the students. It was sad to not be there in person to cheer." Several participants noted how "detached" they felt during the events. For example, "I felt very detached. Nothing can replace cheer in person for your children." A final participant discussed how anxious they were, "Being virtual made me nervous as a parent. If an injury or something occurred I would not be there to help my child."

Concerns About the Child

Participants indicated their children also experienced varied emotions as a result of the virtual spectating experience. Participants (n=9) shared their child experienced negative and undesired emotions because of limited parental presence. Whether it be for reassurance or desire for an audience, participants voiced how much their children wanted them to be in attendance. One participant shared, "My biggest concern was how athletes experienced the process without support in the stands." A second participant echoed this, "My child did not feel supported during competitions." An additional participant wrote, "My child was heartbroken that I could not be there. They wanted me to be there." A participant provided a summary, "While announcers reminded kids, parents were watching from home, the changing atmosphere of no parents in the stands affected the athletes more than we can know." Comments from these various themes highlight a broader point about the pandemic's toll on youth sport spectators. Covid-19 led to an increase in virtual spectating, which ultimately led to a variety of positive and negative biopsychosocial reactions as a result virtual spectating. The experience evoked many emotions and experiences that warrant further investigation of how the family sports experience changed as a result of the pandemic and the impact of virtual spectating on family engagement in youth sports. Figure 1 summarizes these experiences.

Discussion

Study Findings

This study represents one of the first known studies to explore youth sport parent spectating dynamics in both the virtual space and in the context of the Covid-19 pandemic. The researchers collected data to share with a variety of stakeholders and guide future research on parenting practices as virtual spectators. The grounded theory revealed parents had both positive and negative experiences spectating in this modality. These psychosocial experiences were not limited to personal opinions, but also shared how sports activities were engrained in family life and relationships with children.

Consistent with the research of Wiersma and Fifer (2008) and Stefansen et al. (2018), this research revealed both emotional experiences and varied challenges associated with spectating in a virtual context. Some found the experience to be enjoyable and one in which they were able to manage both their adult responsibilities and family roles more effectively. The virtual spectating experience permitted parents to view competitions from the comforts of their home and increase broader family engagement to those who are traditionally unable to see their relatives or friends through in person participation. Others simply appreciated the opportunity to witness their child's engagement in a sport, even if they were not able to be physically present as a spectator, due to safety concerns.

Conversely, participants shared several negative experiences with inconsistent guidelines and technological interruptions and reported experiencing some undesired emotions, such as anger, disconnection from the "live" game experience, or sadness. Sadness was also experienced with their children, as a result of not being physically present and sharing the lived experiences of youth sports with their child. Findings from this research also suggest evidence of "deep involvement" (Stefansen, Smette, and Strandbu 2018). The virtual experience challenged parents to manage their own emotions and their child experiences related to sports participation in the pandemic. This prompts future exploration of factors contributing to parent involvement in youth sports. Sport-based settings create a vehicle for family interaction and their development as children. Participants voiced a desire to attend their child(ren)'s sporting events, to engage their children in feedback about their performance, and as a method for bonding as a family. This study found this behavior pattern consistent across genders of both youth and parents and sports settings.

Future Directions

The study is not without limitations. The study relied upon a convenience and snowball sample from predominantly two regions of the U.S. The Covid-19 pandemic impacted youth sports and spectators on a global scale. A broader sample would reveal more global findings, especially considering the nuanced local and state restrictions related to Covid-19 protocols. Researchers were unable to find prior research to guide the study, as the pandemic was the first in over 100 years to cause widespread shutdowns and impact youth sports operations. This study is among the first on virtual spectating experiences.

Conversely, the study provides researchers with a framework for future study of family behavior in youth sports. In future studies, researchers may replicate the grounded theory approach to compare and contrast parent reactions to alterations in their spectator behavior practices. Sports organizations will also have the opportunity to use this approach to gather more locally based data that can guide them as they balance safety and wellness protocols while providing sports experiences for children. A closer examination of more sport specific studies, gender focused studies (of parents and child participants) and factors influencing both the spectator experience of both parents and children is also warranted. Researchers must also keep in mind that changes in spectator protocols can generate both positive and negative experiences for parents and consider how these experiences impact the collective family experience in youth sports.

Table 1: Participant Demographics

Variable	N	M	Sd
Parent Age (Male)	19	42.3	6.70
Parent Age (Female)	91	46.63	6.35
Parent Age (Non-Binary)	1	45	
Parent Race			
White	95		
Other (African-American, Hispanic, or Biracial)	17		
Child Athlete Age	112	13.10	3.03
Child Athlete (Female)	41		
Child Athlete (Male)	70		
Child Athlete (Non-Binary)	1		
State of Residence			
IN			
LA	64		
MI	19		
AL, TN (each)	8		
MD, NC, PA, TX (each)	3		
CA, CO, FL, IL, IA, MO,	2		
SC, WA (each)	1		

Table 2: Qualitative Themes and Quotes

Theme	Quotes
Enjoyable Experiences	"I thought it was great. The experience was cost effective and I had no worries about crowds or other spectators." "I got to watch my son from the comfort of my own home. I could cook dinner while waiting for his next race." "It was nice to watch from the comfort of our home. It was great to watch them play and did not cost money or travel time." "I appreciated the option to watch virtually. It was great for higher risk spectators and grandparents." "A big advantage was that family and grandparents from out of town were able to watch." "I got to watch my niece. I had not seen her play before. We live far away and are thankful the school was willing to do this." "Although there is nothing like in person sporting experiences and supporting/cheering on athletes, virtual was not bad considering the pandemic concerns. The broadcast made the experience possible for individuals to still be a part of the game."

Negative Experiences	"I tried watching my son play indoor basketball virtually and it was a disaster. Facebook had several glitches and it was a frustrating experience." "There were significant technical difficulties, which included no sound and a lack of a clear picture." "Virtual spectating was very difficult. It was hard to see who was swimming and what their times were." The quality was not the best, but it was better than nothing." "It was difficult to follow due to poor video quality; however, just being able to see any part of the game let us remain grateful." "I was devastated that we would only be able to watch on Facebook. I cried, my daughter cried, and we cried together. I was angry, but ultimately sad that I would be missing out." "It was heartbreaking to not be able to watch my child and their teammates compete." "I miss interacting with others and talking about the students. It was sad to not be there in person to cheer." "I felt very detached. Nothing can replace cheer in person for your children." "Being virtual made me nervous as a parent. If an injury or something occurred I would not be there to help my child."
Concerns about the Child	"My biggest concern was how athletes experienced the process without support in the stands." "My child did not feel supported during competitions." "My child was heartbroken that I could not be there. They wanted me to be there." "While announcers reminded kids, parents were watching from home, the changing atmosphere of no parents in the stands affected the athletes more than we can know."

REFERENCES

Anderson-Butcher, Dawn, Allie Riley, Aidyn Iachini, Rebecca Wade-Mdivanian, and Jerome Davis. 2021. "Sports and Youth Development." In *Encyclopedia of Adolescence,* edited by R.J.R. Levesque, 2846-2859. New York: Springer.

Anderson-Butcher, Dawn, Allie Riley, Aidyn Iachini, Rebecca Wade-Mdivanian, Jerome Davis, and Jerry F. Reynolds II. 2016. "Sports and Youth Development." In *Encyclopedia of Adolescence,* edited by R.J.R. Levesque, 2846-2859. New York: Springer.

Aspen Institute. n.d. "Project Play State of Play 2020." Aspen Institute Project Play. https://www.aspenprojectplay.org/state-of-play-2020/pandemic-trends

Bach, Greg. 2006. "The Parents Association for Youth Sports: A Proactive Method of Spectator Behavior Management." *Journal of Physical Education, Recreation & Dance* 77 (6): 16-19.

Block, Steven, and Eric Lesneskie. 2018. "A Thematic Analysis of Spectator Violence at Sporting Events in North

America." *Deviant Behavior* 39 (9): 1140-1152.

Blom, Lindsey C., and Dan Drane. 2008. "Parents' Sideline Comments: Exploring the Reality of a Growing Issue." *Athletic Insight: The Online Journal of Sport Psychology* 10 (3): 1-25.

Blom, Lindsey C., Amanda J. Visek, and Brandonn S. Harris. 2013. "Triangulation in Youth Sport: Healthy Partnerships Among Parents, Coaches, and Practitioners." *Journal of Sport Psychology in Action* 4 (2): 86-96.

Buman, Matthew P., Jens W. Omli, Peter R. Giacobbi Jr, and Britton W. Brewer. 2008. "Experiences and Coping Responses of "Hitting the Wall" for Recreational Marathon Runners." *Journal of Applied Sport Psychology* 20 (3): 282-300.

Center for Disease Control (CDC). 2020. "Considerations for Youth Sports Administrators." Center for Disease Control. Accessed December 31, 2020. https://www.cdc.gov/coronavirus/2019-ncov/community/schools-childcare/youth-sports.html

Charmaz, Kathy. 2014. *Constructing Grounded Theory*. London: Sage.

Creswell, John W., and J. Creswell. 2003. *Research Design*. Thousand Oaks: Sage Publications.

Witt, Peter A., and Tek B. Dangi. 2018"Why Children/Youth Drop Out of Sports." *Journal of Park and Recreation Administration* 36 (3): 191-199.

Dorsch, Travis E., Alan L. Smith, Jordan A. Blazo, Jay Coakley, Jean Côté, Christopher R.D. Wagstaff, Stacy Warner, and Michael Q. King. 2020. "Toward an Integrated Understanding of the Youth Sport System." *Research Quarterly for Exercise and Sport*: 1-15. https://doi.org/10.1080/02701367.2020.1810847

Dorsch, Travis E., Michael Q. King, Charles R. Dunn, Keith V. Osai, and Sarah Tulane. 2017. "The Impact of Evidence-Based Parent Education In Organized Youth Sport: A Pilot Study." *Journal of Applied Sport Psychology* 29 (2): 199-214.

Dorsch, Travis E., Alan L. Smith, Steven R. Wilson, and Meghan H. McDonough. 2015. "Parent Goals and Verbal Sideline Behavior in Organized Youth Sport." *Sport, Exercise, and Performance Psychology* 4 (1): 19-35.

Fields, Sarah K., Christy L. Collins, and R. Dawn Comstock. 2007. "Conflict on the Courts: A Review of Sports-related Violence Literature." *Trauma, Violence, and Abuse* 8 (4): 359-369.

Fiore, Dianna K. 2003. "Parental Rage and Violence in Youth Sports: How Can We Prevent Soccer Moms and Hockey Dads from Interfering in Youth Sports and Causing Games to End in Fistfights Rather Than Handshakes." *Villanova Sports and Entertainment Law Journal* 10 (1): 1-28.

Frankl, Daniel. 2007. "Youth Sports: Innocence Lost." Los Angeles: California State University.

Fredricks, Jennifer A., and Jacquelynne S. Eccles. 2004. "Parental Influences on Youth Involvement in Sports." In *Developmental Sport and Exercise Psychology: A Lifespan Perspective*, edited by M. R. Weiss, 145–164. Morgantown: Fitness Information Technology.

Goldstein, Jay D., and Seppo E. Iso-Ahola. 2008. "Determinants of Parents' Sideline-rage Emotions and Behaviors at Youth Soccer Games 1." *Journal of Applied Social Psychology* 38 (6): 1442-1462.

Gray, David E. 2004. *Doing Research in the Real World*. London: Sage.

Harwood, Chris G., and Camilla J. Knight. 2016. "Parenting in Sport." *Sport, Exercise, and Performance Psychology* 5 (2): 84-88.

——. 2015. "Parenting in Youth Sport: A Position Paper on Parenting Expertise." *Psychology of Sport and Exercise* 16 (1): 24-35.

Hedstrom, Ryan, and Daniel Gould. 2004. "Research in Youth Sports: Critical Issues Status." *Michigan: Michigan State University*: 1-42.

Hellstedt, Jon C. 1987. "The Coach/Parent/Athlete Relationship." *The Sport Psychologist* 1 (1): 151-160.

Henson, Steve. 2012 "What Makes a Nightmare Sports Parent--And What Makes a Great One." *The Post Game*. Last modified February 15, 2012.

Holt, Nicholas L., Katherine A. Tamminen, Danielle E. Black, Zoë L. Sehn, and Michael P. Wall. 2008. "Parental Involvement in Competitive Youth Sport Settings." *Psychology of Sport and Exercise* 9 (5): 663-685.

Holt, Nicholas L., Katherine A. Tamminen, Danielle E. Black, James L. Mandigo, and Kenneth R. Fox. 2009. "Youth Sport Parenting Styles and Practices." *Journal of Sport and Exercise Psychology* 31 (1): 37-59.

Intrado Globe News Wire. 2019. "Youth Sports Market Projected to Reach $77.6 Billion by 2026 Comprehensive Industry Analysis & Insights" *Intrado Globe News Wire*. Last modified December 26, 2019. https://www.globenewswire.com/fr/news-release/2019/12/26/1964575/0/en/Youth-Sports-Market-Projected-to-Reach-77-6-Billion-by-2026-Comprehensive-Industry-Analysis-Insights.html

Jeanfreau, Michelle M., Chelsey L. Holden, and Jacob A. Esplin. 2020. "How Far is Too Far? Parenting Behaviors in Youth Sports." *The American Journal of Family Therapy* 48 (4): 356-368.

Kelly, Adam L., Karl Erickson, Scott Pierce, and Jennifer Turnnidge. 2020. "Youth Sport and COVID-19: Contextual, Methodological, and Practical Considerations." *Frontiers in Sports and Active Living Journal*, 2: 1-4.

Knight, Camilla J. 2019. "Revealing Findings in Youth Sport Parenting Research." *Kinesiology Review* 8 (3): 252-259.

National Council of Youth Sports (NCYS). 2021. "Youth Sport's Greatest Resource." National Council of Youth Sports. Accessed May 28, 2021. https://www.ncys.org/

Oktay, Julianne S. 2012. *Grounded Theory*. Oxford: Oxford University Press.

Oliver, Carolyn. 2012. "Critical Realist Grounded Theory: A New Approach for Social Work Research." *British Journal of Social Work* 42 (2): 371-387.

Omli, Jens, and Nicole M. LaVoi. 2009. "Background Anger in Youth Sport: A Perfect Storm." *Journal of Sport Behavior* 32 (2): 242-260.

———. 2012. "Emotional Experiences of Youth Sport Parents I: Anger." *Journal of Applied Sport Psychology* 24 (1): 10-25.

Pierce, David, Jessi Stas, Kevin Feller, and William Knox. 2020. "COVID-19: Return to Youth Sports: Preparing Sports Venues and Events for the Return of Youth Sports." *Sports Innovation Journal* 1:62-80.

Pulla, Venkat. 2016. "An Introduction to the Grounded Theory Approach in Social Research." *International Journal of Social Work and Human Services Practice Horizon Research* 4 (4): 75-81.

Ryan Dunn, C., Travis E. Dorsch, Michael Q. King, and Kevin J. Rothlisberger. 2016. "The Impact of Family Financial Investment on Perceived Parent Pressure and Child Enjoyment and Commitment in Organized Youth Sport." *Family Relations* 65 (2): 287-299.

Shields, D., Brenda Light Bredemeier, Nicole M. LaVoi, and F. Clark Power. 2005. "The Sport Behavior of Youth, Parents and Coaches." *Journal of Research in Character Education* 3 (1): 43-59.

Solomon, Jon. 2020. "Survey:50% of Parents Fear Kids Will Get Sick By Returning To Sports." *Project Play*. Accessed May 12, 2020. https://www.aspenprojectplay.org/coronavirus-and-youth-sports/reports/2020/5/12/survey-50-percent-of-parents-fear-kids-will-get-sick-by-returning-to-sports

Stefansen, Kari, Ingrid Smette, and Åse Strandbu. 2018. "Understanding the Increase in Parents' Involvement in Organized Youth Sports." *Sport, Education and Society* 23 (2): 162-172.

Strauss, Anselm, and Juliet Corbin. 1990. *Basics of Qualitative Research*. Thousand Oaks: Sage Publications.

Thrower, Sam N., Chris G. Harwood, and Christopher M. Spray. 2019. "Educating and Supporting Tennis Parents Using Web-based Delivery Methods: A Novel Online Education Program." *Journal of Applied Sport Psychology* 31 (3): 303-323.

Trussell, Dawn E., and Susan M. Shaw. 2012. "Organized Youth Sport and Parenting in Public and Private Spaces." *Leisure Sciences* 34 (5): 377-394.

Walters, Simon, Philip Schluter, Daniel Stamp, Rex Thomson, and Deborah Payne. 2016. "Coaches and Referees' Perspectives of Sideline Behavior in Children's Team Sports: A Cross-sectional Study." *International Journal of Sport Management, Recreation & Tourism* 23: 51-74.

Weed, Mike. 2007. "The Pub as a Virtual Football Fandom Venue: ¿An Alternative to 'Being There'?". *Soccer & Society* 8 (2-3): 399-414.

——. 2008. "Exploring the Sport Spectator Experience: Virtual Football Spectatorship in The Pub." *Soccer & Society* 9 (2): 189-197.

——. 2020. "The Role of The Interface of Sport and Tourism in the Response to the COVID-19 Pandemic." *Journal of Sport & Tourism* 24 (2): 79-92.

Wiersma, Lenny D., and Angela M. Fifer. 2008. "'The Schedule Has Been Tough but We Think It's Worth It': The Joys, Challenges, and Recommendations of Youth Sport Parents." *Journal of Leisure Research* 40 (4): 505-530.

Witt, Peter A., and Tek B. Dangi. 2018. "Helping Parents Be Better Youth Sport Coaches and Spectators." *Journal of Park and Recreation Administration* 36 (3): 200-208.

Wuerth, Sabine, Martin J. Lee, and Dorothee Alfermann. 2004. "Parental Involvement and Athletes' Career in Youth Sport." *Psychology of Sport and Exercise* 5 (1): 21-33.

Chapter 14

Antigonish Multisport and the Maritime Bubble: A Commentary on the Possibilities of Youth Sport Programming in Post-Pandemic Rural Canadian Society

Tom Fabian

Rarely do we mention the benefits of a societal "lockdown." Granted, as the Covid-19 pandemic ravaged the globe, there was little to be optimistic about. In fact, as I write this, in May 2021, my rural, maritime, Canadian province implemented a province-wide lockdown to try and decrease the third-wave spread of the virus. Notwithstanding the carnage that the virus, and its variants, have waged, there are silver linings in our new reality. For instance, many people have been forced to reconsider their priorities in life. The "little things," which have always deserved our focus, are now what we hold on to for hope: time with family, personal space and introspection, comfort in one's domicile, reconnecting with nature, watching children play. It is to this latter "simple pleasure" that this essay is dedicated. In 2015, a youth sporting movement was initiated in my small community. It, along with everything else in the world, shut down in the spring of 2020. In the convening summer and autumn months, however, community sport administrators had the opportunity to reassess and take stock of their accomplishment. The "little things" are getting their due, even in rural Nova Scotia.

Antigonish Multisport is a collaborative, community, youth sport project in the small town of Antigonish, located in rural, northeastern Nova Scotia, Canada. In an oversaturated youth sport system, Antigonish Multisport is a breath of fresh air. In contrast to the detriments of early single-sport specialization, the norm in most youth sport clubs, the Multisport program introduces children to multiple sports in an effort to broaden movement development. It was initiated by the provincial umbrella organization Sport Nova Scotia in 2015, which facilitates and supports fifty-six Provincial Sports Organizations (PSOs) in the province. It was a pilot project—first of its kind in Canada—aimed at children ages five and six, whereby ten Community Sport Organizations (CSOs) came together to offer their programing in concert: parents pay a one-time registration fee, children participate in one sport at a time for nine months, programing occurs during the same time/day of the week, and children get exposed to a variety of sports from an early age. The initiative has ballooned, with multisport programs popping up in another fifteen communities throughout the province, and other communities across Canada are taking notice. The Antigonish Multisport program is a crucial social outlet for young children, an organizational tour de force in the muddled Canadian youth sporting landscape, and a foundation for well-rounded, life-long athletic development.

The aim of this chapter is to question what the implications of an absence of youth sport programing during the pandemic have been and to situate the "restart" of the Antigonish Multisport program within the exemplary "Atlantic Travel Bubble" infrastructure. The Nova Scotian government and the wider "Maritime bubble" (New Brunswick, Nova Scotia, Prince Edward Island, and Newfoundland and Labrador) have been lauded for their stringent pandemic protocols, which have led to a relatively normalized social and economic system for the Maritime province populations during the course of the global Covid-19 pandemic. Implementing stricter restrictions than other provinces, such as the partial closure of the land border between the Maritimes and the rest of Canada (Quebec-New Brunswick), was effective in maintaining a lower infection rate within the region. As such, restrictions were lifted sooner than in other areas, resulting in the creation of the "Atlantic Travel Bubble," which enabled inter-provincial movement by Maritime residents, the opening up of the restaurant and food services industry, and larger outdoor gatherings. Within this seemingly-utopian "Covid-free world" (Nolen 2020), families, communities, and businesses were able to function relatively normally and consistently since mid-summer 2020. Albeit under revised restrictions and conditions, sport was also slowly reintegrated into the social fabric of the community.

Interviews were the main methodology used to collect data for this study. Five in-depth, semi-structured, qualitative interviews took place in May 2021 with key stakeholders (local, regional, and provincial) in the development and operation of Antigonish Multisport. Questions were open-ended in nature, allowing participants to share information in their own words, which was useful for gathering detailed information about the development of the program and understanding the underlying contexts in which it was created. These stakeholders will be identified with the following pseudonyms and titles: (1) Taylor, Regional Sport Advisor; (2) Morgan, Community Sport Organization Coordinator; (3) Pat, Municipal Recreation Manager; (4) Sam, Multisport Program Officer; and (5) Alex, Provincial Multisport Consultant. Their individual feedback, and the collective themes drawn from them, frame the narrative in the three sections of this chapter: A history and theory of multisport; how the program reacted to the pandemic; and future directions for community sport programing. This chapter, about the restart of Antigonish Multisport, and its impact and influence on youth sport in rural Canadian environments, is an intriguing case study of "new norms" in rural sport, promoting communitarian values, healthy active living, and safe post-pandemic sporting interactions. Moreover, the combination of the effective "Maritime bubble" pandemic protocols and the unique pilot multisport project yields an important commentary on the possibilities of youth sport programing in post-pandemic rural Canadian society. In effect, the "pause" in programing has enabled stakeholders to reassess and reimagine the possible objectives and outcomes for rural community sport. Through this introspective process, multisport theory has gained momentum.

History and Theory of Multisport

The entire Canadian sport system is buoyed by a plethora of CSOs. Also known as sport clubs, these volunteer-led CSOs are the local, granular-level, grassroots foundations for any child interested in participating in sport (Doherty and Misener 2008). CSOs are, generally, affiliated with PSOs (provincial), which are affiliated with NSOs (national) and serviced by provincial multisport service organizations– in this case, Sport Nova Scotia. If a youth were to embark on the elite, high-performance pathway (Collins and Buller 2003; Sotiriadou et al. 2016), then they would play on "select teams" (with recruitment, selection, and training camps) at the CSO, PSO, and NSO levels, before being selected by a national (Olympic) team to represent the country in international competition. This pathway is rigorous, competitive, time-consuming, expensive, and all-encompassing, as can be gathered from the stories of dedication, sacrifice, and discipline many Olympians retell (Wilding et al. 2002). In recent years, however, a number of Canadian NSOs have joined efforts through the "Change It Up" campaign to promote the diversification of athletic portfolios and gaining competencies from multiple sports, rather than specializing in a single sport (Active for Life n.d.). At the CSO-level, where networks are somewhat siloed, this idea has only recently started to gain traction (Barnes et al. 2007). Sifting through layers of bureaucracy to implement national standards at local levels is an uphill battle. As confirmed by Taylor, a regional sports advisor, "often when you're passing down best practices from the Provincial Sport Organizations, sometimes there's a disconnect with how they'll work at the community level." Hence the need for a comprehensive multisport program established through grassroots efforts.

Participation in youth sport is often taken as a net positive for youth and community development (Bloom et al. 2005; Donnelly and Kidd 2003; Fraser-Thomas et al. 2005; Nova Scotia Sport and Recreation Commission 2001). However, many youth's experiences in community sport are influenced by parents' past experience in sport (Knight et al. 2016): You play what your parents played. And, in rural communities where sporting options are limited, youth end up pigeon-holed in the dominant sport, which, in most Canadian locales, is hockey. Moreover, the positive outcomes of sport participation can often be overshadowed by the negative psychological effects of early sport specialization (Baker 2003; Baker et al. 2009; Brenner 2016; Gould 2010; Hecimovich 2004; Hill and Hansen 1988; Horn 2015; Jayanthi et al. 2013; Malina 2010; McFadden et al. 2016; Myer et al. 2015; Normand et al. 2017; Padaki et al. 2017; Smith

2015; Waldron et al. 2020; Wiersma 2000). As I have written elsewhere, "the opportunity to capitalize on a robust professional sports market, through the early specialization of athletic skills, with the potential to develop an exceptional talent, exemplifies the indelible capitalist ethos of the contemporary sports industry" (Fabian 2021, 95). In recent years, however, research shows that children who participate in multiple sports not only stay in sport longer, but also develop the various object control, body control, and motor control skills that will encourage them to continue in their sport(s) of choice (Farrey 2019; Popović et al. 2020; Rugg et al. 2017; Strashin 2018; Swanson 2004). As such, notes Alex, a provincial multisport consultant, the mission of the Antigonish Multisport program is to "grow children through sport by creating an 'I can play anything' attitude. The idea was to expose them to multiple experiences and opportunities to be physically active in different spaces (ice, air, ground, water)."

Many youth sport administrators have been preaching the multisport creed for a number of years. Like other youth sport programing, the benefits of a multisport experience are generally accepted and understood, especially by former high-performance athletes (Buckley et al. 2017). Although multisport is a sound theory, the practical implications of such a program have been a barrier to its development at the local level until recently. As reported through the Sport Information Resource Centre (SIRC), an evidence-based Canadian sport advocacy organization, "given that community sport associations, recreation departments, schools, and health agencies tend to operate in separate silos, it can be difficult to bring together the different players needed to create and coordinate the kind of boundary-breaking programing that multi-sport represents" (Grove 2018). Taylor, a regional sport advisor, commented that "sport is something, at least locally, that the municipalities were not really delivering." As such, in rural communities, there has always been a strong dependence on volunteer groups, as municipalities focused on recreational initiatives. With its strong sport-volunteer base, then, Antigonish was the target of a May 2014 community sport summit, during which hypothetical scenarios were proposed to better the community sport delivery model. Some of the issues that CSOs faced included program capacity, early specialization, lack of sporting opportunities, and scheduling conflicts. It was at these meetings that the nascent concept of a multisport program first gained traction, as proposed by CSO stakeholders. As recalled by Morgan, a community sport coordinator present at this summit, the idea was that "rather than working against each other, let's work together." In essence, Antigonish Multisport developed partnerships so as to reduce competition–for space, prime times, and registrations–between CSOs with the sole purpose of "getting kids active."

The Antigonish Multisport program was piloted a year later, in 2015, by Sport Nova Scotia, in partnership with local CSOs, the municipal recreation department, and the Communities, Sport, and Recreation Division of the Nova Scotia Department of Communities, Culture, and Heritage. The main impetus was to reduce the barriers of cost, registration, and scheduling. The Sport Fund, managed by Sport Nova Scotia, supported the development of a sustainable and accessible community model, costing parents $325 CAD for a ten-month program. However, funding from KidSport, a national non-profit youth sport funding program, aided in the achievement of a sustainable model that could continue to grow year-over-year. With the support of Sport Nova Scotia, program participants are eligible for KidSport funding, ensuring that cost would not represent a barrier to participation. The second obstacle was the combined barrier of registering for multiple sports and ensuring that schedules were not overlapping amongst the different CSOs. According to Sam, a guiding question was "how do we provide an opportunity for youth that want to try and develop physical literacy skills in multiple environments and sports, but make it so that it's possible with one registration?" The answer: task-sharing.

Alex explained that Antigonish Multisport is "a model that partners municipal recreation together with multiple community sport organizations to provide more opportunities to kids in the community." Current partnerships are aligned with the four pillars of Sport Nova Scotia's Sport Development Tool (SDT): participation, coaching and officiating, excellence, and organizational effectiveness (Shooting Federation of Nova Scotia n.d.). This last pillar, however, is the most important to the implementation of a multisport program. Antigonish Multisport is elegantly set-up, collaborative in nature, and provides a tremendous benefit from the sharing of tasks by key partners. Until recently, noted Taylor, "municipalities would often run one-off programs for different age groups." As such, delegating the municipal recreation department the responsibilities of organizational logistics and operational oversight (hiring, registration, insurance, etc.) freed up capacity for effective sport delivery. The implementation of the Municipal Physical Activity Leadership (MPAL) program, by the then-Department of Health Promotion and Protection, in 2006, made this task-sharing possible. The MPAL program is a cost-sharing partnership between municipalities and the provincial government to hire dedicated recreation leads (Town of Antigonish 2021). Multisport programs are, therefore, operated by these MPAL coordinators. With this partnership in place, CSOs are able to focus on sport, not the administration of the program. For those who deliver the multisport modules, explained Taylor,

> It's the most fun program to deliver because all you have to do is go in and coach, whereas usually you're doing all the other admin pieces on top of coaching, and sometimes coaching is left to the night before. But for this program, organizations can think of just the coaching aspect.

Multisport sports, as opposed to all other sport programs within a CSO's purview, became the favorite sessions for volunteer sport coaches to conduct.

The ways in which children, parents, CSOs, and the wider sporting community have reacted to the Antigonish Multisport program has been overwhelmingly positive. Pat, a municipal recreation manager, was "surprised in how receptive they all were to the idea of the multisport program." The ten original CSOs approached—badminton, baseball, basketball, gymnastics, hockey, soccer, swimming, taekwondo, tennis, and athletics—were based on their organizational capacity and resource availability to add another program. However, the CSOs all quickly recognized the benefits of the physical literacy and enjoyment outcomes of the program. Jim Grove, a Senior Contributing Editor and Content Strategist at Active for Life, a national non-profit physical literacy advocacy group, wrote that the program "also mirrors the ultimate vision of the Canadian Sport for Life (CS4L) model" (2015). As much of a benefit it has been for children (physical literacy) and parents (convenience), "the trickle-down effect is more than just the program," noted Sam, a multisport program officer, "the program is the vehicle for so many other opportunities for community networking." The partnerships through Antigonish Multisport have helped propel collective decisions, which is an important development for rural community sport. In this vein, Sam provided the following insight: "our partners make an agreement about the community values that we believe in and, from those values, shape the program that speaks to the needs of our community." The greatest benefit of the Antigonish Multisport program has been the development of intracommunity network capacity and "interorganizational linkages" (Thibault and Harvey 1997). The program highlighted the ability to connect CSOs through effective rural networks. Stephanie Spencer, one of the key figures in organizing Antigonish Multisport, remarked that "we ended up with the perfect combination of energy, support and opportunity to do something outside of the box of typical sport delivery" (Grove 2015).

Lockdown and Restart

Between July 3 and November 26, 2020, the "Atlantic Travel Bubble" was created as a travel-restricted zone in an effort to bolster the economies of the Canadian Maritime provinces (Government of Prince Edward Island n.d.). With a combined population of about two and a half million people, the provinces of New Brunswick, Prince Edward Island, Nova Scotia, and Newfoundland and Labrador decided to allow unrestricted travel among provincial residents only. Those traveling from outside the bubble were required to self-quarantine for two weeks. Other regions around the world also experimented with travel bubbles, including the Baltic States (Mzezewa 2020) and New Zealand (Trnka and Davies 2020). The effects of the "Maritime bubble" were, to an extent, positive and 81% of Atlantic Canadians were against lifting the travel restrictions in October 2020 (Gow 2020). Granted, the economy of the Maritime provinces, which relies heavily on tourism from central Canada, took a large hit, as did most tourism sectors around the globe (Nhamo et al. 2020). However, a 2020 Reuters poll noted the forecasted economic shrinkage in the region would be less than the Canadian average (CIBC Capital Markets 2020). In fact, if the real-estate market was any indication of future growth, then it seems that many mobile workers fled the traditional economic centers of Toronto and Montreal to the relative safety of the East coast. It is within this "magical, virus-free world" (Nolen 2020), then, that we investigate the "return to play" initiatives within Nova Scotia.

The restart in community sport was, in Pat's experience, "a bit of a rollercoaster." When the initial lockdowns were implemented in March 2020, the role of Sport Nova Scotia was to simply communicate the need to wait on further instruction from provincial health officials. With regard to the Antigonish Multisport program, parents received refunds and some videos were released to encourage children to stay active, but virtual events for five- and six-year-olds were more for socialization than physical activity. Understandably, as elucidated by Morgan, "people weren't necessarily looking for sport at that point in time." Lockdown restrictions were initially lifted in June 2020, but the Antigonish Multisport program had already ended in May. However, sport and recreation programs of other kinds were permitted to implement "return to play" protocols in an effort to restart physical activity initiatives throughout the province. Municipal recreation departments were the first ones to react to loosened restrictions, shifting initially to equipment loans. With the "back-to-nature" ideals of many Canadians during the easing of restrictions during the summer of 2020, biking, hiking, and general outdoor activities increased (Lesser and Nienhuis 2020). The Antigonish recreation department was able to operate half-day camps during the month of August (all outdoor, with ten campers per group). And, in an effort to build community capacity (Chaskin 2001), the recreation department also facilitated a number of outdoor leadership opportunities to enable community-run outdoor programing. Sports, on the other hand, followed much stricter provincial "Return to Sport" guidelines, which required PSOs to account for physical space restrictions (physical distancing, facility capacities, washrooms/change rooms, etc.), cleaning shared equipment, personal protective precautions, and how to communicate with participants (Sport Nova Scotia 2020). For instance, Soccer Nova Scotia (2020) was operating under a five-step planning process, relying on permissions and consultation from the provincial government, municipalities, Canada Soccer, and its constituent clubs. Hockey Nova Scotia (2020) offered a three-period "Rebound Plan": until October 1, after October 1, and then a to-be-determined third period (which we are to assume is a "back-to-normal" scenario). Baseball Nova Scotia (2020) proposed a four-phase plan with incremental returns to training, competition, events, and the ominously titled "new normal." All PSOs were required to submit, and continually amend, these "return to play" plans with Sport Nova Scotia before community sporting activities could resume.

Even with these protocols and precautions in place, there were many risks associated with restarting youth sports, including limited information about Covid-19, the young age of participants, and lack of adequate facility space. As such, Antigonish Multisport based its programing decisions off of the local elementary schools and modified as needed. Considering the age of participants, explained Alex, it was important for them to learn proper safety precautions (mask-wearing, social-distancing, etc.) in their familiar classrooms, as sport administrators did not feel comfortable "asking community sport organizations to also teach Covid regulations on top of teaching basketball," for instance. Attempting to keep young children apart from each other during sport sessions in non-pandemic times is a near impossible feat, thus there were understandable concerns regarding physical distancing. Taylor lamented that "it was tough because at that point we just didn't know a lot about the virus, we thought that touch was a big component of transmission, so most organizations did not offer programming for that age group." Facility space, however, was the greatest limiting factor. Access to school gymnasia was limited, because of the inability to disinfect appropriately. St. Francis Xavier University, where much of the programing occurred, did not rent any facility space to outside organizations during this planning cycle. It took until November 2020 for local schools to re-open their gymnasia for rental opportunities.

Antigonish Multisport officially resumed in January 2021, offering a shortened schedule (two or three sessions per sport, as opposed to the normal six) at a reduced registration fee of $50 CAD. As per Sam, it quickly became evident that youth sporting opportunities were a "need of the community." The thirty available spots in the program filled via the online registration system within seven minutes of opening–the first twenty registrations claimed within sixty seconds–and there was a waiting list of twenty families. Sam, who is affiliated with a newer multisport program, observed that "in [our region] parents were reaching out and asking when the next multisport program was happening." Multisport proved the power of community relations, as all stakeholders–parents, administrators, program volunteers, etc.–played their part in restarting a safe and healthy youth sport environment. Antigonish Multisport successfully navigated the pandemic because of the advantage of having administrative and support work outsourced to the municipality. Protocol documents, scheduling, and registrations were not the responsibility of volunteer coaches, which enabled them to focus on the mission of keeping children safe and active.

Not only did the Antigonish Multisport program react appropriately and effectively to the Covid-19 pandemic, but an underlying theme in all five interviews was that the lockdown benefited the delivery of community sport. The four benefits suggested by the interviews were: (1) no parent spectators; (2) opportunity to reevaluate; (3) increased parental support; and (4) localized programing. First, and somewhat controversially, CSOs, on average, took advantage of not having parents on-site during program delivery. This proved to have several unexpected advantages. "Not having parent spectators helps [children] stay engaged," relayed Taylor, noting that,

> In the past, with parents being able to watch around the side, you would get a lot of the little ones running back to their parent, checking in, then coming back into the sport. Whereas this time, when it was offered in January, they were all really comfortable leaving their parents.

This comment highlights an issue in youth sport programs: The trepid independence of young children in the presence of their parents. Without parents, children were forced to engage with peers, focus on the activity, and work on independent play. The second benefit is that the time away from everyday activities allowed sport administrators to reassess their programs, processes, and policies. Returning in January after an eight-month hiatus forced some introspection about the youth sporting experience; "you almost had to relearn to get yourself back in that creative mode," opined Morgan. As with teaching, taking time away from the classroom or field allows facilitators to reassess best practices, learning outcomes, and effectiveness. With a hiatus in programing, youth sport administrators and coaches had an opportunity to rethink age-old ideas about the sport delivery system. Third, because of the hardships of the pandemic, many volunteer coaches and administrators noticed that parents were much more amenable to accepting and supporting changes to programing, such as last-minute schedule changes.

The last benefit, as per Alex, is the "stay and play in your community" approach. Understandably, local club teams are not as readily traveling to away games, an issue that was getting out of hand for younger athletes on select teams prior to the pandemic. Some questioned the benefits of eight-year-old boys traveling ninety minutes to play against a basketball team of comparable caliber. "Travel teams" were being organized for younger age groups to conform to the high-performance pathway, but that is not what is best for youth sport development. Pandemic restrictions essentially forced club teams to "stay and play" in their local communities, challenging the purpose of this "travel team" paradigm. The benefits of the lockdown on community sport in Nova Scotia can be summed up as an opportunity to reimagine the youth sporting system: less parental pressure, time and space to plan appropriately, and developing strong local sporting communities.

The Multisport Movement

In his history of Nova Scotian sport, Sandy Young (1988) observed that "Nova Scotian kids were feeling as if coming from elsewhere was some kind of an advantage" (11). Young's motivation to write his book was to educate young Nova Scotian athletes about local opportunities and local sporting heroes. With efforts to increase physical activity participation amongst youth (Harding 2009) and a history of innovative recreational sport development in the province (Pitter 2009), the Nova Scotian community sporting environment provided an ideal incubator for Antigonish Multisport. The first of its kind in Canada (and possibly the world), the program has been deemed, as per Alex, a national best practice by the Sport for Life Society. As such, the pilot program has grown to fifteen other communities throughout the province. As elucidated by Sam, these communities "have seen the concept and [it] helped them reimagine what sport may look like." The counties of Colchester and Lunenburg, for instance, organized multisport programs in 2016, and the former is currently in the process of organizing an adult program. The Antigonish program has been a template in terms of processes, quality, and program mandate. As endorsed by Jim Grove (2019), "at a time when the costs of many youth sport programs are spiraling upwards, the Antigonish model is providing more for less. It represents a promising practice that many other Canadian communities may want to emulate."

The "best practice" label has gained momentum, as communities outside Nova Scotia (and Canada) have also been reaching out to Sport Nova Scotia to learn about the concept, organization, and delivery. Alex commented that other communities are "seeing the same thing: it's a really great thing in theory and concept, but it's really difficult to do. You can't do it by yourself, you need all these multiple partners to make it happen, because the problems are cutting across organizations." Over seventy communities have reached out since the 2015 pilot, including Port Moody (British Columbia), Southport (Manitoba), the Ottawa Sport Council, North Salem (New York), as well as the United States Tennis Association (USTA) and even a sports council in Indonesia. This frenzy of interest, however, comes with some drawbacks, mainly that the Nova Scotian multisport programs are organized with public funds, by a public institution, with the interests of the public top of mind. Therefore, private models undermine the accessible nature of the youth sport philosophy. Moreover, facility space and scheduling amongst CSOs still pose as obstacles to effective programing.

A solution for these continued problems is the next phase of community sport development, also piloted in Antigonish, referred to as Sport HUB Antigonish (Town of Antigonish 2020). HUB is a registration portal which streamlines CSO processes by standardizing waivers, bylaws and policies, gender asks on registration forms, safe sport messaging, etc. Essentially, HUB takes the fundamental principles of the multisport program in an effort to create a multisport system. This type of systemic development will enable growth in other aspects of youth sport in Nova Scotia as well. For instance, offering multisport programing for older age groups, experimenting with non-mainstream sports (like curling, sledge hockey, or orienteering), and expanding into Indigenous communities. Some community multisport programs are already introducing these developments. In effect, if knowledge sharing has become multidirectional, as opposed to centralized in Antigonish, then the ideals of the system have already been met.

In the development of this multisport system, sport administrators learned several important lessons (Grove 2018). First, cross-sectoral working committees were crucial in engaging all stakeholders, including provincial and municipal governments, CSOs, and facilities. Second, communicating the values of multisport theory generated buy-in from parents and demand for the programs. Third, the use of existing resources reduced the need for excess funding and utilized the expertise of municipal recreation departments through MPAL coordinators. Fourth, accessibility, affordability, and inclusivity were the key selling points. Fifth, program sustainability, as monitored by Sport Nova Scotia and its six regional sports consultants, enabled the multisport programs to not only survive during the pandemic, but thrive. In effect, the intracommunity network capacity that was developed through the Sport Nova Scotia system, and championed through the multisport programs, dispelled many of the negative effects of the pandemic on community sport in the province. Interorganizational linkages, research momentum in multisport theory, and the backing of Sport Nova Scotia combined as a perfect storm of factors to support the effective development of a unique multisport system that benefits volunteer-based CSOs, "chauffeur" parents (Knight et al. 2016), and, most importantly, the children who will gain fundamental physical competencies and baseline experiences for a lifetime of physical activity and enjoyment in sport.

Rural community sport has benefited greatly from the relationships developed as a direct result of Antigonish Multisport. One of the chief aims of the program is to build community through sport (Vail 2007). The intracommunity rural network was always there, but a collaborative project like Antigonish Multisport was the impetus to urge CSOs, and other sport stakeholders, to work in concert. Sam concurred that, "overall, it has heightened community sport more than ever, knowing that we need to unify and work closer together, because if you can't travel outside of your jurisdiction, you need to have really great relationships within it to make sure that youth are given the best experience." And this is one of the key takeaways from a pandemic-restricted sporting environment. With limits on travel and physical contact, relationship-building is essential to interorganizational linkages, which the multisport system has established effectively. The successful restart of the Multisport program is an ideal case study of the resiliency of intracommunity network capacity in unprecedented times. This tour de force program is reimagining rural community sport, a fresh perspective on youth sport program delivery, and a hopeful light in the idealizations of a post-pandemic sporting experience. In years to come, historians may well point to Antigonish, Nova Scotia, as the origins of the modern multisport movement.

REFERENCES

Active for Life. n.d. "Change It Up." Play More Sports. Accessed March 2, 2021. https://playmoresports.activeforlife.com/.

Antigonish, Town of. June 22, 2000. "The Antigonish Sport Hub." Latest News. Accessed January 20, 2021. https://www.townofantigonish.ca/the-antigonish-sport-hub.html.

---. 2021. *Active Living Strategy*. February 2021. https://townofantigonish.ca/departments/recreation/969-toa-active-living-strategy-final-17-feb-2021-final/file.html.

Baker, Joe. 2003. "Early Specialization in Youth Sport: A Requirement for Adult Expertise?" *High Ability Studies* 14 (1): 85–94.

Baker, Joe, Stephen Cobley, and Jessica Fraser-Thomas. 2009. "What Do We Know About Early Sport Specialization? Not Much!" *High Ability Studies* 20 (1): 77–89.

Barnes, Martha, Laura Cousens, and Joanne MacLean. 2007. "From Silos to Synergies: A Network Perspective of the Canadian Sport System." *International Journal of Sport Management and Marketing* 2 (5/6): 555-571.

Baseball Nova Scotia. 2020. *Return to Play* 2020. June 3, 2020. http://baseballnovascotia.com/clientuploads/RTP%202020/BNS_Return_to_Play_2020_Final_Version_UPDATED_June_3rd.pdf.

Bloom, Michael, Michael Grant, and Douglas Watt. 2005. *Strengthening Canada: The Socio-economic Benefits of Sport Participation in Canada*. Ottawa: The Conference Board of Canada.

Brenner, Joel S. 2016. "Sports Specialization and Intensive Training in Young Athletes." *Pediatrics* 138 (3): 1–8.

Buckley, Patrick S., Meghan Bishop, Patrick Kane, Michael C. Ciccotti, Stephen Selverian, Dominique Exume,

William Emper, Kevin B. Freedman, Sommer Hammoud, Steven B. Cohen, and Michael G. Ciccotti. 2017. "Early Single-Sport Specialization: A Survey of 3090 High School, Collegiate, and Professional Athletes." *Orthopaedic Journal of Sports Medicine* 5 (7): 1-7.

Chaskin, Robert. 2001. "Building Community Capacity: A Definitional Framework and Case Studies from a Comprehensive Community Initiative." *Urban Affairs Review* 36: 291-323.

CIBC Capital Markets. 2020. "Select Canada Real GDP Forecasts." Reuters Graphics. Accessed May 3, 2021. https://graphics.reuters.com/CANADA-ECONOMY/jbyprxekqpe/.

Collins, Michael F., and James R. Buller. 2003. "Social Exclusion from High-Performance Sport: Are all Talented Young Sports People being given an Equal Opportunity of Reaching the Olympic Podium?" *Journal of Sport and Social Issues* 27 (4): 420-442.

Doherty, Allison, and Misener, Katherine. 2008. "Community Sport Networks." In *Sport and Social Capital,* edited by Matthew Nicholson and Russell Hoye, 113-141. London: Elsevier Butterworth Heinemann.

Donnelly, Peter, and Bruce Kidd. 2003. "Realizing the Expectations: Youth, Character, and Community in Canadian Sport." *The Sport We Want: Essays on Current Issues in Community Sport*. Ottawa: Canadian Centre for Ethics in Sport, 25-44.

Fabian, Tom. 2021. "Jocks and Nerds: The Role of Sport in the North American Education System." In *Duelism: Confronting Sport Through its Doubles*, edited by Brittany Reid and Taylor McKee, 91-110. Champaign: Common Ground Research Networks.

Farrey, Tom. 2019. "Does Norway Have the Answer to Excess in Youth Sports." *New York Times*, April 28, 2019. https://www.nytimes.com/2019/04/28/sports/norway-youth-sports-model.html?fbclid=IwAR0SJgPj2CrlIGOGsO2TmddxrHCB6g-klcvWv008qlIQkHVgetSnLxikDHo#click=https://t.co/Uc9AoUiyQj.

Fraser-Thomas, Jessica L., Jean Côté, and Janice Deakin. 2005. "Youth Sport Programs: An Avenue to Foster Positive Youth Development." *Physical Education and Sport Pedagogy* 10 (1): 19–40.

Gould, D. (2010). Early sport specialization: A psychological perspective. *Journal of Physical Education, Recreation,* & Dance, 81(8), 33–37.

Government of Prince Edward Island. n.d. "Atlantic Provinces Travel Bubble." Health and Wellness. Accessed May 19, 2021. https://www.princeedwardisland.ca/en/information/health-and-wellness/atlantic-provinces-travel-bubble.

Gow, Steve. 2020. "Nova Scotians Steadfast on Keeping Borders Shut: Poll." *Halifax Today*, October 9, 2020. https://www.halifaxtoday.ca/local-news/nova-scotians-steadfast-on-keeping-borders-shut-poll-2781360.

Grove, Jim. 2015. "Antigonish, Nova Scotia Kids Get the Right Start with Multisport Program." Active for Life. September 28, 2015. https://activeforlife.com/antigonish-multi-sport-program/.

---. 2018. Promising Practices to Support Multi-sport Programming. Sport Information Resource Centre. October 18, 2018. https://sirc.ca/blog/promising-practices-to-support-multi-sport-programming/.

---. 2019. "Multisport Programs are Thriving in Nova Scotia." Active for Life. January 29, 2019. https://activeforlife.com/multisport-programs-in-nova-scotia/.

Harding, Andrew. (2009). "Physical Activity Participation: An Exploration of What it will Take to Get Nova Scotia South Shore Youth more Physically Active." PhD diss., Dalhousie University.

Hecimovich, Mark D. 2004. "Sport Specialization in Youth: A Literature Review." *Journal of the American Chiropractic Association* 41 (4): 32–41.

Hill, Grant M., and Gary F. Hansen. 1988. "Specialization in High School Sports the Pros and Cons. *Journal of Physical Education, Recreation,* & Dance 59 (5): 76–79.

Hockey Nova Scotia. 2021. *Rebound Plan*. February 11, 2021. https://5647e90c-cdn.agilitycms.cloud/HNS_Rebound_Plan_Feb_2021.pdf.

Horn, Thelma S. 2015. "Social Psychological and Developmental Perspectives on Early Sport Specialization." *Kinesiology Review* 4 (3): 248–266.

Jayanthi, Neeru, Courtney Pinkham, Lara Dugas, Brittany Patrick, and Cynthia LaBella. 2013. "Sports Specialization in Young Athletes: Evidence-based Recommendations." *Sports Health* 5 (3): 251–257.

Knight, Camilla J., Travis E. Dorsch, Keith V. Osai, Kyle L. Haderlie, and Paul A. Sellars. 2016. "Influences on Parental Involvement in Youth Sport." *Sport, Exercise, and Performance Psychology* 5 (2): 161-178

Lesser, Iris A., and Carl P. Nienhuis. 2020. "The Impact of COVID-19 on Physical Activity Behavior and Well-Being of Canadians." *International Journal of Environmental Research and Public Health* 17 (11): 3899.

Malina, Robert M. 2010. "Early Sport Specialization: Roots, Effectiveness, Risks." *Current Sports Medicine Reports* 9 (6): 364-371.

McFadden, Taylor, Corliss Bean, Michelle Fortier, and Courtney Post. 2016. "Investigating the Influence of Youth Hockey Specialization on Psychological Needs (Dis)Satisfaction, Mental Health, and Mental Illness." *Cogent Psychology* 3 (1): 7–16.

Myer, Gregory D., Neeru Jayanthi, John P. Difiori, Avery D. Faigenbaum, Adam W. Kiefer, David Logerstedt, and Lyle J. Micheli. 2015. "Sport Specialization, Part I: Does Early Sports Specialization Increase Negative Outcomes and Reduce the Opportunity for Success in Young Athletes?" *Sports Health* 7 (5): 437–442.

Mzezewa, Tariro. 2020. "3 Baltic States Announced a 'Travel Bubble.' What Is It and Could It Work in the U.S.?" *New York Times*, August 6, 2020. https://www.nytimes.com/2020/04/29/travel/coronavirus-travel-bubble.html.

Nhamo, Godwell, Kaitano Dube, and David Chikodzi. 2020. *Counting the Cost of COVID-19 on the Global Tourism Industry*. Cham: Springer Nature.

Nolen, Stephanie. 2020. "I Am Living in a Covid-Free World Just a Few Hundred Miles from Manhattan." *New York Times*, November 18, 2020. https://www.nytimes.com/2020/11/18/opinion/covid-halifax-nova-scotia-canada.html.

Normand, Jonathan Michael, Andrew Wolfe, and Kayla Peak. 2017. "A Review of Early Sport Specialization in Relation to the Development of a Young Athlete." *International Journal of Kinesiology & Sports Science* 5 (2): 37–42.

Nova Scotia Sport and Recreation Commission. 2001. *Active Kids, Healthy Kids: A Nova Scotia Physical Activity Strategy for Children and Youth*. Halifax: Author.

Padaki, Ajay S., Charles A. Popkin, Justin L. Hodgins, David Kovacevic, Thomas Sean Lynch, and Christopher S. Ahmad. 2017. "Factors that Drive Youth Specialization." *Sports Health* 9 (6): 532–536.

Rugg, Caitlin, Adarsh Kadoor, Brian T. Feeley, and Nirav K. Pandya. 2017. "The Effects of Playing Multiple High School Sports on National Basketball Association Players' Propensity for Injury and Athletic Performance." *American Journal of Sports Medicine* 46 (2): 402-408.

Pitter, Robert. 2009. "Finding the Kieran Way: Recreational Sport, Health, and Environmental Policy in Nova Scotia." *Journal of Sport and Social Issues* 33 (3): 331-351.

Popović, Boris, Milan Cvetković, Draženka Mačak, Tijana Šćepanović, Nebojša Čokorilo, Aleksandra Belić, Nebojša Trajković, Slobodan Andrašić, and Špela Bogataj. 2020. "Nine Months of a Structured Multisport Program Improve Physical Fitness in Preschool Children: A Quasi-experimental Study." *International Journal of Environmental Research and Public Health* 17: 1-10.

Smith, Maureen M. (2015). "Early Sport Specialization: A Historical Perspective." *Kinesiology Review* 4 (3): 220–229.

Soccer Nova Scotia. 2020. "Soccer Nova Scotia's Return to Soccer Activity 5 Step Process." Soccer Nova Scotia. May 29, 2020. https://www.soccerns.ca/soccer-nova-scotias-return-to-play-5-step-process/.

Sotiriadou, Popi, Jessie Brouwers, and Veerle De Bosscher. 2016. "High Performance Development Pathways." In *Managing Sport Development: An International Approach*, edited by Emma Sherry, Nico Schulenkorf, and Pamm Phillips, 63-76. London: Routledge.

Shooting Federation of Nova Scotia. n.d. "Sport Development Tool (SDT)." Accessed May 13, 2021. https://www.sfns.info/sport-development-tool.html.

Strashin, Alex. 2018. "Kids Should Probably Play More Sports, but It's Easier Said than Done." CBC Sports, June 6, 2018. https://www.cbc.ca/sports/change-it-up-campaign-1.4693781.

Swanson, John R. 2004. "Periodization for the Multisport Athlete." *Strength and Conditioning Journal* 26 (4): 50-58.

Trnka, Susanna, and Sharyn Graham Davies. 2020. "Blowing Bubbles: COVID-19, New Zealand's Bubble Metaphor, and the Limits of Households as Sites of Responsibility and Care." In *COVID-19:*

Global Pandemic, Societal Responses, Ideological Solutions, edited by J. Michael Ryan, 167-183. London: Routledge.

Vail, Susan E. 2007. "Community Development and Sport Participation." *Journal of Sport Management* 21: 571-596.

Waldron, Shelby, J.D. DeFreese, JOhna Register-Mihalik, Brian Pietrosimone, and Nikki Barczak. 2020. "The Costs and Benefits of Early Sport Specialization: A Critical Review of Literature." *Quest* 72 (1): 1-18.

Wiersma, Lenny D. 2000. "Risks and Benefits of Youth Sport Specialization: Perspectives and Recommendations." *Pediatric Exercise Science* 12 (1): 13–22.

Young, A.J. 'Sandy.'1988. *Beyond Heroes: A Sport History of Nova Scotia*. Hantsport, NS: Lancelot Press.

Thibault, Lucie, and Jean Harvey. 1997. "Fostering Interorganizational Linkages in the Canadian Sport Delivery System." *Journal of Sport Management* 11: 45-68.

Wilding, Amanda J., Laura Hunter-Thomas, and Roger Thomas. 2012. "Sacrifice: The Lonely Olympic Road." Reflective Practice: *International and Multidisciplinary Perspectives* 13 (3): 439-453.

Chapter 15

Change and Challenge: A Case Study of Distance and Touch in a Fitness Club After Lockdown

Dominika Czarnecka

On March 14, 2020, all fitness clubs in Poland were closed for an indefinite period due to the Covid-19 pandemic. They were only allowed to reopen on June 6, with the last stage of the post-lockdown unfreezing of the economy. Fitness centers operated under new, tighter sanitary regulations until October 17, 2020, when the rise in Covid-19 cases prompted the Polish government to order the closure of the fitness industry once more, again for an indefinite period.

The long list of government guidelines and procedures regulating the operation of clubs and gyms under strict sanitary conditions also defined new rules for organizing time and space within fitness clubs, affecting how the bodies of gym goers were managed. One aspect that proved to be of crucial importance in the context of altering gym participants' experiences associated with the development of physical skills and interacting with others in the new conditions was the obligation to keep a safe physical distance. It meant that the bodies of the exercising gym participants could not be touched, either by instructors or by other clients. Although most fitness enthusiasts tried to adapt to the new circumstances, not all of them followed the post-lockdown restrictions to the letter.

Based on the results of ethnographic research conducted in one of Warsaw's fitness centers, this chapter aims to present, in the local context, how the mandated social distancing affected the social practices, including touch, developed within fitness club spaces. It also illustrates how fitness instructors and their clients reacted to the changes introduced between the first and the second lockdowns of the fitness industry in Poland, how they experienced them, engaged in or negotiated them (either accepting or resisting), and finally, what meaning they ascribed to the changes and how they interpret them.

As this chapter intends to present a local case study, I shall endeavor to demonstrate the so-called intersection of scales, i.e., the collision of various forces (local, national, and global) influencing social actors in a given location. This study employed the theoretical framework of social change (Alexander 2004), sensory anthropology (Blake 2011), and the concept of disciplinary power (Foucault 1995). It was guided by a case study approach (Stake 1995), which allowed me to obtain detailed information about daily practices in the setting of interest: the fitness club.

This study was based on ethnographic qualitative methods: participant observation; ten semi-structured, in-depth interviews—recorded and transcribed (five with fitness instructors and five with clients); informal conversations; analysis of Internet sources (among others, Polish government guidelines; statements by experts). Eight of the interviews were conducted face-to-face and two took place online through the Facebook Messenger app. The field research was carried out from June to October 2020, between the first (spring) and second (autumn) lockdowns; the interviews concluded one month later, in November 2020.

Since the data used in the present study were acquired as a part of a broader research project in which fitness culture in Poland is analyzed as a gendered phenomenon, all participants were women[1]. For the sake of anonymity, the names appearing in the article have been changed.

Managing Bodies in Gym Spaces

Commercial fitness clubs are heterogeneous spaces, developed around a complex net of connections between the public and the private, the material and the imaginary, the permissible and the forbidden. According to some scholars, the fitness club may be defined as a space designed to provide gym goers with the possibility of engaging in embodied actions that might be seen as improper/inappropriate in other social settings (Brighton et al. 2021). Others perceive fitness clubs as "reinventive institutions," where individuals can transform their body–self identities (Dawson 2017) or as "panoptic" or disciplinary institutions in which various disciplinary techniques towards the creation of docile bodies are developed (Markula and Pringle 2006). This does not alter the fact that discipline and empowerment are often interconnected, and thus need not be seen as opposites (Sassatelli 2011). Given the simple conclusion that fitness clubs are, first and foremost, spaces filled with numerous bodies in motion, what becomes important are the methods of their management.

According to Michel Foucault (1995), obedient and useful bodies are produced through the application of various disciplinary techniques, which include the managing of bodies through the organization of space and time. It should be emphasized that the use of disciplinary techniques through which power is exercised is by no means tantamount to gym bodies being oppressed or passive. Fitness enthusiasts play an active role in the power relations in which they engage

---

[1] The research was funded by the National Science Center Grant No. UMO-2018/29/B/HS3/01563, within the project "Through body in motion. Anthropological study of embodied experiences and identity transition of female fitness culture participants."

and are aware of the beneficial effects of disciplinary power (on corrective touch as a disciplinary technique see Czarnecka 2021a). While disciplinary techniques vary, the present analysis focuses on the managing of bodies through the organization of space and time, since it is these techniques that have a strong connection to the introduction of mandatory social distancing in fitness clubs.

Foucault states that disciplinary spaces are enclosed, functional, partitioned, and ranked (1995: 141–146). A fitness club meets all the above specifications. The space of the club is organized in a certain manner for the purpose of achieving the proper distribution of gym bodies, as well as making sure that gym goers may perform their embodied actions unimpeded. This is achieved by dividing the gym into distinctly different spaces, as well as creating "formal and informal boundaries and distinctions which serve to privilege some bodies and separate, order or exclude others" (Brighton et al. 2021: 67). The specific construction of fitness club space is composed of clearly distinguished sections, including front desks, changing rooms, and studio spaces. Each of these sections has its own social relations, cultural codes, and performances, which affect the embodied experiences of gym goers. The present analysis focuses primarily on studio spaces, as the main spaces in which group fitness practices take place.

In principle, studio spaces are organized to ensure that each person has enough room to be able to exercise with unimpeded motions and to receive the information provided by the instructor. At the beginning of the class, the instructor stands away from the other participants. During training he/she often moves around the space. Participants of group classes choose their spots in the studio space themselves, yet the instructor may, at least to some extent, introduce changes in the configuration of gym bodies in space.

Individual gym bodies are disciplined by the organization of not only space, but also time. Fitness clubs structure time through schedules that define the beginning, end, and duration of each training session, as well as their frequency throughout the day and the week. Every session is divided into segments. The time allotted to training does not involve unnecessary breaks and is used to the maximum, in order for specified goals to be achieved.

Since fitness culture is a significant cultural phenomenon with its global/local variations, "the rules of membership, knowledge shared on the body, and embodied fitness practices undertaken upon them are uniquely dependent on the type, geographical location and membership of the gym" (Brighton et al. 2021: 83). Before describing the changes introduced to the local context due to the epidemiological situation, this chapter will provide a brief overview of the principles of gym bodies management that the Warsaw fitness club followed before the lockdown. This is a necessary step towards a more detailed presentation and deeper understanding of the transformations brought on by the Covid-19 pandemic.

Pre-Lockdown Regulations and Post-Lockdown Restrictions

The mid-size fitness club in which I have been employed as an instructor for various group classes is located in the center of Warsaw. It offers membership packages at affordable prices, which is why the club's clientele consists of a broad spectrum of men and women. The first point of contact upon entering the single-floor building is the front desk. The workout area is situated opposite the "overseeing eye," next to the studio space. Both the workout space and the studio space feature a glass wall, which means that, once inside, gym bodies and their performances can be observed, both by other fitness enthusiasts and by outsiders. Moreover, two other walls in the fitness room are covered with full-length mirrors. Mirrors play a very particular role in the promotion of self-monitoring, and therefore also bodily (Sassatelli 2011), as well as in the development of "pictorial competence" (Bourdieu 1991). They provide "visual evidence of the progression made towards one's self-reflexive body project" (Brighton et al. 2021: 87). The basement, accessible by stairs, accommodates a second (smaller) studio space and the room for personal training sessions. As a low-cost gym, the club only has basic facilities and offers only the most essential equipment. The arrangement of equipment is, in fact, one of the fundamental material methods of managing gym bodies in space.

The delineation of separate gym sites within the club is based not only on material, but also on immaterial boundaries, including idealized gendered body work. Officially at least, gendered spatial segregation is only legitimized when it pertains to toilets and changing rooms. The workout space and the gym room are formally available to all gym goers. However, an informal division has emerged, with the space of the workout room dominated by men, and the studio space occupied mostly by women. The division is also reflected in the sensory landscape (e.g., the sounds and smells predominant in a given gym section).

Before the lockdown, group training sessions were organized regularly throughout the day, seven days a week. A standard class was fifty-five minutes long, with five-minute breaks between each session. To ensure a smooth exchange of gym bodies in each of the spaces, and to avoid overcrowding in the bathrooms and changing rooms, the sessions in the smaller studio space began fifteen minutes later than those in the larger room. The maximum number of participants allowed in the studio space was twenty in the larger room and nine in the smaller. However, the limitations were not always followed in practice. The state of affairs had is consequences. One of them was participants accidentally "bumping into" one another during their embodied practices, which inadvertently led to touch. It must therefore be emphasized that, before the pandemic, gym bodies were everywhere in the club, often crowding together—and nobody so much as took note.

The outbreak of the pandemic brought a significant reorganization of the local landscape. The reopening of fitness centers in Poland was conditional and associated with the introduction of procedures imposed by the government under the Ordinance of the Council of Ministers of May 29, 2020, and the precise guidelines issued by the Minister of Economic Development and the Chief Sanitary Inspector. According to the official justification presented by the central government, the principal aim of the restrictions was to reduce physical interaction, thereby minimizing the risk of transmission of the Covid-19 virus. The list of new sanitary measures to be followed by clients of fitness centers included the obligation to wear a face mask and disinfect surfaces and equipment on a regular basis. The rule that merits particular attention in the context of the present analysis was social distancing, also called physical distancing. This public health practice, defined as keeping a safe distance from other people, has become a key strategy to combat Covid-19 in Europe (Williams 2020). Its principal aim was to prevent direct contact between potentially infected and healthy individuals (Black Larcom 2020). The national authorities of Poland initially imposed the following restrictions to that effect:

1. Maximum limit of persons in indoor spaces: one person per ten square meters;

2. Maintaining a distance of at least two meters between the gym goers.

These stipulations corresponded not only to the recommendations of the national healthcare and sanitation institutions, but also to the guidelines issued by international bodies including the World Health Organization (WHO 2021). However, the instructions of the Polish government regarding social distancing were not permanent but changed over time. As early as June, the Minister of Health announced that the maximum limit for indoor spaces was one person per seven square meters. Another change came in August, when it was stated that "Depending on the dimensions of the gym/fitness club, a limited number of clients is allowed to be present in the rooms, so that a distance of 1.5 meter could be maintained" (Table of alterations to the guidelines in 2020).

As soon as the spring lockdown ended, agents of the fitness industry invoking expert opinions from Poland and abroad (e.g., studies conducted under the supervision of Professor Michael Bretthauer at the University of Oslo) commenced their efforts to persuade the general public that fitness clubs were safe (Siłownie są bezpieczne [Gyms are safe] 2020). In the summer of 2020, the campaign entitled #zdrowiepotrzebujeruchu (#healthneedsexercise) was initiated by the Federation of Fitness Employers, with the support of the Ministry of Sport and the sport clubs affiliated in the organization (including fitness chains). The principal objective was to encourage people to return to training floors (Wracajcie na siłownie [Come back to the gyms] 2020).

The recommendations of international institutions and the restrictions imposed on the Polish fitness industry by the national authorities were soon reflected in social practices undertaken on the local level. In the studied fitness club in Warsaw, all the equipment that used to be located in the workout room was distributed throughout different gym sites. Group training was only organized in the larger studio space (the smaller one was off limits), and the number of participants allowed per session was reduced to ten. The floor of the room was marked with X signs to indicate where the participants should be standing.

The changes pertained to the management of gym bodies in space, but also in time. Although the club's opening hours remained as they had been before the lockdown, the number of group training sessions was limited to only four per day. The classes were shortened to forty-five minutes, with the breaks between them extended to at least fifteen minutes, to facilitate the effective distribution of gym bodies throughout the various gym sections and to minimize the probability of close physical contact. Classes for senior citizens were removed from the schedule. Most seniors did not return to the club after the spring lockdown, yet they were not the only group of clients to take that decision.

The lists of regulations displayed around the club and the containers with disinfectant that had become a fixture of the local landscape served as a constant reminder of the epidemiological situation and the restrictions in force.

Adaptation to Change II: Social Distancing

This section illustrates how the official guidelines pertaining to obligatory social distancing were implemented and negotiated in practice by the employees and clients of the club under analysis.

Despite the increased security measures, only a fraction of the club's clients returned after the reopening of the fitness industry. The decision was taken mainly out of fear of infection, as corroborated by the following statements by one of the gym's clients:

> I am not afraid; if I was, I would not have come. As for someone leaving the virus on the mat, I'm also not afraid, because there are various, I don't know if it even exists. There are fewer people, much fewer. They're afraid, or they don't want to, or they haven't paid [for their membership packages]. (Interview with Roberta, October 14, 2020)

The fitness chain offered online classes during lockdown, but they were discontinued when the clubs started operating again. Informal conversations indicated that some women who did not return to the club after the reopening took part in online training organized privately by fitness instructors (for more on the instructors' situation during the pandemic see Andersson et al. 2021; Czarnecka

2021b). Significantly, however, at least in some cases, fitness enthusiasts chose to continue attending online training sessions due to fear of infection.

Meanwhile, the approach gym goers displayed towards the obligation to keep a safe physical distance in the club evolved over time. Generally speaking, in the first weeks after the lockdown most people tried to follow the new regulations to the letter. The club staff controlled the number of participants in each class, making sure that the limit was not exceeded. The exercisers were counted at the beginning of each session, both by the instructor and by the receptionist (regardless of the automatic number control stemming from the online registration system). This is not to mean that every fitness enthusiast followed the same patterns of behavior in the gym room. One instructor noticed:

> There are individuals who are visibly afraid and prefer to move away. There are those who did not wear a mask in the communal rooms, and those who entered the room wearing a mask and only took it off later, and moved away, and made sure the proper distance was maintained. there's no physical closeness anymore. In the past, for instance exercises in pairs were the standard, but now I think I wouldn't dare do these, because the group might include a person who'd simply be afraid (Interview with Jane, October 19, 2020).

Nevertheless, asked whether she was afraid to come to training sessions during the pandemic, and whether she kept the prescribed distance, one of the club's clients replied:

> I mean, with the distance, I always keep it, because I'm in the cooler [she has always stood close to the fan—D.C.]. So, I'm not afraid of that. I simply adopt a "whatever will be, will be" attitude. It doesn't bother me, actually. Because, in general, everyone has their place, during these classes which I attend, well, everyone has their bit of space where they exercise. And when [the instructor] gets in this space, I don't mind. Because to get infected you'd have to be spitting on one another for, I don't know, fifteen minutes (Interview with Amy, October 15, 2020).

The first of the cited statements indicates that the epidemiological situation not only brought a change in the reactions and behaviors displayed by exercisers in the studio space, but also affected the way the instructor chose to conduct her classes. The second statement illustrates that the subjective sense of danger felt by gym goers in connection with the use of preventive strategies of dealing with the threat of infection (which include rationalizing or suppressing affect—the threat may exist, but there is nothing to worry about [Alexander 2004]), influenced the manner in which these people interacted with other gym goers, as well as their attitude towards the obligatory social distancing measures.

In general, limiting the number of exercisers and dividing the floor into designated "zones" for each person increased the distance between gym goers and practically eliminated the probability of physical contact (i.e., all manner of accidental touch resulting from bumping into other people during exercises).

However, despite the introduction of these new methods of managing gym bodies within the club and attempts at following the sanitary regime undertaken by fitness enthusiasts, the principle of social distancing was not always adhered to in practice. While nobody disrespected the restrictions repeatedly or on purpose, some bodily habits and patterns of behavior associated with training (e.g., walking around the room during class and correcting the exercisers' posture by touch) made instructors forget the new rules. A statement by one of the instructors corroborated this claim:

> When the clubs reopened in June, there was this general emphasis, not to approach the clients, not to touch, but truth be told, it's hard not to. When you're among living people, then, shoot, you either forget yourself, you come closer, too close sometimes, it's just, when you're working with a living person, in a group, then it's really damn hard, you need to check yourself all the time (Interview with Catherine, November 5, 2020).

With every passing week, more and more women—especially regular clients—began to approach one another, paying little attention to the prescribed distance. They frequently gathered several minutes before the class and engaged in lively discussions (without their face masks, as the regulations allowed these to be taken off in the exercise room). The safe distance zone was also breached when clients approached the instructor to ask a question, or after classes, when they walked around the room passing bottles with disinfectant to one another. In a sense, the spaces delineated with the X signs on the floor were only respected during training, but disregarded before and after the classes began.

Significantly, changes in the approach to the social distancing rules were also apparent in the club's policy and the conduct of its employees. The number of clients grew with every passing week, and although the official limits regarding the number of people were not changed, they were exceeded with increasing regularity. Receptionists no longer counted the clients entering gym rooms, often asking instructors for permission to allow more people in. Interestingly, most clients did not mind such practices. Thus, in time the designated zones ceased to serve their purpose, as the increased number of gym bodies in the room translated to less distance between each person. Despite the changes in the space organization of the club, gym goers that were not supervised in any consistent manner failed to abide by the rules of social distancing. Official guidelines were disregarded in a more or less deliberate fashion. From the Foucauldian perspective, the new regulations for managing gym bodies were not internalized to an extent that would enable gym goers to perform them automatically and without hesitation.

Adaptation to Change I: Touch

This section illustrates how the introduction of mandatory social distancing affected touch as a social practice, and how gym goers reacted to changes in this respect.

Touch constitutes one of the coding variables within proxemics measures (Hall 1963). The rules of social distancing introduced following the lockdown were directly associated with the prohibition to touch other gym bodies. The relevant changes did not escape the notice of gym goers, as illustrated by the following statement given by one of the instructors: "Okay, now we need to distinguish between two time zones. The first time zone is before the pandemic, and the second refers to after the pandemic" (interview with Eve, September 20, 2020).

Before the pandemic, fitness enthusiasts experienced different kinds of touch (e.g., sociable, pedagogical), which served a number of different functions. As a significant element of the sensory landscape, touch constituted and structured embodied experiences in fitness culture. In the present chapter, touch is understood as a significant social practice (Blake 2011) and one of disciplinary techniques (Czarnecka 2021a), which requires physical proximity and, as such, was officially forbidden due to the risk of virus transmission.

In the fitness club under scrutiny, before reopening the management notified all instructors that they were forbidden from approaching clients (which implied the prohibition of touch). It should, however, be noted that even before the pandemic corrective touch as a method for disciplining gym bodies had not been employed by all instructors. Similarly, not every instructor was willing to engage in the sociable practices of public, intimate touch (e.g., hugs, high fives, handshakes). To those for whom touch played an important role, the prohibitions stemming from the new sanitary regime proved extremely challenging to bear. On the one hand, instructors tried to limit all forms of touch to the absolute minimum—especially the ones related to social interactions. "There's no hugging me anymore. You know, I would love for it to come back, but I really don't want to do them [clients] a disservice" (interview with Eve, September 20, 2020). The situation resulted not only from the new regulations, but also—or perhaps primarily—from the instructors' own perception of the virus as a real danger, and their sense of care and responsibility for their own health and the well-being of other gym goers. On the other hand, despite the restrictions, corrective touch and other forms of physical contact were not entirely eliminated. This is corroborated by the following statements given by instructors:

> I try to remember about it, but it keeps slipping my mind (laughs). I am the kind of person who, you know, happily comes up to people to fix their posture and help. So, while I know that, well, theoretically I shouldn't be correcting by touch, still, because we've known one another for so long, I don't feel any reservations at all (Interview with Jane, October 19, 2020).

> Yes, but I go about it in a slightly different way than before. First of all, I only touch clothed body parts. I take more time to demonstrate. I myself try to touch less and provide more verbal instructions, but I decided that since these people actually came to classes then we have agreed, that we go back to how things used to be, more or less. But, yeah, I try not to get too close to their faces, but more from the side, maybe like this. To consider their health and my own. But the distance is not 1.5 meter (laughs), let's just say (Interview with Eve, September 20, 2020).

In spite of all prohibitions, some instructors still used various forms of touch in the studio space, though they did so much more seldom than before the lockdown. Their actions were met with acquiescence from many clients, especially regulars, yet many gym goers still declared that during the pandemic all forms of touch ought to be eliminated. One client stated: "I don't mind it. But, generally speaking, when it comes to other people, they shouldn't do it. Because, well, if the distance is to be maintained, the instructor shouldn't be coming up to anyone, or touching, just talking because you don't know how others view the matter, right?" (Interview with Roberta, October 14, 2020).

To minimize the risk of infection, fitness coaches took the initiative to modify their habits, for instance refraining from touching certain body parts or changing the relative position of the touching body and the touched. As far as touch is concerned, many instructors emphasized that they established a practice of more frequent hand washing, which they justified with the wish to protect themselves and other people. Their attempts at eliminating corrective touch had not only negative, but also positive consequences (e.g., led to improvement in the instructors' skill in presenting verbal instructions).

Furthermore, various forms of touch were still observable between gym goers, including instances where efforts were made to limit them. On the one hand, accidental touch occurred when clients attending training sessions passed items to one another. On the other, the gym experience also involved sociable forms of touching. As one instructor noted: "Of course they touch one another. They do, because they're friends, they talk to one another, pat one another's shoulder, or something" (interview with Eve, September 20, 2020).

For some gym goers, the increased duration of time spent together in the club alleviated the subjective sense of danger, which in turn led to them becoming less cautious during interaction. At the same time, the changes introduced to the gyms changed the local tactile landscape experienced by fitness enthusiasts, which also affected their development of corporeality.

Conclusion

Only a fraction of gym goers returned to studio spaces after the reopening of the industry. The introduction of a new sanitary regime proved insufficient to convince those afraid of contracting Covid-19 to take up exercising again.

The epidemiological situation led to a reorganization of the way gym bodies were managed in space and time. Officially imposed changes in bodily comportment and social practice were aimed to help gym goers adapt to the new circumstances. Although, in the local context, not all gym goers fully followed the new restrictions, the majority did try to keep the prescribed distance and avoid touch. The fact that adherence to regulations was not checked constantly or consistently contributed to the loosening of discipline among gym goers; the obligation of social distancing was disregarded especially in the cases where it stood in opposition to earlier bodily habits and the needs or values prioritized by a given person in a given situation.

The pandemic transformed physical proximity and contact (also through touch), which had been an integral element of fitness culture and the embodied experiences of gym goers before the lockdown, into something undesirable and essentially forbidden. The obligation to keep a safe physical distance between gym bodies was directly related to the prohibition of touch, which began to undergo transformations as a result of the epidemiological situation. Increasingly often, it was presented not as an interface allowing for contact with the other or as a didactic "tool," but as a medium of contagion. An interesting phenomenon that could be observed was the clash of values apparent in the behavior of the women who tried to negotiate and modify the existing restrictions in various ways. It is entirely conceivable that careful compliance with these regulations may eventually lead to a remodeling of fitness culture towards a more "disembodied" phenomenon. In an "individual but together" modality, the embodied experiences of fitness enthusiasts are shaped and shared collectively. If enforced for longer periods of time, the obligation to keep more and more physical distance and the prohibition of touching other gym bodies will likely affect the transmission of non-verbal knowledge and gym goers' experiences, which develop differently in situations of close physical contact.

REFERENCES

Alexander, Jeffrey. 2004. *Cultural Trauma and Collective Identity*. Berkeley and Los Angeles and London: University of California Press.

Andersson, Karin, Ulrike Vogl, and Jesper Andreasson. 2021. "Working out Covid-19: Being a Les Mills Instructor and Managing Health in Times of Quarantine." In *Time Out: Global Perspectives on Sport and the Covid-19 Lockdown*, edited by Jörg Krieger, April Henning, Lindsay Parks Pieper, and Paul Dimeo, 107–18. Champaign, US: Common Ground.

Black Larcom, Alexandra. 2020. "Social Distancing in Your Health Club." Accessed May 3, 2021. https://www.ihrsa.org/improve-your-club/social-distancing-in-your-health-club/#.

Blake, Rosemary. 2011. "Ethnographies of Touch and Touching Ethnographies: Some Prospects of Touch in Anthropological Enquiries." *Anthropology Matters* 13 (1): 1–12.

Bourdieu, Pierre. 1977. *Outline of a Theory of Practice*. Cambridge: Cambridge University Press.

Brighton, James, Ian Wellard, and Amy Clark. 2021. "Introducing (Our) Gym Bodies and Fitness Cultures." In *Gym Bodies. Exploring Fitness Cultures*, edited by James Brighton, Ian Wellard, and Amy Clark, 1–19. London and New York: Routledge.

Czarnecka, Dominika. 2021a. "Instrumental Touch: A Foucauldian Analysis of Women's Fitness." *Suomen Antropologi. Journal of the Finnish Anthropological Society* 45 (4): 23–43.

———. 2021b. "'Stay Fit to Fight the Virus': Ethnographies of Change in the World of Fitness Instructors (Selected Case Studies)." In *Time Out: National Perspectives on Sport and the Covid-19 Lockdown*, edited by Jörg Krieger, April Henning, Lindsay Parks Pieper, and Paul Dimeo, 203–14. Champaign, US: Common Ground.

Dawson, Marcelle. 2017. "CrossFit: Fitness Cult or Reinventive Institution?" *International Review for the Sociology of Sport* 52 (3): 361–79.

Foucault, Michel. 1995. *Discipline and Punish. The Birth of the Prison*. New York: Vintage Books.

Hall, Edward T. 1963. "A System for the Notation of Proxemic Behavior." *American Anthropologist* 65 (5): 1003–26.

Markula, Pirkko, and Richard Pringle. 2006. *Foucault, Sport and Exercise: Power, Knowledge and Transforming the Self*. London and New York: Routledge.

Sassatelli, Roberta. 2011. *Fitness Culture. Gym and the Commercialisation of Discipline and Fun*. New York: Plagrave Macmillan.

Siłownie są bezpieczne [Gyms are safe] 2020. Accessed May 3, 2021. https://kobietyimedycyna.pl/silownie-sa-bezpieczne/.

Stake, Robert. 1995. *The Art of Case Study Research*. Thousand Oaks, CA: Sage.

Tabela zmian w wytycznych dla siłowni, klubów fitness, obiektów wspinaczkowych gov.pl/rozwój [Table of alterations to the guidelines for gyms, fitness clubs, wall-climbing centers] 2020. Accessed April 24, 2020. https://www.gov.pl/web/rozwoj-praca-technologia/silownie-i-kluby-fitness.

WHO 2021. "Coronavirus Disease (Covid-19) Advice for the Public." Accessed May 3, 2021. https://www.who.int/emergencies/diseases/novel-coronavirus-2019/advice-for-public.

Williams, Nerys. 2020. "Social Distancing in the Covid-19 Pandemic." *Occupational Medicine* 70 (5): 305.

Wracajcie na siłownie i do fitness klubów. Namawia także resort sportu [Come back to the gyms and fitness clubs. The Ministry of Sport joins in the encouragement] 2020. Accessed May 3, 2021. https://biznes.wprost.pl/gospodarka/10350510/wracajcie-na-silownie-i-do-fitness-klubow-namawia-takze-resort-sportu.html.

Chapter 16

Global Perspectives on Group Fitness Post Lockdown: Reflections of Les Mills' Trainers

Karin Andersson, Jesper Andreasson, and Ulrike Vogl

Introduction

After more than a year of restrictions and social distancing following the Covid-19 pandemic, societies gradually began to open up in June 2021. Clearly, the opening and closing of societies have had a great impact on people's routines, lifestyles, and work. One commercial branch that was greatly affected was the fitness industry, which, in the course of the pandemic suffered severe losses in revenue, manifesting its dependence on sponsorship and further external support (Rowe 2020). However, the situation in gyms and sport clubs has varied greatly depending on countries' own policies and individual gyms' interpretations of restrictions. Across Europe, during spring 2020, many gyms were temporarily closed until summer 2020, and further lockdowns followed in autumn 2020. Notable exceptions were Sweden (no closures) and Finland (only regional temporary closures) (RMD 2021). Reopening began in some regions in February 2021, in parts of Spain for example, while not until May in Austria, Poland, and Belgium (Czarnecka 2021). In contrast to the overall situation in Europe, Australia's gyms were allowed to reopen by November 2020, and in the United States, responsive measures varied between states. These global differences imply that the "restart" of fitness centers have happened at different points in time and under varying circumstances.

The New Zealand-based company, Les Mills International (henceforth LMI), is one of the most successful providers of group fitness activities around the world. LMI workout routines can be found in over 20,000 gyms and fitness clubs, consisting of a community of approximately 140,000 group fitness instructors globally (Les Mills, 2021). Importantly, the company is not only a provider of pre-choreographed workout routines, but also a central stakeholder in the global fitness market—a producer of lifestyles and health ideals. However, following mandatory guidelines and recommendations of social distancing, the company has been forced to partly reinvent itself and adapt to a changed "fitness arena." Unsurprisingly, LMI's exercise programs are designed for face-to-face interaction between customers and instructors, which has largely been impossible during the Covid-19 pandemic. Therefore, virtual fitness activities have enabled customers and trainers, who used to frequent gyms, to comply with guidelines concerning social distancing, while simultaneously continuing their fitness journeys from their private homes. Yet, the substantial changes may have altered instructors' understandings of their occupation and their professional identity.

Therefore, the aim of this chapter is to map how LMI group fitness instructors reason around their occupation after one year of Covid-19, and how they imagine group fitness will continue. The instructors, whom we have followed through focus group discussions since the outbreak of Covid-19, reflected on the changes and challenges they have experienced, and how this affects their group fitness profession. At the time of the interviews for this text, vaccinations had only just begun, and many countries had been closed for several months following new waves of infections that forced re-closing many facilities. Without a scheduled date for reopening's (see method section for further information), respondents speculated freely on how they thought that the situation would develop.

A thematic analysis of the transcribed focus group discussions in NVivo points toward three overarching main topics; (i) reflections concerning what has happened to group fitness so far, (ii) effects on local and global community, and (iii) reasoning around fitness-related Covid-19 restrictions. Consequently, this text will mainly discuss two sub-topics that respondents stressed frequently within all three main topics; restrictions in gyms (e.g., facemasks and reduced classes), and online fitness (e.g., on-demand services and live streamed sessions, all grouped under the term "virtual fitness" (Lupton 2017).

The results point toward two substantial changes. Firstly, due to extended closures of gyms, several instructors have gone from actively teaching fitness classes to being participants online. Secondly, although fitness services online are generally described as sub-optimal alternatives, they are likely here to stay, compelling instructors to either adapt or navigate their fitness enthusiasm elsewhere. Furthermore, the outcomes indicate that additional research is needed to explore how the recently added virtual dimension to fitness classes may affect fitness professions, as well as the professional identity of trainers.

Background

Since the 1980s, everyday exercise has mainly been marketed as an individual responsibility that should be pursued in one's spare time (Crawford 2006). Since physical activity often entails practices in need of large spaces or specialized equipment, it commonly takes place in gyms or sport clubs. Notably, Covid-19 could be classified as an involuntarily imposed and unexpected transition (Schlossberg 1981) that has brought such facilities to a standstill, forcing fitness personnel and laypeople to change habits and venues. Group fitness professionals often identify as highly physically active, maintaining that fitness is a lifestyle rather than an isolated health-practice (Sassatelli 2014). This means that the closure of gyms could cause a loss of community and sense of belonging, but it could also be an opportunity for upskilling. Szabo et al. (2020) write that,

> those who exercise in large volumes, including those at risk of exercise addiction and group/team exercisers, are forced to cut down on their exercise. However, individuals addicted to exercise will presumably find alternative means of training (p. 190).

Consequently, in search of possibilities to be active, trainers may be especially willing to navigate their physical activity towards alternative spaces, such as the internet. According to statistics, the use of virtual fitness and e-health applications have skyrocketed during the pandemic (Mutz et al., 2020; Andersson et al. 2021; Malcolm & Velija 2020). E-health applications are distinguished by providing short and intensive workouts that can be performed in small spaces. They stand out as interactive alternatives where users may share their activities on social media (Marchant 2021). Although fitness online during the pandemic has been described as a new lifestyle trend that is here to stay in China (Ling 2020), it is more commonly portrayed as a last resort (Andersson & Andreasson 2021; Ibrahim et al., 2021), mainly used by well-to-do younger people and women (Mutz et al., 2021). However, respondents within this study underlined that they think online fitness will remain popular post-lockdown, mainly because it is a convenient option. In the findings section, we will present a discussion around online fitness that has, admittedly, provided a space where group fitness classes have been able to continue.

Method and Analysis

This chapter builds on a longitudinal case study (Yin 2014) that was initiated in March 2020, at the outbreak of Covid-19, and continued until fall 2021. Data was collected through focus group discussions (Morgan 2018) with LMI certified group fitness instructors. A total of 18 participants contributed their narratives. Among the participants, eleven respondents identified as women and seven as men (aged between 27 and 56 years old). Seven instructors work full-time as fitness instructors while the other eleven instructors also employed outside of the fitness industry (e.g., schoolteacher, photographer, or college professor). The participants were active LMI instructors from eleven countries: Austria, Belgium, Finland, Israel, Sweden, Spain, Switzerland, Jordan, Australia, England, and U.S. In the sampling process, participants were invited to participate on a voluntary basis after having filled out an online questionnaire concerning their fitness careers (see Andersson, Vogl, and Andreasson 2021).

Interviews were conducted in three sets. The first round of interviews took place in April 2020, the second in November 2020, and the third round in

February 2021. This chapter mainly builds on data gathered in the last set of interviews, conducted while the pandemic was ongoing, but restrictions were less strict in many countries and gyms had restarted face-to-face classes.

Due to the ambition of gathering contrasting experiences of LMI instructors operating in different countries in different time zones, all interviews were conducted using online video conferencing platforms, such as Zoom and Skype. The interviews, ranging between sixty and ninety minutes, were audio recorded and transcribed. Subsequently, the interviews were processed using a thematic analysis (Braun & Clarke 2020), on the program NVivo (1.4.1).

In this chapter, we attempt to capture how professional identity was negotiated during the pandemic, causing some trainers to redefine themselves and "go virtual," whereas others maintained their prior preference for face-to-face teaching. To understand why fitness online might feel unnatural, we employ Randal Collins' (2004) concept of interaction ritual chains. This concept was developed in order to explain how group belonging comes about, namely, through co-presence, mutual focus of attention, and rhythmic entrainment (Collins 2020, p. 478) these are not necessarily successful components via technical devices (e.g., faulty internet connection, lack of eye-contact).

Findings

Professional Challenges in the Local Fitness Studios

This section will highlight the most frequently mentioned challenges of the past and present year, which had an impact on the respondent's fitness professions. As gyms reopened, various restrictions, such as whether or not teaching with a facemask would be required, followed. For Kenny, a teacher and part-time instructor living in San Francisco, masks became mandatory as soon as gyms began reopening again, "I teach outdoors with six feet distance and I'm in a mask, so I can't wait until the moment where I don't have to teach in a mask," whereas Pekka, a full-time entrepreneur located in Helsinki, could choose himself and commented, "I've been using a mask indoors, not while instructing, I tried it but it was more or less impossible." Adding to this, one respondent narrated, "teaching in a mask is more dangerous than corona" (Jamal, full-time trainer, Jordan), while two other instructors based in Vienna referred to teaching in facemasks as a "before the apocalypse last resort situation" in September 2020. Since facemasks received a lot of attention during the discussions, one could consider how the mask affects an instructor. For instance, a facemask limits communication with participants. According to LMIs' concept, instructors are supposed to be theatrical in order to spread energy and positivity (e.g., smiles and other facial expressions), which is potentially impossible while wearing a face covering. Wearing the mask could also be physically demanding, distracting the instructor from teaching altogether. Peter, a British instructor residing in Barcelona elaborated:

> I am guilty of being not as diligent or conscientious about correcting people cause I'm fighting with the elements a bit, so there's people at the back that don't get the sort of connection, and I can only do as much. I feel that it's counterproductive with masks and teaching. They get wet, they fall down. In Bodypump where I touch equipment that is probably dirty then I'm touching my face to pull it back up, I'm thinking this is worse.

He continues by saying that he currently prefers teaching his classes in the solarium area, since he is not obliged to wear a mask there.

The group fitness business concept commonly follows a neoliberal model where trainers work on a freelance basis, and several instructors informed us that the reduction of classes has resulted in financial setbacks. Due to this, monthly salaries may have changed while the regular expenses for LMI licenses (containing the rights to choreography and music from LMI) remained. Kenny recollects, "as the months went on by it was hard for me to justify seven certifications and still paying for certain releases when we're not allowed to teach them, so it was hard to stay motivated." Laura, who is based in Switzerland and also works as a national trainer for LMI Italy, points toward the same issue, "it is difficult to keep the instructors motivated at home." Pekka, however, who used to teach several classes every day, exclaims that he will not let the situation discourage him, but confesses, "if this will continue, I'm running out of money. Then I maybe have to get another job, at least on a temporary basis, and that's a thing I really don't want to think about." Pekka hopes that the fitness classes will soon return to normal in Helsinki before his situation becomes financially precarious.

The reduction of classes following reopening has resulted both in financial losses and feuds at gyms where many trainers now must compete for the few classes available, which causes competition among instructors. Bruce, a student of informatics residing on the Gold Coast in Australia who teaches one weekly class, adds that, although his gym remained open almost throughout, "the availability becomes the challenge, that everyone is trying to get the classes, the few classes that are running." His comment draws attention toward the fact that the distribution of classes is an issue when gyms are not operating at full capacity. Importantly, due to legal regulations, teaching the classes with the licensed music online has not been allowed, and although far from everyone conveyed to be financially reliant on the income from classes, some still expressed disappointment in LMI for not providing discounts. Klaus, a photographer and part-time instructor in Vienna disclosed:

> we've been shut down for four months and there was an entire release that we were never able to teach in a class, and I think lots of countries have the same

situation at the moment, and I'm disappointed that Les Mills haven't reacted more to that. No discounts or anything.

Klaus maintained that it is a matter of principle and that he would have bought the releases as soon as his gym opened again. However, he feels somewhat cheated by the global community, which has resulted in some alienation on his behalf[1]. This means that in the current study, professional identity is contingent on the cultural practices and specific contexts within the LMI community.

In sum, this section has highlighted the most frequently mentioned challenges of the reopening/re-closing period: closed gyms (as well as gyms switching between open and closed) and at times when gyms were (partially) open, having to wear facemasks, reduced capacity for classes, as well as the financial difficulties that followed as a consequence. Facemasks were described as disturbing when teaching, and, by some, even as counterproductive. Yet, more instructors seemed willing to wear a facemask at this point (February 2021) in comparison to our talks in November 2020. Accordingly, one can see how, although a facemask may allow their profession to continue, is simultaneously something that restricts some practices. By extension, the mask comes to symbolize a negotiation between health and performance that may impact professional identity negatively. The instructors only have body language, voice, and facial expressions at their disposal to create a performance, which has also been referred to as a spectacle for the participants to consume (Parviainen 2011). This means that wearing a face-mask limits two of the three possibilities that are necessary to perform the job. Therefore, teaching in facemasks illuminates how two different paradigms of health must merge. The mask comes to represent health from a short-term perspective; prevention of more Covid-19 cases. The classes rather signify a long-term health endeavor prevention of obesity and related diseases through exercising. The mask has clearly become the compromise that allows both undertakings to coexist. For this reason, it is accepted, but also leaves instructors feeling like they are not "doing a good job."

Finally, it is difficult, at this stage, to speculate on how the economic consequences will affect instructors. During our conversations, no one directly expressed that they would give up the profession or contemplated teaching in non-LMI formats (that may be cheaper). Yet, many interviewees did not seem to make clear distinctions between themselves as trainers and themselves as participants. It seems that most considered themselves as both, which hints toward the fact that their professional identities are intertwined with their personal identities, allowing LMI fitness to become something more than an occupation "it is difficult to

---

[1] We define professional identity along the lines of Charles Goodwin's professional vision, which he defines as "socially organized ways of seeing and understanding events that are answerable to the distinctive interests of a particular social group" (p. 606). This means that in the current study, professional identity is contingent on the cultural practices and specific contexts within the LMI community.

imagine a life without LMI" (a statement a majority of the interviewed instructors agreed with).

Fitness Online: A Trend that is here to Stay

A further central theme within our conversations has been virtual fitness, which entails all online fitness, such as on-demand services or live streamed classes via Zoom. Virtual options have, up until this point, predominantly been discussed by the interviewees as a suboptimal spatial transition for the practice of group fitness that, however, may allow their profession to continue (Andersson & Andreasson 2021). Although the conveyed sentiments are still generally skeptical, nuances are noticeable. For example, Klaus described the phenomenon in September 2020 as an "absolute last resort," yet, in February 2021 he commented, "I tried it twice, and it was better than I expected, but it wasn't good enough to keep me going and doing it again." He further explained, "it was like trying some type of foreign food which wasn't bad, but I prefer the homemade stuff and I'll stick to that (laughs)." However, as he learned that his gym was reopening again soon, he began preparing himself with two on-demand classes a week. Significantly, his comments capture the fact that virtual fitness was, to many, a new fitness practice at the outset of the pandemic. Over time, virtual fitness has, to some extent, become normalized, although in Klaus's opinion, teaching face-to-face is still the norm, "online it's not the way it was intended, not the way it was made for basically. So, it feels like you're doing something within the wrong framework." Some other instructors, for example, Laura and Pekka, both share the opinion that virtual fitness is here to stay, yet Pekka, who gave classes online before the pandemic, underline, "I've always thought of it as just an additional service." There were also instructors who changed their minds regarding online classes despite initially disliking it:

> In the beginning I didn't do virtual classes, and it was the same for home workouts, and I thought "I hate it, I won't do it," but after one year of corona it's like I do lots of this. I think it's not the same as the classes in presence, but I would say that my opinion on that completely changed. In the beginning I thought it was ridiculous and now I think it's ok, I can train with friends, so it's really nice (Linda, Vienna).

Linda participates in several classes online each week and accentuates its social dimension—being able to train with friends digitally, which is interesting, since the social dimension is often the aspect that instructors claim that virtual fitness lacks. The sociologist Randall Collins (2020) has underlined that online interaction via Zoom or similar applications lack the usual components of a successful social exchange—co-presence, mutual focus of attention, rhythmic entrainment (478), which became evident when Helga commented that she cannot follow fast workouts online, "the internet lags and you cannot be on the beat."

Laura touched upon the element of co-presence, "it's frustrating cause you don't have feedbacks, so you do but you don't know, and it takes a lot of energy for me, cause you don't have the second part, you give but you don't receive."

Accordingly, within a year, the instructors have transitioned from a premise where some had never tried virtual fitness, to currently making distinctions between various sorts of online training. Bruce narrated:

> I do feel like I have an idea of what virtual fitness targets, I just don't think it works for me personally. There are also different types of it. You have people doing it over Zoom, or the ones like Les Mills on demand where it's just a video feed.

Bruce highlighted the difference between utilizing on-demand classes, which are pre-recorded and can be played at any time, on any electronic device, and contrasts these to live streamed classes that are unique in the sense that they are happening in the moment. Live streamed classes, as Linda pointed out, appear to come the closest to a face-to-face class, since interaction is possible. For example, Joy, a Brazilian trainer teaching over Zoom in Washington D.C. said during our first round of conversations that she employed the chat function at the beginning of the classes to mimic the small talk that would otherwise take place before a class begins. A further social dimension of a live-streamed class is that participants can see other exercisers if they have their cameras turned on. Bruce admits that, "sometimes I swap the pictures around to see who's there more than actually doing the workout." Along these lines, it seems as if live-streamed classes could develop further and become online social events, possibly similar to Twitch or eSport, which have become a popular phenomenon where people watch other people play online-games live. Yet, for the instructors teaching the classes, it has been a new situation that demands advanced skills. Laura reflected:

> I can still teach everything, but with streaming, and it's hard to keep the people motivated without the connection to them. We are communicating on Facebook, Instagram, and other platforms, so I can't see the participants. Sometimes I think that I am lucky because I have lots of experience, lots of hours of teaching, so I can imagine what they are doing, I say keep your back straight, but I can't see what they are doing. It boils down to experience now.

This comment sheds light on the fact that instructors who teach online need to foreshadow what participants are doing without actually observing it. Laura refers to the fact that an experienced trainer could anticipate what could go wrong in certain exercises and employ prophylactic cues. However, as Bruce clarified, not all participants in a live-streamed class might even be actively exercising. Participants may observe while having no obligations to actually perform the routines themselves. Up until this point, being an authentic instructor during a class had been about perfecting participants' technique and motivating them to "go harder." Accordingly, when the instructor cannot see the participants, or when participants are not participating in a traditional sense, other skills for being a successful instructor are needed.

In summary, this section has discussed respondents' reasoning around some virtual fitness alternatives. A significant aspect is that attitudes have clearly changed over time. At the outset of the pandemic, Klaus stated that he would "rather go to a park and do a workout by himself before joining a virtual class," but then, six months later, confessed to have tried live streamed classes, and he is also doing on-demand fitness to get in shape for the reopening of his gym. His colleague Linda similarly went from "hating the idea" to doing it on a daily basis.

In contrast, full-time entrepreneurs like Pekka and Laura, who began teaching online before the pandemic, seemed to embrace the idea of virtual fitness as an additional service and potentially profitable lasting endeavor. The discussions indicated that trainers who are part-time workers seem reluctant to invest time in upskilling their techniques and "go virtual." This is explained by the lacking social dimension, since these trainers pursue the classes as a sociable hobby, which became very clear through Klaus' statement:

> I think there are two types of people. People who just go to the classes and then leave and go back home, and for these people, the online classes are probably just right. For the people who go to the gym cause they wanna socialize, they want the whole package kind of thing, it just doesn't work.

Klaus constructs an "out" group of people who allegedly just wish to exercise and then go home, and for these people virtual fitness is suitable, whereas those who come to also spend time with peers (an important aspect of instructorhood according to LMI), virtual fitness is insufficient. Although far from everyone teaches fitness classes online, everyone has accepted it as a to-be-taken-seriously alternative to face-to-face instruction. It is noteworthy that many seem to wish to reproduce their accustomed habits online, attempting to recreate rituals they are used to. For instance, as in the case of Joy, employing the chat function to mirror a pre-class talk, or Bruce, swapping pictures around to see other participants (something one would otherwise use a mirror to do). This points toward a relocation of instructorhood into the virtual, however, executed with the same ideals as face-to-face instruction. This, in turn, indicates that virtual fitness is hierarchically lower than face-to-face instruction.

For example, Pekka stated he "miss the live classes" and considered virtual fitness as "just another service." This exemplifies the general sentiment that virtual fitness is an alternative, but the real magic happens and remains live.

Discussion and Conclusion

This chapter clearly points toward the enforced contingency between instructors, LMI as a company, and the global virus. Depending on their region, an instructor is influenced by local on-site restrictions. But it also follows that gyms are conditioned by governmental regulations, which in turn are influenced by global health organizations, and the omnipresent virus itself (Vogl et al. 2022). For LMI and their trainers, this alters the status quo of performing the LMI group fitness profession: from teaching a fairly straightforward, standardized product where a trainer's manual produced and restricted the behaviors of an "authentic" instructor, to local regulations and a global pandemic deciding or perhaps redefining several key components of instructorhood. LMI has, during the pandemic, given increased attention to on-demand fitness. Due to the forced navigation of fitness into the virtual sphere, many of the respondents slipped into roles of being participants, since most are not teaching actively anymore, but rather joining classes online while waiting for their gyms to reopen.

The analysis also shows that there is a clear dichotomy between the traditional face-to-face teaching concept and the virtual sphere, possibly, since the emotional payback of interpersonal interactions change, or even fall flat through the use of electronic devices (Collins 2020). Additionally, the key components of an instructors' duty during a class (coaching with music, choreography, and motivation) can only be done on "autopilot" through streaming, since the instructor do not have the possibility of reacting to things they see (unless participants switch on their cameras). As Laura reflected, "it comes down to experience now." Nevertheless, virtual fitness seems to have become compulsory; although not everyone teaches online, everyone actively engaged in the debates around so-called home workouts, which are often assisted by online services. The digital alternatives seemed to emerge as innovative alternatives to keep up health in pandemic times through which instructors can seemingly remain in control over their fitness journeys. Fitness online has also developed into a phenomenon where further distinctions are necessary to make; pre-recorded on-demand classes, live streamed classes, and hybrid models are terminology that appeared in our talks. Consequently, the pandemic seems to have accelerated a process of digitalizing fitness services, which creates expectations of instructors to join this development and reinvent themselves by "going virtual." However, as Laura narrated, teaching online demands advanced skills that newer instructors may lack, which could exclude some instructors from the profession if gyms insist on blending live and online class formats. In addition, the virtual classroom may come to include further dimensions than face-to-face instructing do. For instance, Bruce pointed out that one can just as well join a virtual class to observe and/or interact with fellow participants rather than to exercise per se, which could develop into an online space where fitness enthusiasts come together with less commitment to performing physical labor than in a fitness studio. While participants may gain agency as consumers through such a development, instructors would possibly need to construct a new or extended "persona" for teaching such classes, assuming the purpose of classes becomes more complex and multidimensional.

Finally, this study has some limitations. Due to the amount of space given, the discussion of Covid-19 challenges is mainly concerned with obstructions to professional identity (e.g., virtual fitness and face masks), but the authors are aware that there are also other concerns of importance. Furthermore, one could say that the text mainly considers Western perspectives of being a fitness instructor. The perspectives presented are also limited to LMI fitness professionals and do not include impressions of gym-goers or administrative personnel.

REFERENCES

Andersson, Karin, and Jesper Andreasson. 2021. "Being a Group Fitness Instructor During the COVID-19 Crisis: Navigating Professional Identity, Social Distancing, and Community." *Social Sciences* 10 (4): 118. https://doi.org/ 10.3390/socsci10040118

Andersson, Karin, Anna Fabri, Peter Fredman, Susanna Hedenborg, Alexander Jansson, Sara Karlén, Jens Radmann, and Daniel Wolf-Watz. 2021. "Idrotten och Friluftslivet under Corona Pandemin: Resultat från två Undersökningar om Coronapandemins Effekter på Idrott, Fysisk Aktivitet och Friluftsliv." *MISTRA Sport & Outdoors*, Rapport. ISBN 978-91-88947-96-3.

Andersson, Karin, Ulrike Vogl, and Jesper Andreasson. 2021. "Working out Covid-19: Being a Les Mills Instructor and Managing Health in Times of Quarantine." In *Time Out: Global Perspectives on Sport and the Covid 19-Lockdown*, edited by Jörg Krieger, April Henning, Lindsay Parks Pieper, and Paul Dimeo, 107-118. Champaign: Common Ground Network.

Braun, Virginia, and Victoria Clarke. 2020. "One Size Fits All? What Counts as Quality Practice In (Reflexive) Thematic Analysis?" *Qualitative Research in Psychology* 18 (3): 328-352. https://doi.org/10.1080/14780887.2020.1769238

CDC (Centers for Disease Control and Prevention). "COVID-19 Employer Information for Gyms and Fitness Centers. U.S. Department of Health & Human Services." Accessed June 30, 2021. https://www.cdc.gov/coronavirus/2019-ncov/community/organizations/gym-employers.html.

Collins, Randall. 2004. *Interaction Ritual Chains*. Princeton: Princeton University Press.

——. 2020. "Social Distancing as a Critical Test of the Micro-Sociology of Solidarity." *American Journal of Cultural Sociology* 8 (3): 477-497.

Crawford, Robert. 2006. "Health as a Meaningful Social Practice." *Health* 10 (4): 401-420. https://doi.org/10.1177/1363459306067310

Czarnecka, D. 2021. "'Stay Fit to Fight the Virus': Ethnographies of Change in the World of Fitness Instructors." In *Time Out. National Perspectives on Sport and the Covid-19 Lockdown*, edited by Jörg Krieger, April Henning, Lindsay Parks Pieper, and Paul Dimeo, 203-214. Champaign: Common Ground.

Goodwin, Charles. 1994. "Professional Vision." *American Anthropologist* 96 (3): 606-633. https://doi.org/10.1525/aa.1994.96.3.02a00100.

Ibrahim, A., M. C. Chong, S. Khoo, L. P. Wong, I. Chung, and M. P. Tan. 2021. "Virtual Group Exercises and Psychological Status among Community-Dwelling Older Adults during the COVID-19 Pandemic-A Feasibility Study." *Geriatrics* (Basel) 6 (1): 31. https://doi.org/10.3390/geriatrics6010031

Fisher, Kilian. 2021. "Health Club Closures & Openings by Country." IHRSA (The Global Health and Fitness Association). Accessed May 26, 2021. https://www.ihrsa.org/improve-your-club/health-club-openings-closures-by-country

Les Mills. "We´re for a Fitter Planet." Accessed May 21, 2021. https://www.lesmills.com/about-us/

Ling, Ping. 2020. "Interpretation of leisure sports in the pandemic situation of COVID 19." *World Leisure Journal*, 62:4, 319-321, https://doi.org/10.1080/16078055.2020.1828786

Lupton, Deborah. 2017. *Digital Health: Critical and Cross-Disciplinary Perspectives*. London: Routledge.

Malcolm, Dominic, and Philippa Velija. 2020. "COVID-19, Exercise and Bodily Self-Control." *Sociologia del Deporte* 1 (1): 29-34. http://doi.org/10.46661/socioldeporte.5011

Marchant, G., F. Bonaiuto, M. Bonaiuto, and E. Guillet Descas. 2021. "Exercise and Physical Activity eHealth in COVID-19 Pandemic: A Cross-Sectional Study of Effects on Motivations, Behavior Change Mechanisms, and Behavior." *Frontiers in Psychology*, 12: 147. https://doi.org/10.3389/fpsyg.2021.618362

Morgan, David L., and Kim Hoffman. 2018. "Focus Groups." In *The SAGE Handbook of Qualitative Data Collection*, edited by Uwe Flick, 250-63. Los Angeles: SAGE.

Mutz, Michael, and M. Gerke. 2020 "Sport and Exercise in Times of Self-Quarantine: How Germans Changed Their Behavior at The Beginning of the Covid-19 Pandemic." *International Review for the Sociology of Sport* 56 (3): 305-316. https://doi.org/10.1177/1012690220934335

Mutz, Michael, Johannes Müller, and Anne K. Reimers. 2021. & "Use of Digital Media for Home-Based Sports Activities during the COVID-19 Pandemic: Results from the German SPOVID Survey." *International Journal of Environmental Research and Public Health* 18 (9): 4409.

Parviainen, Jaana. 2011. "The Standardization Process of Movement in the Fitness Industry: The Experience Design of Les Mills Choreographies." *European Journal of Cultural Studies* 14, (5): 526-41. https://doi.org/10.1177/1367549411412202.

Pollan, Michael. 2006. *The Omnivore's Dilemma: A Natural History of Four Meals*. New York: Penguin.

RMD (The Response Measures Database). 2021. "European Centre for Disease Prevention and Control." Accessed May 26, 2021. https://www.ecdc.europa.eu/en/publications-data/download-data-response-measures-covid-19.

Rowe, David. 2020. "Subjecting Pandemic Sport to a Sociological Procedure." *Journal of Sociology* 56 (4): 704-713. https://doi.org/10.1177/1440783320941284

Sassatelli, Roberta. 2014. *Fitness Culture: Gyms and the Commercialisation of Discipline and Fun*. New York: Palgrave Macmillan. https://ubdata.univie.ac.at/AC12116207

Schlossberg, N. K. 1981. "A Model for Analyzing Human Adaptation to Transition." *The Counseling Psychologist* 9 (2): 2-18.

Szabo, A., and A. M. Parkin. 2001. "The Psychological Impact of Training Deprivation in Martial Artists" *Psychology of Sport and Exercise* 2 (3):187-199. https://doi.org/10.1016/S1469-0292(01)00004-8

Vogl, Ulrike, Geert Jacobs, Karin Andersson, and Jesper Andreasson. 2022. "Choosing to Stay Fit? Glocalized Ideologies of Health and Fitness During a Pandemic." In *Pandemic and Crisis Discourse. Communicating COVID-19*, edited by Ruth Breeze, Kayo Kondo, Andreas Musolff, and Sara Vilar-Lluch, 453-69. Bloomsbury Academic.

Weinstein, Joshua I. 2009. "The Market in Plato's Republic." *Classical Philology* 104 (4): 439-58. https://doi.org/10.1086/650979

Yin, Robert. 2014. Case Study Research: Design and Methods. Los Angeles: Sage.

Part Five

Media and Technology

Chapter 17

"A Hellish Version of Snakes and Ladders": Print Media Reporting on the Impact of Covid-19 on Professional Sport in England

Kay Biscomb and Kath Leflay

Introduction

In response to the pandemic, on May 30, 2020, the English Culture Secretary announced "Project Restart," a road map to a phased restart of professional sport. After the initial lockdown it enabled sport in England to resume behind closed doors starting on June 1, with guidance published first by the Department for Digital, Culture, Media & Sport (DCMS), followed by sporting bodies overseeing their individual restarts. Although the opening of sport involved compromise, news of the government's proposal to reinstate professional sport was widely welcomed in the U.K. and was seen as a reason for optimism that sport and life were returning to normal. Although initially plans called for sport to return behind closed doors, they also suggested sport could start to re-open with additional safety measures once testing was in place (Grix et al. 2021). There was intense debate about the restart of sport in the media, with key arguments focused on the need to restart the sporting economy and provide entertainment for fans, balanced against the safety risks any return might pose. Throughout the pandemic, professional sport faced a significant loss of income from media revenue, gate receipts, and match day spending, leaving many clubs and leagues in financial turmoil (Parnell et al. 2020). Professional sport's financial troubles were exasperated by the refusal of the government to offer wide scale financial support that other industries received.

Following the announcement of Project Restart, the media reported a discourse of early optimism in response to a series of pilot events, approved by the government, to test crowd viability. These included a Surrey v. Middlesex cricket match (July), snooker's World Championship at The Crucible in Sheffield (July), and Glorious Goodwood racing (August). Accounts saw spectators as an integral part of the successful return of professional sport because of their financial impact and presence. This optimistic view that professional sport with spectators would resume was reported. For example, the Mail announced, "Fans are back!" (Mokbel 2020) with hopeful predictions that spectator events would be in place by October

2020 and that social distancing would be lifted by November (Ziegler 2020). However, throughout the various phases of Project Restart, there was uncertainty and ambiguity about sports return to normal, as well as the return of fans to stadiums. Early optimism about the resumption of sport quickly dissipated, leading one journalist to describe the restart as a "hellish version of snakes and ladders" (Sandbrook 2020). There were many false starts and unfulfilled promises. The media increasingly voiced frustrations as tensions grew between professional sport organizations and the U.K. government, until a second National lockdown started in December 2020. This chapter reviews the British print media reporting of Project Restart, from June to December 2020, to explore the framing of sport, politics, fans, clubs, and National Governing Bodies' (NGBs) responses to a resumption of professional sport in the context of the pandemic. Using a "Propaganda Model" (Herman and Chomsky 1988) approach, this chapter explores the "fractured messages" (Mirabito, Hardin, and Joshua 2020) of "snakes and ladders" to demonstrate the fluctuations in optimistic reporting about the return of professional sport through political criticism on the government's stance, concluding with scientific hope promised by the vaccine.

Snakes and Ladders

The early pilot events provided an optimistic projection for the rest of the year, but this optimism did not last as the virus continued to spread, resulting in changes to anticipated live sporting events. Following the second lockdown (November – December 2020), the potential for further spectator events was limited by a tier system. All areas of England were placed within a tier (1-4) by the government, which identified the restrictions for that area. Tiers ranged from medium alert, with restrictions on social distancing and limited gatherings, to the highest restriction, categorized as "stay at home." The announcement of the tier system caused frustration for organizations. For example, "Extended Tier 3 and 4 restrictions mean crowds are banned, causing heartbreak for the likes of non-League Marine FC, who were planning to welcome 2,000 fans for their FA Cup tie against Tottenham" ("Covid Slams the Doors" 2020). The changes in ministerial advice, guidance, and the uncertainty that these changes brought resulted in a clear trajectory of spiked optimism, ambiguity, and then negativity as the goal posts continually moved and changed during the autumn period. The continual changes led to the description of snakes and ladders, a reference to the popular children's board game. At times the optimism, the "ladders" offered a potential resumption of crowds; at other times, the restrictions, the "snakes," threatened either crowds entirely or financially viability. The uncertainty of the spread of the virus, as well as the changes to both infection figures and ministerial advice, led to a general sense of conflicting and contrasting progress that was exacerbated in professional sport because of the implications for mass gatherings. As a result, the World Health Organization eventually produced guidelines for mass gatherings that sports leaders followed and impacted the way in which sport operated (Parnell et al. 2020). As England faced a second lockdown, the welcome news of a vaccine presented a more positive picture, and the sporting industry was quick to embrace that optimism. The description of snakes and ladders framed the reporting from the summer until the end of the year, as seen in the media reports during this time period.

Media Reporting in a Time of Crisis

It is widely acknowledged that topics given attention by sports media often stretch well beyond the game itself to intersect with broader issues in society (Schmidt 2018). Of relevance to this chapter is the way that sport is reported upon in times of crisis in society and how such representation allows for the exploration of meaning and cultural power dynamics contained within media texts (Rowe 1999).

The tendency for media reporting to reflect the dominant political position in any given society has been referred to as the Propaganda Model (Herman and Chomsky 1988). According to the Propaganda Model, selectivity occurs because the media perform hegemonic roles that advance the economic, social, and political agendas of privileged groups (Petersen 2002). The media serve this purpose in several ways, including through the selection of topics, framing of issues, filtering of information, and by keeping debates within acceptable parameters (Herman and Chomsky 1988). Clear examples of a dominant political position being used in media framing can be found in the way that sport is reported upon during times of crisis, for example, during wars or following terrorist attacks.

Media reporting during the Cold War provides a wealth of examples of how sport was used to reflect dominant political positions. Spyropoulis (2004) suggested that throughout the Cold War, sport and politics were played out in tandem, with media outlets in the U.S. promoting the merits of democratic political systems. A specific example of the Propaganda Model reflected in reporting is highlighted in Seifried's (2010) work that explored how the media reported on the U.S. hockey team during the 1980 Olympics. In this paper, he argued that the wider power struggle of the Cold War was used to frame the U.S. hockey team as protectors of freedom. The portrayal of the U.S. athletes within the media might therefore be considered symbolic of the core value of democracy. Conversely, the Soviet identity was portrayed as machine like, corrupt and destructive, a trend reflective of popular political narratives of the time in the U.S. media (ibid.).

Media coverage during the war in Iraq provides a further example of the attempts of the government to manage public opinion through persuasive reporting. In his book, Weapons of Mass Persuasion, Paul Rutherford (2004) summarized the prevailing hegemonic interpretation of Iraq news coverage, "Once the bombing started, the big media rallied to the cause of war, as did much of the public, leaving even less room for dissent" (188). Most scholars writing about Western media reporting acknowledge that power is not absolute and that powerful groups, including the government, must work hard to maintain their hegemonic position in the face of resistance. However, research suggests that the government is most powerful with respect to managing public opinion through media coverage during times of crisis (Schmidt 2018).

Similar trends of dominant framing within media reporting were identified by Toohey and Taylor (2006) in their analysis of sport related media reporting following the 9/11 terror attacks in the U.S. in 2001. Toohey and Taylor observed a strong trend in reporting to promote to the public that sport should be used to stand up to terrorism and attempts to strike at the Western way of life. The continuation of professional sport was celebrated in reports as being symbolic of a nation that would not be defeated by terrorists. They observed that another prominent reporting strategy in the immediate aftermath of 9/11 was to promote the notion that the entertainment provided by professional sport was a place to escape the world's ills, offering the American public a distraction to the more serious concerns of national security created by the attacks. This style of reporting is more consistent of the assumption that the media is somewhat of an "opiate for the masses," and this premise assumes a different type, but no less powerful, form of social control--control through distraction rather than control through persuasion (Abercrombie and Longhurst 1998).

Although it may be more likely that the media reflect a dominant political position, it is important to recognize that the media are a contested space and therefore a dominant position may be challenged. Media reporting in contemporary society is likely to be influenced by wider media developments, including the launch of a wide range of social media platforms, which are characterized by more democratic styles of reporting and the blurring of boundaries between producer and consumer. Rather than resistance being large scale and absolute, it has been argued that power played out through media reporting has become more contradictory and ambivalent (Lichfield and Kavanagh 2019).

Using a "Propaganda Model" (Herman and Chomsky 1988) approach, this chapter draws upon the Propaganda Model and the "fractured messages" (Mirabito, Hardin, and Joshua 2020) of "snakes and ladders" to explore the trends in media reporting during the stages of Project Restart.

Methods

Print Media Trends

Print media research in sport sociology has been prevalent since the mid-1980s with a considerable focus on the gendered nature of reporting (Crossman, Vincent, and Speed 2007; Biscomb and Matheson 2017). This chapter extends the current field by focusing on the media during the unique circumstances of the Covid-19 pandemic, which resulted in a dramatic change to the global sporting landscape. It adds to the understanding of crisis reporting and how reporting is framed when sport is under threat.

Four British national newspapers were selected for the study: Daily Telegraph (2.6 million); The Times (4 million); Daily Mail (2.3 million); Daily Mirror (3.3 million)[1]. These papers were chosen as a representative sample of broadsheet and tabloid newspapers available that had the largest circulation figures for print versions (Newsworks 2021; Leflay and Biscomb 2020). To identify articles that emphasized the importance of fans to sport, Proquest Newspapers (UK Newstand) database was used initially to search for the following key terms:

- Sport
- Covid
- Fans/audience/spectators

The date range for the search was from June 1, 2020 to December 31, 2020. The rationale for this decision was that on the May 30, Culture Secretary Oliver Dowden announced that sport in England would resume from behind closed doors. From June 1 onward, sporting bodies made their own individual announcements about returning to play. Organizations followed the DCMS published guidance on the phased return of elite sport (DCMS 2020), which prompted much media speculation about the recovery phase for elite sport.

All articles were retrieved, downloaded, and converted to a word document and then uploaded into NVivo 10, a software package used to assist coding and analysis of qualitative data. Total data set included 239 articles. Once uploaded, each individual article was coded for the base data, such as type of newspaper and sport, and were then analyzed inductively for emerging themes. This entailed reading each section and assigning codes to the content, which were not pre-determined by literature. Coding was undertaken by both researchers at the beginning of the process to clarify the agreed upon understanding of codes. Once all the reports were coded in this way, each individual code was then examined further to explore the breadth and depth of the detail to identify prevalent themes. Coding was undertaken by both authors simultaneously.

Discussion of Results

Throughout the media reporting of the pandemic, a strong and ever-present theme emerged reflecting an on-going debate between the government and NGBs of

---

[1] Circulation figures are monthly for print versions of Telegraph, Times and Mirror and daily for Mail.

sport about the return of crowds to live sports events. Although this was a constant theme from March to December, what was notable was the change in tone in reporting. Initially following the announcement of Project Restart, the style of reporting was consistent with the Propaganda Model, showing overt support for the government and encouraging the public to do the same. In this early reporting the voices of NGBs were used by media reporters to show a united front between the government and professional sport. However, in a trend not seen as explicitly in previous work that has explored media reporting in times of crisis, the media coverage shifted from September onwards, becoming progressively more critical of the government's decision making using a range of strategies to undermine their authority. The precarious financial position that NGBs found themselves in at this stage in the year was used by reporters to highlight the shortcomings of the government, and in particular the Prime Minister's Leadership. This section will first explore the ladders of reporting that mirror a traditional Propaganda Model. Following that we will then explore the snakes of ambiguous and negative reporting, which does not follow the traditional Propaganda Model.

Ladders

After three months of professional sport played behind closed doors, Prime Minister Boris Johnson announced in June that he expected a gradual return of crowds to live sport, subject to Covid-19 health and safety measures (Hughes 2020). Consistent with the Propaganda Model, media reports suggested that the reopening of live sport and the return of crowds represented a significant milestone in the "healing of society" ("Special Report" 2020) and providing reason for optimism that better times were ahead. Given its popular following, sport has frequently been used by governments to form connections and to build trust with the voting public. Previous examples of this strategy used by the Prime Minister were included in media reports to frame him as a charismatic leader worthy of public support. For example, one account explained that "As Mayor of London, he was heralded by Time magazine as the 'biggest winner of the 2012 Olympics,' a man who at the closing ceremony, drew a louder cheer than the Spice Girls" ("Timidity and Paralysis" 2020).

This extract from the media report also served as a reminder of the Prime Minister's previous role in London 2012 Olympic Games, an event that could be assumed to be particularly important to the British people. A subtle reminder of nationalistic fervor associated with London 2012 and the part that Johnson played in this significant sporting event might be considered an editorial strategy to portray the Prime Minister in a positive light and to encourage the public to show support for him during the pandemic.

The Prime Minister's announcement regarding the re-opening of sport was met with "cautious optimism" by NGBs that welcomed the government's positive update. The voices of NGB leaders were included in media reports to show backing for the government's decision to re-open slowly and to acknowledge the "difficult balance" faced in controlling the virus, while enabling parts of society and the economy to remain open. Although the test events had very limited numbers of spectators, they were viewed as a "small, but important step" in the right direction and an opportunity to "mitigate missing out on revenue" (Greechan 2020). Through this messaging there was clear public support from NGBs for the government. Specific reference was made within the reports to the role that sport needs to play in following governmental advice and keeping the virus under control. The fact that professional sport bodies appeared keen to "play their role" perhaps reinforced the government's messaging about collective responsibility for controlling the virus and getting back to normal.

There was clear evidence of a persuasive tone within reporting, a style consistent with the Propaganda Model that presumes that media coverage is likely to represent the interests of elite groups. The tone of these articles stressed the importance of collective responsibility for beating the virus. Reports suggested that this would be achieved through "continuing to follow the rules, getting tested and isolating when instructed, remembering hands, face and space" (Crerar and Glaze 2020). The wording within this article draws on and clearly reinforces official government guidance messaging in wider circulation. NGBs were keen to emphasize their compliance with government recommendations to ensure the safety of fans, outlining a range of measures they would put in place, including sport specific codes of conduct, a formalized way to exert control over an audience. Government officials and inspectors from the Sports Ground Safety Authority, an independent organization that advises the government on fan safety, were reported on in the media as surveyors of the pilot events keeping a "close eye" on proceedings (Dickson 2020). With surveillance often being associated as a mechanism of social control, particularly if people know they are being watched, the media reported that NGBs and fans seemed keen to play their respective roles and to adhere to the rules.

A science-based approach to monitoring the pilots and any potential growth in infection rates was emphasized in reporting to give credibility to the government's approach to the re-opening. Nauman et al. (2020) suggested that how legitimate a policy is viewed by the public is important to compliance. The more someone supports a policy, the more someone is likely to follow it. The use of quotes from the government's scientific advisors within media reporting were also significant in this respect, adding support and credibility to their decision making.

Snakes

However, from September onwards, coinciding with rumors of a second lockdown, there was a clear shift towards a more critical tone in reporting of the British Government's handling of the return of professional sport (Ziegler and Lowe 2020). One editorial strategy used by reporters to frame criticism of the government was to use direct quotes from NGB, club, or league representatives to illustrate the impact of the government's decisions from an insider perspective. The use of an insider perspective is reflective of wider trend in print media reporting of sport and is seen as particularly credible (Biscomb and Griggs 2013).

Unlike earlier in the year when NGBs appeared to largely offer public support for the government's cautious re-opening, by September there were clear frustrations being voiced regarding a decision by the government to drastically reduce the numbers that had previously been approved for the pilot events. When advised that Wembley stadium, a venue with the capacity of 90,000 would only be able to host 1,000 fans, Christian Purslow, the CEO of Premier League Football Club Aston Villa, was reported to launch a "fierce attack" on the government claiming that "the only thing you learn from having 1000 fans in a stadium is that football clubs lose huge amounts of money." Given the precarious financial predicament of many clubs and leagues, continuing to keep sport locked down was framed within the reporting as unsustainable, especially given the absence of a government bailout for the sector (Clarkson et al. 2020). The precarious position of professional sport was reflected in a particular comment from Tony Rowe, Chairman at Exeter Chiefs, who expressed his surprise that England hadn't witnessed the demise of any clubs in Rugby's Premier League. There was frustration from the NGBs that the government were operating under the assumption that professional sport across the board had significant financial reserves, despite evidence to the contrary. Professional sport was treated as a single entity despite significant differences in financial positions between sports and even within sports, between leagues especially in football. In certain sports such as football, there was a growing pressure from the government for the more lucrative Premier League to take responsibility for supporting the lower leagues.

Another editorial strategy used to criticize the government was to draw the public's attention to inconsistencies in the way that rules were being applied to mass gatherings. This strategy typically made direct comparisons between sport and other events or illustrative examples. Examples used by reporters included the number of passengers using the Tube in London, the planned Royal Choral Society Christmas Carol concert, and Arsene Wenger's book launch at the London Palladium, all activities that had government approval to go ahead with crowds (Martin 2020). These examples provided concrete evidence of inconsistencies allowing criticism of the government within the media to gain momentum. A quote in The Daily Mail summarizes this perspective; "the Government loves to tell us that they are following the science. But this is a bit disingenuous because the science is far from settled (Sandbrook 2020). Such arguments and clear evidence of an inconsistent approach to mass gatherings undermined the government's continual insistence that the decision to shut sport was based on objective scientific recommendations (Menish et al. 2019).

It has widely been suggested that the pandemic highlighted economic and cultural inequalities in society (Bond et al. 2020). Such inequalities were placed under the microscope within media coverage of the handling of the pandemic. As well as using direct comparisons with other non-sporting events or examples to point out discrepancies in how guidance was being applied, criticisms leveled at the government were also based on inconsistencies between sporting activities, with more lenient measures applied to sports or leisure activities that were associated with middle or upper-class audiences (Grix et al. 2021). As Martin (2020) suggested "it is almost as if this Government are looking after their own constituents." Reporters were incredulous that grouse shooting, a leisure pursuit of the upper classes, could go ahead whilst working class sports such as football remained closed. To ridicule the differentiation of rules between football and grouse shooting, Martin presented the following point within a media article: "maybe football clubs could heavily arm fans, release 200 grouse on the pitch and get spectators back that way. Call it a shoot, with a match attached. All perfectly legal." (ibid.). This type of argument was clearly more targeted at a working-class audience who was encouraged to consider how they had been disproportionately affected by the government's rules. The class-based argument also brings into question whether the different rules reflect an assumption by the government that people from upper classes were more likely to follow rules and therefore less surveillance and control was needed for activities involving these groups. This perspective was clearly reflected in the following newspaper quote: "I see lots of snobbery claiming football fans can't be trusted to observe social distancing. Maybe government scientists think that if it's the rugger or some nice improv theatre the risk will evaporate" (Zieglar 2020).

Other criticisms were framed through comparisons to other countries with commentary stating that the situation had been handled better elsewhere. The tone of one article suggested that the government was displaying a sense of unnecessary fright in its response. Given that the government, and in particular, the Prime Minister were responsible for leading the U.K. out of the pandemic, the use of words such as "timidity," "fearful," and "paralysis" in media reports were part of an editorial strategy designed to damage public confidence in their leadership. In comparison to what was happening elsewhere in Europe, reference was also made in the reports to the less restricted sizes of crowds and a lack of local flare ups. In these events, the capacity of the crowd was reduced to mitigate risk whilst at the same time allowing for a real test of the effectiveness of measures that had been put in place. With similar protocols in place for health and safety that had been proposed by NGBs of sport in the U.K., the evidence of what was happening elsewhere in Europe again brought into question the credibility of the government's science-based evidence that was being used as a justification for keeping sport closed. Reporters proposed that the real concern of the government was that it did not trust clubs to manage the return of socially distanced, part full crowds. The suggestion that clubs were not ready for the return of fans was ridiculed by reporters who were keen to highlight the stringent measures that sport had been ready to put in place, thereby undermining the government's decision. Reference was also made to Brexit (the term used for Britain's withdrawal from the European Union) with the suggestion that "it probably delights this Brexiteer government not to fall in line with France, Germany, Holland, Austria, Belgium or Denmark, who have all allowed back fans" (Reade 2020). In this editorial strategy, the government was accused of petty one-upmanship, putting sending a political message of independence to Europe ahead of the best interests of professional sport in the U.K.

Conclusion

It is clear that the media used voices from the NGBs as a tool to change their reporting from optimism to ambiguity to negativity, which is in contrast to previously reported styles of Propaganda Model. Initially the media adopted a response that mirrored the Propaganda Model of supporting the government's position in a time of crisis. This shifted throughout the year, however, as the position of fully open spectator events for professional sport became less certain. This contrasts to previous examples of the Propaganda Model as the support for the government was not consistent.

From the media reporting during 2020 it was clear that there was considerable emphasis placed on the importance of the crowd and the view that spectators added additional dimensions to the sporting experience. The economic importance of the return of fans gathered momentum as the year progressed and as the British government provided funding for other areas of social life but not professional sport. The media framed the government with a critical response using international examples as alternative solutions. Governing bodies and sports officials continued to express their frustration about the lack of real progress towards spectator events. The promise of a vaccine on the horizon offered a surge of new hope, which changed the discourse of reporting again.

The snakes and ladders of the progress of the return of social life versus virus restrictions was mirrored in the sports reporting. This resulted in a trajectory of spiked optimism, ambiguity, and then negativity, which ultimately translated to political criticism of the government's failure to support professional sport, especially football. As the year concluded these frustrations and criticisms came to no avail as social life in England was halted one again with lockdown three in January 2021.

References

Abercrombie, Nicholas, and Brian Longhurst. 1998. *Audiences: A Sociological Theory of Performance*. London: Sage Publications.

Biscomb, Kay, and Gerald Griggs. 2013. "A Splendid Effort! Print Media Reporting of England's Women's Performance in the 2009 Cricket World Cup." *International Review for the Sociology of Sport* 48 (1): 99-112.

Biscomb, Kay, and Hilary Matheson. 2017. "Are the Times Changing Enough? Print Media Trends Across Four Decades." *International Review for the Sociology of Sport* 54 (3): 259-281. https://doi.org/10.1177/1012690217716574

Bond, Alexander. J, Cockayne, David, Ludvigsen, Jan, A.L., Maguire, Kieran, Parnel, Daniel, Plumley, Daniel, Widdop, Paul, and Rob Wilson. 2020. "COVID-19: The Return of Football Fans." *Managing Sport and Leisure*, https://doi.org/10.1080/23750472.2020.1841449

"Covid Slams the Doors Shut on Crisis-hit Sport." 2020. *The Daily Telegraph*, December 31, 2020. Proquest.

Crerar, Pippa, and Ben Glaze. 2020. "Escape Route is in Sight." *The Daily Mirror*, November 24, 2020. Proquest.

Crossman Jane, Vincent, John, and Harriet Speed. 2007. "'The Times They Are A-Changing.' Gender Comparisons in Three National Newspapers of the 2004 Wimbledon Championships." *International Review for the Sociology of Sport* 42 (1): 27–41.

Clarkson, Beth G., Culvin, Alex, Pope, Stacey, and Keith Parry. 2020. "Covid-19: Reflections on Threat and Uncertainty for the Future of Elite Women's Football in England." *Managing Sport and Leisure*. https://doi.org/10.1080/23750472.2020.1766377

DCMS. 2020. "Guidance Elite Sport Stage 3." Accessed January 18, 2021. https://www.gov.uk/government/publications/coronavirus-covid-19-guidance-on-phased-return-of-sport-and-recreation/elite-sport-return-to-domestic-competition-guidance.

Dickson, Mike. 2020. "Return of the Fans: Sport in the Bubble 1,000 Lucky Spectators Get Golden tickets as Oval is First to Welcome Back a Crowd." *Daily Mail*, July 27, 2020. Proquest.

Greechan, John. 2020. "DON'T BLOW IT: Doncaster Urges Fans to Behave at SPFL Test Events, Doncaster in Warning Over Return of Fans." *Daily Mail*, September 9, 2020. Proquest.

Grix, Jonathan, Brannagan, Paul, M., Grimes, Holly, and Ross Neville. 2021. "The Impact of Covid-19 on Sport." *International Journal of Sport Policy and Politics* 13 (1): 1-12, https://doi.org/10.1080/19406940.2020.1851285

Herman, Edward, and Noam Chomsky. 1988. *Manufacturing Consent*. New York: Pantheon.

Hughes, Matt. 2020. "Counties lose £25m with Fans Locked Out of T20 Blast." *Daily Mail*, July 18, 2020. https://www.dailymail.co.uk/sport/cricket/article-8534303/Cricket-counties-face-huge-25m-loss-overnment-rules-fans-watching-Twenty20-Blast.html.

Leflay, Kath, and Kay Biscomb. 2020. "England's Summer of Sport 2017." *Sport in Society* 24 (9): 1633-1648. https://doi.org/10.1080/17430437.2020.1764538.

Lichfield, Chelsea, and Emma Kavanagh. 2019. "Twitter, Team GB and the Australian Olympic Team: Representations of Gender in Social Media Spaces." *Sport in Society* 22 (7): 1148-1164. https://doi.org/10.1080/17430437.2018.1504775

Martin, Samuel. 2020. "Royal Albert Hall Reopens While Our Football Clubs are Used and Abused." *Daily Mail*, October 3, 2020. https://www.dailymail.co.uk/sport/football/article-8800061/MARTIN-SAMUEL-Royal-Albert-Hall-reopens-football-clubs-used-abused.html.

Mokobel, Sami. 2020. "Fans Are Back. Cricket, Racing and Snooker Test Events Set for End of This Month. Football Hopes to Have Reduced Crowds from October but County Cricket Still Facing £25m losses. FA's Delight as Planning for Crowds Goes Ahead." *Daily Mail,* July 18, 2020. Proquest.

Menish, Ziad. A., Steffen, Robert, White, Paul, Dar, Osman, Azhar, Esam, I., Sharma, Avinash, and Umla Alimuddin. 2019.

"Mass Gatherings Medicine: Public Health Issues Arising from Mass Gathering Religious and Sporting Events." *The Lancet* 393: 2073-2084.

Mirabito, Timothy, Hardin, Robin, and Joshua, R. Pate. 2020. "The Fractured Messaging of the National Collegiate Athletic Association and Its Members in Response to COVID-19." *International Journal of Sport Communication* 13(3): 324-335 https://doi.org/10.1123/ijsc.2020-0249

Nauman, Elias, Mohring, Katja, Reyenscheid, Maximiliane, Wenz, Alexander, Rettig, Tobias, Lehrer, Roni, Krieger, Ulrich, Juhl, Sebastian, Friedel, Sabine, Fikel, Marina, Cornesse, Carina, and Annelies Blom. 2020. "Covid-19 Policies in Germany and Their Social, Political and Psychological Consequences." *European Policy Analysis* 6: 191-202 https://doi.org/10.1002/epa2.1091

Newsworks. 2021. Titles at a Glance. Accessed January 18, 2021, www.newsworks.org.uk.

Parnell, Daniel, Widdop, Paul, Bond, Alex, and Rob Wilson. 2020. "COVID-19, Networks and Sport," *Managing Sport and Leisure*. https://doi.org/10.1080/23750472.2020.1750100

Peterson, Paul-Mark. 2002. "Examining Equity in Newspaper Photographs: A Content Analysis of the Print Media Photographic Coverage of Interscholastic Athletics." *International Review for the Sociology of Sport* 37 (3): 303-318.

Reade, Brian. 2020. "Johnson Should Give Clubs Hope that Fans Can Return This Season." *The Daily Mirror*, October 1, 2020. Proquest.

Rowe, David. 1999. *Sport, Culture and the Media: The Unruly Trinity*. Buckingham: Open University Press.

Rutherford, Paul. 2004. *Weapons of Mass Persuasion*. Toronto: University of Toronto Press.

Sandbrook, Dominic. 2020. "How Will This Ultra-cautious, Hellish Version of Snakes and Ladders Ever Get Britain Back on its Feet?" *Daily Mail*, September 10, 2020. https://www.dailymail.co.uk/debate/article-8715881/DOMINIC-SANDBROOK-Britain-feet.html.

Schmidt, Hans. 2018 "Sport Reporting in an Era of Activism: Examining the Intersection of Sport, Media and Social Activism." *International Journal of Sport Communication*.11: 2-17.

Seifried, Chad. 2010. "An Exploration into Melodrama and Sport: The miracle on Ice and The Cold War Lens." *International Journal of Olympic Studies* 19: 118-128.

"Special Report Sport's Healing Begins After a Shattering Year? The Welcome Return of Supporters Represents a Symbol of Hope for Those Affected but Impact on the Financial Crisis Will Be Limited." *The Daily Telegraph*, December 2, 2020. Proquest.

Spyropoulis, Evangelos. 2004. "Sport and Politics: Goodbye Sydney 2000 - Hello Athens 2004." *East European Quarterly* 38 (1): 65-84.

"Timidity and Paralysis in Sports' Darkest Hour? Test Events are Vital for Securing Supporters' Return- But the Government is Running Scared of Trying." *The Daily Telegraph*, September 10, 2020. Proquest. Toohey, Kristine, and Tracy Taylor. 2006. "Here Be Dragons, Here Be Savages, Here Be Bad Plumbing: Australia Media Representations of Sport and Terrorism." Sport in Society 9 (1): 71-93. https://doi.org/10.1080/17430430500355816

Ziegler, Martyn. 2020. "Test Events to Target October Return for Fans." *The Times*, July 18, 2020. https://www.thetimes.co.uk/article/fans-could-return-to-sport-stadiums-in-october-gclzkww2z

Ziegler, Martyn, and Alex Lowe. 2020. "Clubs' Anger at Government: Top-flight Anger at U-turn Over Crowds. *The Times*, September 23, 2020. Proquest.

Chapter 18

Ghost Games and Artificial Soundscapes: Sports Media and Fan Reactions to the Return of European Soccer Matches in Empty Stadia

Jeffrey W. Kassing, Mary Helen Clark, Carrie Kaput, Trinity Winton, Keara Katayama, Suzanne Day, Isaiah Utley, and Aleah N. Fisher

Introduction

The first and biggest leagues to restart competitive play after a lengthy and unprecedented interruption induced by the Covid-19 pandemic were the soccer leagues in Europe—including the German Bundesliga, Spain's LaLiga, and the English Premier League (EPL). All restarted matches after a several-month stoppage and only when leagues, governing bodies, and local municipalities deemed that it was safe to do so (Duckworth 2021; McDougall 2021). Serie A in Italy returned shortly thereafter, whereas France's Ligue 1 suspended play for the remainder of the season and did not resume. For the first three leagues to return, the 'safe' restart included a plan to play the remaining league matches of the 2019-2020 season in empty stadia without fans present. This chapter examines media coverage of, and fan reactions to, the restart of European soccer without the presence of fans in stadia. More specifically, to understand the implications of empty stadia, the lack of sound and atmosphere, and the absence of fans, we considered media reports about soccer's return to play, viewers' impressions of the introduction and use of artificial sound, and fans' responses to celebrating a specific club's championship in a pandemic-adjusted season.

European Soccer's Restart

Typically, European supporters fill stadia and animate them with motion, color, and boisterous sound (Doidge, Kossakowski, and Mintert 2020). For this reason, football/soccer matches played in empty stadia create an unusual effect for observers, whereby those elements disappear, and viewers hear sounds emanating from the pitch and the sidelines instead of the stands. Prior to the Covid-19 pandemic, playing matches in empty stadia occurred only in rare, exceptional cases. For example, Football Club Barcelona, historically associated with Catalan identity and nationalism (Shobe 2008a), deliberately chose to play their match behind closed doors without fans present after violence erupted when local citizens participated in the Catalan independence referendum held in early October of 2017 (Kassing 2019). In other cases, soccer's global governing body Federation Internationale de Football Association (FIFA) has mandated that matches be played in empty stadia as a punitive sanction in response to acts of fan violence or overt racist behavior (FIFA Disciplinary Code 2017). Nevertheless, European soccer's return during the Covid-19 pandemic required the absence of fans, making the uncommon occurrence of matches played in empty stadia the norm for spring 2020. Given the widespread popularity of soccer internationally, the global branding it encompasses, and the television contracts leagues secure (Richelieu, Lopez, and Desbordes 2008), the idea of playing in empty stadia was understandable as it allowed massive audiences the opportunity to still view live matches from home. However, it meant that those viewers, supporters, and fans would be subjected to soccer's new environment, with not only the stands empty, but the sound and atmosphere altered considerably.

After the restart, and in response to the novelty of playing games in empty stadia, leagues and networks experimented with producing artificial soundtracks to replicate the sound of full crowds. The public's reaction, media and fans alike, was quite mixed. Despite the German Football League's stern stance discouraging clubs from using artificial sound because "fans can't be replaced by any virtual audience" (Homewood 2020, 24), it soon appeared in Bundesliga broadcasts. German supporters took offense and some pundits called the effort disingenuous (Brewin 2020; Creditor 2020). Yet others welcomed the innovation. For example, Alexi Lalas, a former member of the U.S. National Team and an analyst for Fox Soccer's broadcast team said: "I love it. We all know it's not real, but it is enhancing the viewing experience. And right now without crowds, that's all there is, is the television viewing experience" (Wamsley 2020, 11). Similarly, U.S.-based soccer journalist Grant Wahl added, "The crowd whistles are a great touch" (Scott 2020, 8). And English commentator for NBC Sports, Arlo White, acknowledged that "It sounds in our ears like an actual game" (Reedy 2020, 13). Initially, artificial sound was regenerated from previous broadcasts and orchestrated anew. Indeed, one report complimented "the sound mixer, operating from Sky Germany's studio in Munich" for conducting "a knowledgeable if partisan crowd" that applauded on queue when a defender made a key clearance and booed when claims for a penalty went unheeded (Brewin 2020, 3). Broadcast providers of the EPL and LaLiga in Spain took note of the ambivalence and prepared several options for viewers including team-specific crowd noises and the choice to enjoy the broadcast with or without artificial sound (Brewin 2020; Silverman 2020). Both leagues reached out to video game company Electronic Arts (EA), creators of the popular and influential FIFA video game (Kassing 2020a), to "help enliven their sports broadcasts" (Nair 2020, 1). The soundtracks

EA provided derived from their recordings of actual matches that were cataloged as part of the company's sound library. These, in turn, had been cleaned to remove any obscenities and afforded broadcasters the ability to manually manipulate them for specific effects. The EA's sound library, compiled over a decade, is comparatively robust allowing for adoption of specific fan chants for particular clubs and incorporation of sound from varying size stadia (Davidson, 2020).

Stadia, Supporters, and Sound

The pandemic disrupted fan culture considerably by severing the communal experience it produces (Schallhorn and Kunert 2020), whether that be socially gathering to view telecast matches in pubs or bars (Dixon 2014; Weed 2007), interacting with other supporters in virtual communities (Lawrence and Crawford 2019), or consuming news coverage that shapes fan identities (Lopez-Gonzalez, Guerrero-Sole, and Hayes 2014). Broadcasters and clubs mobilized to recover and restore these connections. In Germany, for example, in the absence of new matches media outlets began to re-broadcast past live matches including classic national team victories, regional rivalry games, and even previous games that featured the two teams that would have faced one another according to the pre-pandemic matchday schedule. In some cases, commentators provided new narration for the re-broadcast matches. Comparatively low ratings indicated that not all fans appreciated these offerings, but for those who did the efforts reproduced the look of normally scheduled programming and offered "fans a structured Saturday" (Schallhorn and Kunert 2020, 518). Clubs and The Bundesliga, in turn, also developed activities to keep supporters engaged. This involved emulating matchdays by broadcasting fans playing one another using the FIFA video game. Clubs promoted the outcomes of these matches, posting content and sharing interviews of contestants (Ibid 2020). These endeavors somewhat mitigated the broader impact that the cessation of soccer had on the larger fan community. The return of soccer, however, presented another wave of challenges given the relevance of crowds and sound at live matches (Doidge, Kossakowski, and Mintert 2020; Perasović and Mustapić 2017; Kassing 2014).

Football/soccer fandom manifests as a significant, continual, and stable identity component that exerts considerable influence over one's overall identity profile (Porat 2010). It becomes an additional and serious relationship in one's life that provokes joy and depression, demands loyalty, and prescribes a self-constructed social role. Accordingly, soccer fandom configures "a way of life" that dictates and prescribes the past, present, and future of supporters (Ibid, 287). The most ardent supporters develop "a long-term personal and emotional investment in the club" (Giulianotti 2002, 33), characterized by thick personal solidarity, obligatory support, and a familial relationship with the club. Moreover, attending matches becomes routine and directs the leisure time of supporters because "supporting the club is a lived experience" (Ibid, 33). Supporters, consequently, achieve social capital through consistent match attendance, particularly through periods of poor performance and decline, and come to consider their club's stadium as home. In addition, geographically dispersed, but devoted fans travel to stadia as a form of pilgrimage (Kassing and Nyaupane 2019). Pilgrims, in turn, attribute sacrality, realized through reverence and a deep sense of wonder, to stadia. They also experience sociality by immersing themselves in the public atmosphere of stadia, which in turn produces feelings of affiliation and authentication. For passionate supporters, then, physical presence in stadia is tantamount to a religious, communal experience (Doidge, Kossakowski, and Mintert 2020; Giulianotti 2002).

Sound is part of the performative dynamic soccer fans generate within stadia (Doidge, Kossakowski, and Mintert 2020). Terrace chants play a key role in how supporters enact their social identities (Clark 2006; Giulianotti 2002; Poulton 2016), differentiate rivals (Benkwitz and Molnar 2012), and create the stadium atmosphere (Antonowicz, Jakubowska, and Kossakowski, 2020). Undeniably, chants and songs are a "fundamental characteristic" (Spaaij and Viñas 2005, 80) of "boisterous and partisan fan culture" (Poulton 2016, 1984), that demarcates authentic supporters from those who merely practice mimicry (Perasović and Mustapić 2017). Supporters use terrace chants and songs to denigrate rivals (Clark 2006), voice political views (Irak 2018), and, unfortunately at times, spew racist and sexist sentiments (Doidge 2015; Jones 2008; Kacem 2013; Poulton 2016). Fans often dismiss this latter tendency as a mere tactic to gain a competitive advantage for their teams (Magrath 2018). And some female fans, particularly those supporting women's soccer, deploy hyper-masculine chants to demonstrate deviance against gender norms (Henderson 2018). Stadium chants also signal adoption of a global tradition, while affording supporter groups the opportunity to localize that tradition (Wagner and Shobe 2017).

Specific supporter groups form acoustic communities through the use and interpretation of communally shared sounds and thereby add to the soundscape of soccer matches (Kytö 2011). Additionally, fans contend that the sounds they manufacture can change the course, and even the outcomes, of matches (Marra and Trotta 2019). Hence, sound plays an important role in shaping and defining the experience of soccer fans. Indeed, expectations of sound associated with soccer matches are quite entrenched. An examination of the use of vuvuzelas by supporters during the 2010 World Cup in South Africa revealed that fans adhered to, and prescribed, a specific soundscape that should accompany broadcasts of live matches. The overwhelming drone of vuvuzela-filled stadia proved troubling for many European viewers who argued that it disrupted the traditional soundscape that augments games. Furthermore, they asserted that the vuvuzela should be used sparingly, before and after games or to celebrate goals, instead of continuously throughout matches. Ostensibly, fans essentialized a specific innate soundscape that should accompany soccer (Kassing 2014), further evidencing the fundamental connection between stadia, sound, and soccer fandom.

To better gauge the impact empty stadia, the lack of sound, and the absence of fan communities had on soccer once it returned from hiatus, we explored several distinct aspects of the phenomenon across three separate phases. First, we examined media reports about the return of the first three major European leagues in empty stadia. Second, we studied the effect introducing artificial sound had on viewers. Third, we considered how the Covid-19 pandemic affected supporters' perspectives on a club's championship achieved during an altered season.

Methodology: Sampling, Data, and Analysis

The analysis took part in three phases designed to address the research objectives. Each phase involved purposive sampling. In the first phase, we sought print media sources in English covering European soccer games played in empty stadia during the Covid-19 pandemic during 2020 to determine how media framed the restart of soccer and the conditions in which it occurred. Framing entails the deployment of language, images, metaphors, selected examples, descriptions, and arguments into a network of meaning making and social construction negotiated by media sources and audience members (Van Gorp 2007). As such, framing involves selecting particular aspects of perceived reality so that they become more salient and effective at promoting particular definitions, interpretations, and evaluations (Entman 1993). Therefore, unearthing dominant frames related to specific cultural events can be informative. To locate articles for analysis we searched the library databases available through Arizona State University using the terms empty, some variation on stadium (i.e., stadium, stands, seats or stadia), and soccer, while restricting the search to articles published between the first of April and the first of August. The final sample consisted of twenty-one relevant newspaper articles, ranging from 191 to 1628 words with a mean of 730 words. Admittedly, only accessing and examining English-language sources is an inherent limitation given coverage of the phenomena would exist in news outlets in other languages. Language barriers and time constrains, however, limited our ability to include non-English sources.

In the second phase, authors examined content available publicly on the social media platform Twitter. By some estimates over 80% of sports fans check Twitter daily, and a sizeable portion multiple times a day (Clavio and Kian 2010). Sports fans use Twitter to connect with and communicate about their favorite sports, teams, and athletes (Hambrick et al. 2010). They also police one another with regard to team and athlete loyalty and use social media to disparage athletes (Kassing and Sanderson 2015). Hence, Twitter is a key site for enacting and displaying fandom and a favorable location to explore fans' reactions to the introduction of artificial sound. This involved searching for tweets that included the term 'crowd noise' on three different dates: May 26, June 11, and June 17, 2020. We selected these dates because they represented different points in time when the Bundesliga, LaLiga, and the EPL respectively introduced artificial soundscapes for televised matches. We intentionally sought tweets that advanced a clear opinion about artificial sound and assembled a total of forty for analysis, which ranged in length from eight characters to 278 characters.

In the third and final phase, the authors examined data that related to Liverpool Football Club (LFC) winning their first league championship in thirty years. For a club with a decorated past and clear success in European and domestic cup competitions during that same timeframe the elusive league title was considered long overdue. In addition, the championship run was remarkable as it set records for the earliest a team had clinched the league (with seven games remaining) and for the latest a club had claimed the title (in June due to the delayed season). Additionally, fans were unable to be present to celebrate with the team. The long absence of a championship combined with Covid-19's effect on it produced an unusual situation for fans that warranted discussion. Reddit is a social news website that on average generates over 1.5 billion unique visitors per month (Clement 2021). The website enables posting links, articles, images, videos, or text within topic-based communities called subreddits. Users comment on posts within subreddits, thereby building discussion on a topic germane to specific social communities. The popularity and accessibility of the website attracts users seeking to engage with others in discussion about particular topics, often across cultures and ideological divides (Lagoria-Chafkin 2018). Sport researches have used the platform to investigate public grieving related to the untimely death of Kobe Bryant and public opinion about Megan Rapinoe's activism (Bingaman 2020; Gallagher, Wright, and Kassing 2022). Therefore, we examined four discussions on the social media platform Reddit that related to Liverpool's championship. From these particular conversations the authors identified 156 comments that referenced empty stadia. On average comments were two sentences long, ranging from a single word to a full paragraph in length.

Across all phases, working in smaller teams of two or three, we used constant comparative methodology to uncover the major frames embedded in the selected news articles and the emergent themes apparent in tweets and discussion posts. Utilizing a grounded theory approach (Glaser and Strauss 1967), authors independently reviewed texts to determine which frames or themes became evident across accounts. The authors then met to confer and collapse the separate analyses into a single analysis. This involved clustering data into emergent frames or themes apparent to all authors working in the team, refining frames or themes as necessary, and locating examples of each identified frame or theme. Development, clarification, and refinement of frames and themes continued until the data reached saturation and observations did not add substantively to existing frames and themes or introduce new ones.

Phase 1: That Empty Feeling

How media framed the return of soccer in empty stadia advanced particular understandings that helped structure and define the phenomenon. Four prominent frames emerged in print media articles covering empty stadia. The safety frame included content related to restrictions placed on players and precautions taken to maintain safety during game play. The return to play frame emphasized how important soccer, and its reappearance, was for fans. The fan absence frame referenced how unusual empty stadia proved to be for players and coaches, particularly with regard to the aural incongruity they introduced. And the play(er) impact frame concerned the (un)anticipated effects playing without crowds had on games generally and the performance of athletes specifically.

Safety

Safety was a prevalent theme throughout news reports. Several outlets reported about the continued need for social distancing, wearing masks, and maintaining proper hygiene. As the first to return, the German Bundesliga became a reference point for other leagues and the primary focus of the media. For example, one report profiled the compromises that the Bundesliga needed to make to return to action. Managing director Christian Seifert explained how league administration decided to forego a two-week quarantine requirement for each team because players were undergoing regular tests (Reuters 2020a). As more teams returned, several outlets noted new protocols like the sanitization of benches and balls and mask-wearing by anyone not on the field. Apparently, the most challenging safety adjustment involved the restrictions on goal celebrations. A number of news outlets sympathized with the teams given the passionate response scoring provokes, despite players being "warned to keep their emotions in check" and refrain from "spitting, hugging, and handshakes" (France 24 2020, 6). Content which reminded readers that precautions were necessary to prevent another suspension of play, however, offset this apparent empathy. The safety frame, then, instrumentally emphasized the need to return to play in a controlled and directed manner, stressing the implementation of protocols and the restrictions on activities like celebrating.

Return to Play

While judgments about the appropriateness of soccer's return were apparent, news outlets tended to frame the return of soccer as a symbol of hope and an economic necessity. A number of articles emphasized that fans were grateful for the return of soccer, particularly as it provided a sense of distraction in trying times. A journalist from The New York Times described how "the Bundesliga became the first major league in any sport in the world to tread gingerly into the light of the post-coronavirus world and attempt to play on" (Smith 2020, 1). Media also espoused the importance of soccer returning as an economic necessity because the delay in play had proved "existence threatening" to many clubs (Reuters 2020a, 17). Putting a constructive spin on the return to play without fans, one outlet pointed out that empty stadia would result in the "erasure of the racist and abusive chants that have long plagued the sport in Europe" (Deighton 2020, 14). The return to play frame served to offset concerns about restarting. Highlighting the symbolic importance and economic necessity of restarting substantiated soccer as a global cultural experience (Giulianotti 2002; Porat 2010).

Fan Absence

In contrast, media also framed soccer as hollow or wanting without the presence of fans and empty stadia as 'weird' and 'bizarre' (Beaton and Robinson 2020; Deighton 2020). The extraordinary situation was reflected in the English-language media's adoption and use of the German term, 'Geisterspiele' or 'ghost games,' (which references matches played in empty stadia without fans) to refer to the restart of Bundesliga play in empty stadia (Deighton 2020). Media portrayed fans as instrumental to the sport experience and empty stadia as antithetical to it. This depiction, for instance, involved reporting on the statement released by Bayern Munich fan groups, claiming "Football without fans is nothing" (France 24 2020, 28). Media sources relied on the opinions of players and coaches to advance this framing, with Jose Mourinho, manager of Tottenham Hotspur, suggesting that the situation produced "an unknown for all of us" (The Guardian 2020, 2). Several articles noted the effect empty stadia had on players, discussing their connection to the fans and the sense of melancholy they experienced celebrating in the absence of supporters. For example, the media reported about Borussia Dortmund players applauding in front of an empty stand in an effort to acknowledge missing fans and to address those watching on television (France 24 2020). The fan absence frame presented an orthogonal position to the return to play frame. It (re)confirmed the role and place of fans in orchestrating the full soccer match experience, affirming that anything less was a perversion of the game (Doidge, Kossakowski, and Mintert 2020; Perasović and Mustapić 2017).

Play(er) Impact

The most prevalent theme observed referenced the impact that empty stadia had on player performance and overall game play. This stemmed from the understanding that the presence of a home crowd contributed to how well teams played and to the outcomes of matches, echoing the sentiment that fans do believe that the noise they generate can influence games (Marra and Trotta 2019). Thus, their absence proved noteworthy as pundits suggested it neutralized this suspected advantage. For example, London-based Arsenal Football Club's coach, Mikel Arteta said that losing the fan energy meant that "things balance much more" (Reuters, 2020b, 5). One outlet discussed the absence of fans as a new phenomenon, referring to it as the negative home field advantage, forwarding the possibility that teams were performing poorly in their home stadia without fans and better at away matches because "for the first time in soccer history" it might "be easier to be playing on the road" (Smith 2020, 8). Additionally, pundits speculated that missing the pressure home fans apply to referees could result in the loss of favorable calls.

Media reports also described how the suspension of the season resulted in different dynamics once it returned. During the lockdown players spent nearly two months "entertaining themselves with push-ups and target practice" (Cohen and Robinson 2020, 16). Once approved to return to practice, players were limited to individual workouts and skill development, which surfaced in their play. For example, sources noted that players felt less pressure to entertain without crowds, and as a result, their performance could be more calculated (Smith 2020) and observed how players were "more clinical from the penalty spot and more accurate from long range" (Cohen and Robinson 2020, 17). The play(er) impact frame brought unintended consequences of the lockdown and return to play in empty stadia to the fore by highlighting the effects the absence of vibrant fan atmospheres within stadia had on players, teams, and match outcomes.

Overall the four frames shaped understanding of the restart for soccer audiences and the general public by serving varying purposes and different audiences. Some frames concerned the overall societal impact with regard to public safety, the important role soccer plays in culture, and the economic crisis it faced, whereas others focused on the impact the lockdown and restart had on specific audiences like fans and athletes.

Phase 2: A Game Changing Experience

Soccer fans socially construct communities of fandom via social media by developing and enacting social identities (Gibbons and Dixon 2010), celebrating or disparaging athletes (Gallagher, Wright, and Kassing 2022), and demeaning rivals (Kassing 2020b). Our analysis indicated how fans framed empty stadia and artificial sound via two main themes that emerged from the selected tweets: appreciation for artificial sound and dissatisfaction with it. With regard to appreciation, fans reported gratitude for sound versus the alternative of silence, acceptance and affinity for artificial soundscapes, and recognition of artificial sound's capacity to produce a sense of normalcy for viewers. Dissatisfaction, in turn, manifested in fan commentary that stridently opposed artificial sound, fans' suggestions that deemed it to be merely superfluous, and their efforts to humorously attack both simulated noise and its execution.

Whereas appreciation and dissatisfaction provide a simple bifurcation of fan reactions to artificial sound, these distinctions reflect the more subtle and embedded associations fans maintain with regard to the aural components of live matches. Fans not only have specific expectations about sound accompanying matches, but also how it should unfold during those matches. Appreciation for sound derives from the simple premise that sound enhances viewers' experience of matches (Cummins, Berke, Moe, and Gong 2019), and that any disruption to it nullifies "the drama that the crowd's reaction brings to the game" (Kassing 2014, 129). Yet, sound alone is not enough to satiate viewers as some expect sound to be "emitted at precise moments by particular supporters in the cause of specific players or teams"—including but not limited to applause as players emerge before the match, songs and chants sung in unison by supporters, and stadium-wide quite tension accompanying key plays (Ibid). These sonic expectations suggest that sound should not only be present, but also appropriately scripted to the match as a reflection of fan engagement with the live experience. Artificial sound, then, deployed as a surrogate for live audiences proved problematic for viewers who felt that it dislocated sound from those who create stadium atmosphere.

Appreciation: Gratitude, Acceptance, and Normalcy

In mid-May of 2020 Bundesliga matches returned accompanied by the amplification of sounds from the pitch and the sidelines with no crowd noise whatsoever. Not long after broadcasts introduced artificial soundscapes and fans seemed grateful for their presence compared to the alternative of no sound. For example, one viewer commented, "This is so much better than silence" (@BarstoolBigCat, May 26, 2020) and another "I actually don't mind the crowd noise. It's far better than the echoing sound of the empty stadium" (@Mitchellturner8, June 11, 2020). For many fans 'fake noise' was preferable to the awkwardness of silence during games. Gratitude for some sound, even fake sound, was evident in one particularly enthusiastic tweet, which read: "Hey there, Fox Sports employees pumping crowd noise into these Bundesliga games, I hope you see this: FANTASTIC job. Y'all are CRUSHING it. These games are 100% less weird because of YOU" (@acrossthepond, May 26, 2020). The effusiveness of this user attested to how artificial sound addressed the awkwardness of silence during matches. For some fans, then, artificial sound was a welcome alternative to silence, an analog for recapturing the ambiance and atmosphere of live matches characterized by boisterous noise (Antonowicz, Jakubowska, and Kossakowski, 2020).

Other fans outwardly expressed their affinity for artificial soundscapes, but did so without making a comparison necessarily to silence. Instead they openly offered their acceptance and appreciation of artificial soundscapes. For instance, one user tweeted "I like the crowd noise pumped in tbh [to be honest]" (@Tykircher (May 26, 2020). Another proclaimed, "I have to say I quite like the virtual fans and crowd noise!" (@Nbonfieldgolf, June 11, 2020). This post references another, arguably less successful, attempt to recreate stadium atmosphere by adding representations of fans in the form of either cardboard cutouts or digital images. Some fans parsed their opinions, suggesting that "crowd noise improves the watching experience" whereas the virtual crowd "in the background is just poorly done" (@TheExpertChels, June 11, 2020). Effectively, and perhaps ironically, these fans appreciated artificial soundscapes as a natural and necessary extension of broadcast games and did so without comparing against the seemingly intolerable option of silence.

Artificial sound also drew appreciation from fans because it reminded them of how sport sounded and felt prior to the pandemic. Viewers reported that the artificial soundscape brought a sense of normalcy back to their viewing experience. Thus, sound became a key component signifying normalcy, even to the point of overcoming skepticism about its use. For instance, one fan tweeted: "I was skeptical of fake crowd noise. Watching Dortmund-Bayern with it, I'm completely sold. Feels normal, forgot all about it in minutes" (@SneakyJoeWGR, May 26, 2020). Another user provided a similar comment about the Spanish league suggesting that "what laliga [sic] has done with the stands and the crowd noise is commendable, seeing the Sevilla game on TV and it looks somewhat like pre Covid" (@Btomzz, June 11, 2020). Interestingly, these same viewers not only recommended the use of artificial sound, but endorsed it by claiming that "every league should copy this" and "100% pipe it in." (@Btomzz, June 11, 2020; @SneakyJoeWGR, May 26, 2020). Comments such as these revealed how the presence of artificial sound grounded the experience of viewers in a sense of normalcy that was absent otherwise. That is, despite being artificial the soundscape authenticated their viewing experience much like it would for fervent live audiences within stadia (Perasović and Mustapić 2017). Moreover, it also appeased viewing audiences that maintain specific expectations regarding "a particular sonic backdrop" that should accompany live matches (Kassing 2014, 129). These connections reflect how the aural component of sports broadcasts can increase fans' impressions of match excitement (Cummins, Berke, Moe, and Gong 2019).

Dissatisfaction: Distasteful, Unnecessary, and Ridiculous

While some fans appreciated the use of artificial noise, others found it distracting and strange. One user stipulated that "fake crowd noise in the premier league [sic] is creepy" (@cyalm, June 17, 2020). Another exhibited outright disdain, saying that it was "stupid and just plain wrong" (@ARMO ARF, June 17, 2020). Others were more abrasive in their condemnation of it, claiming that it was "really shit" (@thomaspeters203, June 17, 2020), "dog shit" (@flemo53, June 17, 2020), or simply that "Its horse shit!!" (@periculumin, June 17, 2020). Such strong reactions to artificial sound gave some users pause, requiring them to recognize that "fans actually being there is real important and we take it for granted" (@CFCTerence, June 17, 2020). Fans also demonstrated their dissatisfaction with artificial crowd noise by making the argument that it was unnecessary. For example, a viewer watching a Premier League match affirmed, "glad to have football back don't need to jazz it up with recorded singing" (@yankgeordie, June 17, 2020). Another argued that "you can't replicate crowd" before asserting that fans could still enjoy a match without sound because "it's raw, it's real and it's still exciting" (@Ricardo40656182, June 17, 2020). For these viewers, matches provided ample excitement, and therefore, did not warrant nor need artificial sound. The sentiment underlying this position suggested that the requisition of disembodied sound from actual fans was an unwelcome and misguided proxy for authentic supporters who create vibrant soundscapes within stadia through chants and songs (Poulton 2016; Spaaij and Viñas 2005).

Additionally, fans showed their displeasure with the introduction of artificial soundscapes via mockery. This could take the form of ridiculing the misappropriation of sound against the backdrop of live action during matches. For instance, one fan chided sound technicians for overplaying a routine save by Manchester United's goalkeeper, stating "they turned up the crowd noise for a standard Dean Henderson save like someone had scored an injury time winner" (@thesaltishere, June 17, 2020). Or it might entail humorously revealing its inaccuracies. For example, another viewer declared that vociferous artificial sound was "very unrealistic" because "the Etihad is never that loud" (@stevey mac, June 17, 2020). This jibe foregrounds the reputed lackluster noise produced by Manchester City fans within their home stadium to underscore how misguided artificial sound could be. This tactic involved not only humor, but a deliberate deployment of it that leveraged in-depth contextual knowledge in the same manner as supporters who used Internet sports memes to antagonize and demean their major rivals (Kassing 2020b).

Phase 3: Winning it in a Toilet

Mercantile pursuits, pop music, humor and football have shaped the civic identity of Liverpool and its "history of difference and apartness" (Rookwood 2012, 100). Subsequently, LFC's success in European competitions afforded the development of an international reputation and further differentiated the city and club from its English counterparts. Symbolism engulfs the club, characterized by the Kop end (reputedly the first large terrace inhabited by the most fervent supporters), the Hillsborough disaster that resulted in the crushing death of ninety-seven supporters in 1989, and the symbolically-charged singing of the "You'll Never Walk Alone" anthem (Power 2011). Understood most readily by local fans, LFC supporters have ensured that newer global, consumer-oriented fans learn of and appreciate these traditions (Rookwood and Millward 2011). All of which suggests that support for LFC is widespread, unwavering, and considerable (Rookwood 2012).

Sport generally, and soccer in particular, prompts imagined communities whereby people across time and space collectively associate despite the likelihood of never meeting in person (Anderson 1991; O'Brien 2013; Shobe 2008b). This is particularly true for clubs, like Liverpool, that have secured a strong sense of place and locality while fostering an international following (Kassing 2019; Kassing and Nyaupane 2019; O'Brien 2013; Rookwood and Millward 2011). The sensemaking that occurred among LFC fans in the Reddit conversations illustrated how a large-scale, geographically-distributed community responded to the excitement of winning a championship and the challenge and inconvenience of celebrating it without traditional laudatory practices (e.g., a trophy presentation in a crowded boisterous stadium, a festive parade within the city). Accordingly, two major themes appeared in the Reddit conversations about Liverpool's championship. Indifference surfaced when fans determined that the pandemic would not diminish the club's success. Virtual or delayed gratification entailed suggestions about postponing celebrations until social distancing requirements had been relaxed, which engendered a degree of optimism about celebrating the championship and returning to in-person matches.

Indifference

Liverpool fans, who had not witnessed a championship since the 1989-90 season, stated that they happily would claim the title even if it occurred in an empty stadium. They routinely made this point by suggesting the championship could be won in a variety of settings, none of which would detract from the enthusiasm generated by winning an elusive, but well-deserved title. Comments that characterized this sentiment included: "I'd take them lifting the trophy in a broom closet over them not getting it" (Splash of Cold Brew, April 6, 2020), "I'd take winning it in a toilet at this rate" (BullisBull, April 6, 2020), "I don't care if we have to do our trophy lifting celebration over on Microsoft Teams, just let us win it" (KinnyRiddle, April 6, 2020), and "Hendo [nickname for team captain Jordan Henderson] could lift it on a stage made out of toilet paper rolls" (J539, April 6, 2020). Evidently, winning overwhelmed all else as fans admitted that receiving the championship was paramount regardless of where or when the club captured it. One participant boosted the extremity of such claims by proposing that, "Hendo could pick it up by himself, in an isolation chamber, in an empty stadium on a dead volcano under a frozen sea of a planetoid in orbit of a star somewhere in the vicinity of Betelgeuse and still we'd all be there for the ride" (mahan42, April 7, 2020). In this instance, the closing remark offsets the extravagance of the preceding claim by proposing a simple and indisputable belief. That is, that bona fide fans would universally celebrate the championship despite their dislocation from it (Rookwood 2012; Rookwood and Millward 2011). Moreover, the fact that many fans had not witnessed a championship bolstered their willingness to acquire it whenever and wherever it occurred. One fan reminded readers of this powerful emotion by declaring, "All I want is to see them lift the trophy once in my life" (cmn3y0, April 6, 2020). Basically, commenters showed an indifference to the team winning the championship in an empty stadium, asserting that the historical accomplishment superseded any seemingly inconsequential pandemic-induced obstacles. Despite the absence of long-established traditions like singing and chanting from the Kop end (Power 2011), LFC supporters still felt immeasurable satisfaction with the outcome. The pandemic and restart failed to stunt the outpouring of global support for the club and its dispersed supporters (Rookwood and Millward 2011).

Virtual or Delayed Gratification

Similarly, fans heartily acknowledged that their raucous, in-person celebrations would need to be replaced with something virtual or delayed. Accordingly, some contributors suggested ways in which fans could virtually join one another or the team in celebration. For instance, one suggested turning the circumstances "into a positive" by taking advantage of modern technology and orchestrating "some sort of live stream thing/video production where you see all the screaming fans reaction across the world at the same time" (mrchuckbass, April 6, 2020). Another argued for live streaming "the fans when we lift it [the trophy]" (Deeco7, April 6, 2020). Other fans opted for delaying gratification and collective celebration, reasoning that "we will eventually return to a packed Anfield and when we do we'll have the party of a lifetime" because people needed "to be patient in these really really sh*t times" (SafePay8, April 6, 2020). Another supporter queried if the celebrations could be postponed in order to "do the actual trophy lift at the first home game next season" (Splash of Cold Brew, April 6, 2020).

Generally, fans accepted that their enthusiasm might need to be postponed and their gratification delayed. This realization inspired optimism about the future, specifically with regard to celebrating the championship with fellow fans. One fan lamented the situation before suggesting that "when all this hopefully blows over there WILL be a huge party/parade/celebration in Liverpool" (Reddit, April 6, 2020). Other fans echoed this conclusion, joining in the argument that once the pandemic subsided, 'proper' celebrations would occur. The championship drought informed fans' patience with regard to celebrations. In fact, one confessed that "I've waited my whole life, another 6 months to a year is fine" (deanlfc95, April 6, 2020). For the LFC community, that had engaged in a protracted battle to seek justice for the victims lost in the Hillsborough disaster against initial accusations of hooliganism (Power 2011), patience and determination apparently materialized instinctively. Indeed, fans simultaneously braced for triumphant celebrations, with one supporter predicting that, "The people will more than make up for these strange times! It's gonna be a hell of a party!" (LFC2020Buzzzing, April 6, 2020). Thus, delayed gratification and patience, characteristics already well forged in the community (Power 2011; Rookwood and Millward 2011), coalesced into optimism for future prospects and excitement for imminent celebrations. Overall, the implications of the pandemic seemed to do little to dampen the enthusiasm of LFC's robust and seasoned fan community (Power 2011; Rookwood 2012; Rookwood and Millward 2011), which showed remarkable indifference and strong solidarity by accepting that their celebrations would be virtual, delayed, or both. The collective ethos shared among members of the community demonstrated a cohesiveness, even within an imagined community, that overpowered the obstructions presented by the pandemic.

Conclusion

In summary, media reports recognized the importance of soccer's return by forwarding social and economic arguments, while revisiting the need to do so in accordance with explicit safety regulations in place. Simultaneously, articles confirmed the awkwardness that empty stadia created, realized through comments provided by coaches, players, club officials and league administrators. They also pointed out the unexpected byproducts of empty stadia including the diminishment of home field advantage, the inability to unnerve referees, and the reduced pressure players felt. Thus, reports shifted between the unfamiliarity of the situation and the unexpected outcomes it produced. These particular frames provided sensemaking apparatus for the audience to decipher and determine the impact of Covid-19 on the restart of European soccer (Entman 1993; Van Gorp 2007).

Another important development involved the introduction of artificial sound for broadcast coverage. This innovation divided fans, with some supporters grateful for its presence, particularly as it addressed the sonic awkwardness audible to viewers in empty stadia and reintroduced a sense of normalcy for them, underscoring the entrenched understanding of how filled soccer stadia should sound (Kassing 2014). But it also offended others who found it unnecessary, poorly executed, and excessive. Fans used social media to express their disdain and to mock artificial soundscapes, both their presence and execution. Interestingly, responses exposed a paradoxical association with disembodied sound. Some fans welcomed it as a necessary aural enhancement, whereas others explicitly rejected it as an inappropriate substitution for actual supporters. This contradiction reflects current concerns about commercialization of the sport and the displacement of more heavily vested supporters by ones that merely enjoy and expect the trappings of commodified fandom (Giulianotti 2002; Perasović and Mustapić 2017). The implication being that the comfort which artificial sound offers, should neither eclipse nor obscure the fundamental connection between supporters and clubs (Doidge, Kossakowski, and Mintert 2020; Kennedy 2013).

Champions of each league emerged at the end of the unusual season, but none was more significant than LFC's title in the Premier League. In response, fans used humor, hyperbole, goodwill, enthusiasm and delayed gratification to ensure that the pandemic would not disrupt their celebratory mood or overall experience. This may be representative of the distinctive fanbase that supports the club (Power 2011; Rookwood 2012; Rookwood and Millward 2011), or simply indicative of how most imagined communities, particularly ones forged through sport, identity, and affiliation (Kassing and Nyaupane 2019), would respond. In the other leagues considered, Real Madrid and Bayern Munich added titles to their growing list of achievements. They also did so within the same abnormal milieu—absent of fans, noise, and communal celebrations. Future research could address this question by considering how fan communities across leagues and sports recognized and celebrated championships.

While the three phases of this research provide a broad view of how the pandemic affected the return of European soccer that approach includes some limitations. We chose to consider different facets of the pandemic's effect, rather than concentrating specifically on any single one. As a consequence, our analysis is less comprehensive and more anecdotal, providing mere snapshots of the various aspects of the pandemic's impact on the return of European soccer. It certainly could be improved upon by thoroughly examining, with larger data sets, each of the specific attributes considered. For example, the media analysis is limited by exclusively English language sources and a small sample size. Additionally, the LFC case should be recognized as an outlier compared to other league champions. Consequently, while the occasion provides a fascinating juxtaposition to explore (i.e., an overdue championship achieved in a season where celebrations will be subdued), it is not necessarily representative of other fan communities who confronted the challenge of celebrating championships during pandemic-influenced seasons.

Overall, our analyses reveal that the pandemic upended sport, not only by creating widespread stoppages in play, but by dictating the circumstances when it resumed. The return of soccer transpired with matches staged in empty stadia, which disrupted the fundamental connection between fandom, match attendance, and sound (Kytö 2011; Marra and Trotta 2019). Put succinctly, our findings suggest that stadium presence and crowd noise matter. The return of soccer dislocated these indispensable elements of fandom and brought their absence into relief. All of which (re)confirms the importance of not just fans, as they were still able to view their respective clubs via broadcasts, but of their presence in stadia and the atmosphere they create (Doidge, Kossakowski, and Mintert 2020). Essentially, matches returned to stadia, but the supporter-driven spectacle that complements them was missing—indicating that soccer could be restarted but not fully realized until crowds followed.

REFERENCES

Anderson, Benedict. 1991. *Imagined Communities: Reflections on the Origin and Spread of Nationalism*. London: Verso.

Antonowicz, Dominik, Honorata Jakubowska, and Radoslaw Kossakowski. 2020. "Marginalized, Patronized and Instrumentalized: Polish Female Fans in the Ultras' Narratives." *International Review for the Sociology of Sport* 55 (1): 60-76.

Beaton, Andrew, and Joshua Robinson. 2020. "The 90,000 Fans Who Screamed in an Empty Stadium." *The Wall Street Journal*, May 26, 2020. https://www.wsj.com/articles/the-90-000-fans-who-screamed-in-an-empty-stadium-11590494401

Benkwitz, Adam, and Gyozo Molnar. 2012. "Interpreting and Exploring Football Fan Rivalries: An Overview. *Soccer & Society* 13 (4): 479-494.

Bingaman, James. 2020. "Dude I've Never Felt This Way Towards a Celebrity Death: Parasocial Grieving and the Collective Mourning of Kobe Bryant on Reddit." *OMEGA-Journal of Death and Dying*. https://doi.org/10.1177/0030222820971531

Brewin, John. 2020. "Bundesliga's Virtual Crowd Gives a Game Context for the TV Onlooker." *The Guardian*, June 7, 2020. https://www.theguardian.com/football/2020/jun/07/bundesligas-virtual-crowd-gives-a-game-context-for-the-tv-onlooker

Clark, Tom. 2006. "'I'm Scunthorpe 'til I Die': Constructing and (Re)Negotiating Identity Through the Terrace Chant." *Soccer and Society* 7 (4): 494-507.

Clavio, Galen and Ted M. Kian. 2010. "Uses and Gratifications of a Retired Female Athlete's Twitter Followers." *International Journal of Sport Communication* 3 (4): 485-500.

Clement, J. 2021. "Total Global Visitor Traffic to Reddit.com 2021". *Statista.com*, July 29, 2021. https://www.statista.com/statistics/443332/reddit-monthly-visitors/

Cohen, Ben, and Joshua Robinson. 2020. "The World's Best Athletes Are Now Better at Shooting." *The Wall Street Journal*, August, 4, 2020. https://www.wsj.com/articles/nba-bubble-shooting-soccer-empty-stadiums-11596539693

Creditor, Avi. 2020. "Fake Crowd Noise on Soccer Broadcasts Provides Comfort, but it's Disingenuous." *Sports Illustrated*, May 27, 2020. https://www.si.com/soccer/2020/05/27/fake-crowd-noise-soccer-tv-broadcasts-bundesliga

Cummins, R. Glenn, Collin K. Berke, Alexander Moe, and Zijian Gong. 2019. "Sight Versus Sound: The Differential Impact of Mediated Spectator Response in Sport Broadcasts." *Journal of Broadcasting & Electronic Media* 63 (1): 111-129.

Davidson, Neil. 2020. "EA Sports Providing Sound at Empty Soccer Stadiums in England, Spain." *The Canadian Press*, June 11, 2020. https://www.chroniclejournal.com/sports/national_sports/ea-sports-providing-sound-at-fill-empty-soccer-%20stadiums-in-england-spain/article_eeb08326-eb94-5d42-a07f-c225cfdaef8b.html

Deighton, Katie. 2020. "TV Sports Executives Warm to Canned Crowd Noise, but Give Viewers an Out." *The Wall Street Journal*, June 17, 2020. https://www.wsj.com/articles/tv-sports-executives-warm-to-canned-crowd-noise-but-give-viewers-an-out-11592366400

Dixon, Kevin. 2014. "The Football Fan and the Pub: An Enduring Relationship." *International Review for the Sociology of Sport* 49 (3/4): 382-399.

Doidge, Mark. 2015. "'If You Jump Up and Down, Balotelli Dies': Racism and Player Abuse in Italian Football." *International Review for the Sociology of Sport 50 (3): 249-264.*

Doidge, Mark, Radoslaw Kossakowski, and Svenja Mintert. 2020. *Ultras: Passion and Performance of Contemporary Football Fandom*. Manchester: University of Manchester Press.

Duckworth, Austin. "Gegenpressing: The Bundesliga's Tactical Response to the Coivd-19 Lockdown." In *Time Out: National Perspectives on Sport and the Covid-19 Lockdown* edited by Jörg Krieger, April Henning, Lindsay Parks Pieper, and Paul Dimeo, 29-40. Champaign, IL: Common Ground Research Networks.

Entman, Robert M. 1993. "Framing: Toward Clarification of a Fractured Paradigm." *Journal of Communication* 43 (4): 51-58.

Federation Internationale de Football Association. 2017. *FIFA Disciplinary Code. Zurich.*

France 24. 2020. "Surreal Day for European Football as Germany's Bundesliga Returns to Empty Stadiums." *France 24*, May 16, 2020. https://www.france24.com/en/20200516-surreal-day-for-german-football-as-bundesliga-returns-to-empty-stadiums

Gallagher, Hayley F., Caroline Wright, and Jeffrey W. Kassing. 2022. "I'm Not Going to the F***ing White House: Fan Discourse about Megan Rapinoe During the 2019 Women's World Cup. In *Athlete Activism: Contemporary Perspectives*, edited by Rory Magrath. London: Routledge.

Gibbons, Tom, and Kevin Dixon. 2010. "Surf's Up!: A Call to Take English Soccer Fan Interactions on the Internet More Seriously." *Soccer & Society* 11 (5): 599-613.

Giulianotti, Richard. 2002. "Supporters, Followers, Fans, and Flaneurs: A Taxonomy of Spectator Identities in Football." *Journal of Sport & Social Issues* 26 (1): 25-46.

Glaser, Barney, and Anselm Strauss. 1967. *The Discovery of Grounded Theory*. Hawthorne, NY: Aldine.

Hambrick, Marion, Jason M. Simmons, Greg P. Greenhalgh, and T. Christopher Greenwell. 2010. "Understanding Professional Athletes' Use of Twitter: A Content Analysis of Athlete Tweets." *International Journal of Sport Communication* 3 (4): 454-471.

Henderson, Chris W. 2018. "Two Balls is Too Many: Stadium Performance and Queerness among Portland's Rose City Riveters Supporters Club." *Sport in Society* 21 (7): 1031-1046.

Homewood, Brian. 2020. "Carboard Fans, Piped Applause: Football Looks to Liven up Empty Stands." *Reuters*, May 12, 2020. https://www.reuters.com/article/uk-health-coronavirus-soccer-stadiums/cardboard-fans-piped-applause-football-looks-to-liven-up-empty-stands-idUKKBN22O2GG

Irak, Dağhan. 2018. "'Shoot Some Pepper Gas at Me!' Football Fans vs. Erdoğan: Organized Politicization or Reactive Politics?" *Soccer & Society* 19 (3): 400-417.

Jones, Katharine W. 2008. "Female Fandom: Identity, Sexism, and Men's Professional Football in England." *Sociology of Sport Journal* 25 (4): 516-537.

Kassing, Jeffrey W. 2014. "Noisemaker or Cultural Symbol: The Vuvuzela Controversy and Expressions of Football Fandom". In *African Football, Identity Politics and Global Media Narratives: The Legacy of the FIFA 2010 World Cup*, edited by Tendai Chari and Mhiripiri Nhamo, 121-139. Basingstoke: Palgrave Macmillan.

———. 2019. "'Mes Que un-Club' and an Empty Camp Nou: A Case Study of Strategic Ambiguity and Catalan Nationalism at Football Club Barcelona." *International Journal of Sport Communication* 12 (2): 260-274.

———. 2020a. "Overcoming American Exceptionalism and Media Antipathy via the Digital Pitch: Soccer, Attitudinal Change, and Video Game Play." *Soccer & Society* 21 (7): 778-787.

———. 2020b. "Messi Hanging Laundry at the Bernabéu: The Production and Consumption of Internet Sports Memes as Trash Talk." *Discourse, Context & Media* 34 (April). https://doi.org/10.1016/j.dcm.2019.100320

Kassing, Jeffrey W., and Pratik Nyaupane. 2019. "I Just Couldn't Believe I Was There": An Exploration of Soccer Pilgrimage." *International Journal of Sport Communication* 12 (2): 167-184.

Kassing, Jeffrey W., and Jimmy Sanderson. 2015. "Playing in the New Media Game or Riding the Virtual Bench: Confirming and Disconfirming Membership in the Community of Sport." *Journal of Sport and Social Issues* 39 (1): 3-18.

Kennedy, David. 2013. "A Contextual Analysis of Europe's Ultra Football Supporters Movement." *Soccer & Society* 14 (2): 132-153.

Kytö, Meri. 2011. "'We are the Rebellious Voice of the Terraces, We are Çarsi': Constructing a Football Supporter Group through Sound." *Soccer & Society* 12 (1): 77-93.

Lagorio-Chafkin, Christine. 2018. We are the Nerds: *The Birth and Tumultuous Life of Reddit, the Internet's Culture Laboratory*. New York: Hachette Books.

Lawrence, Stefan and Garry Crawford. 2019. "The Hyperdigitalization of Football Cultures." In *Digital Football Cultures. Fandom, Identities and Resistance* edited by Stefan Lawrence and Garry Crawford, 1-16. London: Routledge.

Lopez-Gonzalez, Hibai, Federic Guerrero-Sole, & Richard Hayes. 2014. "Manufacturing Conflict Narratives in Real Madrid versus Barcelona Football Matches." *International Review for the Sociology of Sport* 49 (6): 688-706.

Magrath, Rory. 2018. "'To Try and Gain an Advantage for My Team': Homophobic and Homosexually Themed Chanting among English Football Fans." *Sociology* 52 (4): 709-726.

Marra, Pedro S., and Felipe Trotta. 2019. "Sound, Music and Magic in Football Stadiums." *Popular Music* 38 (1): 73-89.

McDougall, Alan. 2021. "Between Self-Interest and Solidarity: European Football and the Covid-19 Lockdown." In *Time Out: Global Perspectives on Sport and the Covid-19 Lockdown* edited by Jörg Krieger, April Henning, Lindsay Parks Pieper, and Paul Dimeo, 197-210. Champaign, IL: Common Ground Research Networks.

Nair, Roshini. 2020. "EA Sports Lends its Recorded Stadium Sounds to Bolster Crowd-deprived Soccer Matches." *CBC,* July 12, 2020. https://www.cbc.ca/news/canada/british-columbia/ea-sports-crowd-sounds-1.5645848

O'Brien, Jim. 2013. "'El Clasico' and the Demise of Tradition in Spanish Club Football: Perspectives on Shifting Patterns of Cultural Identity." *Soccer & Society* 14 (3): 315-330.

Perasović, Benjamin, and Marko Mustapić. 2017. "Carnival Supporters, Hooligans, and the 'Against Modern Football' Movement: Life within the Ultras Subculture in the Croatian Context." *Sport in Society* 21 (6): 960-976.

Porat, Amir. 2010. "Football Fandom: A Bounded Identification." *Soccer & Society* 11 (3): 277-290.

Poulton, Emma. 2016. "Towards Understanding: Antisemitism and the Contested Use and Meanings of 'Yid' in English Football." *Ethnic and Racial Studies* 39 (11): 1981-2001.

Power, Ben. 2011. "Justice for the Ninety-Six: Liverpool FC Fans and Uncommon Use of Football Song." *Soccer & Society* 12 (1): 96-112.

Reedy, Joe. 2020. "Enhanced crowd audio adds another dimension to fanless games." *The Washington Post,* July 5, 2020. https://www.washingtonpost.com/sports/soccer/enhanced-crowd-audio-adds-another-dimension-to-fanless-games/2020/07/05/4c545f14-bec8-11ea-8908-68a2b9eae9e0_story.html

Reuters. 2020a. "Bundesliga Soccer to Resume on May 16 in Empty Stadiums." May 11, 2020. https://www.reuters.com/article/us-health-coronavirus-soccer-germany/soccer-bundesliga-season-resumes-on-may-16-with-empty-stadiums-idUSKBN22J1U4

———. 2020b. "Empty Stadium Might Help Us at Man City, Says Arsenal Boss Arteta." June 11, 2020. https://www.reuters.com/article/uk-soccer-england-ars/empty-stadium-might-help-us-at-man-city-says-arsenal-boss-arteta-idUKKBN23I1QX

Richelieu, André, Sibylle Lopez, and Michel Desbordes. 2008. "The Internationalization of Sports Team Brand: The Case of European Soccer Teams." *International Journal of Sports Marketing & Sponsorship* 10 (1) 29-44.

Rookwood, Joel. 2012. "We're Not English, We are Scouse!: Examining Civic Loyalty and Collective Fan Identities at Liverpool Football Club." In The Role of Sports in the Formation of Personal Identities, edited by John Hughson, Clive Palmer, and Fiona Skillen, 95-120. New York: Edwin Mellen.

Rookwood, Joel, and Peter Millward. 2011. "We All Dream of a Team of Carraghers: Comparing 'local' and Texan Liverpool fans' talk." *Sport in Society* 14 (1): 37-52.

Schallhorn, Christiana and Jessica Kunert. 2020. "Football without Football: Creativity in German Football Coverage by TV Broadcasters and Clubs During the Coronavirus Crisis." *International Journal of Sport Communication* 13 (3): 514-522.

Scott, Nate. 2020. "Opinion: German Bundesliga Broadcast Uses Fake Crowd Noise, and it's Actually Great." *USA TODAY*, May 24, 2020. https://www.usatoday.com/story/sports/ftw/2020/05/24/bundesliga-broadcast-uses-fake-crowd-noise-and-its-actually-great/111859288/

Shobe, Hunter. 2008a. "Place, Identity and Football: Catalonia, Catalanisme and Football Club Barcelona, 1899-1975." *National Identities* 10 (3): 329-343.

———. 2008b. "Football and the Politics of Place: Football Club Barcelona and Catalonia, 1975-2005." *Journal of Cultural Geography* 25 (1): 87-105.

Silverman, Alex. 2020. "La Liga, BeIn Sports Let Viewers Choose Fake Crowd Noise or Natural Sound for Empty Stadium Matches." June 10, 2020.

Smith, Rory. 2020. "Do Empty Stadiums Affect Outcomes: The Data Say Yes." *The New York Times*, July 1, 2020. https://www.nytimes.com/2020/07/01/sports/soccer/soccer-without-fans-germany-data.html

Spaaij, Ramón, and Carles Viñas. 2005. "Passion, Politics and Violence: A Socio-Historical Analysis of Spanish Ultras." *Soccer & Society* 6 (1): 79-96.

The Guardian. 2020. "'An Unknown for All of Us': Mourinho on Spur's Premier League Return." *The Guardian*, June 18, 2020. https://www.theguardian.com/football/video/2020/jun/18/an-unknown-for-all-of-us-mourinho-on-spurs-premier-league-return-video

Van Gorp, Baldwin. 2007. "The Constructionist Approach to Framing: Bringing Culture Back In." *Journal of Communication* 57 (1): 60-78.

Wagner, Jesse H., and Hunter Shobe. 2017. "Identity, Scale and Soccer Supporter Groups: The Case of the Timbers Army." *Sport in Society* 20 (9): 1150-1166.

Wamsley, Laurel. 2020. "As German Soccer Restarts, Broadcasters Use Crowd Sounds to Replace Missing Fans." *National Public Radio*, May 29, 2020.

https://www.npr.org/2020/05/29/865685683/germanys-soccer-league-resumes-season-offers-feeds-with-fake-crowd-sounds

Weed, Mike. 2007. "The Pub as a Virtual Football Fandom Venue: An Alternative to 'Being There'?" *Soccer & Society* 8 (2/3): 399-414.

Chapter 19

Esports, Repositioning and Enhancing Profitability Post Covid-19 Sports Lockdown: An Australian Case

Michelle O'Shea, Sarah Duffy, and Daniel Roman

Introduction

Recent world events brought on by Covid-19 have highlighted the commercial complexities professional sport organizations face. Australian sport leagues and teams are in an unstable position due to falling match day attendances, a simultaneous reduction in gate receipts, and an overreliance on revenue generated through the sale of television broadcast rights (Anderson 2020; Colangelo and Samios 2021; Mason 2019; Wildie 2020). The precariousness of this position has been exacerbated by sport's global lockdown. Some event organizers, teams, and athletes took to eSports as a means to keep their commercial entities alive or simply pass the time in ways that, fortuitously brought commercial returns.

As Australian sport leagues reboot their Covid-19 disrupted season fixtures, the prospect of further localized outbreaks, protracted lockdowns, and border closures has commentators and sport leaders questioning the sustainability of the current sports business model.

While professional Australian sport leagues and teams have busily kept their core product alive through "player bubbles," "league hubs," and strict biosecurity protocols given the competitive Australian professional sport and entertainment marketplace, new revenue opportunities should be front of mind. In the current Covid-19 induced resource scarcity, the authors of the present chapter explore eSports' salience as a commercial opportunity for the professional sport marketplace.

eSports' interactive nature has commercial potential by virtue of retaining and developing highly identified sports fans, particularly millennials whose preferences and sport consumption habits are evolving and increasingly technology-centered (Anderson et al. 2021). Even before the pandemic, Australian sports fan engagement was shifting with more fans than ever consuming sport via digital platforms and devices (Nielsen 2021).

eSports' defining features are perfect for a pandemic that demands physical distancing. That is, the main facets of the sport are enabled by electronic systems;

player inputs and teams and the eSports system outputs are facilitated by human-computer interfaces (Carter et al. 2017). The reluctance of many Australian sport organizations to strategically engage with eSports during and prior to Covid-19 warrants investigation. The central question underpinning the chapter is: how have Australian sport organizations engaged with eSports to date and what does the nature and degree of this engagement mean for the future?

Defining and Conceptualizing the Esports Domain

Fan motivations, expectations, and tastes continue to evolve. For example, younger fans are no longer satisfied by the thrill of a live sports contest alone. Indeed, today viewership of major eSports tournaments often exceeds that of traditional sporting events (Cranmer et al. 2021). A catalyst for this change has been the rapid integration of technology into people's daily routines. This technological shift has forced sports marketers to expand ancillary activities from sports trading cards and memorabilia (Williams 1995) to a new arena, one facilitated by the internet and allied platforms.

Originally a "niche past-time" (Taylor 2012, 33), video games have emerged as one of the most popular recreational activities (ESA 2018), especially for the 18 to 30 demographic (Nielsen 2019). The popularity and ubiquity of video games has in part paved the way for eSports. However, defining, and conceptualizing eSports is a challenge due to its "convergence of culture, technology, sport, and business" and perhaps its absence of traditional hallmarks such as physical activity and athletic prowess (Jin 2010, 68).

Hemphill (2005, 199) first conceptualized eSports as an "alternative sport reality, that is, to electronically extend athletes in digitally represented sporting worlds". More recent scholarship (Bányai et al. 2019) has signposted how eSports is fundamentally challenging how we define and conceptualize sport (Cranmer et al. 2021).

eSports can be identified as a new form of sport. That is, an activity usually conducted in a competitive manner where the participation of players and teams is mediated by human-machine interfaces made possible by the Internet (Jonasson and Thiborg 2010; Weiss 2011; Hamari and Sjöblom 2017). Moreover, scholars have argued how formalized governing bodies and standardisation are considered necessary to define esports as a sport (Funk et al. 2018; Jenny et al. 2017).

During the 2000s, eSports's transition from a fringe hobby to a commercial business with international eSports organizations and competitions began to emerge (Hope 2014). The evolution of the Internet and the transformation of sport led to "a fast-moving consumable experience that fits neatly into the iPod society" (Smith and Stewart 2010, 6) and continues to shape sport in new and nuanced ways. High-speed internet has enabled live streaming platforms like YouTube and Twitch to promote and present eSports events at no cost, making video games and eSports even more appealing to event organizers and "next-generation" fans.

Fortnite and League of Legends are examples of games with significant prize pools, in-demand tournaments, and identifiable players. The mainstream popularity and reach of these two games have helped grow the eSport scene. The League of Legends 2020 World Championship averaged more than 1.1 million viewers, with a single match attracting 3.8 million viewers (Dixon 2020).

Perhaps in the ultimate endorsement of eSports, the International Olympic Committee (IOC) has partnered with five International Sports Federations (IFs) to produce the Olympic Virtual Series (OVS). This will be the first ever Olympic-licensed event for physical and non-physical virtual sports and provides the IOC with a new way to engage directly with audiences in the field of virtual sports. This tactic is an impactful seeding campaign amongst youth, an important demographic for ensuring the longevity of the Olympics.

Game publishers, broadcasting platforms, competitions, branding, and advertising have all played an integral role in providing a structure for eSports' growth as a mainstream entertainment product. eSports is the fastest-growing market segment within the sports industry, attracting billions in commercial revenue (Nagel and Sugishita 2016). Such is the speed of growth that Grand View Research (2020) expects the global eSports market size to reach $USD6.8 billion by 2027, with eSports viewership expected to hit 646 million in 2023.

eSports Enabled Professional Sport Reboot: The Australian Context

In the proceeding chapter sections, three case studies are presented to highlight how Australian sport organizations drew on eSports in various ways to reboot their sports during and after the Covid-19 lockdown. Following the presented case studies and discussion, data emerging from interviews with sport managers and marketers are critically discussed.

Internationally, motorsport was dramatically affected by Covid-19. The 2020 season-opening Australian Formula One (F1) event's last-minute cancelation left F1 enthusiasts locked out with paid tickets in hand. Australian event administrators were left reeling, but internationally, the F1 led the rollout of eSport contingencies with the Virtual Grand Prix series.

In Australia, the Supercars Championship organizers scanned the domestic and international market in a bid to find tactics to combat the Covid-19 shutdown. We here discuss their first mover advantage.

Case Study 1

Racing Ahead: Supercars Takes Pole Position in Australia

> "Broadcast skill and motor-racing passion fused to make literally the world's best virtual racing broadcast product." Neil Crompton, Supercars Hall of Fame

Securing "pole position" or "leading the pack" are phrases synonymous with motorsports. Characteristically associated with on-the-track action, these phrases are increasingly associated with strategic virtual initiatives. In response to evolving fan needs and expectations, motorsports have redesigned their product to include an eSports component, expanding their interactions with fans.

In the years prior to when Covid-19 struck, the Supercars Championship had created and refined their eSports platform, allowing them to sustain their existing fans' interest and seek out new fans in lockdown. This opportunity arose due to forward thinking, with Supercars envisioning eSports "as a crucial way to reach and engage the younger demographic" (Bartholomaeus 2017). In 2019, with Gfinity Australia's (eSports and gaming solutions provider) investment and knowledge, Supercars Pro Eseries moved to a new gaming platform and expanded to twelve teams. The driver draft and championship were broadcast live on FoxSports and streamed on Kayo (Supercars 2019). These efforts meant they weren't scrambling to establish an online presence when the pandemic struck.

Leveraging Their "First Mover" Advantage

In a bid to keep fans engaged during the pandemic, Supercars transitioned its Eseries from a side attraction to the main event. Utilizing the iRacing platform and conducted in the safety of their homes, all 24 professional drivers competed in the Supercars All Stars Eseries.

The championship consisted of ten rounds of virtual racing (two races per round) at traditional supercar racetracks as well as some of the most famous racetracks from around the world. Whilst the drivers' inclusion and enthusiasm added to the series' attraction and authenticity, how the championship was staged was also vital. Nathan Prendergast (GM Television and Content at Supercars) said he wanted the "product to look, feel and sound like a true Supercars broadcast" (Gravity Media 2020). To achieve this, drivers raced in realistic racing set-ups, outfitted in team branding. The coverage of the Eseries included graphics, statistics, and commentary as if it was a normal race day.

For the opening round, 158,000 viewers tuned into the Fox Sports broadcast (Supercars 2020) while 210,736 viewers watched the championship online through Supercars' Facebook and Twitch channels (Newton 2020). The championship attracted 130,000 views on replay demonstrating Supercars' advantage during a period when sport was "dead."

The success gained international interest. Overseas drivers, such as Max Verstappen, Marcos Ambrose, and Joey Logano participating, as well as the creation of an extra "celebrity" round, garnered new Supercars fans from around the world.

Esports: A Brand Extension for Traditional Sports

When an established brand implements a strategy to launch a new product to reach a mass market it is known as a "diffusion brand" or "brand extension" (Broniarczyk and Alba 1994). Brands do so in a bid to leverage their existing goodwill and reputation to enter a new market, most often to defend their territory or to grow their sales (Riley et al. 2004). Usually, the transition direction is from exclusive to a more mass-market appeal to gain critical mass and increased revenue (Reddy et al. 2009). It is important to maintain a meaningful distinction between the two brands, taking a physical sport into the online domain maintains this distinction. The application of this approach is discussed through the following case study of Australia's topflight soccer/football competition, the A-League.

Case Study 2

A Whole New Ball Game for Australia Football

In 2018, well before Covid-19 brought sport to a standstill, the A-League, Australia and New Zealand's professional soccer league, celebrated its inaugural E-League series. The online simulated series was an initiative to connect fans of the EA SPORTS™ FIFA 18 game with the Australian Hyundai A-League.

The FIFA18 competitors represent the A-League's elite top-tier clubs to compete for a new E-League championship for both Xbox and PlayStation. Like their professional on-field counterparts, E-league competitors wear their team strip and battle it out through E-League Premiership Rounds before qualifying for the E-League Final Live Event.

The E-League's success was immediate with opening online fixtures attracting an audience 16% higher than the average A-League match (Bossi 2018). The code's earlier strategic move online had, in part, enabled the sports administrators to weather the Covid-19 storm. As avid sports fans were self-isolating at home with cabin fever setting in, the E-League kept them entertained and engaged with the sport.

Proof of Success: A Lucrative Naming Rights Sponsorship

Despite the E-League's infancy, its popularity and commercial appeal was reflected through Nivea Men's 2021 naming rights sponsorship. For the Australian Professional Leagues chief commercial officer, Ant Hearne, the deal signified the league's growth (Warren 2021). From an A-League perspective, the move online is a bridge between the gaming world and the Hyundai A-League.

While the E-League forges ahead, the A-League struggles to attract large numbers of fans to matches and commercial support. "The game unfortunately is probably at one of its lowest ebbs, certainly since the A-League started so it's not easy to get airtime. It's not easy to get coverage because it's not easy to get sponsors to pay for it," said commentator Simon Hill (Thomas 2021).

As Australian sport administrators grapple with incentivizing live game-day attendances, eSports fit easily into the online lives many millennials lead. Other countries are already seeing this shift. The U.S.'s Major League Soccer (MLS) administrators found 65% of their most devoted fans highlighted FIFA gaming as driving their interest in soccer. "Gaming is actually more important to us than people playing soccer itself," said MLS senior director James Ruth (Cohen 2019).

In Australia, commercial growth through eSports investment is an underutilized strategy. The A-League's E-League has the capacity to assist with addressing the codes commercial challenges. Despite the signing of a new broadcast deal, television viewership remains problematic. As crowd numbers at stadiums continue to rapidly decline, A-League administrators should continue to look to new possibilities.

Case Study 3

Has the NRL Dropped the Ball on Esports?

Although Supercars and A-League administrators are astute to the commercial benefits of eSports investment, two of Australia's most popular professional football codes National Rugby League (NRL) and Australian Football League (AFL) have failed to invest. As demonstrated through the two earlier case studies, Supercars and the A-League were able to pivot when the pandemic hit due to their prior investment in eSports and existing institutional knowledge. Within the context of the NRL, it was the athletes themselves and a rogue state-based league that were leading the charge. To date, the NRL HQ has shown little interest in offering eSports content to its fans. They have dipped a cautious toe in the water organizing the odd eSports event to add spectacle to their game-day experience, but nothing ongoing. This is surprising, as minimal meaningful action is contrary to the national and international sporting norms, as demonstrated throughout this chapter. However, some individual athletes and even a state-based league have shown greater initiative and foresight with successful forays into eSports, which we will now outline.

Turning Passion into $$$

Individual athletes within the NRL have signaled their own enthusiasm for online gaming. The most famous example was Josh Dugan who struck a Fortnite pose after scoring a goal in 2018. Dugan has parlayed his enjoyment of online gaming into an additional income stream and he is now a sponsored online gamer for a professional eSports organization in addition to his on-field contract. Dugan has been followed by the Captain of the Brisbane Broncos, Alex Glenn, who, in March 2021, signed with an eSports team and will similarly benefit from an additional income stream, a diversified fan base, and an ongoing career prospect when age or injury sets in.

A Bit of eSports on the Side?

Image 1: NRL Fortnite Promotion 2019
Source: https://letsplay.live/event/leagueroyale/

In 2019, the NRL partnered with an eSports media company to host a Fortnite tournament for fans as part of the NRL grand final day spectacle. The event took place after prior successful collaborations to promote off-season test matches in Auckland in 2018. Gamers had the opportunity to be flown to the event to compete for $18,000 in prize money, as well as the chance to play alongside NRL and gaming stars.

The New Zealand Warriors are the only NRL team that has their own dedicated eSports team that shares the same name and branding. The team was established in 2019 and continues to build momentum.

*Image 2: Cross promotion between the NRL Warriors and the eSports Warriors
Source: https://www.facebook.com/WarriorsESC*

The QRL Shows the Potential of eSports

During lockdown, the QRL (Queensland Rugby League), a state-based rugby league competition, created an eSports challenge, sponsored by the naming rights sponsor of the on-field competition–Intrust Super. The competition involved star athletes from the on-field competition playing the Rugby League Live 4 game for their respective teams over two seven-minute halves, weekly over seven rounds with the famous rugby league commentator and host of the Wide World of Sports, Peter Psaltis calling the games. Like Supercars, it was important to replicate the game day experience and closely as possible and provide fans with a digital outlet to keep their engagement with the sport when there were no live games.

Do NRL Executives Need a HIA (Head Injury Assessment) Test on eSports?

To date, the NRL is lagging in the eSports arena. While the longer-term effects of this lag remain unknown, the teams and state-based leagues that have embraced the potential of this new frontier are succeeding. Based on the viewership numbers of the QRL final there is an appetite for eSports amongst rugby league fans. If this potential remains untapped, someone else may seize the advantage.

Key Findings

In this section, an analysis of the key themes and findings emerging from interviews with Australian sports administration professionals are presented. In total, thirteen respondents participated in a forty-five-minute interview that was firstly digitally transcribed and then verbatim transcribed for accuracy.

Respondents originated from either top-tier or second-tier sport organizations and were employed in positions ranging from CEO and General Manager to Membership, Marketing, and Digital Analysts. The categorization of the sport as top or second tier was based on its popularity and familiarity with Australian sport fans. Refer to Table 1 for an overview of participant characteristics.

The interviews sought to elicit information relevant to respondents' current knowledge and understanding of eSports. Interviewees were asked to reflect on how within their organizational and/or league contexts eSports were operationalized for strategic imperatives including fan acquisition, engagement, and retention.

Table 1: Participant Characteristics

TOP-TIER SPORT OR SECOND-TIER SPORT	MALE OR FEMALE	OCCUPATION	YEARS WITHIN SPORT INDUSTRY	TENURE AT ORGANISATION
TOP-TIER SPORT	MALE	MATCH DAY AND EVENTS, LOGISTICS AND OPERATION	6	4
TOP-TIER SPORT	MALE	MARKETING AUDIENCE AND INSIGHTS MANAGER	5	4
SECOND-TIER SPORT	MALE	SPORTS COORDINATOR	7	3
TOP-TIER SPORT	MALE	HEAD OF CONSUMER	8	6
TOP-TIER SPORT	MALE	GENERAL MANAGER COMMUNICATIONS	7	7
SECOND-TIER SPORT	FEMALE	ASSISTANT GENERAL MANAGER	9	7
TOP-TIER SPORT	FEMALE	COMMUNITY ENGAGEMENT MANAGER	16	3
SECOND-TIER SPORT	FEMALE	CEO	10	3
TOP-TIER SPORT	MALE	PARTNERSHIPS MANAGER	5	2
TOP-TIER SPORT	FEMALE	DIGITAL INSIGHTS AND MARKETING SPECIALIST	5	2
TOP-TIER SPORT	MALE	MEMBERSHIP MANAGER	7	3
TOP-TIER SPORT	MALE	MEMBERSHIP & TICKETING MANAGER	6	3
TOP-TIER SPORT	MALE	COMMUNITY AND EVENTS COORDINATOR	5	3

The interviews were conducted immediately prior to and during the pandemic. The emerging findings show that while managers acknowledged that eSports would play a major role in shaping sport's future, there was little to no financial investment as the "threat" posed by eSports was conceived of as "many years away." This interpretation was in part due to a widely held attitude that eSports are not "real sports." The pandemic emphasized an increasing gap between the perceived readiness for the future and the need for an alternative and/or complimentary digital reality which we discuss next.

Redefining "Sport" in Modern Times

One of the key developments triggered by sports Covid-19 shutdown was a review of the meaning and practice of sport. Sport was typically conceived of by industry respondents as an activity involving physical exertion and skill. However, this perspective no longer reflects how the sport landscape is changing with the advent of video games combined with internet-driven connectivity fundamentally reshaping sport participation, fandom, and spectatorship. Most participants (67%) shared the view that how we define sport "needs to grow." This is encapsulated by respondent interpretations such as: "we are past the point where physicality goes hand in hand with sport."

Participants interpreted that competition and athlete commitment are fundamental components for an activity to be considered a sport: "a real eye-opener people actually travel to come and watch [others] play games that was my sort of first realization that [it's] actually a thing that people do." While less frequently, several participants highlighted how top-tier eSports athletes have elite skills, endurance and have dedicated hours of training to their sport, with an observation being made that "it's on par with most sports in terms of commitment." Furthermore, from their perspectives, eSports events, much like traditional sports, demonstrate great competition and unpredictability, with a respondent stating, "there's no reason to say that an eSports participant wouldn't be doing the same things a traditional sportsperson would." Indeed, these interpretations are in part reflected through international sport federations' recategorization of member federation sports into five groups: physical, mind, motorized, coordination, and animal supported (GAISF 2021). However, it was found that overall, in Australian sporting organizations, eSports are not given the same standing and respect afforded to traditional sports.

Visionaries Fail to Capitalize to Grow their Brand

For industry professionals, eSports is not a new phenomenon. But, translating awareness of eSports into new fans, entertainment, and engagement during and following the on-field sports hiatus has proven to be an obstacle too great for many. The QRL, Supercars, and the A-League were quick to utilize eSports during the pandemic as a means to keep in touch with fans, deepen their engagement and garner new fans. In comparison, the response from the AFL and NRL was lackluster, largely relying on social media platforms to maintain fan connections. This was principally due to a lack of groundwork in eSports. Interviewees from these codes considered eSports "a niche offering compared to traditional sport" or remarked how they "do not see eSports as a threat for another 5-10 years."

Despite eSports' impact on the international sporting landscape, there was for many organizations a complete absence of strategic imperatives or long-term planning to move into the digital sport age. When asked whether internal discussions had been held about eSports' uses, all participants stated that there had been, with some even mentioning that they had been discussing eSports for two to three years prior to Covid-19. Problematically, in the face of Covid-19, some participants stated that eSports is "too small to have someone dedicated" and that it was not "worthwhile." This shows interviewees' reluctance to change and inertia to maintaining the status quo.

Risk-Takers Rewarded

While the pandemic had devastating financial impacts on many leagues and teams, it forced other sport organizations to fast track their strategic plans. This development was especially visible in regards to how organizations adopted modern technology platforms to promote themselves in order to maintain and expand their fan base. With people forced to stay at home, streaming services such as Netflix and Amazon Prime experienced exponential growth. The continued appeal of on-demand video entertainment options has spread to sport as well, with football departments placed in "Covid bubbles" to ensure their survival. Whether rediscovering clubs' largely untouched YouTube channel or entering new platforms like Snapchat and TikTok, some leagues and clubs quickly reconfigured their resources in order to either remain relevant or capitalize on an opening in the public's attention. This highlights that when clubs must fight to survive, they are able to effectively and efficiently utilize digital platforms to engage fans.

The changes triggered by the Covid-19 pandemic highlight an important outcome. Sporting organizations, such as the Supercars and A-League, who recognized the impact of technology in sport and prepared for it, were rewarded. By establishing a foundation in unknown areas and platforms, like eSports, they were not as severely impacted when the pandemic suspended sport. Instead, they were able to build on their current offering to appeal to younger demographics. Through a "different kind of strategy," they attracted the next-generation fan to traditional sport through a virtual approach, which may well be something of the future as Covid-19 leaves a lasting impact.

Conclusions & Recommendations

eSports have been successfully used as a complementary offering by Supercars, the QRL, and the A-League. It has helped to promote traditional sports to younger fans and offer an avenue to deepen the relationship with existing fans by providing more content and more active ways for fans to engage with their team when and how it suits the fan. It is also an additional revenue stream for sports that are struggling to grow attendance and find sponsorship in a hotly contested space. eSports' appeal and novelty could be a source for sports regeneration. This is particularly important for the struggling NRL and A-League.

Time to Get-Off "Sleep Mode" and Press Play on eSports in Australia

eSports have been discussed by sports administrators for years, however, its potential has not been realized due to a lack of commitment. Athletes themselves, especially during the Covid-19 postponements, transitioned to eSports. By live streaming eSports, athletes could build their personal brands and connect directly with their fans. For many athletes, the suspension of leagues meant the suspension of playing wages. Consequently, athletes in underfunded sports were struggling to make ends meet. Live streaming platforms that have a subscription method, like Twitch, provided athletes an alternative means to earn an income.

Without the internet, athletes lacked a direct avenue to fans. The Covid-19 sports lockdown demonstrated that administrators could learn from a bottom-up approach and add a new income stream to their revenue via eSports. Many athletes are younger and consume eSports out of interest. Who is better positioned to advise their club than their own athletes who have a genuine affinity with eSports?

Reconceptualizing of the Sports Model

eSports as a brand extension for traditional sporting leagues to better serve their customers might not be enough to convince administrators to invest. For years, the gaming industry has operated using a loss-leading product strategy. In other words, Microsoft (XBOX) and Sony (PlayStation) have produced consoles that have either lost money or broke-even. Yet, these two companies consider their gaming division critically important because of the profits generated from locking a consumer into purchasing games for either console. Traditional leagues could be loss-leading products funded by profit-generating eSports, and this perspective may be enough to secure the attention of sport managers. eSports could provide struggling sports leagues a lower-cost and more profitable product to financially support their on-field competitions.

In addition, eSports' "plug and play" approach means that sporting organizations are provided with a risk management strategy for when external situations threaten their traditional championships. Alternative options that replicate the original offering, allow leagues and clubs to diversify their business and spread their risk. Replicating the commentary and theatre of the game day experience seemed to be an important part of the success of the Supercars and QRL eSports competitions. Additionally, by emulating the traditional sport, club identities are preserved, fan bases are renewed, and new fans may be gained. For investors, sport becomes more attractive to invest in, as it no longer is a single product catering to a narrow market, but is now a future-ready, diversified product. Finally, taking into account the environmental impacts of traditional sports, eSports could be a necessity. Motorsports in particular faces increasing questions about how they are reducing their greenhouse emissions. Whilst Formula E was established in 2014, much of the greenhouse emissions associated with motorsports originates from travel and logistics, not the cars themselves (O'Shea et al. 2020). Thus, eSports could be a more environmentally sustainable option for the future.

Based on this research, Australian sport organizations are faced with a choice invest resources now, catch-up, and make eSports a viable brand extension for their traditional league that may have the additional benefit of funding the traditional sport. Or they can continue as they are and let eSports grow in the Australian sporting landscape for it to become a direct threat or superior competitor.

REFERENCES

Anderson, Devin, Kevin Sweeney, Erica Pasquini, Brent Estes, and Ryan Zapalac. 2021. "An Exploration of Esports Consumer Consumption Patterns, Fandom, and Motives." *International Journal of eSports Research* 1 (1): 1-18. http://doi.org/10.4018/IJER.20210101.oa3.

Anderson, Jack. 2020. "How COVID Caused Chaos for Cricket and May Force a Rethink of All Sport Broadcasting Deals." *The Conversation*, January 6, 2021. https://theconversation.com/how-covid-caused-chaos-for-cricket-and-may-force-a-rethink-of-all-sport-broadcasting-deals-145246.

Bányai, Fanni, Mark Griffiths, Orsolya Király, and Zsolt Demetrovics. 2019. "The Psychology of Esports: A Systematic Literature Review," *Journal of Gambling Studies* 35 (2): 351-65. http://doi.org/10.1007/s10899-018-9763-1.

Bartholomaeus, Stefan. 2017. "Supercars plans virtual racing plunge." Accessed February 10, 2021. https://www.supercars.com/news/championship/supercars-plans-virtual-racing-plunge/.

Bossi, Dominic. 2018. "FFA's E-League Proves a Bigger Hit Than A-League Games." *The Sydney Morning Herald.* April 15, 2021. https://www.smh.com.au/sport/soccer/ffas-eleague-proves-a-bigger-hit-than-aleague-games-20180216-h0w87y.html.

Broniarczyk, Susan, and Joseph Alba. 1994. "The Importance of the Brand in Brand Extension." *Journal of Marketing Research* 31 (2): 214-228. http://doi.org/10.2307/3152195.

Carter, Marcus, Robbie Fordyce, Martin Gibbs & Emma Witkowski. 2017. "eSports Futures in Australia." Paper presented at the *Digital Games Research Association Conference, Melbourne, Australia.*

http://digra2017.com/static/Extended%20Abstracts/84_DIGRA2017_EA_Carter_Australian_eSports.pdf.

Cohen, Andrew. 2019. "FIFA Video Game Is Attracting Fans to MLS More Than Real Soccer." March 10, 2021. https://www.sporttechie.com/fifa-mls-soccer-fans-video-games/.

Colangelo, Anthony and Zoe Samios. 2020. "AFL Extends Foxtel and Telstra Broadcast Deal by Two Years." *The Age*, January 27, 2021. https://www.theage.com.au/sport/afl/afl-extends-foxtel-and-telstra-broadcast-deal-by-two-years-20201223-p56prx.html.

Cranmer, Eleanor, Dai-In Danny Han, Marnix van Gisbergen, and Timothy Jung. 2021. "Esports Matrix: Structuring the Esports Research Agenda." *Computers in Human Behavior*, 117, April. https://doi.org/10.1016/j.chb.2020.106671.

Dixon, Ed. 2020. "2020 LoL World Championship Draws 3.8m Peak Viewers." *SportsPro Media*, November 5, 2020. https://www.sportspromedia.com/news/league-of-legends-world-championship-2020-final-audience-viewing-figures#:~:text=Esports%20tournament%20racks%20up%20139m,up%20from%20last%20year's%20137m.&text=The%202020%20League%20of%20Legends, year's%20high%20of%203.9%20million.

Entertainment Software Association (ESA). 2018. "2018 Essential Facts About the Computer and Video Game Industry." December 1, 2019. https://www.theesa.com/esa-research/2018-essential-facts-about-the-computer-and-video-game-industry/.

Gibbs, Martin, Carter Marcus and Witkowski Emma. 2017. "Understanding Esports Spectatorship: players, fans and recruits." Paper presented at the *18th Annual Conference of the Association of Internet Researchers Tartu, Estonia / 18-21*.

Grand View Research. 2020. "Esports Market Size, Share & Trends Analysis Report by Revenue Source (Sponsorship, Advertising, Merchandise & Tickets, Media Rights), By Region, And Segment Forecasts, 2020 – 2027." June 30, 2020. https://www.grandviewresearch.com/industry-analysis/esports-market.

Gravity Media. 2020. "Supercars All-Stars Eseries." August 5, 2020. https://www.gravitymedia.com/projects/2020/supercars-all-stars-eseries/#:~:text=The%20Supercars%20All%20Stars%20Eseries,world's%20leading%20motorsport%20racing%20simulation.

Hamari, Juho and Max Sjöblom. 2017. "What is eSports and Why Do People Watch It?" *Internet Research* 27 (2): 211-232. http://doi.org/10.1108/IntR-04-2016-0085.

Hemphill, Dennis. 2005. "Cybersport." *Journal of the Philosophy of Sport* 32 (2): 195-207. http://doi.org/10.1080/00948705.2005.9714682.

Hodson, Joshua. 2019. "Supercars Unveil 2019 Esports Competition." *Ministry of Sport*, February 10, 2021. https://ministryofsport.com.au/supercars-unveil-2019-esports-competition/.

Hope, Anders. 2014. "The Evolution of the Electronic Sports Entertainment Industry and Its Popularity." *Computers for Everyone* 1 (1): 87-89. Emerald Insight.

International Olympic Committee. 2021. "IOC Makes Landmark Move into Virtual Sports by Announcing First-Ever Olympic Virtual Series." April 22, 2021. https://olympics.com/ioc/news/international-olympic-committee-makes-landmark-move-into-virtual-sports-by-announcing-first-ever-olympic-virtual-series.

Jin, Dal. 2010. "ESports and Television Business in the Digital Economy." In *Korea's Online Gaming Empire*, edited by Dal Jin, 59-79. MIT Press: Cambridge.

Jonasson, Kakke, and Jesper Thiborg. 2010. "Electronic Sport and Its Impact on Future Sport." *Sport in Society* 13, (2): 287-299. http://doi.org/10.1080/17430430903522996.

Mason, Max. 2019. "The Game has Changed for Australian Sports." *Financial Review*. March 12, 2021. https://www.afr.com/companies/media-and-marketing/the-game-has-changed-for-australian-sports-20190613-p51x90.

Nagel, Mark, and Kenny Sugishita. 2016. "Esports: The Fastest Growing Segment of the 'Sport' Industry." *Sport & Entertainment Review* 2 (2): 51–60. Emerald Insight.

Newton, Bruce. 2020. "Hundreds of Thousands Tune into Supercars Eseries." *AutoAction*. March 10, 2021. https://autoaction.com.au/2020/04/09/hundreds-of-thousands-tune-into-supercars-eseries.

Nielsen. 2019. "eSports Playbook for Brands 2019." Nielsen Report. December 15, 2019. https://www.nielsen.com/wp-content/uploads/sites/3/2019/05/esports-playbook-for-brands-2019.pdf.

⸻ 2018. "The Esports Playbook: Australia Maximising Your Investment Through Understanding the Fans." Insights. https://www.nielsen.com/wp-content/uploads/sites/3/2019/04/Esports20Playbook20Australia20-20Nielsen.pdf.

O'Shea, Michelle, Chloe Taylor, and Jessica Richards. 2020. "Stadiums are Emptying Out Globally. So Why Have Australian Sports Been So Slow to Act?" *The Conversation*, March 13, 2020. https://theconversation.com/stadiums-are-emptying-out-globally-so-why-have-australian-sports-been-so-slow-to-act-133354.

Reddy, Mergen, Nic Terblanche, Leyland Pitt, and Michael Parent. 2009. "How Far Can Luxury Brands Travel? Avoiding the Pitfalls of Luxury Brand Extension." *Business Horizons* 52 (2):187-197. https://doi.org/10.1016/j.bushor.2008.11.001.

Riley, Francesca, Wendy Lomax, and Angela Blunden. 2004. "Dove vs. Dior: Extending the Brand Extension Decision-Making Process from Mass to Luxury." *Australasian Marketing Journal* 12 (3): 40-55. https://doi.org/10.1016/S1441-3582(04)70105-6.

Seamus, Byrne 2019. "Esports Don't Need Your Approval as They Represent a New Digital Mainstream." *Financial Review*, February 8, 2021. https://www.afr.com/technology/esports-dont-need-your-approval-as-they-represent-a-new-digital-mainstream-20190322-h1cozo.

Smith, Aaron, and Bob Stewart. 2010. "The Special Features of Sport: A Critical Revisit." *Sport Management Review* 13 (1): 1-13. https://doi.org/10.1016/j.smr.2009.07.002.

Supercars. 2019. "Supercars Eseries Schedule, Broadcasts Locked In." News. Last modified July 7, 2019. https://www.supercars.com/news/eseries/supercars-eseries-schedule-broadcasts-locked-in/.

⸻ 2020. "Strong audience tunes in for opening round of BP Supercars All Stars Eseries." News, April 9, 2021. https://www.supercars.com/news/allstars-eseries/strong-audience-tunes-in-for-opening-round-of-bp-supercars-all-stars-eseries/.

Taylor, T.L. 2012. *Raising the Stakes: E-Sports and the Professionalization of Computer Gaming*. Cambridge: The MIT Press. ProQuest Ebrary.

Thomas, Josh. 2021. "Makes Me Weep' Simon Hill's Advice to Revive A-League Active Support," *Sporting News*, April 25, 2021.https://www.sportingnews.com/au/football/news/makes-me-weep-simon-hills-advice-to-revive-a-league-active-support/nfzkvjzqc1ih1mvivkq7fh4uv.

Warren, Jordan. 2021. "Nivea Men Announced as Naming Rights Partner For E-League," *Ministry of Sport*, May 26, 2021. https://ministryofsport.com.au/nivea-men-announced-as-naming-rights-partner-for-e-league/.

Wagner, Michel. 2006. "On the Scientific Relevance of eSports." Paper presented at *International Conference on Internet Computing: Computer Games Development, Las Vegas, 26-29 June 2006*. 437-442. London: CSREA Press.

Walter, Brad. 2020. "From Shutdown to Restart: How NRL Walked Tightrope to Get Season Going Again." *National Rugby League*, January 21, 2021. https://www.nrl.com/news/2020/05/25/from-shutdown-to-restart-how-nrl-walked-tightrope-to-get-season-going-again/.

Weiss, Thomas. 2011. "Fulfilling the Needs of eSports Consumers: A Uses and Gratifications Perspective." Paper presented at *Bled eConference eFuture: Creating Solutions for the Individual, Organizations and Society, Bled, 12-15 June 2011*. https://aisel.aisnet.org/bled2011/30.

Wildie, Tom. 2020. "Coronavirus Leaves Sporting Codes Facing an Uncertain Future and Bracing for a Financial Hit." *ABC News*, March 16, 2021. https://www.abc.net.au/news/2020-03-16/coronavirus-pandemic-leaves-sport-bracing-for-financial-hit/12059402.

Williams, Pete. 1995. Card Sharks: How Upper Deck Turned a Child's Hobby into a Billion-Dollar Business. New York: Macmillan.

www.ingramcontent.com/pod-product-compliance
Lightning Source LLC
Chambersburg PA
CBHW062025290426
44108CB00025B/2785